GREAT HOLLYWOOD MOVIES

TED SENNETT

GREAT HOLLYWOOD MOVIES

HARRY N. ABRAMS, INC., PUBLISHERS, NEW YORK

CONTENTS

INTRODUCTION

Movies are many things: recurring dreams of beauty and adventure; kaleidoscopic visions of what life is, was, or could become; shafts of light illuminating the dark corners of the human heart; invitations to hearty laughter—and just plain fun. They delight us, inspire us, move us, infuriate us, and make us wonder. And some of the movies we see linger in our minds long after their original release, imprinting themselves permanently on our consciousness. The reasons for their durability, for our willingness to watch them whenever they turn up, range from frivolous (a favorite film of a favorite star) to profound (a movie that broke important new ground in the art). Whatever the reasons, these are the movies we cherish, the films that refuse to fade from memory no matter how much time passes. These are the "great Hollywood movies."

It is difficult, of course, to explain what makes a movie great. Films are elusive, and, despite the noble efforts of critics, they will always remain so. What strikes one person as cinematic splendor may be dreary dross to another. The work of a major comedy figure may induce helpless laughter in one viewer and leave another bristling with irritation or numb with boredom. Ultimately, each moviegoer will construct his or her own storehouse of great movies, built to withstand the heat of controversy or the chill of someone else's rejection.

In this book, I have been pleased to open my personal movie storehouse to readers. From a collection that ranges over many years of moviegoing, I have selected several hundred films from the earliest days to the present and ventured to determine why I continue to remember them, or to pinpoint the qualities that have kept them popular for decades. These are films from virtually every genre; like every movie buff, I have my favorite genres, but I hope they are undetectable. Some of the films covered have been subject to minute scrutiny by scholars and critics since the day of their release, but, with a touch of trepidation and a dash of audacity, I have added my own thoughts about them.

The films I have chosen can be said to fall roughly into three categories: those films, judged great by general consensus, that have altered or advanced the history of the art (*The Birth of a Nation* and *Citizen Kane* come quickly to mind); those that have special qualities of excellence, a confluence of brilliant acting, direction, writing, and production that forms the entity called a "great" movie (*On the Waterfront* and *Nashville* are examples); and, finally, films that have little to do with cinematic art but much to do with the charisma of movies. Those are the legendary films that surprise even their creators with their never-fading appeal. (The primary example is probably *Casablanca*, that imaginary city of romance and intrigue.) We should probably reserve a fourth category for films that may belong to neither art nor legend but that represent a peak of achievement by the screen's mythic performers (W. C. Fields's *The Bank Dick*) or directors (John Ford's *How Green Was My Valley*).

A few qualifications and explanations: this book is by no means intended to cover *all* great Hollywood movies. There are many films that, for various reasons, could not be fitted into the framework of the book. One might mention such films as MGM's spectacular *San Francisco*, with its classic earthquake sequence; John Ford's excellent biographical drama *Young Mr. Lincoln*, richly flavored with Americana; or William Wyler's melodrama *The Letter*, starring Bette Davis as a mendacious murderess. Every film buff or scholar will be able to supply his or her own list of omitted films. I welcome their suggestions, asking only that they understand the conditions imposed by the limitations of space.

It should also be noted that the word "Hollywood" in the title is used in a generic sense. Many American movies since the 1950s have been made partially or wholly on location; a delightful side benefit of films over the past few decades has been the opportunities they provide for armchair traveling. Yet, for all its connotations of glitter over substance, Hollywood has been the lifeblood of American movies, the source of its professionalism and technical wizardry. Brouhaha and tub-thumping aside, American movies qualify as a national—and exportable—treasure.

"National treasure" sounds formidable indeed, but movies are also an accessible and personal treasure. At a time of multiplex theaters, unruly audiences, and high-priced refreshment stands, it is pleasant to recall the circumstances under which I saw many of the films in this book. Often my neighborhood Bijou was the hectic gathering place for every preteen who could coax a coin or two out of mother. Not even the clattering machine gun of James Cagney could be heard over the din of shrieking voices; it was blissful chaos. But as I grew older (and came to love and admire films), the experience became calmer, quieter, and infinitely more rewarding as I basked in the glow emanating from the screen. The maturing movie buff is a giddy soul, probably indiscriminate in his love but learning all the time. Once in a great while, as a kind of pilgrimage, I would venture to the golden movie palaces of Manhattan to gaze with awe at the vast screens in an atmosphere that positively reeked with "class." The education continued; the affection never faltered.

This book, then, is a product of those vanished years and the years since: a tribute to many of the films that represent the unique art of motion pictures and its combination of talent, magic, ballyhoo, and dreams.

Opposite: How Green Was My Valley *(Fox, 1941). Young Huw Morgan (Roddy McDowall) and his father (Donald Crisp) walk among the hills near their Welsh mining town. It hardly mattered that the background was actually California.*
Overleaf: City Lights *(Charlie Chaplin/United Artists, 1931). One of the most sublime moments in film history: the Little Tramp (Charlie Chaplin) shyly acknowledges his identity to the girl (Virginia Cherrill) whose sight he helped to restore.*

DIVERSIONS

THE SOUND OF LAUGHTER
Great Comedy Movies

What is as refreshing, as soothing to one's wavering sanity and peace of mind, as the sound of laughter? Tragedy stirs our emotions and cleanses our souls; melodrama quickens our pulses. But comedy lifts our hearts and makes the gray days bearable.

Across the decades, happily, Hollywood has given us a generous supply of laughter in the form of witty, outrageous, and joyful comedy films. Years after they have departed the scene, the great comedy performers continue to brighten our lives with their images. (Of course some are still around to exercise their franchise on humor, to everyone's gratitude.) We can try to determine why they make us laugh; certainly the art of comedy has been analyzed and explicated to a fare-thee-well. Yet nothing can speak as eloquently as Chaplin's twitching moustache, Keaton's stony visage, or Harpo's honking horn. And no essay on Woody Allen's comic persona can replace the risible sight of his urban *Angst*.

It is true that comedy is usually one step away from tragedy. A building collapses (in any number of disaster films) and we are filled with pity and terror for the victims. Harpo leans against a wall, and a policeman asks, "Say, what do you think you're doing? Holding up the building?" Harpo nods, the policeman takes him away, and the wall crumbles. We roar with laughter. Edward G. Robinson's brutal gangster Enrico Bandello is pursued by the cops and shot to death in the street; justice has been grimly served. The Little Tramp is forever scampering from the law, but his ridiculous costume and absurd gait make him a comic figure. Yet in comedy as well as tragedy, the characters are faced with a world that is indifferent at best, hostile at worst. Generally, comedy ends in survival; tragedy ends in defeat and death.

How characters respond to their plight determines the two major strands of comedy. In the silent era of the teens and twenties, the principal comedy figures were resourceful innocents who learned to cope with injustice and adversity through any means at their disposal: dogged persistence, ingenuity born of desperation, or even a touch of wide-eyed larceny. Objects and people could do them in for a while, but they landed on their feet, hoping for better tomorrows. There was no greater innocent in the silent era than Harry Langdon—he was practically infantile—but the others were sophisticated only in their developing film techniques and not in their personae. The indelible images of that period include Chaplin bravely eating his shoe as if it were a gourmet dish, or Keaton struggling to keep his beloved train the General on course while saddled with a dim-witted girlfriend.

In the thirties, the world grew even more hostile, more dangerous, and a new group of talented comedians emerged to take up the fray. Unlike their silent predecessors, they were not ready to be trampled on or ignored, and whether it took a quip or a whip, they held the enemy (whoever that was) at bay. And so we had the Marx Brothers, leering and joking their impudent way through mythical countries, opera houses, race tracks, or any place that could embrace their lunacy. We had W. C. Fields, contemptuous of people as he brayed his way to the main chance, or Mae West laughing at sexual reticence and hypocrisy. Along the way there were other comic performers, equally knowing but less grotesque, who brought elegance, charm, and wit to their romantic films. If the world was awry, there was comfort and pleasure in the wryly amusing attitudes of Cary Grant, Irene Dunne, William Powell, Myrna Loy, Carole Lombard, Spencer Tracy, and Katharine Hepburn. There was pleasure, too, in the comic creations of Frank Capra, whose innocent lambs triumphed over the wolves, and Preston Sturges, who took a satirical, "damn-you-all" view of both victims and victimizers.

In recent years, the most innovative film comedies have come from Woody Allen. Slight, owlish, and unprepossessing, he is a brilliant amalgam of both comic traditions: on the one hand, he is the put-upon innocent of the twenties, faced with a world bent on doing him harm. (He may abhor his innocence and spend all of his time trying to lose it, but he is basically good-natured and generous.) On the other hand, in the style of the thirties, he is determined to deflect pain and suffering with a wisecrack or a satirical put-down. He arrived at his ultimate portrait of the hopelessly neurotic, urbanized *schlemiel* in *Manhattan* (1979), his best film to date.

Opposite: The Graduate *(Joseph E. Levine/Embassy, 1967). Benjamin Braddock (Dustin Hoffman), looking forlorn and foolish in his new scuba diving outfit, a graduation present, prepares to meet his parents' friends. The shot emphasizes Benjamin's alienation.*
Above: The General *(Buster Keaton/United Artists, 1927). In his efforts to take his beloved train, the General, out of enemy territory, Southerner Buster Keaton experiences another of many difficult—and uproarious—moments. This epic comedy was Keaton's personal favorite.*

American film comedy spans over seven decades, but it covers more than time. It embraces changing attitudes and mores, the transition from silence to sound, and many unforgettable comic personalities. One thing remains constant: what is truly funny remains funny forever; it disregards trends and styles to remain fixed in the unchanging absurdity of mankind.

The indisputable master of American film comedy was not American at all but an Englishman, known affectionately by various names throughout the world: Charlie, Charlot, Carlo, Carlitos, the Little Fellow. To immortality, he is Charlie Chaplin, a unique artist who created the single most memorable character in international cinema. From a poverty-stricken childhood in London, through his apprenticeship with Mack Sennett, to classic feature films, Chaplin evolved the heroic figure of the Tramp, a shabby, resourceful, indomitable fellow with a ridiculous moustache, a curious walk, and a heart filled with compassion for suffering humanity. The Tramp is a natural prey of burly policemen, an inevitable prison inmate, and the obvious butt for a practical joke. But bullies beware. In his eyes there is a mischievous twinkle, and his battered shoe houses a foot ready with a swift kick. This ludicrous fellow is also gallant: he is ready to befriend children and young girls who have been struck down by adversity; shyly, he offers them shelter and sometimes sacrifice.

There is probably no film artist who has been discussed more than Chaplin, or so often emulated. Often his deficiencies have been glossed over or completely ignored. His early films for Keystone and Essanay contain glimpses of the evolving comedian but they are generally crude and primitive. Even his later feature films suffer from meager production values and mediocre supporting players. Chaplin's taste occasionally faltered, and his sentimentality could become excruciating. Yet his shortcomings fade beside the durable glow of his achievements.

It is generally agreed that *The Gold Rush* (1925) is the golden summit of Chaplin's art in the twenties, a masterpiece that offers up new rewards or renewed delight with every viewing. In its miraculous combination of slapstick and poignancy, it has no peers. It distills the very essence of the Tramp, that sweetly innocent fellow known here as the Lone Prospector. In Chaplin's familiar tramp costume, this prospector cuts a foolish figure, but when his Alaskan adventures are over, we have seen and been moved by his perseverance, resourcefulness, and gallantry. *The Gold Rush* is perhaps Chaplin's purest statement of the triumph of man over the dispassionate cruelty of nature and the calculated cruelty of man.

Having placed it in the pantheon of motion pictures, and not only of the silent era, we should add that the movie is also riotously funny. Chaplin is able to draw uproarious laughs from the most improbable situations—he turns calamity into triumph by refusing to accept it. He is the ultimate survivor. In a sublime sequence—one of the best in all his films—he is trapped in a cabin with two starving prospectors and must resort to boiling and eating one of his grimy shoes. With the utmost finesse and the slight smile of a satisfied gourmet, he twirls the laces as if they were spaghetti and nibbles daintily at the nails as if they were succulent bones.

Throughout the film, Chaplin succeeds in turning his pantomimic art into something funny, moving, and transcendent. We are touched when the Tramp is rejected by the dance-hall hostess he loves (Georgia Hale), but we laugh when she rushes toward him with outstretched arms, then passes him to embrace someone else. Waiting alone for Georgia and her friends at his New Year's Eve party, he is a lonely, pathetic figure—but not in his dreams. In his fantasy, everyone is having a gala time, and to express his joy, the Tramp spears two rolls with forks and performs an ingenious variety of dance steps on the table to the tune of the "Oceana Roll." When Georgia kisses him, he topples from his chair in embarrassment, only to discover that it was all a dream. Once again the Tramp is a solitary soul buffeted by the strong winds of adversity. No other comic artist could combine tears and laughter in such delicate proportion.

Chaplin began work on *City Lights* late in the twenties, but when sound swept Hollywood he halted production, then decided to complete the film using only a few moments of gibberish speech and his original musical score. It was the only way he could demonstrate his profound belief in the viability of silent film. By the time he had finished working on the movie in painstaking—and expensive—detail, it was 1931, and sound was in full force. Nevertheless, the film was hailed as one of Chaplin's greatest achievements, a judgment still

The Gold Rush (Charlie Chaplin/United Artists, 1925). In a busy Alaskan saloon, prospector Charlie Chaplin gazes at the girl (Georgia Hale) he adores from afar. Chaplin's comedy masterpiece overflows with memorable moments.

current today. It has probably been admired out of proportion to its considerable merits, and its faults—some vulgar moments and a few comic bits that might be dismissed if a comedian other than Chaplin had used them—have been forgotten in the general enthusiasm.

As in so many of his films, the central story of *City Lights* smacks of Victorian melodrama, with the Tramp, down on his luck as usual, befriending a pretty blind girl (Virginia Cherrill) who sells flowers. He also becomes involved with a millionaire (Harry Myers), his bosom buddy when drunk and a surly plutocrat who doesn't recognize Charlie when sober. The intrepid Tramp surmounts all obstacles to obtain money for an operation to cure the girl's blindness. At the end, her sight restored, the girl realizes that this shabby but dignified Tramp is her secret benefactor. Puzzled, she places her hand over his and can only bring herself to ask, "You?" He nods slightly and, embarrassed, lifts his fingers to his lips. "You can see now?" he asks. She nods her head slowly, tears in her eyes. In one of the most famous close-ups in film history, the Tramp gazes at her with a mixture of shyness, delight, adoration, and hope.

By the mid-thirties, Chaplin was still not ready to accede to the demands of sound, and his first, anxiously awaited film since *City Lights* contained only sound effects, a musical score (his own), a few scattered lines of dialogue, and one song delivered by Chaplin near the end of the film. As in many earlier films, in *Modern Times* (1936) the Tramp finds himself at odds with society, and fights to hold on to

the remnants of his tattered dignity and individuality. Once again, he befriends a homeless waif and extricates himself from perilous situations. Apart from the fact that Chaplin was working from a shooting script for the first time, the major difference between this and previous films came from Chaplin's strongly increased social awareness: behind the slapstick and the sentimentality is a pointed spoof of the dehumanization of man in an industrialized society. (Despite the controversy it caused at the time of its release, *Modern Times* is really much more of a spoof than an indictment—it derides mechanization, not capitalism, and it appears to advocate a return to the bucolic life rather than revolution.)

The movie begins with a heavy hand—a shot of a herd of sheep dissolves into one of workers marching into a factory of the Electro Steel Corporation. Enter Charlie on the assembly line, tightening nuts at breakneck speed—the perfect cog in the wheel of misfortune. Hilariously, he becomes the guinea pig for a bizarre "feeding machine," which is intended to feed the workers on the job. The not-exactly-perfected machine continually goes berserk, wreaking havoc on poor Charlie. At one point, a corn-eating device runs across his mouth like an electric buzz saw—the ultimate expression of a mechanized age gone mad. When a nervous breakdown forces Charlie to leave the factory—he finds he cannot stop tightening nuts even when there are none to tighten—he hurtles from one disastrous job to another. Along the way, he takes under his wing a wistful gamine (Paulette Goddard) whose father has been killed in a labor riot.

Modern Times is uneven—it veers into Chaplin's shameless sentimentality, and it occasionally makes its point with a trowel—but there are probably more inspired moments in the film than in any other by Chaplin. Some involve primitive slapstick, but others either have a sharply satirical edge or touches of visual poetry. Retrieving a red flag that has fallen from a truck, Charlie finds himself leading a Communist demonstration and is hauled away by police. In a

Left: City Lights *(Charlie Chaplin/United Artists, 1931). Charlie prevents tippling millionaire Harry Myers from leaping into the river. They become close friends—but only when Myers is drunk. The implied social commentary runs throughout the movie.*
Right: Modern Times *(Charlie Chaplin/United Artists, 1936). Driven to near-madness by his routine, mechanical job in the factory, Charlie Chaplin alarms his coworkers by going merrily berserk. Chaplin's comedy was, among other things, a hilarious satire on the industrial age.*

lovely sequence in a department store, he and the gamine romp happily through every department until Charlie, blindfolded and on roller skates, comes perilously close to falling four stories. Back in the factory, Charlie becomes Chester Conklin's cheerfully inept assistant, resulting in a scene of extraordinary comic variety. The mechanic becomes caught up in the vast machinery, ending up on his back and unable to move. Charlie's efforts to serve him lunch while he's in this position are achingly funny.

Chaplin's closest rival in the silent years was a comedian in an entirely different mode. Unlike Chaplin, Buster Keaton had no complex, multilayered persona and little of Chaplin's pathos, impudence, or concealed pain. His humor came out of what he did to extricate himself from life's dilemmas and not out of what he was. But Buster Keaton was funny, often uproariously so, as well as a painstaking artist. His stoic manner and his famous poker face were as familiar to audiences of the twenties as Chaplin's baggy trousers, moustache, and walking stick.

From 1923 on, Keaton starred in and codirected (with the exception of *Sherlock, Jr.*, which he directed alone) eleven silent films that centered on his abrupt collision with a series of disasters and the comic measures he used to survive them. Often he narrowly escaped death, or he was obliged to run swiftly to avoid calamity, but his deadpan features never betrayed fear or alarm, only the faintest flicker of irritation or disapproval. All of his considerable energy and acrobatic prowess went into the creation of the most elaborate gags in silent film history.

The General (1927) is usually regarded as his greatest film, and with good reason. A lavish and carefully constructed film, with authentic sets that provide flavor and atmosphere, it works as both a straightforward Civil War melodrama complete with chases and last-minute rescues and as a compendium of hilarious Keaton set pieces. Filmed largely on location in Oregon and based on a true incident, *The General* told the story of Johnnie Gray (Keaton), an engineer on the train known affectionately as the General. At the height of the Civil War, the General is stolen by Union soldiers and Johnnie, a true-blue Southerner, fights to get it back. He is hindered more than helped by his dim-witted fiancée, Annabelle Lee (Marian Mack). Johnnie succeeds after a series of wild adventures and becomes a lionized hero.

The obstacles that confront Johnnie as he races to retrieve the General are both harrowing and hilarious. He must cope with a cannon that refuses to fire or insists on aiming at him. (When it does go off, it hits the rear of the train.) He tries to suppress his irritation with Annabelle Lee, who, when they are aboard the recovered General, insists on sweeping the engine floor and discarding any wood with knotholes. (In one wonderful moment, Johnnie throttles her briefly, then decides on a kiss instead.) Through all the comedy, there is suspense as well, and also spectacle—the film's most celebrated scene involves the demolition of a bridge, which brings a Northern train crashing down in ruins. (No faking here —Keaton would never allow it.) Keaton even manages a few moments

of beautiful repose—at one point, he is caught up in a platoon of Southern soldiers rushing off to battle. When they leave, he stands alone, looking after them, a forlorn and pathetic man.

Certainly another distinctive comedian of the silent era was Harold Lloyd. With his horn-rimmed glasses and straw hat and his irrepressibly cheerful manner, Lloyd represented the clean-cut American boy who wanted success and an admiring girlfriend. His grit and determination usually put him in dire peril so that Lloyd could work out elaborate, hair-raising gags. He lacked the finesse and intricate comedy timing of Chaplin and Keaton, and the laughter he induced came more from nervous anxiety (will he fall? will he make it?) than from his eager-beaver character, but he had a wide and loyal following. His best film was probably *The Freshman* (1925), which satirized college life in the twenties with its lighthearted atmosphere and lightheaded students.

With *City Lights* and *Modern Times*, Chaplin had defied sound, asserting that the visual aspect of comedy was all-important. (Actually, his own light British-accented voice was not especially distinctive.) But there were other comedians—even some who had had their beginnings in the silent years—who were not so bold, and they sought to develop a comic persona that was both aural and visual, one that matched the moods and attitudes of their time. For them, sound gave their work a new dimension, made it possible to confront a hostile world in a way that they never could in silent films: with a quip, a wisecrack, or a cynical aside. Groucho Marx's magnificent leer required no words, but that dry, nasal voice was needed to demolish fools and pompous dowagers. W. C. Fields muttered wicked remarks under his whiskey breath and audiences roared at his misanthropy. Mae West's nasal twang contained an unromantic, unashamed invitation to sex. (Harpo Marx's innocent devil needed no words to chase women or to work his wiles, and Laurel and Hardy, innocents as well, had voices that were only appropriate extensions of their silent personae. It is possible to argue that they fared best in silent films.)

To single out one or two films that best represent these gifted comedians is a perilous task subject to invective from their fans. Virtually all of their movies contain pearly moments. Nevertheless...

By general agreement, *Duck Soup* (1933) is the Marxes' funniest and certainly their wildest film. In its own day, this uproarious spoof of warmongering and diplomacy had its champions but most often it was either mildly accepted or roundly panned. Considering the film's steady flow of inspired sight gags and celebrated set pieces, this view is astonishing. *Duck Soup* is emphatically not the comic equivalent of *All Quiet on the Western Front*—its antiwar stance really has no satirical teeth—but it is a merry and outrageous lark that looks better with every passing year.

With Groucho the newly appointed ruler of Freedonia, Chico as his Minister of War, Harpo as his chauffeur, and Zeppo (in his last role before retiring from films) as his secretary, can madness be far behind? Hardly, and *Duck Soup* abounds in joyfully lunatic scenes that director Leo McCarey handles briskly. (Did anyone ever really

Opposite, above: A lobby card for The Gold Rush *(Charlie Chaplin/United Artists, 1925).*
Opposite, center: A lobby card for Duck Soup *(Paramount, 1933).*
Opposite, below: A lobby card for The Bank Dick *(Universal, 1940).*

CHARLIE CHAPLIN in "THE GOLD RUSH"

THE FOUR MARX BROTHERS in 'Duck Soup'

Directed by LEO McCAREY

A Paramount Picture

UNIVERSAL PICTURES presents

W.C. FIELDS in THE Bank Dick

handle the Marxes?) There is not a whit of reason, sentiment, or romance in the Bert Kalmar–Harry Ruby screenplay, as Freedonia and neighboring Sylvania stumble idiotically into all-out war. Long before the battle begins, however, the brothers engage in their unique brand of horseplay. They mock ceremonial pomp at a lavish reception for Groucho ("Oh, your Excellency," murmurs the indispensable Margaret Dumont as the powerful Mrs. Teasdale. "You're not so bad yourself," Groucho responds coyly.) They take aim at governmental red tape (at a Cabinet meeting, a bored, contemptuous Groucho plays jacks), and—best of all—they make nasty fun of patriotic fervor in an almost hallucinatory musical number called "The Country's Going to War," complete with minstrels, chorus girls, and a choir. The war itself is pure delirium: a compendium of Marxian quips, sight gags, non sequiturs, and pure sappiness. The movie also contains the extraordinary sequence, a miracle of timing, in which Harpo and Chico dress up like Groucho and try to convince him that he is looking into a mirror.

There are those who would opt for *A Night at the Opera* (1935) as the Marxes' best film, and the brothers themselves seemed to have held this opinion. Their first film for MGM, it was also their first to have a reasonably coherent story line, including a subsidiary love story and several songs. The Marxes were worried about this new concept, which was contributed by the studio's "boy wonder," Irving Thalberg, and even today many critics and Marx fans prefer the pure anarchy of *Duck Soup*. But *A Night at the Opera* is still a riotously

funny film. With a script by George S. Kaufman and Morrie Ryskind (assisted by Al Boasberg) and direction more or less by Sam Wood, the boys plunged into the world of grand opera and virtually demolished it. Groucho was leering fortune hunter Otis P. Driftwood, and Chico and Harpo were two hustling friends, Fiorello and Tomasso. They become involved with Mrs. Claypool (Margaret Dumont), an imperious patron of the arts, and a pair of singing lovers (Allan Jones and Maureen O'Sullivan).

In between harp and piano solos or romantic duets, *A Night at the Opera* demonstrates the comic genius that made the Marx Brothers unique. Like their contemporaries W. C. Fields and Mae West, they thumbed their noses at society, and they were even capable of a bit of larceny to reach their goal. But they also went several steps further than the others, turning impudence into iconoclasm that reached almost surrealistic heights. Nothing was too trivial or too sacred to be spared by the brothers—everything was fodder for their joyous assault on propriety and convention. They also defied gravity and common sense, as in the immortal stateroom scene, widely regarded as the funniest few minutes on film, in which the boys and virtually an entire ship's staff crowd into a tiny room. (Harpo sleeps blissfully through the entire ruckus, remaining unconscious even as he honks for food or grabs at the nearest available female.) Not even grand opera was safe in their hands—in a wild climax, they destroy a performance of *Il Trovatore* in ways that must be seen to be appreciated. The message was theirs alone: the world is an inflated balloon floating on the hot air expended by pretentious, self-serving fools. Why not puncture the balloon with laughter?

Left: The Freshman *(Harold Lloyd/Pathé, 1925). In the big game, college freshman Harold Lloyd scores a touchdown and becomes the school hero. The bountiful gags include Harold running the wrong way and dropping the ball when he hears the whistle from a local factory.*

Right: The Bank Dick *(Universal, 1940). As Egbert Sousé, the world's most unlikely bank guard, W. C. Fields expresses his feelings about children. He had a similar attitude toward dogs and families.*

While the Marxes were running rampant at Paramount in the early thirties, the studio also housed another genuine original of quite a different stripe. W. C. Fields had been a vaudeville juggler, a Ziegfeld star, and a silent film comedian when he made his sound debut in 1930. By 1933, his inimitable, whiskey-soaked voice, his wicked asides, muttered sotto voce, and his sardonic outlook on life were so popular with large segments of the movie audience (he was by no means universally popular) that the studio starred him in a series of knockabout comedies, often from his own stories. From all reports, Fields was very much like his film persona: a misanthropic man battered by life and scornful of sentiment and wholesomeness, whose only weapons were a caustic wit and a penchant for larcenous activity.

His best film was probably *The Bank Dick* (1940), made after he moved to Universal Studios in 1939. Written by Fields under the pseudonym of Mahatma Kane Jeeves, the movie revolved about Egbert Sousé, a small-town drunk saddled with a miserable family who becomes a hero when he is mistakenly credited with thwarting a bank robbery. The fact that Sousé is acutally a misanthropic liar and crook is cheerfully swept away in a series of complications, which include nasty entanglements with his wife (Cora Witherspoon) and mother-in-law (Jessie Ralph) and his attempts to get inquisitive bank examiner J. Pinkerton Snoopington (Franklin Pangborn) drunk with a barrage of "Michael Finns." The movie ends with an out-of-control car chase with Fields at the wheel and a bank robber in the back seat. *The Bank Dick* is vintage slapstick out of Mack Sennett, laced with Fields's contempt for small-town life, family life, and simple honesty: a bitter pill coated with laughter.

Incredibly, Paramount's roster of comedians in the early thirties was not exhausted by the Marx Brothers and W. C. Fields. There was also a lady (she might dispute the word) who gave sound comedy its first true contact with hearty, uninhibited sex. Like Fields, Mae West concocted most of her own story ideas, but she also wrote the screenplays, feeling that nobody understood her unique style as well as she did. (She was probably right.) Never exactly models of craftsmanship, they merely provided enough plot on which to hang her array of suggestive quips, her comments on life, love, and men, and possibly a song or two. Any way one wishes to interpret her, she was an original: a parody of sex, a free spirit mocking convention and propriety, or a tough, overweight blonde with only a few repetitious tricks in her bag.

None of Mae West's movies qualify as art, but her best is probably *I'm No Angel* (1933). Although not substantially better than some of the others, it has a flavorsome, disreputable carnival background in the early scenes, a generous sprinkling of Westian one-liners, and her best leading man (Cary Grant, before he turned to comedy; coping with Mae is serious business). Mae plays Tira, an independent-minded carnival queen with social aspirations—she moves from honky-tonk to the big time, where she entrances socialite Kirk Lawrence (Kent Taylor), but it is Lawrence's cousin Jack Clayton (Grant) who eventually wins her. The movie is essence of West: Mae at the

Above: Duck Soup *(Paramount, 1933). All hail Rufus T. Firefly, the new ruler of Freedonia!*
He happens to be Groucho Marx, and so the country is in deep trouble.
Center and below: A Night at the Opera *(MGM, 1935). Bedlam reigns in the celebrated scene*
in which the Marx Brothers and a ship's entire staff crowd into a tiny stateroom. Below: Harpo Marx,
Chico Marx, and Allan Jones make unconvincing Russian aviators, but the only one
apparently not fooled by their disguise is Groucho Marx, leering at bottom right.

If the screwball comedy often reveled in the racy, raucous rich—*My Man Godfrey* (1936) was the best of many examples—it was also clear that life in the Depression years was not all dinner parties and scavenger hunts, and once in a while, a dizzy heiress had to learn that bitter fact. In no film was the lesson more divertingly taught than in Frank Capra's landmark comedy *It Happened One Night* (1934). With a perceptiveness that seems like inspiration in hindsight, Capra took comedy out of the drawing rooms and placed it squarely in middle America. Robert Riskin's screenplay, from a story by Samuel Hopkins Adams, was a refreshingly new-style tale of a runaway heiress (Claudette Colbert) and a newspaper reporter (Clark Gable) who share adventures and a love affair on a cross-country bus ride. Released without fanfare, loathed by its stars, dismissed by its studio, *It Happened One Night* was a rousing success, winning five Academy Awards, and it has lost little of its status as one of Hollywood's greatest comedy films.

One may well ask why. The film reinforced the idea that rich folk were scatterbrained and irresponsible, and that poor people harbored most of the virtues, including decency, honesty, and compassion (this would remain Frank Capra's theme for many years), but so had many other movies of the day. The screenplay is more engaging than witty, and the cast, though expert and winning, is not measurably superior to that of other screwball comedies. But *It Happened*

carnival, bumping and grinding on the runway or taming lions with a whip and a gun while keeping up a running commentary with the beasts ("Where were *you* last night?"); Mae surrounded by admiring, giggling black maids; Mae exchanging quips with Grant ("Do you mind if I get personal?" "I don't mind if you get familiar"). She plays her best scene in the courtroom, suing Grant for breach of promise. Wearing a fur stole, a black gown, a rope of beads, and a feathered hat, she brazenly questions the male witnesses with damaging evidence against her, reducing each of them to total bewilderment. Mae treats men with open contempt, but she loves them, nonetheless. Tira's life's creed and her own are interchangeable: "When I'm good, I'm *very* good. But when I'm bad, I'm better."

All these sublime figures of thirties comedy existed in their own self-created worlds. But there *was* a real world out there, where people (or most people) struggled to make a living, fell in love and married, and grappled with daily problems. Magazines and newspapers also told us that, in the midst of poverty and pain, there were immensely wealthy people with not a worry on their minds or a thought in their heads: arrogant tycoons with flighty wives and frivolous daughters who fell in and out of love on a regular basis. They were amusing, they were exasperating, and they made good copy. Out of this heady mixture of middle and upper classes (the lower class was largely reserved for social drama) came a body of films known compositely as the screwball comedy.

With a set of attitudes and conventions as stylized as Restoration comedy, the screwball comedy skipped its nimble way through the thirties (and, greatly diminished, into the forties), thumbing its nose at the Depression either by ignoring it or by turning it into a background for fairy tales (Cinderella marries rich prince; heiress falls for proletarian). The characters in screwball comedies reacted in the same way as the great comic stars, but within recognizable settings of living rooms, bedrooms, and trains. If the world had turned irrational, why not behave irrationally? Cheerful but also laced with cynicism, the screwball comedies were inhabited by dizzy heiresses, slap-happy reporters, addled butlers, dippy dowagers, and other assorted eccentrics.

Left: I'm No Angel *(Paramount, 1933). The incomparable Tira (Mae West) plays havoc with courtroom procedure when she acts as her own lawyer in her breach-of-promise suit against Cary Grant.*
Right: It Happened One Night *(Columbia, 1934). Weary travelers Peter Warne (Clark Gable) and Ellie Andrews (Claudette Colbert) are about to share a carrot. Frank Capra's romantic comedy was a surprise hit.*

One Night struck a responsive chord (and still does) because it recognized and appreciated the lives of ordinary Americans. Instead of in a Cadillac, the principals traveled on a bus; instead of in a drawing room, they cavorted in a cramped cabin of an auto court. The movie also presented some home truths: one could be resourceful and learn to cope with trouble, and life could be tolerable if its simple joys were savored whenever they turned up.

The longevity of *It Happened One Night* also stems from its many scenes that have become a permanent part of movie lore: the "walls of Jericho" scene in which Gable places a blanket on a clothesline between himself and Colbert in the cabin they are forced to occupy; Gable teaching Colbert how to dunk a doughnut ("Dunking's an art. Don't let it soak so long. A dip and plop into your mouth"); Gable and Colbert hitchhiking, in which she proves conclusively that "the limb is mightier than the thumb." Despite their grudging participation, the stars are immensely skilled and likable. In his twenty-first film in only three years, Gable gave his easy masculinity a humorous edge and Claudette Colbert projected an ingratiating warmth behind her haughty demeanor. She set the pattern for many other actresses who relished playing madcap heiresses, including Myrna Loy and Katharine Hepburn.

After too many years in lofty dramas, Katharine Hepburn emerged as one of the most successful comediennes of the period, bringing her eccentric style to a succession of rich-girl roles. In RKO's *Bringing Up Baby* (1938), directed by Howard Hawks from a screenplay by Dudley Nichols and Hagar Wilde, she played Susan Vance, a scatterbrained heiress who sets her sights on a serious-minded (and engaged) young paleontologist named David Huxley (Cary Grant). She snares him, but not before involving her baffled aunt (May Robson), her aunt's friend (Charlie Ruggles), a big-game hunter, and a large, gentle leopard named Baby. Played at ninety miles an hour, with not a single pause for logic, *Bringing Up Baby* combines the elements for a successful screwball comedy: it has cleverly contrived slapstick (Susan and David scramble through the Connecticut woods singing Baby's favorite soothing song, "I Can't Give You

Anything But Love"); a full quota of eccentric character roles, including an apoplectic constable (Walter Catlett) and a drunken stableman (Barry Fitzgerald); and dialogue that generates laughter by being off-center rather than off-color. (Forced to put on a woman's fluffy robe—don't ask why—David is confronted by Susan's Aunt Elizabeth, who rightfully asks, "Why are you wearing a robe?" David fairly leaps into the air as he replies, "Because I just went *gay* all of a sudden!") Unlike most film comedies of the 1980s, *Bringing Up Baby* steers an even course of lunacy, never veering into sentiment (true screwball comedies don't have the time) or easy bawdry.

After filming *Holiday* (1938) at Columbia and then returning to the stage for Philip Barry's *The Philadelphia Story*, Hepburn starred in the movie version of the play. Released in 1940, it contained her most accomplished, most enchanting portrait of a rich girl. As Tracy Lord, a cold and demanding Main Line heiress (a role written for her by Barry), she discovers the virtues of humility and understanding through the men who love her, a reporter named Mike Connor (James Stewart) and C. K. Dexter Haven (Cary Grant), her ex-husband, who ultimately wins her back. Donald Ogden Stewart's screenplay retains Barry's graceful, civilized tone, but more interestingly, it veers away from the satirical, even spiteful attitude of many thirties comedies toward the rich. Here the wealthy folk are not silly and irresponsible, and Tracy, so hard and unyielding that she might qualify as the nasty "other woman" in thirties comedy, even learns to have some regard for human frailty. (The wealthy largely vanished as a target in the forties.) Given the chance to play a highfalutin woman without the off-putting haughtiness and pretentiousness of her earlier thirties roles, Hepburn is magically right as Tracy; when Mike tells her, "You have a magnificence in you—you're lit from within," you can see the radiance.

When not twitting the foibles of the rich, screwball comedies found humor in the antics of the married, or the about-to-be-unmarried. (On the whole, the province of the married rich was left to the

Left: Bringing Up Baby *(RKO, 1938). Scatterbrained heiress Katharine Hepburn and beleaguered paleontologist Cary Grant confront a leopard that is definitely not Baby.*
Right: The Philadelphia Story *(MGM, 1940). Katharine Hepburn repeated her stage role as Tracy Lord, the imperious rich girl who learns humility, and James Stewart won an Oscar as reporter Mike Connor, who falls in love with her.*

theater.) Probably the best of the marital comedies was Columbia's *The Awful Truth* (1937), an unquestionable change of pace for director Leo McCarey after his moving but commercially unsuccessful production of *Make Way for Tomorrow*. Derived from a play by Arthur Richman that had been filmed twice before, *The Awful Truth* had a bright and amusing screenplay credited to Viña Delmar, but reportedly McCarey reshaped it himself, using improvisation to capture the special chemistry of his stars Irene Dunne and Cary Grant. As a divorced couple who really love each other, they played with irresistible humor and charm, making many of the lines seem better than they were. Dunne's deliciously tongue-in-cheek manner meshes beautifully with Grant's urbane and debonair style. There are classically funny scenes—Dunne trying to hide both Grant and her ardent voice teacher from her new beau (Ralph Bellamy) and his battle-ax mother; Grant interrupting Dunne's song recital—but the film's best scene belongs to Dunne alone: pretending to be Grant's flighty Southern sister, she bursts in on a party attended by the friends and family of Grant's new socialite fiancée and wreaks hilarious mayhem. Like the best screwball comedies, *The Awful Truth* earns its laughs through the absurdity of human behavior: people willfully acting against their own best instincts.

The Awful Truth was good-natured fun—the closest it came to satire was in the characterization of Dunne's new beau, a dim-witted Oklahoma oil millionaire—but other screwball comedies were not so kind. There was definite malice in the film comedies of Ben Hecht, especially in his script for *Nothing Sacred* (1937), but his wicked turn of mind never produced happier results than when Columbia reworked his famed newspaper comedy, *The Front Page* (written with Charles MacArthur), for a second go-around in 1940. Newly titled *His Girl Friday*, this version changed star reporter Hildy Johnson into a woman but kept the machine-gun pace (reportedly, it has the fastest dialogue ever recorded on film) and mordant, cynical humor of the original. Under Howard Hawks's direction, Rosalind Russell played Hildy in her most brittle and frenetic style,

battling editor and ex-husband Cary Grant but keeping an eye out for the hot story. The first version of *The Front Page* was released in 1931, and in many ways *His Girl Friday* is like a throwback to the earlier period in its abrasive and callous attitudes. There is nothing romantic in Grant's scheming to win Russell back—he only needs a good reporter—and the newshawks gathered in the press room of a Chicago prison are a seedy, corruptible lot. Fortunately, Charles Lederer's adaptation of the play is also preternaturally funny, even in its wildly melodramatic portions.

If the dominant note of the screwball comedy was lighthearted or wicked impudence, there was still room for a kindlier, more hopeful view of humanity than that provided by madcap heiresses and cynical reporters. Throughout the thirties, director Frank Capra amply filled this space with a series of populist (and popular) comedies that started with *It Happened One Night*. Perhaps the best representative of the group was Columbia's *Mr. Deeds Goes to Town* (1936), which Capra's favorite scenarist, Robert Riskin, wrote from a story by Clarence Budington Kelland. This genial if overlong comedy centered on a bona fide screwball whose nuttiness comes not from thumbing his nose at the Depression but from completely ignoring it, until circumstances make that impossible. Amiable Longfellow Deeds (Gary Cooper) of Mandrake Falls, Vermont, inherits a fortune but is not impressed—he would rather write greeting card verse and play his tuba. When he realizes that he has become a target for nasty schemers and con men, Deeds decides to use his money to build a cooperative for downtrodden farmers. His enemies try to have him declared insane but he triumphs at a sanity hearing. He also wins the love of Babe Bennett (Jean Arthur), a reporter who was originally out to humiliate him in print.

On the surface, *Mr. Deeds Goes to Town* is a kind of cheerful Depression fantasy: in a grim time, one simple, honest man can make a difference; money is the root of all evil; and so on. Played by Gary Cooper with charming diffidence, Deeds is the Good Man, although eccentric enough to avoid being cloying and unreal. But,

Left: The Awful Truth *(Columbia, 1937). In Leo McCarey's classic screwball comedy, Irene Dunne and Cary Grant play a divorced couple who are destined to get together again. The stars made a compatible team here and in several other films.*
Right: His Girl Friday *(Columbia, 1940). This hilarious, fast-moving version of the stage play* The Front Page *tailored the role of reporter Hildy Johnson, a man in the play, for Rosalind Russell. Here she talks with devious editor (and ex-husband) Walter Burns, played by Cary Grant.*

as in most Capra films, there are ominous clouds in that sunny sky, hints of melancholy and bleakness. Deeds's purity and common sense are tested by the cruelest ordeal: he is mocked, badgered, humiliated, and finally brought to court, where elderly ladies of his town claim that he's "pixilated." As the world grows ugly around him, he withdraws into catatonia. In a sense, Longfellow Deeds harks back to the innocent clowns of the twenties—Capra had his roots in silent comedy—but the difference is significant. Whereas the silent clowns were optimistic and resourceful in a hopeful world, Deeds is thrown into depression by a hostile world. Only the heartfelt support of others and the love of a woman can spur him into fighting back.

Frank Capra was a truly original director of the thirties, but there was another, diametrically opposite to Capra in his tone and approach, whose best work was done during that decade. German-born Ernst Lubitsch had established an international reputation in the twenties with his ironic, elegant sex comedies (*Forbidden Paradise, Kiss Me Again*), and in the early thirties, his musical films, particularly *The Love Parade* and *The Merry Widow*, were enchanting combinations of songs and witty dialogue. In 1932, he directed one of the very best comedies of the period, *Trouble in Paradise*. This glittering masterwork, with a screenplay by Samson Raphaelson and Grover Jones (from a play by Laszlo Aladar), concerned two thieves (Herbert Marshall and Miriam Hopkins) pretending to be aristocrats

Above: Mr. Deeds Goes to Town *(Columbia, 1936). Longfellow Deeds (Gary Cooper) is hailed as a hero of the people. An easygoing eccentric from Mandrake Falls, Vermont, Deeds is subjected to all sorts of tribulations after he inherits a fortune.*
Below: Trouble in Paradise *(Paramount, 1932). The screen's most elegant thieves, Miriam Hopkins and Herbert Marshall, are served dinner by waiter George Humbert. In this witty comedy, directed by Ernst Lubitsch, the dialogue glitters as brightly as the jewels this duo tries to steal.*

With the exception of that rapturous musical *The Merry Widow*, Lubitsch did not match the elegance and wit of *Trouble in Paradise* until 1939, when he directed one of his most celebrated films, *Ninotchka*. If this film is largely remembered for presenting Greta Garbo in her first romantic comedy, that is not to demean the screenplay by Charles Brackett, Billy Wilder, and Walter Reisch (from a story by Melchior Lengyel). Witty and satirical, its story of the thawing of an austere lady Communist—an ex-sergeant in the Russian army—and her romance with a debonair Frenchman is as sparkling as the champagne she downs on a seductive evening in Paris. Helped by a superlative cast headed by Melvyn Douglas and Ina Claire (one of the very best stage comediennes), Garbo proved that her radiance was as suitable for comedy as it was for tragedy.

Ninotchka pokes malicious fun at the Soviets: in the three nervous, impressionable Russian envoys who precede Ninotchka to Paris, in Ninotchka's severe clothing and somber demeanor, in jokes about trials and purges. But the film is essentially a romance, as two people from widely divergent cultures move from attraction to devotion. The melting of Ninotchka takes effect in a series of delightful sequences, none more so than one in which an amorous Leon (Douglas) tries to make love to her. He begins tentatively: "Do you like me just a little bit?" She replies, "Your general appearance is not distasteful." When she claims to be a "tiny cog in the wheel of evolution," he becomes ardent: "You're the most adorable cog I ever saw in my life." Later, in a small café, Ninotchka stubbornly resists Leon's attempts to make her laugh, until he accidentally tumbles from his chair and she roars with pleasure. (The film's ads shouted, "Garbo Laughs!") And Garbo finally in love is a glowing creature who touches the heart as well as the funnybone. She pours forth her feeling for Leon with an intensity every bit as strong as that she gave to the role of Camille, bringing a touch of poignancy to a witty comedy.

With one or two conspicuous exceptions, the forties saw a precipitous decline in movie comedy, for a variety of reasons. It was as if the decade simply could not accommodate the impudent wit, the

who fall in love in Venice and decide to join forces. In Paris, they scheme to steal from a rich and amorous widow (Kay Francis); Gaston (Marshall) takes a job as her secretary. Jealousy causes a rift in their relationship, but eventually the two are reconciled, and they make off with their stolen goods.

Trouble in Paradise is so sly, so deft, so wonderfully civilized that it virtually stands alone amid the sophisticated comedies of the period. The production credits are impeccable—we can cite Hans Dreier's expansive, amusing Art Deco sets, Victor Milner's glistening camerawork, and the principal players, who have never been better. Herbert Marshall's Gaston is mercifully free of the actor's usual stodginess, and Miriam Hopkins is charming and animated as Lily; Kay Francis's Mariette makes excellent use of her throaty voice and regal bearing. But *Trouble in Paradise* sparkles most in its dialogue, which is never less than sharply ironic, graceful, or, when necessary, highly romantic. In a splendid dinner scene, Gaston and Lily spend their time exchanging confidences and blunt truths, while filching items from each other with airy finesse; admiration turns to love before the night is over.

Left: Ninotchka *(MGM, 1939). The ads proclaimed "Garbo Laughs!"—and here is the indisputable evidence. Her tutor in the pleasures of laughter is Melvyn Douglas.*
Right: Adam's Rib *(MGM, 1949). Defendant Doris Attinger (Judy Holliday) is flanked by prosecutor Adam Bonner (Spencer Tracy) and defending counsel Amanda Bonner (Katharine Hepburn).*
Opposite, above: A lobby card for Bringing Up Baby *(RKO, 1938). Opposite, center, left: A lobby card for* Mr. Deeds Goes to Town *(Columbia, 1936). Opposite, center, right: A lobby card for* Ninotchka *(MGM, 1939). Opposite, below: A lobby card for* Woman of the Year *(MGM, 1942).*

sense of inspired lunacy, the verbal and physical eccentricities that made thirties comedy memorable. For one, the great comic artists of the thirties had passed their heyday or could no longer find material to match their best early efforts. In addition, many of the best comedy actresses of the thirties were off their stride in the forties; divested of their sense of humor by high-minded dramas, they often seemed pale echoes of what they once had been.

It was not all drought; there were a number of superior comedy films released during the forties, not all of them from Preston Sturges's acid-tipped pen. One of the first was also one of the best; early in the decade MGM had the apt idea of teaming two of its most popular stars, Spencer Tracy and Katharine Hepburn. Tracy had been a sturdy actor at the studio since 1935, but only occasionally as a romantic lead. Hepburn had just scored an enormous success in the film version of her stage triumph, *The Philadelphia Story*, after years of being labeled "box-office poison." Combined for *Woman of the Year* (1942), directed by George Stevens, his straightforward masculinity played well against her airy, brittle femininity. Together in the same frame, his craggy Irish face made an oddly appealing contrast to her angular New England features. The movie's bright original screenplay (by Ring Lardner, Jr., and Michael Kanin) concerned a renowned political columnist (Hepburn) who falls in love with and marries a rugged sportswriter (Tracy) for the same newspaper. But Hepburn refuses to settle into domesticity, and their opposing life styles result in quarrels and separation, until she sees the light—love is more important than politics or fame—and returns to assume her wifely duties (today's liberated women would recoil in horror). Occasionally sluggish and sentimental, the film had an overall charm provided by the stars' obvious rapport with each other.

The next few teamings of Hepburn and Tracy were not up to *Woman of the Year*—their comedies, although enjoyable, tended to be talky or thin, and their dramas were turgid. But the end of the decade brought their best work together, in a film dexterously guided by Hepburn's first and favorite director, George Cukor. *Adam's Rib* (1949) was much less malicious toward career women than was *Woman of the Year*, but the Ruth Gordon—Garson Kanin screenplay could not resist a touch of condescension toward the independent-minded woman. Tracy and Hepburn played married lawyers who find themselves on opposite sides of a case involving a wife's shooting of her errant husband. Their quarrels and courtroom antics lead to separation but ultimately, of course, they kiss and make up.

Cut to the stars' exact measure, the script of *Adam's Rib* gives them ample room to play against each other in high style: she strident and overconfident, he condescendingly amused until she scores some telling points. They are in top form, but the film is stolen from them by the supporting players. As the gun-toting wife, Judy Holliday created a sensation. Her endearingly pixilated Doris Attinger, never so distraught at her husband's cheating that she can't pause for something to eat, is a unique comic creation, with her very own way of speaking. ("He used to do that a lot. Not come home.") Also memorable were Tom Ewell as her indignant husband ("She's crazy! She's *always* been crazy!") and Jean Hagen as his sluttish mistress (asked whether he had ever touched her before the day of the shooting, she replies, "We used to shake hands a lot").

By far the most original contribution to film comedy in the forties was made by Preston Sturges. A screenwriter in the thirties—his script for *Easy Living* (1937) was exceptionally adroit—Sturges won his first assignment in 1940 when he convinced Paramount to let him direct his screenplay for *The Great McGinty*. For the next four years, Sturges wrote and directed a series of comedies that bore his unique stamp: irreverent, irrational, and ferociously funny, they blended satire and slapstick in happy proportions. They were also daring in their way—audiences may have been laughing too hard to notice that Sturges was poking fun at America's most cherished ideals and pretensions. His targets included heroism, motherhood, politics, romance, and the lofty attitudes of many of his colleagues. His characters were a colorful lot of grafters, bumblers, opportunists, charlatans, and simple eccentrics who spoke in a vernacular that seemed to have been invented by Sturges.

Each of Sturges's Paramount comedies of the forties has its ardent champions, but *Hail the Conquering Hero* (1944) has the most sustained humor and point, and it is perhaps the best example of Sturges's offbeat style. At the height of World War II, he saw fit to aim his fire at America's mindless hero worship, its fondness for turning every serviceman who kills his quota of the enemy into a figure of adulation. It was a bold endeavor, but Sturges, as usual, couched his message in raucous terms that made it much more palatable. His "hero," Woodrow Lafayette Pershing Truesmith (Eddie Bracken), is a glum 4-F with a family history of wartime heroism. Six Marines take him under their wing and insist on bringing him home as a decorated hero, but they (and Woodrow) get much more than they bargained for. Woodrow is given a tumultuous reception—he is lionized and practically canonized. But finally he confesses all, only to find, to his astonishment, that his confession endears him all the more to everyone.

Sturges's screenplay brims with clever, cynical touches; he is

Above: Hail the Conquering Hero *(Paramount, 1944). A highly reluctant Woodrow Truesmith (Eddie Bracken), classified 4-F by his draft board, is pressured into becoming a fake military hero to his fellow townspeople by Marines Freddie Steele and William Demarest.*
Opposite: All About Eve *(Fox, 1950). The scheming, ambitious Eve Harrington (Anne Baxter) faces her "idol," stage star Margo Channing (Bette Davis). Visible in the background are (left to right) Gary Merrill, Celeste Holm, George Sanders, Marilyn Monroe, and Hugh Marlowe.*

funniest when he is most malicious. Thus, his Marines are no clean-cut warriors: the Sergeant (William Demarest) is a fanciful liar and another, cruelly nicknamed "Bugsy" (Freddie Steele), is a shell-shocked fellow with a mother complex. The townspeople are all idiots: the mayor (Raymond Walburn) is a bombastic fraud, the chairman of the Reception Committee (Franklin Pangborn) is a hysterical nincompoop, and a judge (Jimmy Conlin) is shamelessly corrupt. Unlike Frank Capra's lamb-bites-wolf comedies, *Hail the Conquering Hero* does not have a soft center; in many ways, it reverts to the nastier comedies of the thirties such as *Nothing Sacred*, but with an added dose of vitriol. It also differs from the thirties comedies in that it offers little or no romance or sentiment in exchange for its sardonic message. Even when Sturges includes romance in his films, he gives it a slightly mocking tone.

By the end of the forties, the diminishing quality of film comedy, despite some excellent movies, was evident, and it would diminish even further in the fifties. Toward the end of the decade, there was one strong ray of hope in the person of the inordinately clever and perceptive Joseph L. Mankiewicz. Active for many years as a writer and producer, mainly at Paramount and MGM, Mankiewicz joined Fox in the mid-forties and turned to directing as well as writing. Rather static cinematically, his films benefited from unusually literate screenplays that satirized human foibles and attitudes and provided juicy roles for actors.

His first comedy as writer and director, *A Letter to Three Wives* (1949), is a cleverly amusing movie with some sharp commentary on marriage, social barriers, and other contemporary topics. He was even more successful the following year with *All About Eve* (1950), which went a step further in making literate, theatrically styled dialogue the basis of the humor. Appropriately, the subject of the screenplay (from Mary Orr's story) is the theater itself—it deals with Margo Channing (Bette Davis), a forty-year-old stage luminary who becomes the target for a scheming minx named Eve Harrington (Anne Baxter). Swirling about these two ladies are various theater people, including Margo's director and lover (Gary Merrill), a playwright (Hugh Marlowe), his wife and friend to Margo (Celeste Holm), and a poisonous drama critic (George Sanders).

The effectiveness of *All About Eve* depends largely on the marvelously pointed lines of badinage, invective, and bitchiness that Mankiewicz gives to his characters. In some cases, he is extremely fortunate in the actors called upon to deliver them. As the vain, insecure, volatile Margo, Bette Davis gives what may be her best performance; fully aware of her explosive temperament ("Fasten your seat belts, it's going to be a bumpy night!"), she can still reveal her vulnerability in times of stress and pain. George Sanders's Addison De Witt is the perfect summation of all the malicious, spiteful characters this actor had played over the years, and, as Margo's blunt, loyal maid Birdie, Thelma Ritter is given some of the best lines, which she dispatches with relish. Listening to Eve's sad (and also untruthful) tale of woe, she can only comment, "The only thing missing is the bloodhounds snapping at her rear end!" The comments

on the theater, like Mankiewicz's incidental preachments on education in *A Letter to Three Wives*, were amusing, not too intrusive, and not especially profound, but they served the purpose of flattering the audience with their "inside" erudition. The movie won that year's Oscar, as did Mankiewicz for his direction.

The fifties were a sparse decade for comedy—among the better efforts were several likable films starring the talented Judy Holliday—but the end of the decade brought a movie that has taken on classic status since its release in 1959. Billy Wilder's outrageous and consistently hilarious farce *Some Like It Hot* had a one-joke premise that threatened to topple over into bad taste: on St. Valentine's Day in 1927, two down-and-out musicians (Tony Curtis and Jack Lemmon) witness a mass gangland slaying in a Chicago garage. Fleeing in panic, they join an all-girl band heading for a job in Florida, disguised as improbable females. The frantic complications involve the band singer (Marilyn Monroe), a voluptuous but naïve blonde beauty who falls for Curtis in his second disguise as a millionaire. At the same time, Lemmon, coming to believe that he *is* a girl, finds a "suitor" in wealthy but addled old Joe E. Brown. When the gangland killers, led by George Raft, come to Florida, a frenzied chase ensues, but it all ends happily. In the famous ending, Lemmon reveals to the relentless Brown that he's really a guy. The cheerful geezer replies, "Well, nobody's perfect!"

It has been noted often enough that the Billy Wilder–I. A. L. Diamond screenplay (from an old German film) actually trades in less than savory subjects, including transvestism, impotence, murder on a grand scale, and, in Brown's case, near-imbecility. Yet it is all so cheerfully innocent, so gleefully prankish that the only possible response is surrender and enjoyment. It has all of Billy Wilder's rowdiness and hearty vulgarity without the usual bitter aftertaste. The cast could not be better: Tony Curtis reveals an unexpected comic flair (he does an on-target impression of Cary Grant), Monroe invests her good-hearted blonde with a touch of pathos (she always gets "the fuzzy end of the lollipop"), and Brown is a joy. But *Some Like It Hot* belongs to Jack Lemmon, whose performance is awesomely

Overleaf, left: Some Like It Hot *(Mirisch/United Artists, 1959). Billy Wilder's riotous comedy starred Marilyn Monroe as the luscious singer with an all-girls band and Jack Lemmon and Tony Curtis as musicians who dress up as flirtatious flappers to escape gangland reprisal.*
Overleaf, right: M*A*S*H *(Ingo Preminger/Fox, 1970). Donald Sutherland and Elliott Gould as gifted surgeons who relax from patching up wounded soldiers by carrying on in the style of overage Rover Boys. Below: The men of the MASH unit pose in a way that unmistakably duplicates Leonardo da Vinci's* The Last Supper—*evidence of the film's audacious, irreverent humor.*

funny. From his first moment in women's clothing, struggling to stay upright on his high heels, he induces helpless laughter. His Jerry-Daphne is a riotous creation, perfectly timed, impeccably controlled; we need only watch him on the train to Florida, in delicious agony

in the hope of advancement in his job, lends his apartment to company executives for sexual assignations. He becomes involved with Fran Kubelik (Shirley MacLaine), an elevator operator who is the discarded mistress of one of these executives. Ultimately, he recovers

as the girls crowd into his berth, or dancing the tango with his ardent millionaire, or, in perhaps the funniest scene, joyfully announcing his "engagement" to a disgusted Curtis.

Billy Wilder followed *Some Like It Hot* with *The Apartment* (1960), a more characteristic film and that year's Academy Award winner as Best Picture. A comedy with decidedly serious overtones, it concerned C. C. ("Bud") Baxter (Jack Lemmon), an office worker who,

his pride, integrity, and moral sense, and refuses to turn over his apartment. He also wins Fran's admiration and love.

The Apartment has often been compared with the comedies of Ernst Lubitsch (for whom Wilder worked on *Ninotchka*) in its winking attitude toward sexual peccadilloes and its somewhat astringent attitude toward human behavior in general. It is true that there are similarities to Lubitsch in his use of humor to cover or disguise

Some Like It Hot *(Mirisch/United Artists, 1959). "Josephine" and "Daphne" pose prettily for the cameras. They are, of course, Joe (Tony Curtis) and Jerry (Jack Lemmon).*

a basically unsavory situation. There are many scenes that echo Lubitsch's charming and offbeat style: Bud and Fran playing gin rummy after her attempted suicide, with a glum Fran wondering "why people have to love each other anyway"; Bud, happy and no longer lonesome, straining spaghetti through his tennis racket.

Yet *The Apartment* is not a Lubitschean comedy in significant ways; it prompts an ambiguous reaction rather than pure delight. Lubitsch's cheating wives and errant husbands exercise their wit more than their bodies as they play their marital and extramarital games, whereas the characters in *The Apartment* are really not an attractive lot, and their bedroom games result in misery and pain that cannot be completely concealed by laughs. Despite Lemmon's best efforts, his Bud Baxter is not the abused, lonely soul we are expected to find sympathetic; he is actually mealy-mouthed, weak, and opportunistic. His reformation comes somewhat too late to make him lovable. In a paltry decade for comedy, *The Apartment* stands out as an expertly handled and highly enjoyable movie. But, like other Billy Wilder films, it leaves a sour taste in one's mouth.

After *The Apartment*, no other important Hollywood comedy was released until Mike Nichols's landmark 1967 film, *The Graduate*. Widely acclaimed—and also heatedly discussed—at its release, *The Graduate* was a talisman for its time: the first major film to deal with the alienation of young people in the sixties—but emphatically *not* the fierce, rebellious young people who were storming the barricades. Benjamin Braddock (Dustin Hoffman), the twenty-one-year-old hero of Buck Henry and Calder Willingham's perceptive screenplay (from Charles Webb's novel), is "an award-winning scholar," the pride of his upper-middle-class parents, to whom he appears modest, respectful—a model son. Actually, he feels isolated from his environment: inert, melancholy, and totally at sea (almost literally—he floats in his pool like a shipwrecked sailor).

During the course of the movie, Benjamin emerges from his lethargy, spurred on by an affair with the wife of his father's partner, the elegant, alcoholic Mrs. Robinson (Anne Bancroft), but then he falls in love with Mrs. Robinson's daughter, Elaine (Katharine Ross). In the end, having journeyed from empty indifference to frenzied obsession, he abducts Elaine from the bridal altar (she has just married another man). He has finally found a purpose, a sense of destination. But as he rides off on a bus with Elaine, it is ironically not at all clear what that destination might be.

Benjamin's feeling of isolation is brilliantly conveyed in the opening section of the film: his blank face appears over the credits as he rides the airport escalator or as he presses it against a fishbowl, contemplating nothing in particular. Wearing his new scuba suit ("Here's the track star!" "Proud, proud, proud!"), he walks amid his parents' well-meaning but fatuous friends like an alien being. His seduction by Mrs. Robinson is certainly one of the funniest ever recorded on film; her cool, casual sexiness is hilariously contrasted with his fumbling, desperate nervousness. Using his constricted nasal voice and a helpless little squeal, Hoffman makes Benjamin an endearing parody of all the sensitive young men who have soulful "coming-of-age" encounters with older women in more seriously intended movies. It is like Henry Aldrich in *Devil in the Flesh*.

The film's tone darkens considerably when Elaine Robinson returns home and Benjamin, after strong resistance, falls in love with her. Here the screenplay runs into difficulties: the mother-daughter-Benjamin triangle (with a justifiably bitter Mr. Robinson on the sidelines) cannot fully avoid an unpleasant aroma, and Benjamin's obsessive behavior seems amazingly insensitive and not overly bright. It is never made clear whether we are intended to applaud the end of Benjamin's alienation from society or to commiserate with everyone whose path he crosses. Perhaps there are aspects of both in the characterization, which might explain the puzzled, wondering expression on Elaine's face as she rides off to a life with Benjamin Braddock. Still, *The Graduate* deserves its fame, and it is one of the few comedies of the sixties to leave an indelible mark on the decade.

By 1970, after a decade of Doris Day and an absence of truly mean-spirited comedies since the thirties, audiences were ready for the nonstop irreverence of Robert Altman's *M*A*S*H*. The mordantly funny screenplay by Ring Lardner, Jr., adapted from Richard Hooker's novel, used the Korean War as a metaphor for man's absurdity, stupidity, and cruelty to his fellow creatures. Set in a Mobile Army Surgical Hospital (MASH) unit, the movie focused on Captains "Hawkeye" Pierce (Donald Sutherland) and "Trapper John" McIntyre (Elliott Gould), two gifted surgeons whose sole delight, when they are not patching up the broken, bleeding bodies of wounded soldiers, is in carrying on in the style of hyper, overage Rover Boys. They enjoy disrupting army routine, chasing and often catching the nurses, and, especially, humiliating all those they look upon as pompous, holier-than-thou fools. Their outrage at the war is masked by their outrageous behavior; their sorrow is muted by brazen laughter at the edge of the grave.

M*A*S*H is clearly a deadly serious farce, and its mixture of bloodshed and slapstick startled and delighted most critics and moviegoers. It does, in fact, have some audaciously funny scenes:

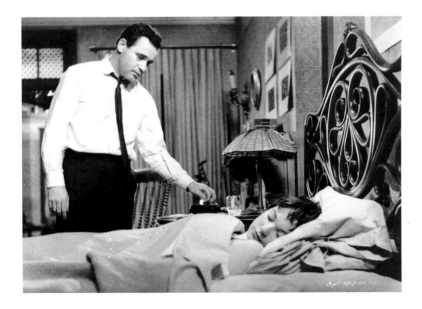

The Apartment (Mirisch/United Artists, 1960). C.B. ("Bud") Baxter (Jack Lemmon) gazes tenderly at Fran Kubelik (Shirley MacLaine), who has attempted suicide in his apartment after being rejected by her lover, Bud's employer. Billy Wilder's dark-hued comedy won that year's Academy Award as Best Picture.

the attempts to help a suicide-minded dentist who is in despair over his impotence; Hawkeye and Trapper John on the loose in Tokyo, dispensing their disrespect to anyone who gets in their way; and a climactic football game, which the MASH unit wins by injecting the rival team's star player with a paralyzing drug. There were many others, however, who were put off by the film's savage cruelty, particularly to Major Margaret ("Hot Lips") Houlihan (Sally Kellerman) and her priggish, Bible-spouting lover, Major Frank Burns (Robert Duvall). For their relatively minor crimes of pomposity, rigidity, and unwavering dedication to the military life, they are afforded shabby treatment that is supposed to be funny: their conversation during sex is recorded and played over the camp's loudspeaker, and a shower is rigged so that "Hot Lips" can be exposed nude to the camp and settle a bet as to the color of her pubic hair. (Actually, the film is rather insulting to *all* women—the nurses seem to serve either as prey or therapy.)

The most talented and original filmmaker to emerge in the seventies was Woody Allen. A comedy writer for years and then a popular nightclub comedian, Allen at first conveyed the image of the put-upon urban *schlemeil* who would like to function as a tower of strength

and a sexual champion. He was the class wit who used jokes to avoid being the class punching bag. But his jokes were not the

The Graduate *(Joseph E. Levine/Embassy, 1967). Young Benjamin Braddock (Dustin Hoffman) has his first tryst with the elegant and alcoholic Mrs. Robinson (Anne Bancroft). Both Hoffman and Bancroft were nominated for Academy Awards. Below: A desperate Benjamin tears Elaine Robinson (Katharine Ross) away from her marriage ceremony, much to the fury of Mrs. Robinson.*

usual patter—they were something fresh and new, with their own unique combination of absurdity and intellect. When he entered filmmaking—as writer and actor in *What's New, Pussycat* (1965) and as director, writer, and star in *Take the Money and Run* (1969)— he unleashed an undisciplined wildness that had its origin in the Marx Brothers, whom he admired greatly. His special blend of cerebral gags and lunatic situations produced films that were completely pleasurable, despite their unevenness.

Although *Sleeper* (1973), Allen's science-fiction slapstick comedy, generated many laughs, *Annie Hall* (1977) was his most successful film to date, embraced by the public and acclaimed by most critics as a major advance for the filmmaker and one of the best comedies in years. It won that year's Academy Award for Best Picture, and Diane Keaton was voted Best Actress for her performance in the title role. (Allen also won as director and co-screenwriter.) Like his earlier films, it is endowed with Allenesque one-liners and a well-developed sense of the absurdities in modern living, but it also has somewhat more form and substance and less of his flights of fancy and self-indulgence (as in *Bananas*). *Annie Hall* is the love story of two hopeless neurotics: a comedian named Alvy Singer (Allen) with a rich fantasy life and a total inability to have a straightforward, uncomplicated relationship with women (or, for that matter, with anyone), and Annie (Keaton), a would-be singer and bundle of hang-ups, endlessly dithering and insecure. Alvy and Annie are meant for each other—and an impossible couple.

Although no masterwork, *Annie Hall* is a totally genial, observant, and often hilarious film sprung full-grown from Woody Allen's disorderly mind. It has a generous sprinkling of Allen jokes that surprise the viewer into laughter ("My grandmother never gave gifts. She was too busy being raped by Cossacks." "Sex is the most fun I've had without laughing"). It has funny snippets of Alvy's autobiography (his bizarre childhood, a 1944 coming-home party for his soldier brother, his disastrous marriages). It has a number of set pieces that viewers remember fondly—Alvy and Annie's kitchen battle with live lobsters, Alvy's visit to Annie's Wisconsin family (Alvy imagines himself looking like an Orthodox rabbi amid anti-Semitic types), a frenetic California house party. But it gets whatever substance it has from the scratchy, neurotic, untidy relationship between the principals. Allen taps a rich vein of humor and extracts a measure of pathos from their secret reflections, their conversations, and their psychoanalytic sessions. Unlike the characters in screwball comedies of the thirties, the messiness of their lives is not a reaction to an irrational outside world but to their own internal irrationality. While the madcap people of screwball comedy reveled in their superficiality, Alvy and Annie are the end products of an intensely introspective generation.

Allen followed *Annie Hall* with a serious drama, *Interiors* (1978), and then with *Manhattan* (1979), a dark-hued comedy that is his best movie so far. Its content was in keeping with Allen's obsession with the hang-ups and neuroses of modern urban men and women. The story revolved around a couple not unlike Alvy Singer and Annie Hall: two intense, apprehensive New Yorkers, both vainly pursuing an elusive happiness: comedy writer Isaac Davis (Allen) and Mary Wilke (Diane Keaton), who writes book reviews and novelizations. Isaac is plagued by an ex-wife (Meryl Streep) who left him for a female lover, and he is having a troubling affair with seventeen-year-old Tracy (Mariel Hemingway); Mary's romance is with Isaac's married friend Yale (Michael Murphy). During the course of the film, Isaac and Mary drift into an intense love affair which, not unexpectedly, ends unhappily when Mary returns to Yale. Isaac tries to return to Tracy, but she is leaving for London to study drama. The pattern of his basically selfish life has left him isolated, rejected, and hurting. The final shot of his face (clearly modeled after the ending of *City Lights*) reflects pain, confusion, and possibly hope.

Manhattan contains the requisite number of funny Allen quips (Yale: "You think you're God." Isaac: "I've got to model myself after *someone*"), but it is his most sensitive and certainly his most beautiful movie. For one thing, it looks and sounds like no other Allen film: the combination of dazzling black-and-white photography by Gordon Willis and the lilting, symphonically arranged Gershwin music creates a love letter to Manhattan, as well as an appropriate background for the strivings of these hedonistic characters. Manhattan is their natural habitat, their playground, and it has never looked better. For another thing, the film, for all its laughter, takes a sober, even rueful look at human relationships; these people live with continual regret, rejection, dissatisfaction. While the scenes depicting the love affair between Isaac and Mary are rhapsodic, their basic selfishness takes its human toll. In the film's most touching scene, Isaac and Tracy meet at a soda fountain, where he must tell her that he loves someone else. She is both a hurt child and a scorned woman as she sits crying over her malted. Nobody really wins, least of all Isaac, whose desolation is complete when he is scorned by his ex-wife, rejected by Mary, and even placed at arm's length by Tracy. ("Don't be so mature," he tells her in their parting scene.) Isaac Davis may not be a profoundly drawn character, but he is Allen's most deeply felt creation: a would-be tiger who is really a timid tomcat lost in a concrete but mightily attractive jungle.

From the first pratfall, the first pie-in-the-face, comedy has been a remedy for pain, a solace against the dark, a buttress against a dangerous world. From Charlie Chaplin's Tramp, pursued by irate policemen and vengeful bullies while dreaming of damsels in distress, to Woody Allen, afflicted with urban trauma and entire bundles of neuroses while dreaming of concupiscent females, comedy has sustained and nurtured life's victims, offering them a shield against disaster. You can deflect a bullet with a gag, either physical or verbal. During the thirties, comedy was used by the not-so-innocent as a weapon, to give the enemy as good as they got. Groucho Marx, Mae West, and W. C. Fields were nobody's victims.

In every decade, American film comedy has been, and, one hopes, will continue to be, a national treasure that brings us possibly the best gift of all: the gift of laughter.

WHAT A GLORIOUS FEELING
Great Musical Movies

There are those for whom the musical film is anathema. They resent the frivolous, often scatterbrained story lines, and they are intimidated by the bursts of music that seem to come out of nowhere, in the midst of the Canadian Rockies or the Austrian Alps, or through the walls of a turn-of-the-century St. Louis parlor. They find the color garish and the performers oppressive.

And then there are many others, happily outnumbering the dissenters, who find the Hollywood musical at its best a constant source of magic. For them, the world of the musical is suspended in its own time and place, far away from the pressures and demands of reality. For them, the response is visceral: intense joy when the music of Gershwin, Berlin, Kern, or Harry Warren fills the air with melody, tingling pleasure in Judy Garland's emotion-charged voice or Fred Astaire's lighter-than-air dancing. Admittedly, these musical fans have dwindled in number over the past few decades. But even in disappointment, their love persists for a genre that remains probably Hollywood's greatest contribution to popular culture.

Detractors have been given fuel for their fire in many of the elephantine musical films since the sixties. (We won't cite the titles—they deserve their anonymity.) But over the decades, and even since the sixties, there have been musical films that triumphantly fused all of their components—music, settings, costumes, performances, even (on occasion) the story—into perfect or nearly perfect entertainment. Inevitably, some components will overwhelm others—there may be a physical production of surpassing beauty (*The King and I*), a musical score overflowing with melody and wit (*My Fair Lady*), or a single performance of transcendent power (Judy Garland in *A Star Is Born*). Occasionally, a sense of fun pervades all components (*Singin' in the Rain*), or the director's vision casts a glow over the entire production (Rouben Mamoulian's *Love Me Tonight*). These are the musicals we cherish, and remember. And if nothing will persuade others to surrender to the movie musical, what does it matter? Those of us who love the genre will continue to revel in its glories, sharing in the dream of singing and dancing along with the performers in the enveloping darkness of the theater.

Al Jolson's fruity baritone on the scratchy soundtrack of *The Jazz Singer* (1927) may have paved the way for sound, but the film was neither the first talkie nor the first movie musical. It was *The Broadway Melody* (1929), MGM's first all-talking film, that actually set the framework for scores of musicals in the next few years. The sentimental backstage plot—two sisters in love with the same song-and-dance man as they seek fame on the musical stage—was imitated so often that it virtually became a subgenre, and the brash, slangy dialogue set a trend that carried well into the next decade. But it was the film's

elaborate musical numbers that created a sensation. Some critics objected to their vulgarity (the *New York Times* man was offended by "show girls in various states of undress"), but the public was immediately taken with the displays of lavish scenery and costumes, especially in the color sequence built around "The Wedding of the Painted Doll."

Less than two years after *Broadway Melody* was released, audiences filled to the bursting point with musical films turned hostile to the genre. But before the flood became a trickle, the screen was deluged with "all-talking, all-singing, all-dancing" movies: offspring of *Melody*, set in the hectic backstage world; film versions of popular stage operettas or contemporary musical comedies; and musicals using original songs and stories. Occasionally, however, an innovative director, intrigued by the possibilities of sound, decided to experiment with the new "toy." Musicals that went several steps beyond the conventional, using sound to implement, enhance, or comment upon a scene, turned up amid the scores of static, heavy-handed efforts.

One such director was King Vidor, widely admired for his silent features *The Big Parade* (1925) and *The Crowd* (1928). Vidor's single contribution to the early sound musical was remarkably daring for its time: a strong drama of sin and redemption in the deep South, featuring an all-black cast and spotted with spirituals and work songs. It even offered new songs by Irving Berlin—"At the End of the Road" and "The Swanee Shuffle"––but these added little to the film's overall impact. *Hallelujah!* (1929) was received with a mixture of admiration and hostility, and today it seems overwrought and (despite Vidor's sincere intentions) unmistakably racist in its depiction of blacks as fearful, sexually obsessed children. Yet its beautiful soft-focus photog-

Opposite: My Fair Lady *(Warner Bros., 1964). As cockney-turned-lady Eliza Doolittle, Audrey Hepburn wears one of Cecil Beaton's lavish creations with rare style and aplomb.*
Above: The Jazz Singer *(Warner Bros., 1927). In this landmark film, Jack Robin (Al Jolson), born Jakie Rabinowitz, must choose between a show business career and filial duty to his cantor father. Influencing his choice are Richard Tucker, May McAvoy, Otto Lederer, and Eugenie Besserer.*

raphy captures life in the cotton fields, and the film retains a crude power that reaches its peak in the climax, when the tormented hero, bent on revenge, chases the villain through a swamp. Here, Vidor heightened the drama by deliberately exaggerating the sounds of the swamp.

The same year in which *Hallelujah!* was released, another director with much different credentials than Vidor also succeeded in moving the musical film from its primitive state. Rouben Mamoulian, already highly regarded as a stage director, came to Hollywood to direct *Applause*, a musical drama concerning an ex-burlesque star (Helen Morgan) at the end of her tether. Mamoulian's use of innovative sound techniques improved a trite story, but his greatest musical achievement came three years later, when he directed one of the screen's most memorable musical films, *Love Me Tonight* (1932). This sparkling movie has the frailest of plots: the romance of a frustrated princess and a tailor who is mistaken for a baron, played by the popular team of Jeanette MacDonald and Maurice Chevalier. Yet around this conceit Mamoulian spins a web of total enchantment, interweaving witty and sometimes risqué dialogue with songs by Richard Rodgers and Lorenz Hart, while adding his own imaginative directorial touches. In few other early musicals is sound (an overheard melody, chattering women, a dropped vase) combined as felicitously with the action, or the camera used with such lighthearted flair to comment on a key scene. The deer hunt, for example, is brilliantly photographed not only to convey its balletic exhilaration but also to reveal its underlying absurdity.

The film's opening section is justly famous: Paris awakens to a symphony of noises, after which tailor Maurice greets the dawn with his "Song of Paree" and welcomes his first customer. A brief exchange with the customer leads to rhymed dialogue and then to one of the screen's greatest musical numbers. Maurice sings "Isn't It Romantic?" and, in dazzling succession, the song is taken up by a taxi driver, a composer, marching soldiers, a violinist in a gypsy camp, and finally by Princess Jeanette, a bored prisoner in her own castle. The hero and heroine are now linked in song, and Mamoulian has demonstrated

how visual and aural effects can be blended skillfully to create a musical number of great charm and beauty.

Love Me Tonight would be a masterpiece in any year but in 1932 it was a perfect diamond with very little competition from other musical gems—a jewel in a display case that was virtually empty. The dearth of musical films due to public indifference finally ended the following year when Darryl F. Zanuck, production head at Warner Bros., decided that audiences would welcome a contemporary musical comedy that brightened the bleak scene with a "so-what" approach to the Depression and a batch of extravagant musical numbers. Winning the support of the Warner brothers after initially strong resistance, Zanuck put together a musical film called *42nd Street* (1933). His judgment proved to be astute, but his choice for the film's dance director proved to be a stroke of genius. To create the numbers, he hired an abrasive but talented Broadway dance director named Busby Berkeley. With only one film credit (*Whoopee*), Berkeley was set loose on the Warners soundstage to indulge his whims and exercise his imagination.

The Warners musicals of the period have long been relegated to the realm of camp, but *42nd Street* has retained its status as the most durable of the group. Other musicals that followed were more lavish, more flamboyant and inventive in the Berkeley style, but none had a sharper or funnier screenplay (written by Rian James and James Seymour, from Bradford Ropes's story). A pungent look at life behind the footlights, the script was studded with one-liners often aimed at the wavering morals of the chorus girls ("She only said 'no' once, and then she didn't hear the question"). It also offered, in theatrical producer Julian Marsh (Warner Baxter), a central character of unusual depth for a frivolous musical. Ill, exhausted, and knowing that his current

Left: The Broadway Melody *(MGM, 1929). Sisters Anita Page and Bessie Love audition their act in this scene from the first true musical movie. Primitive by today's standards, it created a sensation in its day with its slangy dialogue and extravagant musical numbers.*
Right: Hallelujah! *(MGM, 1929). Wicked Chick (Nina Mae McKinney) entertains her friends in King Vidor's musical drama, the first all-black sound feature film. Vidor's experiments with sound influenced many later filmmakers.*

show will be his "last shot," Marsh drives his cast with a ferocity that smacks of desperation. He must cope with a temperamental star (Bebe Daniels), a not conspicuously talented chorine (Ruby Keeler) who replaces her in the show, a weak-willed backer (Guy Kibbee), and several venal ex-wives.

Lloyd Bacon was the director of record, but it was Busby Berkeley's contribution that drew most of the attention. Disregarding the prosce-

Above: Love Me Tonight *(Paramount, 1932). Princess Jeanette MacDonald is beginning to suspect that Maurice Chevalier is not a baron but a tailor with more on his mind than measurements. Right: Maurice Chevalier sings "Poor Apache" at a costume ball.*
Below: 42nd Street *(Warner Bros., 1933). A chorus line, 1933 variety, featuring three actresses on their way up the ladder: Ginger Rogers (second from the left, with suspenders), Ruby Keeler (center), and Una Merkel (to Ruby's left).*

nium arch that had locked most musical numbers into a rigid pattern, he created his own hallucinatory world. His best numbers are crowded into the film's last reel, when Marsh's show finally opens. "Shuffle Off to Buffalo" has newlyweds Ruby Keeler and Clarence Nordstrom prancing about the Niagara Limited, while underclad chorines in their berths make ribald or cynical comments. In the extravagant "Young and Healthy," Berkeley draws on techniques he had first used in *Whoopee*, including the often imitated "top shot," which allowed for kaleidoscopic (and dehumanizing) effects, and the close-ups of smiling chorines.

Most of the critical and public enthusiasm went to the film's title number. A miniature musical melodrama set in New York City's night world, the number is a compendium of Berkeleyesque touches: the startling camera angles, a mammoth set crowded with flashy, faintly disreputable people, and rows of identically dressed chorus girls, tapping in unison—like raunchy Rockettes—down a mythical (and "naughty, gaudy, bawdy") 42nd Street. Berkeley adds a bit of violence to the mix when a girl escapes from her raging lover, only to be knifed in the back by him as she dances with another man.

Gold Diggers of 1933 (Warner Bros., 1933). The Busby Berkeley girls "play" their violins in the extravagant number "The Shadow Waltz." Below: Backstage activity at a musical rehearsal. At left, looking unduly solemn, are actresses Aline MacMahon and Ruby Keeler. Observing them at right is an unduly serious Dick Powell. At the rear, watching the chorus, is producer Ned Sparks, who always looked somber. (Do they all know something about their show?)

Footlight Parade was less inclined to take direct note of the Depression, focusing on the awesome aquacade of "By a Waterfall" and one extraordinary number, "Shanghai Lil," in which the film's dynamic star, James Cagney, fought and danced in a vice-ridden Shanghai bar. The mood in both musicals matched the times: brashness and flippancy superimposed on a deep-seated fear.

While Berkeley musicals continued at Warners for several years, they inevitably lost their novelty, their momentum, and part of their sizable budgets. Audiences were beginning to wake up to the fact that musical numbers did not require a crowd of dancing extras to be entirely pleasing, nor was romance, or the urge to sing and dance about it, confined to the backstage of theaters. The two people responsible for this refreshing new attitude were a reed-thin performer from Broadway named Fred Astaire and a singer-dancer-actress named Ginger Rogers who had already appeared in twenty movies. In *Flying Down to Rio* (1933), their debut as a team dancing to "The Carioca" caught the public fancy, but it was in their first starring film, *The Gay Divorcee* (1934), that their ultimate status as dancing deities was clearly visible. When they danced to Cole Porter's "Night and Day" in the deserted ballroom of a resort hotel, the magic was palpable. Suddenly this angular, unhandsome, supremely gifted dancer and this bemused, cheeky, talented redhead were dancing out their emotions: physical attraction, resistance, surrender, and, finally, adoration were being expressed with elegance and grace on the dance floor. It was not exactly erotic, but it was worlds removed from the regimented and coolly tapping feet of Busby Berkeley chorines.

Following *Roberta* (1935), which had them dancing to Jerome Kern's bewitching music, the team found an ideal vehicle for their special talents in *Top Hat* (1935), generally regarded as the best of their movies together. This favored status is certainly not due to the foolish plot line involving an amorous dancer and a fashion model, but rather to the fact that the film crystallized the relationship between Astaire and Rogers that had begun to form in their first films: the give-and-take, resist-and-surrender of two gifted people who move from wariness to trust, and from trust to complete devotion. And it did so not with words, but with their inimitably dancing feet.

The blend of backstage ribaldry and Berkeley wizardry was clearly so potent that Warners quickly stirred up several more batches with equally successful results. Both *Gold Diggers of 1933* and *Footlight Parade* (1933) retained the hearty vulgarity and the wisecracking attitude toward the Depression of *42nd Street*, but what undoubtedly filled the box-office coffers were Berkeley's large-scale musical numbers. In *Gold Diggers*, nobody seemed to notice (or care) that two of these numbers offered contrasting images of the Depression: on the one hand, Ginger Rogers proclaiming that "We're in the Money!" as she and the chorus dance with oversize coins, and, on the other, Joan Blondell as a streetwalker in slit skirt exhorting us to remember her "forgotten man," the desperate war veteran now on the breadlines.

Left: Footlight Parade *(Warner Bros., 1933). This "human fountain" ended Busby Berkeley's mind-boggling musical number "By a Waterfall." The number featured one hundred chorines splashing and cavorting in a giant pool and forming kaleidoscopic patterns in the water.*
Right: The Gay Divorcee *(RKO, 1934). Ginger Rogers and Fred Astaire lead the chorus in "The Continental," the musical number that ran for a then-record seventeen-and-a-half minutes and featured several reprises of the Con Conrad–Herb Magidson song.*

Top Hat is virtually a catalogue of privileged Astaire-Rogers moments on film. Their dances to Irving Berlin's wonderfully spirited songs, whether solo or in tandem, are not self-contained interruptions to the flow of the movie: they are embodiments of the characters' attitudes toward life and each other. If Astaire plays a carefree dancer who is unattached (to both people and earth itself), he demonstrates his feelings by dancing to "No Strings." When Astaire and Rogers begin to sense (after the usual reluctance) that their destinies may be intertwined, they show their rapport by whirling about a deserted pavilion to the tune of "Isn't This a Lovely Day (To Be Caught in the Rain)?" And when love can no longer be denied, they dance to Berlin's enchanting "Cheek to Cheek"—in an Art Deco setting spun out of some fantasy of romance—a visible manifestation of how legends are born before our eyes.

While Astaire and Rogers gamboled through their RKO musicals, irrepressibly lighter than air, Metro-Goldwyn-Mayer was attempting to give wings to its lavish musical films. However, until Walt Disney proved otherwise with *Dumbo* in 1941, it was difficult, if not altogether impossible, to make an elephant fly. Heavily weighted with tons of scenery, burdened with interminable musical numbers that were ersatz Berkeley at best, they betrayed the studio's shortage of genuine musical talent by casting nonmusical stars (Joan Crawford, Jean Harlow) in singing-and-dancing roles.

Although most of MGM's musical films of the period were clearly not destined to advance movie history, the studio did produce a group of musical films that have entered the realm of legend. Fragrantly (and often flagrantly) sentimental, these were operettas that could hardly fail to please Depression-ridden audiences: they were derived from hardy stage perennials of a more tranquil era and they brimmed with melodies that had been sung around many parlor pianos through the years. They also offered a star who had joined the Mayer galaxy in 1934: the red-headed soprano Jeanette MacDonald. The very same actress who had revealed a piquant appeal in Paramount operettas of the early thirties, she was teamed with Nelson Eddy, a handsome baritone with minimal acting ability.

MacDonald's first assignment at MGM, however, was not with Eddy, but with her costar at Paramount, the jaunty Maurice Chevalier. Despite their mutual distrust and dislike, fostered over their three films together, the stars were signed to appear in a new version of Franz Lehár's evergreen operetta, *The Merry Widow*. Wisely, the studio selected Ernst Lubitsch as the director, on a one-picture loan from Paramount, where he had guided MacDonald and Chevalier in *The Love Parade* and *One Hour with You*. By this time, Lubitsch's ability to suggest wit and sophistication, with or without dialogue, and his skill at heightening the charm and sexuality of his leading players were well known and appreciated.

Erich von Stroheim's 1925 version of *The Merry Widow* had been astringent, mocking, with more than a hint of decadence. It was a cocktail laced with bitters and a drop or two of hemlock. Lubitsch's version was pure sparkling champagne, delicious from first sip to last. The familiar story of Sonia, Marshovia's wealthiest widow, and

her romance with the dashing Count Danilo provided Lubitsch with the springboard to exercise his touches of dry, sly wit and innocently "wicked" innuendo. More often than not, the wit was more visual than verbal: when Sonia decides to give up her widow's weeds and kick up her heels in Paris, everything black in her room (including her dog) suddenly turns white.

The Merry Widow winks rather than leers, and nowhere is its romantic heart exposed more openly than in the enchanting music. (Several new lyrics by Lorenz Hart and Gus Kahn were added to the perennially popular Franz Lehár score.) Sonia's songs of wistful longing ("Vilia") and eager anticipation ("Paris in the Spring") are matched by Danilo's robust hymns to joyful self-indulgence ("I'm Going to Maxim's," "Girls! Girls! Girls!"). In the latter song, the image of Danilo gleefully surrounded by prancing Maxim girls is pure exhilaration. Above all, there is the celebrated sequence centering on the "Merry Widow Waltz." This entire number is staged with astonishing skill, but when the stars give way to dozens of waltzing couples who whirl down a mirrored hallway, every viewer's pulse must quicken in time with the accelerating music.

Although *The Merry Widow* was not an unqualified hit at the box office, it confirmed Louis B. Mayer's belief that he had a major new star in Jeanette MacDonald. Despite her reluctance, she was signed to appear in a new version of Victor Herbert's 1910 operetta, *Naughty Marietta*. Its story is not exactly deathless literature, but the Herbert score ("Tramp, Tramp, Tramp," "Ah, Sweet Mystery of Life," "I'm

Opposite: Top Hat *(RKO, 1935). The inimitable Fred Astaire, demonstrating that his dancing is lighter than air. Below, left: In the eye-popping Art Deco set for "The Piccolino," the boys and girls of the chorus go into their dance. Below, right: In the same number, Ginger Rogers and Fred Astaire whirl to Irving Berlin's infectious music.*
Above: The Merry Widow *(MGM, 1934). Sonia (Jeanette MacDonald), Marshovia's wealthiest widow, and the dashing Count Danilo (Maurice Chevalier) share an amorous moment.*

Falling in Love with Someone") had a lush romanticism that audiences invariably enjoyed. Nelson Eddy, the resident baritone on the MGM lot, was assigned as MacDonald's costar. Released early in 1935, *Naughty Marietta* was received enthusiastically, establishing the team as singing idols of the decade.

It is difficult for present-day audiences to understand the widespread appeal of MacDonald and Eddy, and indeed the last few of their eight films together—ponderous and lifeless—offer very little support for their popularity. We must turn to their third and best movie, *Maytime* (1937), for genuine evidence of their assured place in musical film history. No doubt it is a shamelessly sentimental version of the Sigmund Romberg musical play that had been a sensational success on Broadway back in 1917. Its moist story of the ill-fated romance between two opera singers in the court of Louis Napoleon was virtually submerged in the shower of apple blossoms

that becomes the film's final image. Not even the bracing presence of John Barrymore as MacDonald's fatally jealous mentor (and, later, husband) could make *Maytime* seem much more than a florid, overripe operetta.

Yet it all works beautifully, in a way that makes ridicule pointless and turns easy laughter into something close to tears. The expected lushness of MGM's production, Barrymore's glowering histrionics, and even MacDonald's surprisingly credible performance are all attributes. But what keeps *Maytime* indelible in the memory is one sequence that captures the film's essence as a highly romantic valentine to an imagined yesteryear. Marcia (MacDonald) and her beloved Paul (Eddy) attend a May country fair where they sing "Santa Lucia" and mingle with the dancers. After a shimmering montage of flowers, trees, and sun-dappled water, they sit by a tree where he sings Romberg's "Will You Remember (Sweetheart)." They know they are

Maytime *(MGM, 1937). The most warmly remembered sequence in this popular musical romance: seated by a blossoming tree, Nelson Eddy and Jeanette MacDonald sing Sigmund Romberg's "Will You Remember (Sweetheart)" as a pledge of their eternal love.*

destined to part but she tells him, "I'll always remember you—and your song." Tenderly, she reprises "Will You Remember." The scene is admittedly drenched in the *Weltschmerz* of a bygone era, and yet it remains as curiously affecting as our last view of the lovers, reunited in death, heading toward heaven as they stroll hand in hand along a country lane.

While MacDonald and Eddy were enjoying their popularity, other studios were showcasing the voices of their resident sopranos, such as Grace Moore at Columbia and Deanna Durbin at Universal. Occasionally, Irene Dunne, a talented actress and trained singer whose forte was romantic comedy, was permitted to vocalize on screen, most memorably in the second screen adaptation of the classic Jerome Kern–Oscar Hammerstein II musical play, *Show Boat* (1936).

In most respects, the latter film, directed by James Whale, is the best of the three versions. This *Show Boat* amply featured the musical score that was largely absent from the partly silent 1929 version, and it also avoided the lacquered look that marred MGM's later (1951) adaptation. But most of all, the film conveyed, more than any other version, the emotional resonance that has kept *Show Boat* an enduring musical drama for over five decades. Apart from the film's admirable portrait of a colorful but vanished period in America's past—the showboat chugging down the Mississippi into a jubilant Southern town—there are characterizations that are surprisingly deep and affecting for a vintage musical. We are drawn into the lives of the charming heroine Magnolia (Irene Dunne) and her irresponsible gambler husband Gaylord Ravenal (Allan Jones), and we share in the tragic plight of the mulatto Julie, especially as played by the legendary Helen Morgan, whose expressive voice, with its suggestion of lost hopes and chances, echoed a career already close to ruin. This emotional richness gives an added luster to the lovely

Show Boat *(Universal, 1936). In this best of several versions of the Jerome Kern–Oscar Hammerstein II classic musical play, the showboat is docked on "ol' man river" as roustabout Joe (Paul Robeson) looks up at ingenue Magnolia (Irene Dunne).*

musical score, especially when Paul Robeson, as the showboat roustabout Joe, brings his formidable presence to the singing of "Ol' Man River."

By the end of the thirties, with the loss of Busby Berkeley's awesome production numbers at Warners, and the closing of the Rogers-Astaire series at RKO, new directions were needed for the musical film. They came first from Fox, where Darryl F. Zanuck combined nostalgia for yesteryear with a bouquet of Irving Berlin tunes in *Alexander's Ragtime Band* (1938), then, more importantly, from Metro-Goldwyn-Mayer, where a young singer named Judy Garland skyrocketed to national attention as the wistful heroine of *The Wizard of Oz* (1939). Her wide-eyed Dorothy, traveling over the rainbow to the merry old land of Oz, already projected the vulnerability, the surprisingly strong voice embedded in a fragile psyche, that would define her persona

over the coming years. She became a leading light in the roster of performers at MGM, which dominated the musical genre over the next decade.

The Wizard of Oz is, of course, a legendary film with a luster that repeated showings have not dimmed. Apart from Garland's tremulous performance, the movie offers perfectly realized characterizations by a choice group of character comedians (Bert Lahr, Jack Haley, Ray Bolger, Frank Morgan, Margaret Hamilton). Its few misjudgments (the Witch's flying monkeys, for example, are much too sinister and grotesque for a film of this kind) are far outweighed by its many delightful sequences: the trip down the Yellow Brick Road, the adventures in the Emerald City, the escape from the Witch's castle, and others. The Harold Arlen—E. Y. ("Yip") Harburg songs continue to amuse us, but "Over the Rainbow" has special value, not only

The Wizard of Oz (MGM, 1939). Dorothy (Judy Garland) is welcomed by the Munchkins and the Good Witch of the North (Billie Burke) to the merry old land of Oz. Opposite: Off to see the Wizard in the Emerald City, Dorothy and her friends are warned to proceed no further. Left to right: Judy Garland (Dorothy), Ray Bolger (Scarecrow), Bert Lahr (Cowardly Lion), and Jack Haley (Tin Woodman).

because of its association with Judy Garland but also because it speaks of the universal longing to discover the unknown worlds that exist "away above the chimneytops."

True, the movie's sentiments could be stitched onto a sampler, and its most famous pronouncement—"Oh, Auntie Em, there's *no* place like home!"—may be comforting to those too timid to venture beyond their doorways. Yet the movie appeals to a common need: the need to belong, to have a home that offers warmth and shelter after the world's witches have been conquered. The film may also be telling us, in an admittedly simplistic way, that there are no true wizards, only sham ones, and only one's own resources can help us to triumph in the end.

The Wizard of Oz closed out a decade that had been exceptionally rewarding for the musical film. The forties were to have their share of musical highlights as well, but not until the middle of the decade. The demands of a world war drained money and talent from the Hollywood studios, and for several years audiences were content with lightweight diversions that took their minds off the war: mainly Technicolor baubles starring resident movie queens (Fox's Betty Grable, Columbia's Rita Hayworth) or all-star tributes to the war effort. By 1944, however, with victory in sight, creativity and innovation were again becoming factors in the movie musical. Two films, in particular, marked the beginning of a richly productive period for the genre: *Meet Me in St. Louis* (1944) and *On the Town* (1949).

These two landmark films were produced by MGM, where a unit

headed by Arthur Freed was developing a reputation for its entertaining, crisply professional musicals. Both films are innovative— *Meet Me in St. Louis* in its concern with an ordinary American family rather than the "show business" figures of earlier nostalgic musicals, and *On the Town* in its use of actual locations for parts of the production. Yet they also reflect the differences between relative youth and maturity. Filmed during wartime, *Meet Me in St. Louis* yearns for the America of a more serene era, while *On the Town*, released five years later, looks ahead to the unit's greatest triumphs of the early fifties, when content and film techniques were at their most sophisticated. *Meet Me in St. Louis* reveals the use of color and design to enhance a musical mood that would characterize director Vincente Minnelli's later efforts (this was only his third film, and his first in color), while *On the Town* has some of the drive and exuberance that codirectors Gene Kelly and Stanley Donen would bring to their masterwork, *Singin' in the Rain*, three years later.

Of the two films, *Meet Me in St. Louis* has survived the years with greater ease. Set in an idealized St. Louis at the turn of the century,

Left: Meet Me in St. Louis *(MGM, 1944). Fetching Esther Smith (Judy Garland) pines for*
"The Boy Next Door" in Vincente Minnelli's glowing and perennially popular musical.
Right: On the Town *(MGM, 1949). Sailors Gene Kelly, Frank Sinatra, and Jules Munshin*
pause at the Statue of Liberty during their visit to "a helluva town." The use of actual New York
City locations was innovative at the time.

the musical concerns the familiar rites of passage of the Smith family of 5135 Kensington Avenue. Over the course of one year, as the Louisiana Purchase Exposition nears, members of the family experience job problems (father Leon Ames), budding romance (Judy Garland, ravishing as the middle daughter, Esther), and the innocent —yet troubling—traumas of childhood (Margaret O'Brien, almost eerily marvelous as little Tootie). Under Vincente Minnelli's loving and watchful guidance, their story takes on a timeless quality.

Meet Me in St. Louis marks the first turning point in the genre since the early thirties, not only because of the skill with which the physical production, the plot situations, the music (by Hugh Martin and Ralph Blane), and the performances are all perfectly meshed, but also because of its sensitive concern for the small crises, the fleeting joys and sorrows of a middle-class family at the turn of the century. There are no spangled chorus girls, no straw-hatted songwriters; instead we find young Esther Smith in the lace-curtained parlor, wistfully singing of her longing for "The Boy Next Door," or, in "The Trolley Song," expressing her boundless joy when he joins her on a trolley ride to the fairgrounds. There is no vaudeville razzmatazz, only little Tootie's excursion into the frightening side of childhood as she ventures out on Halloween to face unknown terrors. The family's loving regard for each other shines out of every frame, expressing itself best in song when, on a winter evening, Esther pulls her wrap around Tootie's shivering shoulders as she tenderly sings "Have Yourself a Merry Little Christmas."

On the Town, a belated film version of the Betty Comden–Adolph Green–Leonard Bernstein stage musical of 1944, was innovative in quite a different way. The directors took a major step forward for the genre by photographing some of the scenes in popular New York City locations and by making the dances an integral part of the story. From the early morning opening in the Brooklyn Navy Yard, as a dock worker sings "I Feel Like I'm Not Out of Bed Yet," the film moves with the exhilarating lightness and speed of the dancer's art. This is not surprising, since Gene Kelly's codirector, Stanley Donen, had been a dancer and choreographer for many years.

The refreshingly simple story, and some of the songs, were retained from the stage version: three sailors (Gene Kelly, Frank Sinatra, and Jules Munshin) discover romance and a bit of adventure on leave in New York City. Hurtling from their ship to the tune of "New York, New York!," they cover the requisite tourist spots (instant cutting from location to location was also one of the film's innovations) and, not incidentally, they meet three attractive girls, a dancer (Vera-Ellen), an anthropologist (Ann Miller), and a cab driver (Betty Garrett). Balancing the stretches of inane dialogue and some conventional musical numbers is a sense, throughout the movie, of what a musical film can be, given the right combination of skills and talents.

The dance portions are the best, reaching their peak in an ambitious, innovative dream sequence called "A Day in New York." Against stylized sets of the city, Gene Kelly, Vera-Ellen, and four surrogate dancers for the other principals dance out the day's events. No musical number until that time had drawn so directly on the emotions—the

An American in Paris *(MGM, 1951). As the lights of Paris twinkle in the darkness, a saddened Gene Kelly thinks about his lost love (Leslie Caron). But this was a musical, after all, and a happy ending was in the offing. Below: Gene Kelly and Leslie Caron dance in a Rousseau-like square in the unprecedented ballet that closes the film. Designed by Irene Sharaff and Preston Ames, choreographed by Gene Kelly, and directed by Vincente Minnelli, the ballet was an audacious tour de force.*

hopes and frustrations—of its characters. Fred Astaire's ballroom dances with Ginger Rogers had indeed generated romantic sparks, but never with such scope or dimension. For some, Kelly's story ballets, in this and later musicals, represented a loss rather than a gain, pretentiousness overtaking the sublime simplicity of Astaire's dance numbers. For others, they represented a new direction for dance in films.

At the start of the fifties, the Freed Unit hit its stride with its first prestigious musical of the decade, *An American in Paris* (1951). Conceived from the first as a project built entirely around the music of George Gershwin, the movie offered a bold concept for its closing number: a seventeen-minute ballet to the composer's tone poem "An American in Paris." To carry out a film of such unprecedented scope, the studio assembled an impressive array of talents: director Vincente Minnelli; star Gene Kelly; librettist Alan Jay Lerner, and the unit's imaginative, hard-working team of designers, cinematographers, and technicians. Kelly's leading lady was a pert young French dancer named Leslie Caron.

The result was a stunning achievement that surmounted its glaring faults: principally, a sluggish book by Lerner and an obviously studio-built Paris. Musically, the film is a treasure, blending George Gershwin's shimmering melodies, brother Ira's felicitous lyrics, and imaginative staging by Minnelli with the ingratiating performances of Kelly, Caron, sardonic wit Oscar Levant, and French music hall star Georges Guetary. One recalls so much: the introduction of Leslie Caron to movie audiences as she dances in contrasting moods and styles to "Embraceable You"; Kelly entertaining a group of French children with "I Got Rhythm"; Kelly singing and dancing with Guetary down a street in the Latin Quarter to "'S Wonderful." The lyrical, purely romantic mood created by Kelly and Caron as they dance along the banks of the Seine to "Our Love Is Here to Stay" casts a glow that never fades after many viewings.

The film's controversial ballet turned out to be its most highly praised feature. Both audacious and highfalutin, the number is the hero-artist's extravagant fantasy of romance and Paris—it expresses his sorrow and regret for a lost love, as well as his overwhelming feelings for the City of Lights. As he moves through a stylized Paris in search of the elusive Caron, the settings and costumes (by Preston Ames and Irene Sharaff) adopt the styles of some of France's most celebrated painters. The eyes are dazzled, but ultimately the mind is benumbed by the images, colors, and dancing figures. In March of 1952, the movie won six Academy Awards (including for Best Picture) and an honorary award for Gene Kelly.

An American in Paris won the honors, but the next musical from the Freed Unit won the lasting fame. *Singin' in the Rain* has, by this time, moved far beyond its original status as the best musical film released in 1952 to its exalted position as not only one of Hollywood's greatest musicals but also one of the finest achievements in any genre. Except possibly for some overfancy moments in the "Broadway" ballet, *Singin' in the Rain* wears its mantle of fame with becoming modesty and good cheer. It never claims to be anything more than a

Opposite, above: Meet Me in St. Louis *(MGM, 1944). Esther Smith (Judy Garland) leads her friends in "The Trolley Song" on their way to the fairgrounds.*
Opposite, below: On the Town *(MGM, 1949). Ann Miller and her sailor friends in the "Prehistoric Man" number from this landmark musical.*
Above: Singin' in the Rain *(MGM, 1952). Those "romantic lovers of the screen," Don Lockwood (Gene Kelly) and Lina Lamont (Jean Hagen), greet their rhapsodic fans. Below: Joy abounds as Gene Kelly sings and dances in a downpour.*

friendly, funny, and tuneful example of the American musical film at its summit.

Then why has the reputation of *Singin' in the Rain* survived for over three decades? The books for most movie musicals can be dismissed without harm to the overall impact—but here Betty Comden and Adolph Green's screenplay is essential: a broad spoof of the earliest days of sound, with no claim to accuracy but with many witty satirical swipes at the absurdity and hysteria of the period when movies first learned to talk. It is affectionate parody that gives point and substance to the film's lightweight plot concerning a late-twenties movie star (Gene Kelly), his problems with sound and with his vulgar, shrilly vindictive costar (Jean Hagen), and his romance with a budding actress (Debbie Reynolds). Observing wryly from the sidelines is friend and sidekick Donald O'Connor. Comden and Green have a grand time poking fun at the tribulations of early sound recording, especially the desperate attempts to get silent stars ready to speak on film for the first time.

The film's music, mostly by Arthur Freed and Nacio Herb Brown, works in close harmony with the story, adding touches of romance and knockabout humor. From Donald O'Connor's riotous "Make 'Em Laugh," a matchless mixture of slapstick and dance, to Gene Kelly's legendary dance in the rain to the title song, the movie abounds in

musical riches displayed with pride and professionalism. The film's climactic ballet, built around the songs "Broadway Rhythm" and "Broadway Melody," pokes good-natured fun at the "rags-to-riches" backstage musical, as well as other basic genres.

A number of other musical films emerged from the Freed Unit during the fifties, but none reached the pinnacle of *Singin' in the Rain*. Several, however, came close. *The Band Wagon* (1953) had an abundance of virtues: another witty screenplay by Betty Comden and Adolph Green, this time dealing with the tribulations and rewards of theater life; a melodious score by Howard Dietz and Arthur Schwartz; and the inimitable presence of Fred Astaire, in his best role since joining MGM in the forties. Also aboard were Cyd Charisse as a haughty ballerina, Nanette Fabray and Oscar Levant as writer-performers modeled after Comden and Green themselves, and British musical comedy star Jack Buchanan as an off-the-wall director. Vincente Minnelli, who had spent years in the theater before coming to Hollywood, was the logical choice to direct.

The Band Wagon contains musical moments as good as any during the decade, and they all involve Fred Astaire. As a fading movie star who finds new success on the stage, he joins Cyd Charisse for a romantic number in Central Park to "Dancing in the Dark," cavorts with Nanette Fabray and Jack Buchanan in the hilarious "Triplets" ("We hate each other very much"), and concludes the film with an amusing and beautifully designed jazz ballet called "The Girl Hunt" that parodies Mickey Spillane's hard-boiled detective novels while poking sly fun at Gene Kelly's "serious" dance work. Yet one small solo number is the most memorable, and Astaire dances not a step. Strolling down a railroad platform, he sings "By Myself" without a trace of self-pity and regret, and with all the charm, gallantry, and style that have always resided in that thin frame.

By the end of the fifties, the influence of the Freed Unit was waning, although *It's Always Fair Weather* (1955) and *Silk Stockings* (1957) were better-than-respectable efforts. The decade ended, however, with a musical film that seemed to epitomize the unit's well-honed professional skills. Adapted from Colette's short novel, *Gigi* (1958) was surprisingly "sophisticated" for a Hollywood product; its story of an impish but blossoming teenager (Leslie Caron) in turn-of-the-century Paris who is next in line in a distinguished family of courtesans hardly seemed a suitable subject for MGM's family audience. Yet Alan Jay Lerner's adroit book, winking but never sniggering, and his captivating score with Frederick Loewe made the film, under Vincente Minnelli's sure-footed direction, a great success. It won an unprecedented nine Academy Awards.

Between the photography by Joseph Ruttenberg and the costumes and settings by Cecil Beaton, *Gigi* is entrancing to look at. The performances are impeccable, particularly Louis Jourdan's depiction of a world-weary Parisian who succumbs to Gigi's girlish appeal. (His rendition of the title song demonstrates the art of combining characterization and music.) But what gives the movie its special glow is the inimitable presence of Maurice Chevalier as Jourdan's uncle. As a well-seasoned *boulevardier*, a retired but still amorous

The Band Wagon *(MGM, 1953). Cyd Charisse and Fred Astaire dance in "The Girl Hunt," the jazz ballet that spoofs Mickey Spillane's hard-boiled, lusty detective novels. The ballet was conceived by choreographer Michael Kidd in collaboration with Roger Edens.*

Danilo, Chevalier embodies the intended spirit of the film, insouciant, slightly wicked, but romantic after all. We have only to watch him opening the film with a sly "Thank Heaven for Little Girls," or extolling the virtues of aging by singing "I'm Glad I'm Not Young Anymore," or recalling his romance with Gigi's grandmother (Hermione Gingold) in "I Remember It Well" to recognize that he forms the solid center of the movie.

Above: Gigi *(MGM, 1958).* Gigi *(Leslie Caron), her grandmother (Hermione Gingold), and* Gaston *(Louis Jourdan) express their happiness in the Lerner and Loewe song "The Night They Invented Champagne." Above, right: Playing the debonair Honoré Lachaille, Maurice Chevalier celebrates the virtues of old age in the song "I'm Glad I'm Not Young Anymore." Below:* Seven Brides for Seven Brothers *(MGM, 1954).* Milly *(Jane Powell), bride to the eldest Pontipee brother, shows her brothers-in-law how to dance when they are "Goin' Courtin'."*

While the Freed Unit was creating its memorable musicals at MGM, another unit at the studio, headed by veteran Jack Cummings, had been producing breezy musical entertainments for a number of years. The films lacked the sophistication and high style of the Freed musicals, but the peak of Cummings's achievement came in 1954 with the engaging *Seven Brides for Seven Brothers*. Based on a Stephen Vincent Benét story, "The Sobbin' Women," this musical concerned an Oregon farmer (Howard Keel) in 1850 who takes a wife (Jane Powell) and then convinces his six brothers to do the same. The boys forcibly carry off six town girls who are held as prisoners through the winter until the thawing brings communal romance and marriage.

The idea has a faint odor of perversity, but this is innocent musical comedy country after all, and the emphasis is on well-scrubbed young performers singing and dancing to a tuneful Gene de Paul–Johnny Mercer score. Directed by Stanley Donen, *Seven Brides for Seven Brothers* was the first musical in many years to be so thoroughly dominated by its dances. Keel and Powell are attractive and even animated in the leading roles, but they pale beside the zest, energy, and skill of the professional dancers who play most of the rambunctious Pontipee brothers (Marc Platt, Tommy Rall, Jacques d'Amboise, Russ Tamblyn, and Matt Mattox). The film's undisputed highlight is the barn-raising sequence in which the brothers "challenge" their town rivals in a series of breathtaking acrobatic leaps and ballet steps, then join in raising the barn. The sequence, which ends in an all-out brawl, was staged by Michael Kidd, whose handling of all the dances brought him wide acclaim.

After directing *Seven Brides* and several other films, Stanley Donen left MGM for a plum directorial assignment at Paramount. *Funny Face* (1957) turned out to be one of the best musicals of the fifties, but, curiously, the movie seemed much more of an MGM than a Paramount creation. In addition to Donen, the people involved in the production included star Fred Astaire, producer (and occasional composer) Roger Edens, and singer-composer-arranger Kay Thompson, who had all worked on many MGM musical films. With Audrey Hepburn as Astaire's ravishing costar, the result of their combined efforts was stylish entertainment in the MGM mode.

Style, in fact, is the keynote of *Funny Face*, since the film is set in the world of Paris *haute couture*. (The movie dates more than many musicals of the fifties because of its fashions.) The style extends not only to the setting but also to the performances, the witty Gershwin music (with several additions by Roger Edens), and the production itself, especially the color. Photographer Richard Avedon, hired as special visual consultant, drenched the screen with a dazzling variety of shades, hues, and tones. Long after we have forgotten the silly plot (fashion photographer Astaire turns bookworm Hepburn into a butterfly, then falls for her), we remember the green ribbons in Hepburn's orange-and-yellow hat as she sings "How Long Has This Been Going On?," the glowing red light in Astaire's darkroom as he dances with Hepburn to the title song, or the white of Hepburn's

wedding gown as she whirls with Astaire through the green countryside to the beguiling melody of "He Loves and She Loves."

Although MGM dominated the genre in the fifties, superior musical films emerged occasionally from other studios. In 1956, Twentieth Century-Fox released lavish and reverent versions of two longstanding stage successes by Rodgers and Hammerstein: *Carousel* and *The King and I*, while Warner Bros. offered two notable musical films during the decade: a lively filming of the stage hit *The Pajama Game* (1957) and a musicalization of the 1937 film about Hollywood, *A Star Is Born* (1954). The latter film was designed as a showcase for Judy Garland, whose well-publicized troubles had kept her out

of films since 1950. In the role of small-town girl Esther Blodgett who becomes film star Vicki Lester, Garland gave a tour-de-force performance that demonstrates the power of a single radiant personality to transform soap into gold. Under George Cukor's patient, sensitive direction, she succeeds in conveying all of the hopefulness, vulnerability, and anguish of a woman who watches helplessly while her husband (James Mason, in one of his best performances) makes a humiliating descent into alcoholism and suicide. Musically, she is at the top of her form, her emotionally charged voice giving rare intensity to "The Man That Got Away," "It's a New World," and an astonishing eighteen-minute production number, "Born in a Trunk," which was added after the film was completed.

By the sixties, the musical film was already on the wane, due to the extraordinarily high production costs, the increasing inroads of television (television films were cheaper to make and had a built-in audience), and the decline of the overseas market for Hollywood

Opposite: Funny Face *(Paramount, 1957). Atop the Eiffel Tower, Kay Thompson, Fred Astaire, and Audrey Hepburn hail the City of Lights with the song "Bonjour, Paris!" Below: A memorable musical scene as Fred Astaire and Audrey Hepburn dance through a lovely park setting to the Gershwin song "He Loves and She Loves."*
Above: A Star Is Born *(Warner Bros., 1954). A spotlight catches Judy Garland in her eighteen-minute number, "Born in a Trunk." Added after the film was completed, the number told the story of a singing star's life from her birth to her triumph on the stage.*

musicals. Anxious for at least some return on their huge investments, the studios repeated their mistake of the late fifties: concentrating almost exclusively on mammoth film versions of popular stage successes. Assigning these films to directors with little or no experience in the genre, and often giving the leading roles to unsuitable performers with box-office clout, they managed to extract most of the life out of the original properties.

One of the most notable exceptions came early in the decade. Derived from the stage musical that had electrified Broadway in 1957, *West Side Story* (1961) offered evidence that it was possible to transcribe a theatrical property into a cinematically effective film with slight loss of value. The touching story of young love trampled by intolerance—Shakespeare's *Romeo and Juliet* shifted from Verona to Manhattan's violence-plagued West Side—the varied and stunning score by Leonard Bernstein and Stephen Sondheim, and especially the remarkable dances staged by Jerome Robbins were adapted brilliantly to the screen. Neither a slavish imitation of the stage original nor a top-heavy star vehicle, *West Side Story* builds its own world on its own terms.

True, there is some uneasiness at the start. Immediately after the celebrated opening, in which the camera swoops down on the street gang known as the Jets as they swagger down a deserted Manhattan street, we begin to wonder why these tough boys are performing ballet steps. But once their choreographed fight with their hated rivals, the Sharks, gets under way, we are soon swept up by the vigor and pulsating excitement of the dancing. And the exhilarating feeling generated by the dancing carries into the dramatic portions of the film, which were ably directed by Robert Wise.

The story of the ill-fated romance of Tony (Richard Beymer) and Maria (Natalie Wood) is genuinely affecting, and their songs, both apart and together ("Maria," "Tonight," "One Hand, One Heart"), are lovely and lyrical. Yet it is the dancing that truly galvanizes the film. Led by Rita Moreno as Maria's feisty friend Anita, and by George Chakiris as Maria's volatile brother, Bernardo, the dancers express their charged feelings in bravura style. One recalls the "challenge" dance of the Puerto Ricans between choruses of their wickedly funny song, "America"; the explosive tension of the dance in the school gymnasium; the choreographed fight, bristling with

West Side Story *(Mirisch-Seven Arts/United Artists, 1961). A grief-stricken Maria
(Natalie Wood) runs to the body of her slain lover, Tony (Richard Beymer). Behind her is
policeman Schrank (Simon Oakland). Opposite, above: The Jets leap defiantly down a
New York street. Opposite, below: Anita (Rita Moreno) leads the girls in a rooftop
dance to "America." Jerome Robbins's dances for the stage version were adapted
brilliantly to the screen.*

rage and terror, that kills opposing gang members.

Other long-running stage musicals found their way to the screen in the sixties, with varying success. One of the most eagerly awaited adaptations was *My Fair Lady* (1964), Alan Jay Lerner and Frederick Loewe's musical version of George Bernard Shaw's play *Pygmalion*. For the most part, the long (eight-year) wait was amply rewarded. The film, directed reverently (perhaps too reverently) by George Cukor, succeeded in retaining most of the virtues of the stage play. Cecil Beaton's sumptuous sets and costumes lovingly re-create an idealized Edwardian London. Alan Jay Lerner's screenplay cleverly distills Shaw's prickly wit while eliminating some of the polemics, and his score with Frederick Loewe overflows with entrancing melodies. Above all, the producers had the good sense to cast two of the stage version's stars in their original roles. Rex Harrison's incorrigible Professor Henry Higgins is a masterly portrait, and Stanley Holloway's duplication of Alfred Doolittle, Eliza's

scoundrelly father, is a model of music hall artistry. Replacing the stage's Julie Andrews as the duck-into-swan heroine, Audrey Hepburn brings beauty, charm, and elegance to a role that requires all these attributes—but only after cockney Liza has become lady Eliza.

The songs of *My Fair Lady* are exceptional in their ability to reveal character; music and lyrics combine to convey changing attitudes and feelings. During the course of the movie, we see Professor Higgins, in song, move from petulant pedant ("Why Can't the English") to exasperated mysogynist ("Why Can't a Woman Be More Like a Man?") to out-of-the-closet romantic ("I've Grown Accustomed to Her Face"). Audrey Hepburn (dubbed by Marni Nixon) goes from wistful cockney longing in "Wouldn't It Be Loverly?" to perfectly enunciated romantic joy in "I Could Have Danced All Night." Even Stanley Holloway's rowdy music hall turn in "With a Little Bit of Luck" gives us a close-up view of the sly, lazy, disreputable Doolittle. Yet, for all its magnificent score and impressive production,

Above: Mary Poppins (Disney, 1964). Mary Poppins (Julie Andrews) and Bert (Dick Van Dyke) join the chimney sweeps in dancing about the rooftops of Edwardian London. This number, "Step in Time," is joyful, energetic, and imaginative.
Page 56, above: My Fair Lady (Warner Bros., 1964). Eliza Doolittle (Audrey Hepburn) and Henry Higgins (Rex Harrison) are clearly delighted that "the rain in Spain stays mainly in the plain."
Page 56, below: Mary Poppins (Disney, 1964). Magical nanny Mary Poppins eliminates the competition by causing other nannies to blow away on their umbrellas.

My Fair Lady misses greatness due to the faint aroma of embalming fluid that emanates from this screen reincarnation. It is like Eliza at the ball, exquisitely turned out and well-behaved, but needing a warming touch to spring fully to life.

If Julie Andrews felt any regret at losing the choice role of Eliza to Audrey Hepburn, she was given ample compensation in two sixties musicals that established her as a popular film personality. Her ladylike demeanor, trilling soprano, and reticent British charm captured the public fancy, first in Walt Disney's musical fantasy *Mary Poppins* (1964) and then in the film version of Rodgers and Hammerstein's story of the singing Trapp family, *The Sound of Music* (1965).

As Mary Poppins, P. L. Travers's magical nanny, Andrews was perhaps not ideally cast, but she invested the role with such friendly good cheer that it didn't matter. What did matter was that *Mary Poppins* was the first musical fantasy since *The Wizard of Oz* to master the delicate balance of the real and the unreal required by fantasy, while embellishing the whimsical story of the governess and her two young charges with a batch of attractive songs ("Chim Chim Cheree," "A Spoonful of Sugar," "I Love to Laugh"). Although it lacked the emotional center of *The Wizard of Oz* (Mary, unlike Dorothy, is a rather cool customer), it surpassed the earlier film in technical proficiency and in the richness of its physical production. (The beautiful, slightly stylized sets captured the look of Edwardian London.) The movie's many special effects, never too ambitious and nicely modified by Mary Poppins's sensible attitude toward them, included characters soaring into the air, with or without umbrellas, dancing across rooftops without danger of falling, or cavorting with animated animals in an extended "Jolly Holiday" sequence.

Julie Andrews's contribution to *The Sound of Music* was even greater. As Maria, the mischievous young novitiate who falls in love with and marries the stern paterfamilias Captain Von Trapp (Christopher Plummer) in the early years of World War II, she brought a welcome note of common sense to the heavily sentimental book and treacly, sometimes charming score. *The Sound of Music* is a perfectly apportioned mix of adorable children, breathtaking scenery, operetta-like romance, and religion, cleverly spiked with just the right amount of anti-Nazi feeling, but it is so mired in the theatrical past that even from its beginnings on the stage it seemed like a revival of a fragrant Shubert perennial rather than a modern musical. Still, one must acknowledge its extraordinary popularity; some viewers went back to see it again and again.

By the seventies, the number of musical films was reduced even further than in the sixties. Despite elaborate (and expensive) adaptations of successful stage musicals, audiences were no longer enthusiastic. In place of an idyllic world of music and laughter, they preferred the awesome special effects of "disaster" films such as *The Towering Inferno* or the graphic violence of such films as *The Godfather* and *The French Connection*. It was as if the explosive sixties, with its political assassinations and its senseless, brutal war, had made the depiction of human destruction, either on a one-on-one

or mass basis, not only acceptable but entertaining. In a world more clamorous than glamorous, there seemed to be little room for musical expressions of joy or romance.

Still, there were several films in the seventies that managed to uphold the tradition of great Hollywood musicals. One was the 1971 adaptation of the long-running stage musical *Fiddler on the Roof*. Derived from Sholom Aleichem's wistful, ironic stories, the Joseph Stein–Jerry Bock–Sheldon Harnick musical had offered a touching if romanticized view of Jewish life in an impoverished Russian village at the turn of the century. The film version, under Norman Jewison's capable direction, enriched and deepened the original material as it depicted the descent of the milkman Tevye and his family from poor but cheerful residents of Anatevka to homeless wanderers, victims of cruel persecution.

Beautifully photographed (largely in and around Zagreb, Yugoslavia), the film begins by establishing the village traditions that will be destroyed, one by one, from the sweet family communion of the Sabbath ceremony (the exquisite "Sabbath Prayer") to the all-powerful position of the father in every family. Tevye, played with deep feeling by Israeli actor Topol, has his dreams of glory ("If I Were a Rich Man"), but he watches helplessly as his small world collapses and the old traditions die.

Fiddler on the Roof was criticized for expanding the fragile story to grandiose Hollywood dimensions, but there are so many sequences of exceptional beauty and power, staged with cinematic flair, that the criticism seems negligible. Tevye's dream, in which he convinces his wife that their daughter must marry the poor tailor she loves or face the wrath of the dead, is a stunningly staged evocation of deep-seated fears and superstitions. The wedding of Tevye's daughter, with its candlelit procession, moving ceremony, and song ("Sunrise, Sunset") that indelibly expresses the sad inevitability of time's passing, is a memorable set piece that evokes a vanished world, brutally shattered by Cossack soldiers. Most affecting of all are the many moments of parting, especially the inevitable time when the townspeople must leave their homes forever. There is heart-wrenching sadness in the images of the displaced Jews floating on a raft down the river, and of Tevye and the remnants of his family marching down the dusty road to nowhere.

The following year brought the release of the finest, and also the most unconventional, musical film of the decade. *Cabaret* (1972) had appeared in many other versions, both musical and nonmusical, before reaching the screen, and although the attitudes toward the material ranged from Brechtian to Broadway, the central story always revolved around Sally Bowles, an amoral, hedonistic girl living in Berlin of the early thirties. As the shadow of Nazism looms larger, Sally becomes involved with (among others) a detached, sexually ambiguous young British writer. The image of the cabaret—decadent, sardonic, and dominated by its leering, painted Master of Ceremonies—hovers over everything.

Under Bob Fosse's inspired direction, this *Cabaret* became the

Overleaf, right, above: The Sound of Music *(Fox, 1965). A novitiate on leave from a nearby nunnery, governess Maria (Julie Andrews) takes her charges to the market.*
Overleaf, right, center and below: Fiddler on the Roof *(Norman Jewison/United Artists, 1971). Tevye (Topol) and his friends sing a joyful hymn "To Life." Below: In the vivid dream sequence, Tevye, his wife Golde, and their neighbors in Anatevka are terrified by the spirit of Lazar Wolf's deceased wife, who has come to protest the planned marriage of Lazar to Tevye's daughter Tzeitel.*

move from the brassy cheerfulness of "Willkommen" to the surreptitious nastiness of "If You Could See Her with My Eyes," in which the Master of Ceremonies sings the praises of a girl in a gorilla costume, adding in a stage whisper, "She doesn't look *Jewish* at all!" Most eloquent of all is Sally's closing rendition of the title song, which encapsulates the film's haunting view of a society turning ugly and dangerous, yet laughing at the edge of doom. Outside the walls of the cabaret, a series of isolated occurrences parallel the increasingly "politicized" music: a Jewish vendor is murdered and his bloody body lies in the street covered with his prayer shawl; the word "Jüden" is smeared on a wall; a sweet-voiced blond German boy sings rhapsodically about the future, while the camera pans to a Nazi insignia on his sleeve. As the music and the events interweave into a darkening pattern, Sally and her friends spin in their private orbit. (Only her observant writer-friend opposes the violence, and he is badly beaten for his concern.)

If *Cabaret* was unlike any previous musical film, then a musical drama that appeared at the end of the decade was even more unconventional. *All That Jazz* (1979) had only one thing in common with *Cabaret*: its talented director, Bob Fosse. With the innovative flair that had distinguished his best stage work, Fosse moved from hedonistic Berlin in the thirties to the frenzied world of today's musical theater. Clearly, he knew and loved his field, but there was unmistakable satire and irony as well—barbed wire mixed in with

very model of what a modern musical film can be when all components are merged in a single, brilliantly clear vision. Actually it is a triple vision ultimately merged into one: the lives of Sally (Liza Minnelli) and her friends, heedless and self-obsessed; the enclosed world of the cabaret where the Master of Ceremonies (Joel Grey) and his garish girls invite visitors to surrender to the pleasures of the flesh; and the world outside the cabaret, turning dark and sinister. Inevitably, all three areas overlap, as Sally's friends experience the impact—or at least the side effects—of racial hatred and violence. Sally comes close to reality but never manages to lose her delusions.

Cabaret is unlike the standard musical in almost every way. Virtually all of the music is performed in the Kit Kat Club by Sally and the Master of Ceremonies, and it is used not only to punctuate the events of the film but to comment on them obliquely. Thus the songs

Cabaret (Cy Feuer/Allied Artists, 1972). Liza Minnelli received a well-deserved Oscar for her
performance as the frenetic, hedonistic, but vulnerable cabaret singer Sally Bowles.
Right: Sally Bowles and the Kit Kat Club's Master of Ceremonies (Joel Grey) sing
the praises of hard cash in "Money, Money, Money."

the bouquets. His semiautobiographical account of a fatally driven, egotistical dance director (Roy Scheider) and his hectic activities both on and off the stage is alternately funny and moving, audacious and exasperating, but it is never dull.

As we follow Joe Gideon through a day of auditions, rehearsals, and impulsive womanizing, it becomes evident that, for him, life and show business are one and the same. ("It's show time, folks!" is his daily self-salutation.) Life as theater is the central metaphor of the film, especially after Gideon suffers a heart attack and his hospital becomes a stage for his hallucinatory musical numbers. Brilliantly conceived and startling in their boldness, these numbers are built around standard songs, climaxed by a rousing "Bye, Bye, Life" (originally "Bye, Bye, Love"), in which Gideon, surrounded by family and friends fantastically attired, bids farewell to the world.

Light-years away from Busby Berkeley's backstage milieu, *All That Jazz* is perhaps the screen's best view of that combination of dedication, talent, fear, and egomania called the theater. During the dramatic portions, we witness the sycophancy and the double-dealing of theater folk (a smarmy director tries to take over Gideon's job while professing concern for his health). But even the musical numbers comment obliquely on the insulated world of the theater. In the opening musical sequence, for example, we observe dancers auditioning en masse to the song "On Broadway," as the camera catches their hopefulness, pride, and anxiety.

In recent years, the musical film has not fared well. Moviegoers, who three or four decades ago would have flocked to see Judy Garland or Fred Astaire in their latest film, failed to support the few attempts to resuscitate the genre. Francis Ford Coppola's pretentious *One from the Heart* (1981), a romantic comedy with music, was poorly attended and drew harsh notices from the critics. Herbert Ross's *Pennies from Heaven* (1981), derived from a British television production, was a brave and often stunning attempt to carry out an unusual musical concept. Basically a harsh drama set in a Depression-era Chicago, the film showed its characters fantasizing to songs of the period, their lips moving in synchronization to actual old recordings. The most recent large-scale musical, *Annie* (1982), was a deliberate throwback to the extravaganzas of other years, aimed at the family trade, but more families were attending *E.T.* instead.

Battered and bloated, the musical film may presently be in an unhealthy state, but its condition should not be construed as fatal. As long as there are filmgoers who are eager to respond to its music, who can rejoice in the beauty of its illusions and the peerless talents of its performers, there are filmmakers who will want to reach them. And as long as we can continue to enjoy the musicals of the past, the melody will linger on.

All That Jazz (Fox, 1979). Dance director Joe Gideon (Roy Scheider) converses with Angelique (Jessica Lange), the mysterious and beautiful Angel of Death who is waiting patiently for his demise. She will not have to wait long.

Greta
GARBO
Robert
TAYLOR

Camille

A Metro-Goldwyn-Mayer PICTURE

"Love me a little — only a little!"

A WARNER BROS. PICTURE

CASABLANCA

THROUGH THE EYES OF LOVE
Great Romantic Films

In the year 1896, a highly popular stage comedienne named May Irwin and the actor John C. Rice repeated a scene from their stage success, *The Widow Jones*, for the experimental cameras of Thomas Alva Edison. It was a very brief scene (only fifty feet of film), involving Miss Irwin and the mustachioed Rice in a prolonged kiss. To the shock and dismay of many, including members of the clergy, the couple seemed to be enjoying their on-camera smooch. One indignant writer proclaimed it close to "indecent in its emphasized vulgarity, a lyric of the Stock Yards," and called for police interference.

The Kiss was a sensation, a scandal, and the earliest indication that the subject of romance would clearly flourish on the screen. Since that first demonstration of affection, lovers have met, endured, or separated through choice or tragedy, all to the attendant sighs, swoons, and occasional catcalls of movie audiences. Perhaps the finest romantic films were made in the silent period, when the absence of sound and the necessary emphasis on the visual made high flights of romantic fancy most feasible and convincing. Even into the thirties, when the voices of such actresses as Greta Garbo and Margaret Sullavan cast their own spell, the photography of William Daniels and Gregg Toland brought a special luster to tales of thwarted or fulfilled love. By the forties, the growing exigencies of realism made pure romance less of a regular film commodity. In our time, the screen love story is comparatively rare; perhaps its occasional return is welcomed only by those who recall, or have seen in revival, the radiant glow of Diane waiting patiently for the return of Chico, or Marguerite Gautier dying in the arms of her beloved Armand.

From the early silent years, one film survives as the epitome of romantic tragedy. *Broken Blossoms* (1919), the first film directed by D. W. Griffith after forming United Artists with Douglas Fairbanks, Mary Pickford, and Charlie Chaplin, was a marked contrast to the ambitious scale of *The Birth of a Nation* and *Intolerance*. A small, gentle, and infinitely moving film set in London's Limehouse district, it centered on the love that springs up between Cheng Huan (Richard Barthelmess) and Lucy (Lillian Gish), a pitiful, horribly abused young girl. Cheng Huan rescues her from her sadistic father (Donald Crisp) and tends her lovingly, but her father finds her and beats her to death savagely. A brokenhearted Cheng Huan kills the father in retaliation and then takes his own life.

Filmed in almost impressionistic style, *Broken Blossoms* takes place in a dreamlike world, but one in which the dream, conveyed in the fog-laden London streets, opium dens, and the serene, isolated abode of Cheng Huan, turns into a terrible nightmare. Leaving his country to bring the peaceful message of Buddha to the Western world, Cheng Huan finds only corruption and despair—and he is met with blatantly racist scorn for his efforts. His heart goes out to the forlorn Lucy, who staggers into his store and collapses, the victim of one more unmerciful beating. With mute adoration, he transforms his room into a tiny kingdom for a princess; he brings warmth and gentleness into a life that has never known either.

The last scenes of *Broken Blossoms* are affecting, amazingly so in light of the still-embryonic state of film language and techniques.

Opposite, above: A lobby card for Camille *(MGM, 1937).*
Opposite, below: A lobby card for Casablanca *(Warner Bros., 1942).*
Above: Broken Blossoms *(D. W. Griffith/United Artists, 1919). In D. W. Griffith's tragic romance, Cheng Huan (Richard Barthelmess) gazes tenderly at Lucy (Lillian Gish), the pathetic girl he is protecting from a sadistic father.*

gloss and a confidence that made them internationally admired. Ironically, the year 1927, which saw the release of Al Jolson's historic partial-sound feature *The Jazz Singer*, also witnessed the release of such celebrated silent films as *Wings*, *Seventh Heaven*, *Sunrise*, and *Underworld*. Of these, *Seventh Heaven* and *Sunrise* were romantic dramas involving love both sacred and profane. Apart from their considerable polish, these films also demonstrated the potency of silence in dealing with romantic subjects. Somehow the absence of dialogue, the reliance on facial expression and bodily movements to convey feelings of sexual attraction or undying passion gave the romantic scenes an added conviction and, in some cases, a sense of otherworldliness that diminished or even vanished with sound. There were undeniable advantages in being able to hear voices, but there were disadvantages as well. It may be that, unlike most other genres and subgenres, the romantic film was not substantially improved by sound and may, in fact, have been harmed in some ways.

Frank Borzage's *Seventh Heaven* (1927) is a case in point. Although Charles Farrell tends to overplay as the hero Chico and the war scenes are sketchily staged, this extremely popular film has a matchless romantic aura that can be attributed, at least in part, to the absence of sound. Without spoken dialogue (there are sound effects and a musical score), viewers could project their own romantic imaginations onto the story of Chico and Diane. Of course the film's success is also due to Borzage's characteristically fluid direction, and especially to Janet Gaynor's luminous performance as Diane. She invests the hapless heroine with a sweetness and a surprising spunkiness that are most appealing.

Set in the Paris slums, *Seventh Heaven* concerns Chico, a sewer worker (later promoted to street washer) and a self-proclaimed "remarkable fellow," who rescues the fragile, woebegone Diane from the clutches of her sadistic sister (Gladys Brockwell). He takes Diane to his apartment high above the streets ("I work in the sewers, but I live near the stars"), which becomes "heaven" to them as they fall in love. They plan to marry but on their wedding day, a general mobilization for war (very sudden and dramatically convenient) sends Chico into the army. They hold a daily communion in spirit ("Chico...Diane...Heaven!"), but Diane's fervent belief in his return is shattered when Chico is presumed killed. He returns to her after all, blinded but still a "very remarkable fellow."

There is little doubt that the fame of this *Seventh Heaven*—the 1937 remake was disastrous—rests firmly on the romantic middle section in which Chico and Diane come to love each other. Diane's delight in being treated with kindness, her pleasure in the "heaven" she shares with Chico are touchingly expressed in little scenes of pantomime. In one especially lovely moment, she wraps Chico's jacket around herself and buries her face in the sleeves. When they are forced to part, their scene together has an almost palpable fervor and passion. In a too-obvious suggestion of his future fate, he says, "Let me fill my eyes with you!" The subsequent battle scenes use too many obvious miniatures, and there is some unnecessary cheating that lets the audience believe that Chico has been killed. But when he charges

They are not only a testament to Griffith's art but, even more so, immutable evidence of Lillian Gish's gifts as an actress. Trapped in a small closet as her father rages outside, she whirls in terror like a trapped bird confronted by a predatory cat. A viewer can almost hear her pitiable screams. As she dies, she uses two fingers to force a smile on her face, just as she had earlier in the movie. Richard Barthelmess's Cheng Huan is also fine, so reverent and peace-loving that the violence he resorts to in the end is all the more appalling. After he kills Lucy's father, he brings Lucy back to his room, places flowers on her body, and prepares for his own final destiny. "All the tears of the world pour over his heart" as he stabs himself to death. Cheng Huan has chosen not to live in the Western world of bigotry and violence. Five years after making *Intolerance*, Griffith was still expounding its theme, but on a much more intimate scale.

By the late twenties, cinematic techniques had improved to the extent that the best American silent films had acquired a professional

Seventh Heaven (Fox, 1927). Safe and at peace in the "heaven" she shares with Chico, abused waif Diane (Janet Gaynor) looks out upon the Paris street.

blindly through a crowd, to return (naturally) at the exact moment of their daily 11:00 A.M. communion, the surge of emotion is very real, theirs and the willing audience's.

That same year, Janet Gaynor starred for Fox in F. W. Murnau's *Sunrise*, one of the peak achievements of the silent film, and a drama of exceptional power and lyricism. Its story is actually simplistic melodrama of the sort that was already dated by 1927 (the film is subtitled "A Song of Two Humans"). But Murnau, the distinguished German director of such landmark films as *Nosferatu* and *The Last Laugh*, was able to fuse his stylized techniques and his sense of pictorial beauty with the more naturalistic demands of Hollywood—this was his first American movie—to create a timeless film. The heavily expressionistic touches that might have made the movie remote and baffling are happily offset by the strong emotional content; despite the hard-breathing melodramatics, we come to care about the obsessed farmer (George O'Brien) and his sweetly obliging drudge of a wife (Gaynor).

Sunrise plunges directly into the story. The opening sequence shows the man (he is never given a name) in sexual thrall to a passionate "city woman" (Margaret Livingston), while his wife waits helplessly outside their door. The city woman fills his mind with terrible or seductive images: he imagines himself throwing his wife from a boat, or reveling in the hedonistic life of the big city. Acting on their plot to kill the wife, the man takes her out in a boat—a scene that is exquisitely staged and acted. As they move into the water, the wife is faintly troubled by watching him. Gradually, her coquettish smile fades; she becomes sad, pensive, then frightened. When he lumbers toward her, she is horrified, but then he changes his mind and rows furiously to the shore. Distraught, she rushes from him, and flees to the city, where he follows her, humble and remorseful.

The long section in the city combines stylized sets with moments of heartbreaking tenderness and pain, but this melding of reality and unreality never becomes distracting. In a restaurant, they sit in mute anguish until the wife begins sobbing inconsolably. He brings her flowers, but she continues to sob. Soon, however, they are touched by happy memories of the past and they begin to enjoy themselves. As they watch a wedding, he redeclares his own love for her, and they emerge from the church transported by renewed feeling. On the boat taking them home, they are idyllically content; as she sleeps peacefully, he gently covers her with a scarf.

Then a storm comes and capsizes the boat, and the wife is presumed drowned. These scenes bring images of enormous cinematic power. We see the wife floating unconscious in the water, and the camera remains stationary as her body moves into, then out of the frame. The man finds rushes entangled with the remnants of her scarf, and in despair, he can see only a close-up of her face. When he looks down at their empty bed and falls weeping to his knees, the room is streaked with somber shadows. But she is found alive, and as the sun rises, she opens her eyes and smiles at him. Gaynor's deeply moving performance, along with her performances in *Seventh Heaven* and *Street Angel*, won her an Academy Award.

The romantic ardor generated in silent films of the late twenties carried over into the thirties with the coming of sound. Even when a major upheaval such as war intruded on the isolated, dreamlike world of the lovers, the romance remained intense and idyllic: a momentary suspension of time and place. Accustomed to the perfervid passions of the twenties, movie audiences (and not only its women members) responded to the new, spoken declarations of love with the same tears and sighs they had reserved for Garbo and Gilbert, Gaynor and Farrell.

Sunrise (Fox, 1927). A desolate George O'Brien pleads for forgiveness from wife Janet Gaynor. Below: Farmer George O'Brien, bitterly remorseful at having even thought of taking the life of his wife (Janet Gaynor), sits with her in a city restaurant. The film's cameramen Charles Rosher and Karl Struss won the first Academy Award given for cinematography.

Sound did little to disturb the lyrical romanticism of director Frank Borzage. One of his best-remembered films is the dramatization of Ernest Hemingway's novel *A Farewell to Arms* (1932), the first attempt to bring Hemingway's work to the screen. Gary Cooper and Helen Hayes (in her third sound film) costarred in the story of the ill-fated romance of a British nurse and an American serving in the Italian ambulance corps during World War I.

Hemingway's elliptical dialogue did not translate well to film, and Gary Cooper did not have the range to carry off the role of the smitten Lieutenant Frederic Henry—he looks petulant when he is supposed to be grief-stricken—but somehow the movie still has the quality of a faded but tenderly remembered valentine. Due largely to Borzage's sympathetic direction, Charles Lang's shimmering soft-focus photography, and Helen Hayes's poignant, only slightly affected performance as Catherine Barkley, it has survived the years much better than David O. Selznick's elephantine 1957 version.

In this *Farewell to Arms*, the war serves merely as the backdrop for the tragic romance. The screenplay pays lip service to Frederic's desertion from the army ("What does the war mean to me?"); there is the obligatory, although well-managed montage of trudging, weary soldiers, strafing planes, and rows of white crosses; and a few characters are permitted to express their hatred of the war. But the film is mostly concerned with the fate of Catherine and Lieutenant Henry: their quick but ardent meeting, their mock wedding in a hospital room (a touching, beautifully photographed scene with the couple exchanging their vows while the priest blesses them), their long and painful separation during which Frederic deserts the army, and Catherine's death in childbirth. Their farewell scene, which is similar to the last scene in Borzage's *Three Comrades* six years later, is guaranteed to move an audience to tears. Although the difference in their heights sometimes makes them seem an odd match indeed, Helen Hayes and Gary Cooper are appealing together.

In the early thirties, the screen had only one actress who could rival Marlene Dietrich in romantic allure. In the last years before sound, Greta Garbo had earned a place in movie history with a series of starring roles, usually as a mysterious temptress, that took advantage of her enigmatic beauty. (In *Flesh and the Devil*, she seemed to be playing both title roles.) Then, as a weary prostitute named *Anna Christie* (1930), she sauntered into a waterfront bar and said, "Give me a whiskey, ginger ale on the side. And don't be stingy, baby." Her throaty, seductive, accented voice took her stardom to a new dimension, and she was soon appearing in more romantic dramas.

In 1933, she starred in one of her best films, playing Sweden's ambiguous *Queen Christina* under Rouben Mamoulian's direction. With John Gilbert as her personally requested costar, Garbo tossed history to the winds and transformed the allegedly plain-looking bisexual queen into a stunning woman who renounces her throne out of love for a man. The film is a mixture of artful and tedious scenes, but its ending is legendary: aboard a ship carrying her and her dead lover back to Spain, Christina moves to the bow and the camera advances for an exceptionally long close-up of that immobile, inscrutable face. Mamoulian, in fact, had asked Garbo to make her face "a blank sheet of paper," allowing every member of the audience to make his or her own interpretation.

Several years after *Queen Christina*, Garbo appeared in her most

Left: A Farewell to Arms *(Paramount, 1932). Adolphe Menjou (right) watches with dismay as soldier Gary Cooper and nurse Helen Hayes fall in love.*
Right: Queen Christina *(MGM, 1933). Greta Garbo as the Swedish Queen Christina, who gives up her throne out of love for Don Antonio (John Gilbert), emissary from the king of Spain. Director Rouben Mamoulian seemed to understand Garbo's special mystique.*
Opposite: Camille *(MGM, 1937). Greta Garbo in her greatest role, as the fatally ill, self-sacrificing courtesan Marguerite Gautier.*

famous role, as Marguerite Gautier in *Camille* (1937). The story of the ill-fated courtesan had turned up in many versions since Alexandre Dumas *fils* wrote the play *La Dame aux Camélias* in 1852. MGM dusted off the slightly moth-eaten property, gave it a sumptuous if somewhat overstuffed production, put the fastidious George Cukor in charge of the direction, and starred Garbo as Marguerite, loving and coughing her way into legend. To play her lover Armand, the studio chose Robert Taylor, young, inexperienced, and almost improbably handsome.

Marguerite Gautier is Garbo at her most luminous: an inner light burns in her failing body. We see her first in a carriage on her way to the opera. Lavishly gowned and ravishingly beautiful, she is an ornament of Paris in 1847, when, we are told, "the game was romance." At present, she is the mistress of the cynical, saturnine Baron de Varville (Henry Daniell in a brilliant performance). Marguerite is all gaiety and carefree charm, but she is frequently ill—Garbo is extraordinarily adept at suggesting a hint of pain and mortal illness in her laughter. Even as she flings her head back with joy, there are lines and shadows in that remarkable face. At the opera, she meets Armand, dashing and devoted, and her fate is sealed.

It would be foolish to pretend that the screenplay is anything more than fustian nonsense. In truth, the florid dialogue has a hollow sound amid all those ornate and stifling Cedric Gibbons sets. But Garbo, with the considerable aid of Henry Daniell, manages to bring a surprising amount of subtlety and genuine feeling to the proceedings. Early in the film, when the fiercely jealous Baron de Varville suspects Marguerite of having an assignation with Armand, their mirthless laughter as he plays the piano has a chilling edge.

Garbo's love scenes with Robert Taylor are only minimally handicapped by his stiffness—she is so vibrant, so convincingly amorous that she all but electrifies the screen. In a memorable solo scene, after deciding to sacrifice her own happiness for Armand's sake,

she weeps uncontrollably as she writes the Baron de Varville, asking to return. In the final death scene, Garbo succeeds in turning a clichéd character into a tragic figure. Pale and drawn, but grasping at the last vestiges of hope, the last tattered remnants of her life, she waits for Armand to appear. When he arrives, her desperate attempts to act well are painfully moving—when she swoons, she tells him, "My heart! It's not used to being happy." But she expires in his arms, whispering, "Perhaps it's better if I live in your heart, where the world can't see me." Those who would dispute Garbo's greatness as an actress should watch the changing emotions that pass across her face during this scene, or even the way she moves her failing body. *Camille* may be a cluttered and musty monument to Garbo's art, but it is a monument, nonetheless.

Camille was in the vein of high romance that most viewers found highly palatable during the thirties. Rarely did the demands of real life enter into the lovers' isolated universe, and when they did they remained in the background, as catalysts to the romance's fateful outcome. The war that had separated Lieutenant Henry and Catherine Barkley in Frank Borzage's *A Farewell to Arms* surfaced again some years later when Borzage directed an adaptation of Erich Maria Remarque's novel *Three Comrades* (1938). Here the setting was a bleak, defeated Germany, in a state of upheaval directly after World War I. Remarque's political concerns in his novel were muted, however, to make room for the story of three friends, Erich (Robert Taylor), Otto (Franchot Tone), and Gottfried (Robert Young), and Patricia (Margaret Sullavan), the young girl who affects their lives. The romance and marriage of Pat and Erich ends tragically when she dies of tuberculosis.

The screenplay, by F. Scott Fitzgerald and Edward Paramore (with final revisions by Joseph L. Mankiewicz), is not especially successful in capturing the despairing, violent atmosphere of postwar Germany, nor does the production avoid the stodginess of many MGM movies of the period. But when Pat, a girl of aristocratic background who has fallen on hard times, takes over the film, the effect is so moving as to override the inadequacies. With her throaty voice, her air of fragility and vulnerability, Margaret Sullavan was ideal for the role. Her death scene is an affecting tour de force: she is frightened by the ticking of Erich's watch, and when he destroys it, she tells him, "Now time is standing still!" Just before she dies in his arms, she says, "It's right for me to die, darling. It isn't hard. And I'm so full of love." This remarkable actress, too seldom on the screen, brings stature to a faulty but commendable movie.

Pat's death in *Three Comrades* was echoed the following year in Samuel Goldwyn's adaptation of Emily Brontë's novel, *Wuthering Heights* (1939). Here, in a well-remembered scene, the fragile heroine Catherine Earnshaw breathes her last in the arms of Heathcliff, the darkly brooding man she has loved (and also tormented) over the years. It was the climactic scene of a film that, despite critical carping, can still hold its own as one of the screen's great romantic dramas and an impeccable example of Hollywood craftsmanship.

The screenplay by Ben Hecht and Charles MacArthur generally

Three Comrades (MGM, 1938). Robert Taylor offers love and solace to his critically ill wife (Margaret Sullavan). The film was adapted from Erich Maria Remarque's novel about the years following World War I.

cries, "What do they know of heaven and hell, who know nothing of life?" Long afterward, after Heathcliff has frozen to death in his last desperate search for Cathy, the ghostly lovers can be seen, young again in eternity, gathering heather at their own "castle" on Penniston Crag.

The film output of that remarkable cinematic year of 1939 included two other noteworthy romantic dramas that have survived the years. Warners's *Dark Victory* submerged its essential triteness in a pyrotechnic performance by the studio's leading actress, Bette Davis. As a doomed heiress who marries her compassionate doctor, Davis pulled out all the stops, expressing recklessness, anguish, and beatific resignation in her best bravura style. The film, directed by Edmund Goulding, was actually glossy soap opera, but watching this actress flounce through her early happy scenes ("I'm well and strong and nothing can touch me!"), or rage against her fate, or settle into her wifely ways in one last bid for happiness, a viewer was not likely to resist its emotional pull. Davis played her final scene with such moving restraint that it remains high in her catalogue of memorable moments: blinded by her fatal illness, she sends her husband (George Brent) off on a business trip, says goodbye to her best friend (Geraldine Fitzgerald, in sensitive support), and walks upstairs to die in bed, her eyes staring into space as the scene grows dim. Not even the obligatory heavenly choir can spoil the emotional impact.

follows Emily Brontë's novel up to a point, then moves quickly to the tragic ending twenty years later, when Heathcliff joins his beloved Cathy in death. If the film lacks some of the feverish and haunted atmosphere of the novel, the total effect is still riveting. The film's credits are entirely praiseworthy: William Wyler's expert direction, Gregg Toland's luminous photography, Alfred Newman's lovely score, and a set of first-rate performances. Although Merle Oberon's Cathy has been criticized as too tame and ladylike, she is believable as a girl with two warring natures, one wild and passionate, the other longing for wealth and security, while Laurence Olivier makes a properly fierce and bedeviled Heathcliff. In fact, the most vivid memories of *Wuthering Heights* are concentrated in Olivier's characterization of Heathcliff, the ferocious stableboy-turned-landowner whose reckless love endures beyond death. In no previous movie had he demonstrated such power and romantic appeal. We retain indelible images of his performance: Heathcliff cursing the Lintons for their snobbery and for taking Cathy away from him ("I'll bring this house down in ruins around your head!"), or finally clinging to the dying Cathy and shouting, "My tears don't love you! They blight and curse and damn you!" Cathy's death scene is one of the most unforgettable in film history: with her last breaths, Cathy asks Heathcliff to take her to the window—"Let me look at the moors once more with you." She tells him, "I'll wait for you, until you come," and her body goes slack in his arms. As they all pray, Heathcliff

Left: Wuthering Heights *(Samuel Goldwyn/United Artists, 1939). A despairing Heathcliff (Laurence Olivier) is reunited with his beloved Cathy (Merle Oberon) as she lies on her deathbed. This film version of Emily Brontë's novel surprised everyone by winning the New York Film Critics Award for Best Picture over* Gone with the Wind.
Right: Dark Victory *(Warner Bros., 1939). In the poignant finale, Judy Traherne (Bette Davis) and her best friend (Geraldine Fitzgerald) realize that Judy is losing her sight and therefore about to succumb to her fatal illness.*

Another 1939 release, Leo McCarey's *Love Affair*, has also provoked fond memories over the years. A sentimental and charming comedy-drama, it centered on the romance between Terry Mackay (Irene Dunne) and Michel Marnay (Charles Boyer), who meet aboard an ocean liner and, although engaged to others, fall in love and promise to meet six months later atop the Empire State Building. An accident cripples Terry, and she is unable to keep the appointment. But love will find a way, and they are finally reunited. A simple story, but the screenplay by Delmer Daves and Donald Ogden Stewart has a surprising amount of literacy and wit, especially in the early part of the movie, which is treated with the lightness of romantic comedy. In McCarey's deft style, the film moves from the couple's shipboard attraction to a romantic idyll and a meeting with Michel's knowing mother (Maria Ouspenskaya), and then to their enforced

separation. The final scene, as Michel comes to understand why Terry has not tried to contact him, is slightly soggy but touching. All of the film's elements are first-rate, but what lifts this *Love Affair* far above the ordinary are the performances of the two stars. They play with grace and delicacy, and with commendable adjustment to the shifting moods.

By 1940, the tragic love story was becoming an anachronism. That year, MGM examined the lighter side of romance with Ernst Lubitsch's comedy *The Shop Around the Corner*. A totally charming film, with an adroit screenplay by Samson Raphaelson (from a play by Nikolaus Laszlo), it revolved around two store clerks in Budapest who are unwitting pen pals. Since the clerks were played by Margaret Sullavan and James Stewart, their interplay and eventual romance could not have been handled more winningly. This lovely film even manages to be touching at moments, especially when we see Margaret Sullavan's hand exploring a post office rack for an important letter that hasn't arrived. A delightful bonus was the wit and grace with which the film showed the everyday lives and rituals of the people who worked at Matuscheck and Company. As Matuscheck, the shop's cuckolded proprietor, Frank Morgan gave one of his best, most restrained performances.

In the early forties, an occasional film succeeded in keeping its lovers oblivious to the war raging around the world by offering a major star whose romantic suffering could draw audiences, and by providing a few touches of modernity. These factors converged with resounding success in Warners's adaptation of Olive Higgins Prouty's novel *Now, Voyager* (1942). Designed as a showcase for Bette Davis, its familiar story of an ugly duckling who finds romance was laced with a moderate dose of primer-level psychiatry, a subject just entering into dramatic vogue. Bette Davis played Charlotte Vale, a grim, hysterical Boston spinster saddled with a monstrous mother (Gladys Cooper in a definitive portrait of the mother as ogre). Under the guidance of a compassionate psychiatrist (Claude Rains), she is transformed into a chic but nervous beauty who finds love with Jerry Durrence (Paul Henreid), an unhappily married man. But this is Hollywood, 1942, and they must part, although curiously they now have one permanent thing in common: her lover's troubled teenage daughter.

Like many Warners films of the period, *Now, Voyager* is noisily scored, written in large, bold strokes (by the studio's prolific Casey Robinson), and played (especially by Davis) with firm assurance. Its premise is nonsense—once again romance or, more specifically, one intense sexual encounter is offered as the best form of therapy. But through the years, *Now, Voyager* has triumphantly resisted close criticism. Jerry's gesture of lighting two cigarettes and handing one to Charlotte is now part of movie folklore, but other sequences help to turn kitsch into not art, but something almost as memorable. It is difficult to forget the first view of the miraculously transformed Charlotte as she descends the gangplank to be greeted by astonished relatives, or Charlotte's first encounter with her mother in her altered state. ("Things are much worse than they led me to believe"

Above: Love Affair *(RKO, 1939). Irene Dunne and Charles Boyer share a shipboard romance that later takes a sad turn. Leo McCarey's film had warmth, humor, and superb performances by the leading players.*
Below: The Shop Around the Corner *(MGM, 1940). Charm abounded in this romantic comedy by the masterly Ernst Lubitsch. Here, clerk James Stewart discovers that his secret pen pal is the unfriendly girl (Margaret Sullavan) who works beside him every day.*

four decades. With the possible exception of *Gone with the Wind*, it is Hollywood's most legendary film: a romantic melodrama set in a seething North African city when the war in Europe sent thousands of desperate people in flight from the Nazis, searching for a haven in Lisbon, or at least a point of departure to that haven. The name of the city was *Casablanca*.

A romantic film? Yes, indeed. Although the screenplay (by Julius and Philip Epstein and Howard Koch) touches on topical matters involving such familiar wartime figures as brave underground fighters, sinister Nazi officers, and devious black-market dealers, it is essentially the love story of Rick Blaine (Humphrey Bogart), the sardonic owner of Casablanca's most popular night spot, the Café Américain, and Ilsa Lund (Ingrid Bergman), the beautiful wife of underground leader Victor Laszlo (Paul Henreid). Their fateful meeting in Casablanca, years after their romance ended mysteriously in Paris, not only sets the plot in motion, it also gives the film its resonance, its romantic aura. For Rick, the meeting revives bitter memories of a once-great love. ("Of all the gin mills in all the joints in all the world, she walks into mine!") But by the end of the film, this man who refuses to become involved in the turmoil around him ("I stick my neck out for nobody!") has recovered his lost ideals—he had fought Fascists for years—and he makes the supreme gallant gesture of sending the woman he loves away with another man. This film placed Humphrey Bogart in film legend. It not only turned a

is a line that reverberates with several levels of meaning, all of them sinister.) We may wonder why the early Charlotte must resemble the Goodyear Blimp with glasses, or why there should be such staggering encumbrances to the love affair. We may scoff at the ambiguous ending which has Charlotte and Jerry sharing his daughter but not each other (a *ménage à deux et demi*). But there are valid reasons for the film's longstanding popularity: it is well-cooked and deliciously seasoned corn; its central character speaks to the heart and pipe dreams of those who would transform themselves if they could; and it offers three examples of film acting at its best. Those who would question Bette Davis's versatility in her peak period should watch her two "Charlottes," in this film and in *The Old Maid* released two years earlier. Claude Rains's Dr. Jaquith exudes warmth and sympathy, and Gladys Cooper's Mrs. Vale freezes the blood with her imperious cruelty and cunning. Unable to offer a shred of love or compassion to her daughter, she even dies with Back Bay rectitude—she simply stiffens in her chair as Charlotte regales her with a lifetime of bitterness.

Now, Voyager's moth-into-butterfly story was appealing, but with America's entry into World War II, romance could no longer exist in a cocoon, nor could the war serve merely as a background for isolated lovers. It was too real, too urgent to be ignored or relegated to brief montages or newsreels. Apart from the many combat films or movies concerning sacrifices on the home front, there were stories of wartime lovers triumphing over death (*A Guy Named Joe*, 1943), or seizing every bittersweet moment before parting (*Since You Went Away*, 1944), or surmounting physical adversity (*Pride of the Marines*, 1945).

Yet before all these films, there was one movie, released in the fall of 1942, that captured the romantic imagination of audiences in that perilous time, and it has firmly retained that hold for more than

Left: Now, Voyager *(Warner Bros., 1942). Jerry Durrence (Paul Henreid) lights the cigarette of Charlotte Vale (Bette Davis), who, through the efforts of psychiatry and some movie magic, has been transformed from a repressed spinster into a stylish woman of the world.*
Right: Casablanca *(Warner Bros., 1942). A rare full view of Rick's Café Américain, one of the most famous nightspots in film history. At the right is Rick himself (Humphrey Bogart), and at the piano is his loyal friend Sam (Dooley Wilson).*

The Clock *(MGM, 1945). Soldier Robert Walker holds the broken shoe of office worker Judy Garland in Pennsylvania Station. It was a slight story, but Vincente Minnelli's film made something touching and tender out of their hasty wartime romance and marriage.*

craggy-faced, lisping portrayer of sullen hoods into a viable romantic star, it also made his performance the standard against which all strong but basically vulnerable screen heroes would be measured in the future.

It has been pointed out often enough that *Casablanca* is, at heart, little more than an expert wartime drama of romance and intrigue in an exotic city, with its share of plot loopholes and slightly risible dialogue. But the spell this film has woven on more than one generation of filmgoers cannot be denied, and for perfectly good reasons. Apart from Michael Curtiz's adroit direction, Arthur Edeson's photography, which uses the studio-built settings with exceptional skill, and Max Steiner's stirring if typically bombastic musical score, *Casablanca* contains a set of supporting performances of unusual color and variety. Peter Lorre's trapped little dealer in illegal exit visas, Sydney Greenstreet's black-market kingpin, Conrad Veidt's arrogant German major, and Dooley Wilson's loyal, piano-playing Sam—these roles are etched in broad but satisfying strokes. Most memorable of all among the supporting players is Claude Rains as the charming, opportunistic Captain Renault, whose corruptibility will not go so far as to betray Rick or wreck his plan of escape for Ilsa and Laszlo. (Just listen to the inflection he gives to such a line as "I'm only a poor corrupt official.")

Inevitably, however, we come back to Bogart and Bergman for the true source of *Casablanca*'s fame. Is there any filmgoer who has not succumbed to the irresistible appeal of their relationship? His tough-tender salutation to her, "Here's looking at you, kid," and her fervent plea to hear their song "As Time Goes By"—"Play it once, Sam. For old times' sake"—have gone beyond movie lore to become part of our permanent consciousness of the past. Finally, alone in the café after their years apart, Rick and Ilsa exude a coiled sexual tension compounded of still-warm memories and an edge of antagonism. Their last scene together, when Rick insists that she leave on the plane with Laszlo, can be recited verbatim by many film buffs. "You're part of his work," he tells her. "We'll always have Paris. The problems of three people don't amount to a hill of beans in this crazy world." As Rick and Renault walked off together ("Louis, I think this is the beginning of a beautiful friendship"), the film took its place among Hollywood's greatest efforts, probably to the surprise of everyone who had participated in the production.

Another romantic film from the war years that lingers in the memory —far longer than many grandiose efforts—was MGM's *The Clock* (1945). Vincente Minnelli's first film after his success with *Meet Me in St. Louis*, *The Clock* was an unpretentious movie with a frail plot concerning a shy corporal (Robert Walker) on a brief leave in New York City who meets, falls in love with, and marries an office worker (Judy Garland), all within forty-eight hours. There were no subplots, and only a few complications (the two lose each other for a while, and there are some difficulties in getting a blood test), but love triumphs, and they part with brave hopes for the future. Somehow, within this fragile structure, the Robert Nathan–Joseph Schrank screenplay, lovingly guided by Minnelli, manages to suggest the

poignant plight of young people caught up in events and looking for fleeting moments of happiness. The film also conveys some of the ambiance of New York City in wartime, surprisingly since it was largely shot on studio sets.

As Joe and Alice, boyish Robert Walker and a nicely low-key Judy Garland are an agreeable but unexceptional couple who find themselves attracted to each other from the moment of their meeting. Except for one unfortunate moment, when they kiss in close-up to the sound of a heavenly choir, their day and evening together are resolutely ordinary. The pitifully brief period they can spend as husband and wife marks the highlight of the movie. After being married in a ceremony that is drowned out by the sound of a passing train, they sit uneasily in a restaurant while a man at an adjacent table stares at them blankly. Touched by watching a couple being married in a church, they recite the marriage ceremony to each other in hushed tones (the film's best scene). And in the morning, in their hotel room, they gaze at each other adoringly, going through the breakfast ritual without saying a word. When they finally part, Alice is swallowed up in the crowd at Pennsylvania Station. Unlike many other films of the war period, *The Clock* does not press too hard

Summertime *(Lopert Films/United Artists, 1955). In a Venice street café, spinster Jane Hudson (Katharine Hepburn) will soon meet the man (Rossano Brazzi) behind the newspaper. The combination of Hepburn and Venice, aided by Sandro Cicognini's melodic musical theme, made* Summertime *a pleasurable season.*

to manipulate the audience. It mirrors deeply felt emotions in a way that makes it a small but lovely artifact of its time.

Since the 1950s, the love story *per se* has fallen on hard times. Although occasionally critics and audiences have hailed a movie that returns to "old-fashioned" romance for its essential appeal, the general feeling on the part of filmmakers is that audiences are too sophisticated, too jaded to embrace again the conventions of cinematic romance. Others have blamed the basic lack of that elusive quality called romantic star power among the major actors of the last few decades.

There have been some reasonably effective examples of romantic films since 1950. *Summertime* (1955), filmed in Venice and directed by the British David Lean, had an unmistakably American star in Katharine Hepburn. She played Jane Hudson, a spinster secretary on vacation in Venice who not only succumbs to the city's enchantment but also to the charms of a married man (Rossano Brazzi). Ultimately, she assuages her guilt and resentment and leaves for home happy and fulfilled: yet another example of the Hollywood myth of the spinster who achieves personal fulfillment with her first sexual experience. But the photography of Venice by Jack Hillyard was breathtakingly beautiful—the city was clearly on its best behavior for the occasion—and Hepburn was superb as the lady who discovers love. There were perhaps too many rhapsodic stares, too many tremulous line readings, but when she says, "I don't want to forget a single moment of it. I think I never shall," we believe her entirely. Other romantic films, however, were confined to glossily packaged but shallow remakes of familiar properties that did not exactly have depth in the first place, such as *Magnificent Obsession* (1954), *Back Street* (1961), and *Madame X* (1966), or to pulpish fictions such as *All That Heaven Allows* (1954).

By 1970, audiences appeared to be ready for a moist tale of tragic love, especially one that came prepackaged with the stamp of approval by teary-eyed readers. The screen adaptation of Erich Segal's ingeniously contrived novel *Love Story* (1970) was a vast success, its story of the romance between a rich, young Harvard preppie type (Ryan O'Neal) and a fatally ill Radcliffe girl (Ali MacGraw) touching the heartstrings, as it were, of countless viewers. There was no semblance of real life in the film—not in the idyllic scenes of love and courtship, not in the unidentified "movie disease" that carried off the heroine (her swearing was the only concession to actual time and place)—but audiences did not seem to mind. What it lacked, despite Ryan O'Neal's competent and even occasionally moving performance, was the true romantic charge that comes with authentic star presence.

Such a charge was provided in the 1973 film *The Way We Were*. By no means an exceptional film, it is an entertaining comedy-drama focusing on the romance and marriage of an intensely aggressive, radical-minded Jewish girl and her handsome WASP prince, a writer of books and (later) screenplays. Arthur Laurents's observant and felicitous screenplay (from his own novel) takes them from college

in the thirties to a final bittersweet meeting many years later, and Sydney Pollack's direction keeps things moving briskly, if somewhat confusingly in the later sections. But the stars are Barbra Streisand and Robert Redford, and they demonstrate, with full force, the unmistakable power of star personalities. There are scenes that are deliberately staged to reveal that power: a graduation dance at which heroine Katie expresses her mute worship of Hubbell Gardner; a love scene by the fire in which Harry Stradling, Jr.'s photography captures in close-up the amusing contrast of their profiles, and a "showdown" scene in which they realize that neither can change enough to make their marriage work. Their star quality is evident: a mysterious quality that emanates from the screen and rivets our attention.

The Way We Were is basically the story of the Ugly Duckling and the Prince, but with a contemporary patina. Here the Ugly Duckling never turns into a swan, but neither is she really so ugly; despite her plain features, Streisand looks quite attractive in the changing styles of each decade. Nor is the Prince a man embodying all the virtues: Redford's Hubbell Gardner has feet of clay—he is willing to compromise in his writing, and he also recognizes very quickly the futility of protest. The early scenes between them are the best as we watch their baffled, prickly relationship in 1937 turn into attraction and love in the war years. Their married life in Hollywood, involving the years of blacklisting and the "Red" scare, is much less satisfactory; reputedly, much of this was cut in the final print. But the film has a truly memorable ending: years later, Katie and Hubbell meet again. She is remarried and still pursuing her "causes." He is a successful writer with a pretty blonde girlfriend. With no trace of embarrassment or confusion, they express a mingled love and regret that is extremely touching. They go their separate ways, with memories of the way they were.

Recently, *An Officer and a Gentleman* (1982) has been acclaimed as a welcome throwback to the romantic films of yore, in spite of its highly explicit sexual encounters between hero and heroine. Its strong narrative and likable characters seem to have invited the sort of emotional involvement viewers were able to bring to love stories in the thirties and forties. There is, however, one species of romantic film that is not likely to appear again in its purest form. In our new enlightened age in which women are no longer fragile, acquiescent creatures, we do not expect to see the likes of Marguerite Gautier, sacrificing herself for her lover's sake, or Catherine Earnshaw, expiring as much from unfulfilled love as from tuberculosis, or Terry Mackay stoically keeping the truth about her crippled state from the man she adores. Charlotte Vale would probably agree to continue seeing her married lover, and even Ilsa Lund might give up high-minded nobility for a passionate relationship.

Is this a loss or a gain? We cannot say for sure. But in the far reaches of movie annals, we should reserve a place for the rhapsodic, lovelorn women (and men) who experienced the joys and sorrows of romance.

Opposite, above: Love Story *(Paramount, 1970). Harvard student Oliver Barrett IV (Ryan O'Neal) loves Radcliffe girl Jenny Cavilleri (Ali MacGraw) in Arthur Hiller's adaptation of Erich Segal's popular novel about an ill-fated romance.*
Opposite, below: The Way We Were *(Ray Stark/Columbia, 1973). Barbra Streisand and Robert Redford exuded movie-star charisma in this drama concerning the romance and marriage of a radical-minded Jewish girl and her WASP prince.*

LIGHTS! CAMERA! ACTION!

WARNER BROS. PRESENT THE C.V.WHITNEY PICTURE STARRING

JOHN WAYNE IN "THE SEARCHERS"

CO-STARRING
JEFFREY HUNTER · VERA MILES · WARD BOND · NATALIE WOOD

VISTAVISION
AND
TECHNICOLOR

PRINT THE LEGEND
Great Western Movies

In John Ford's 1962 Western, *The Man Who Shot Liberty Valance*, a reporter learns that there is no factual basis for a longstanding romantic legend. It was not stalwart Senator Rance Stoddard (James Stewart) who had shot down killer Liberty Valance, but Stoddard's crusty old friend, Tom Donophon (John Wayne). The killing earned Stoddard the reputation as "the man who shot Liberty Valance" and won him political office. Before his death, Donophon had urged his friend to perpetuate the myth and use it to do good deeds. Hearing the story, the reporter tears up his notes, and when asked why, he replies, "When the legend becomes fact, print the legend."

Since the earliest days of motion pictures, filmmakers have "printed the legend," and audiences have loved it. (Or at least they did until the early fifties, when the trend was to focus on the melancholy and often ugly truth behind the legend.) In spite of changing attitudes, a mythology has grown up about the old West, fostered not only by movies but also by pulp fiction and later by television. In this mythology, characters become prototypes: time and again, we meet the gunslingers and cowboys, brave or sneaky, the ranchers continually at war with the homesteaders, the grizzled prospectors, the dandyish gamblers, the outlaws, either mean or wronged by society. Their female counterparts come in two varieties: good and bad—schoolmarms or dancehall girls. And then there are the rituals—births, marriages, and funerals—and the events that become rituals: cattle drives, stampedes, gold rushes, Indian raids, barroom brawls, and showdowns in the dusty center of town.

Of course not all Western films are formulaic, and over the years some of them have even contained kernels of truth about the nature of heroism, human resilience, and nobility under stress. A film such as *Fort Apache*, however inadvertently, makes us think about the dangers inherent in printing the legend. *The Searchers* has something to say about loneliness, family ties, and the destructive power of bigotry. *The Wild Bunch* makes us question our feelings about violence. If the essence of the Western still lies in its scenes of forthright action, that is not to say it is a mindless genre. Nor can we deny the pride and pleasure in the beauty of the American landscape it instills in us. The Western film may be dormant in the eighties, but it has earned its place in the cinematic sun.

The Western film has, in fact, perhaps the longest history of any major film genre. At the turn of the century, with motion pictures in their infancy, audiences had a fondness for the lore and legends of the old West. It was, after all, not so many years in the past that actual cowboys and outlaws had roamed the Western plains, and a silent film could at least suggest the grandeur of this setting. In 1903, the landmark film *The Great Train Robbery* created a sensation with its narrative of a robbery and the pursuit and capture of the bandits. Neither the first story film nor the first Western, it was, despite its mere ten minutes of running time, an astonishing achievement in its use of primitive camera techniques. The startling last frame showed gunslinger George Barnes firing twice into the camera and then vanishing behind the smoke.

The Great Train Robbery was followed by many other brief films with "western" locales (actually more New Jersey than Wyoming), and by the end of the century's first decade, Western films were already in vogue. By the following decade, many rising directors such as D. W. Griffith, Thomas H. Ince, and Cecil B. DeMille were making Westerns. DeMille, in fact, began his long career with two Westerns, *The Squaw Man* (1913) and *The Virginian* (1914), both starring Dustin Farnum. Farnum and his brother William were busy Western actors, but neither exceeded the popularity of Tom Mix, who made scores of action-filled Westerns well into the thirties.

Another popular Western hero of the silent era was a dour, intense, middle-aged man named William S. Hart. A stern moralizer who insisted on authentic details in his films, Hart starred in (and, in his early career, also directed) a number of Westerns in which he was reformed from his evil ways by a good woman or a bad conscience, in the process becoming a fire-and-brimstone zealot for law and order. In such movies as *Hell's Hinges* (1916), *The Narrow Trail* (1917), and *Blue Blazes Rawden* (1918), Hart emphasized character and plot over conventional Western action, continuing to do so even after audiences were expressing a preference for more rough-and-ready cowboys such as Tom Mix and Buck Jones. By 1920 his vogue had already passed, but he persisted in making his kind of Western until his very last film, *Tumbleweeds* (1925). Ironically, it was both a critical and popular

Preceding pages: Gunga Din *(RKO, 1939). The intrepid Cutter (Cary Grant) and faithful little Gunga Din (Sam Jaffe, far left) stalk the great hall of the murderously fanatic Thugs in British India.*
Opposite: *A lobby card for* The Searchers *(Warner Bros., 1956).*
Above: Tumbleweeds *(William S. Hart/United Artists, 1925). William S. Hart's only attempt at an outsize Western, this movie included a scene in which Hart watches the cattle herds moving across land that would soon be occupied by homesteaders. He removes his hat and remarks, "Boys, it's the last of the West."*

success, an auspicious forerunner of movies showing that the American West could be not only a setting for hard-riding action but also a rich source of myths and legends recounted on the grandest of scales.

Two years before *Tumbleweeds*, audiences were viewing the first truly epic-size Western, *The Covered Wagon* (1923). Directed by James Cruze, formerly a very busy actor, and photographed by Karl Brown, a former assistant of Griffith, the movie anticipated many later efforts by chronicling a wagon train's two-thousand-mile journey to Oregon in

1848. The scenes of the wagons snaking across the awesome Western landscape were much more impressive than the ordinary plot. The film also paid careful attention to the Western rituals and travails that were to become integral features of the genre: a hazardous river crossing, a buffalo hunt, a simple funeral, wagons struggling to move through a blizzard.

The Iron Horse (1924), an elaborate Western by John Ford, did not duplicate the success of *The Covered Wagon*, but it was a superior

Above: The Covered Wagon *(Famous Players-Lasky/Paramount, 1923). The wagon train moves into uncharted territory. Karl Brown's documentary-like photography foreshadowed the work of such later craftsmen as Russell Harlan and Winton Hoch.*
Below: The Iron Horse *(Fox, 1924). The historic meeting of the Union Pacific and Central Pacific railroads on May 10, 1869, is re-created in John Ford's silent Western. The film's action scenes were staged with a flair that augured well for Ford's future.*

film. Its plot was not much better, and its photography was not up to Karl Brown's in the earlier film, but it contained some of the elements that were to emerge full-blown in Ford's subsequent Westerns: the feeling for outdoor spectacle, pleasure in re-creating (and somewhat idealizing) life in the pioneer West, and even the rowdy Irish humor that later became so oppressive in his films. Made almost entirely on location in the Nevada desert, *The Iron Horse* was Ford's most ambitious film to date—a lavishly detailed account of the building of the great railroads that brought civilization to the West.

Although filmgoers and critics were impressed with *The Covered Wagon* and *The Iron Horse*, the films did not create a trend. The balance of the twenties and, indeed, much of the thirties saw few Westerns of any genuine scope or dimension. Some interesting efforts in the early years of sound included Raoul Walsh's *In Old Arizona* (1929) and *The Big Trail* (1930) and Wesley Ruggles's *Cimarron* (1931). But many filmmakers, obsessed with the idea of talk at any cost, felt that the West, with its accent on action over dialogue, did not warrant more than "B"-level treatment. Later in the thirties, such major Westerns as Cecil B. DeMille's *The Plainsman* (1936) and King Vidor's *The Texas Rangers* (1936), while popular, were few and far between; low-budget Western films dominated the field.

And then, early in 1939, United Artists released the landmark film that gave new direction and momentum to the Western. John Ford's first Western in over a decade, *Stagecoach* restored the genre

to its former position as a source of home-grown American spectacle while demonstrating that characters who moved against a Western landscape could have as much color and variety as those in any other genre. The movie launched a long-lasting cycle of outsize Westerns filmed at least partly in natural settings, and it brought stardom to one of the screen's most durable actors, John Wayne.

Stagecoach *(Walter Wanger/United Artists, 1939). The stagecoach passengers gather for a meal along the way to their destination. Around the table, clockwise from lower left: Claire Trevor, John Wayne, Louise Platt, John Carradine, and Berton Churchill. Below: The stagecoach, followed by an army escort, races through Monument Valley.*

It should be added, however, that by now the historical value of *Stagecoach* exceeds its merits as a film. Its story of a disparate group of stagecoach passengers who share a perilous adventure on their way to Lordsburg was not exactly fresh even in 1939 (there had been many films of what might be called the "Grand Hotel" school of plotting), nor were the characters invented by Dudley Nichols for his screenplay all that original. Other, much less ambitious Westerns had offered such figures as the revenge-driven cowboy (John Wayne), the prostitute-with-a-heart-of-gold (Claire Trevor), the bibulous doctor (Thomas Mitchell), the crooked banker (Berton Churchill), and the suave gambler (John Carradine). Also, although Ford filmed some of his exteriors in Monument Valley for the first time, much of the movie was made on the studio back lot, using rear-screen projection.

Then why has *Stagecoach* retained its lofty status over all these years? For one thing, the film succeeded in crystallizing the elements that became part of the classic Western mold: it set the pattern for depicting the rites of passage in the West (here the birth of a baby, which mellows the passengers) and for filming the archetypal action

scenes of the genre—the Indian attack, the last-minute cavalry rescue, the climactic showdown in the heart of town. For another, the characters have a substance that makes the viewers truly care about their plight. Although they are not necessarily "flesh-and-blood characters whose confrontations symbolized the differences and prejudices of class" (Bosley Crowther, *Vintage Films*), they are certainly more than cardboard. The warm relationship that develops between the cowboy and the prostitute is captured more in glances than in dialogue (the shot of him watching her hold the newborn baby provides a lovely quiet moment), and the courage the characters demonstrate throughout their ordeal gives even the meanest of them a sort of touching nobility. Bert Glennon's sharp photography, an artful musical score fashioned from American folk songs (it won an Academy Award), and skillful performances by a well-chosen cast of character actors help to make the film memorable.

Another 1939 Western film made good use of Technicolor. The vivid hues of Henry King's *Jesse James* seemed entirely appropriate for this prettified and fanciful version of the short life and violent

Jesse James *(Fox, 1939). Brothers Frank and Jesse James (Henry Fonda and Tyrone Power)*
ride out of town after their aborted attempt at a bank robbery. The movie whitewashed the
notorious outlaws, but it was a lively and colorful Western.

demise of the famous outlaw. In whitewashing the lawless career of Jesse (Tyrone Power) and his brother Frank (Henry Fonda)—not the first and by no means the last movie to do so—the film depicted them as hotheaded young men who turn to crime only after their home is destroyed and their mother is murdered by brutal railroad agents. In the popular late-thirties mode—according to which movie criminals blamed a vaguely defined "society" for their behavior—the James boys are rebels against a power that abuses them and wrecks their lives. We are asked to sympathize with them because, after all, we would all enjoy rebelling a little against authority, and besides, they rob the railroads with such thoroughgoing professionalism. At the close of the film, standing over Jesse's grave, newspaper editor Henry Hull puts this dubious premise bluntly: "Jesse was a bandit, an outlaw, a criminal. But we ain't ashamed of him. Maybe because he was bold, lawless, like we all like to be sometime. . . . Or maybe it was because he was so good at what he was."

It is interesting to compare the elegiac closing of this movie with the end of *The Gunfighter*, made a decade later by the same director. Whereas Jesse James is gunned down in the bosom of his regained family, Jimmy Ringo of *The Gunfighter* is never reconciled with his wife and son, and his wife acknowledges their relationship only after his death at the hand of the town bully. *Jesse James* is agreeable Technicolor artifice; *The Gunfighter* is filmed in austere black-and-white. One is movie legend, the other movie reality, which is not to be confused with true reality. Henry King is far from a major director, but we must admire the skill that created two such disparate examples of the Western genre.

One other Western released the same year as *Stagecoach* and *Jesse James* was much different from either of them: an amusing and rowdy spoof of the genre entitled *Destry Rides Again*. A sendup of virtually all of the conventions and clichés of the Western, the movie starred James Stewart as a mild-mannered, gunless sheriff in the wild town of Bottleneck who somehow manages to defeat the town's nasty types. The film suggests an interesting contrast with the later *High Noon*, in which a sheriff is abandoned and scorned for taking up arms against evil forces and not, as in *Destry*, for *refusing* to take up arms against similarly evil forces. In 1939, Tom Destry is mocked for his pacifism until he joins club-wielding women in routing the enemy; in 1952, Will Kane is deserted because of his decision to fight back, and he is only joined in the final shootout by his Quaker wife. The message in both films: pacifism is misguided at best, and cowardly at worst; alone or in concert, we must ultimately fight back.

As the forties began, the Western continued as staple fare, although on a minor scale. During the years of World War II, the studios were much more concerned with turning out patriotic combat films and encomiums to the war effort at home, or, more often, untaxing escapist fare for war-weary Americans. It did not seem wise in wartime to emphasize a genre that featured gunplay and body counts, however far removed in time. (Gangster films were even scarcer, for much the same reason.) There was also the fact that John Ford, the most important director of Westerns, was serving as a lieutenant commander

in the navy. The few major Westerns that did get produced included *The Ox-Bow Incident* (1943), a grim but seriously flawed diatribe against lynching, and *Buffalo Bill* (1944), a glossy Technicolor distortion of history. These films could not be more different in tone and intention, yet oddly enough, they were both directed by the versatile William Wellman.

The years following the war saw a resurgence of interest in the Western and the welcome return of John Ford to the genre he loved best. Of Ford's Westerns of the postwar forties, his first, *My Darling Clementine* (1946), is perhaps the best. Although it lacks the sweeping Technicolor pageantry of *Fort Apache* and *She Wore a Yellow Ribbon*, it also avoids the heavy-handed sentiment and roughhouse

Above: Destry Rides Again *(Universal, 1939). Rowdy times in the town of Bottleneck with (left to right) Brian Donlevy, James Stewart, and Marlene Dietrich.*
Below: The Ox-Bow Incident *(Fox, 1943). Lynching victims Dana Andrews, Anthony Quinn, and Francis Ford face Frank Conroy, the vindictive major who conducted their mock trial. Henry Fonda (right) is a troubled observer. The innocence of the pitiable victims raised an unanswered question: Is a lynching any more justified when the victims are guilty of the crime?*

humor of the later films. Crisply and beautifully photographed in black-and-white by Joseph MacDonald, the film has the quality of legend as it relates the by-now familiar tale of Marshal Wyatt Earp's conflict with the murderous Clanton clan in the Tombstone of 1882, climaxed with the shootout at the O.K. Corral. The steadfast but laconic Earp is aided in his battle by the bitter, alcoholic, and tubercular gunman named Doc Holliday.

Ford brings his customary briskness and assurance to the narrative, but as is so often the case in his Western films, he is more concerned with expressing his abiding affection and even reverence for pioneer America—not the grimy West of violence and corruption (the "revisionist" Western films would cover that many years later), but the legendary West of courage and resilience. The action sequences are well-staged against the awesome vistas of Monument Valley—the final showdown at the O.K. Corral is a model of its kind—but one sooner recalls the quietly eloquent scenes of life and death in the community. (Such scenes are often a central part of Ford's films, as in *The Grapes of Wrath* and *How Green Was My Valley*.) Here, one remembers the funeral of Earp's murdered young brother, with Earp (Henry Fonda) delivering a solemn graveside speech ("Didn't get much of a chance, did you? Maybe when we leave this country, kids like you will be able to live and grow up safe"). Most memorable of all is the sequence of the dance celebrating the opening of the town church. The church bells ring triumphantly as the townspeople sing "Shall We Gather at the River," and later, after the dedication, Earp joins the demure Clementine (Cathy Downs) in an earnest, marvelously funny dance around the floor.

As Earp, Henry Fonda uses his trademarked understated style, making the character forceful and self-confident through the steady intensity of his gaze, the no-nonsense flatness of his voice. Essentially shy behind his cowboy-lawman veneer, he is unable to express his feelings of love directly. ("I sure like the name—Clementine.")

Victor Mature, finally emerging from the unfortunate earlier period of his career as Fox's handsome "hunk" of man, is surprisingly impressive as Doc Holliday, and there is a consummate portrait of unregenerate evil by Walter Brennan as the head of the Clanton family. Only the women fare poorly, as they often do in Ford's Western films. Linda Darnell is improbable—and also much too visible—as an ill-fated Mexican girl named Chihuahua, and Cathy Downs is pallid as Clementine.

Henry Fonda played an entirely different sort of role in Ford's next Western film, *Fort Apache* (1948). Colonel Owen Thursday, a cold, glory-seeking martinet, is bitterly resentful at being placed in command of the remote Fort Apache in hostile Indian country. His affection is reserved exclusively for his young daughter Philadelphia (Shirley Temple). Against the recommendation of his sensible second-in-command, Captain Kirby York (John Wayne), Thursday sends his men on a suicidal mission against the Apaches. During the ensuing massacre, he realizes his tragic error and rides off to die with his soldiers. Afterward, without a trace of irony, York extols him as a gallant and honorable hero.

Fort Apache is a long, sprawling Western that embodies many of John Ford's favorite, most recurrent themes: the necessity for duty and honor in a burgeoning new country, the value of military pomp and ritual, with its sense of order and tradition, and the unchanging beauty of the land itself. These are certainly laudable themes, and if they sometimes lead to dubious conclusions, they also inspire sequences showing Ford's romantic attitude toward the cavalry and pioneer life: a dance at which noncommissioned officers and their women perform a lovingly photographed Grand March, and the troops' departure from the fort to meet the enemy, their voices proudly raised in song. As always, Ford makes his beloved Monument Valley a character as important as any in the film: its imposing vistas become a testimonial to that part of the land that accommodates humanity but will never be conquered by it. Despite a slow first reel, given over to too much boisterous slapstick comedy and a callow romance between Philadelphia Thursday and a young lieutenant (John Agar), there are splendid action sequences, especially the climactic Indian attack.

Where *Fort Apache* falters is in Captain York's deliberate deification of Thursday: the concept that we must choose the legend over the truth. Until he chooses to sacrifice his life in payment for arrogantly leading his men into ambush, Thursday is depicted as a vainglorious, bullheaded man who snobbishly refuses to allow his daughter to marry the son of his sergeant-major, and who deliberately insults the peace-seeking Indian chief Cochise by calling him "an illiterate, uncivilized savage." Yet York's final tribute to this man ("No man died more gallantly—or earned more honor for his regiment!") is meant to be stirring rather than ironic, sweeping our disapproval under a blanket of praise for "the regiment." Ford asks us to dismiss any censure of military miscalculation that costs thousands of lives—a dismissal that would absolve not only Thursday but Custer, the leaders of the charge of the Light Brigade, and more recent military

My Darling Clementine (Fox, 1946). A tense confrontation between Marshal Wyatt Earp (Henry Fonda) and Doc Holliday (Victor Mature) in John Ford's classic Western drama.

blunderers. *Fort Apache* is a lusty Fordian Western but we need to ask: What price the legend? Small wonder that Ford detested the "debunking" Westerns of the fifties and beyond.

She Wore a Yellow Ribbon (1949), Ford's second film in his trilogy on the U.S. Cavalry, is superior to *Fort Apache* and not only because its Technicolor enhances the magnificence of Monument Valley. (Ford's frequent cameraman Winton Hoch won an Academy Award for his photography, which deliberately suggests the Western paintings of artist Frederic Remington.) Although Ford persists in including rowdy Irish humor, he is more concerned with the many facets of his central character, Captain Nathan Brittles. As Brittles, an aging cavalry officer who must finally give up his command, John Wayne gives one of his sturdiest performances. A strong, courageous frontier soldier who leads his men in one last battle against the Cheyennes, he regularly visits the gravesite of his wife and young children to water the flowers and bring his wife up to date on events, and he even sheds a few tears at his moving retirement ceremony. Although Ford, as usual, does not neglect the action his fans had come to expect, his heart is with the rituals and customs of military life and the people who observe them, embodied by Captain Brittles and his loyal men. Some think of this as Ford's sentimentality, others as Ford's humanism. Suffice to say that *She Wore a Yellow Ribbon* is a far distance from the harsh and gritty reality of Howard Hawks's

Red River, the classic Western film that preceded it by a year.

In many ways *Red River* makes an interesting contrast to John Ford's Westerns of the period. Whereas Ford opts for a romantic,

Fort Apache *(RKO, 1948). Captain York (John Wayne, center, at left) meets with the Apaches to negotiate a truce. Below: At a regimental dance, martinet Colonel Owen Thursday (Henry Fonda) confronts Captain York. Between them: Captain Sam Collingwood (George O'Brien). John Ford later justified the film's glorification of a military blunderer (Thursday) by claiming, "It's good for the country to have heroes to look up to" (Bogdanovich,* John Ford, *p. 86).*

legendary view of the old West, bathing Monument Valley in glowing Technicolor hues, Hawks, using black-and-white for his first film in the genre, is more interested in conveying a sense of the dust, the sweat, and the grime that were part of the daily lives of his cattlemen. While Ford continually exults in sequences of epic grandeur—a cavalry charge, a pioneer trek across the pitiless desert—or in Western rituals—funerals, military balls, marches—Hawks, in *Red River*, confines his large-scale sequences to the central event of the film: the cattle drive along the historic Chisholm Trail. The start of the drive on a Texas morning, brilliantly staged by Hawks and photographed with almost documentary realism by Russell Harlan, is followed at various points in the movie by a cattle stampede and a hazardous river crossing. Yet another revealing difference between Ford and Hawks is in their handling of the camaraderie among men that was an integral part of Western life. Ford tends to treat the subject with boisterous sentiment, while the men of *Red River* live under an uneasy truce, their loyalties shaded by expediency and self-interest. (Relationships among men under stress and the responsibilities of leadership are two of Hawks's consistent themes, as in *The Dawn Patrol*, 1930, *Ceiling Zero*, 1935, and *Air Force*, 1943.)

Red River gave John Wayne one of his most interesting Western roles. He plays a determined despot named Tom Dunson, a cattle baron obsessed with driving his herd from Texas to Missouri along an uncharted thousand-mile trail. As the journey progresses, Dunson becomes harsher and more unreasonable until Matt (Montgomery Clift), the young man he adopted as a son after an Indian attack, is forced to take over leadership and drive the cattle to the safer region of Kansas.

Narrated by Walter Brennan, playing Dunson's loyal, plain-speaking old friend ("You was wrong, Mr. Dunson"), *Red River* is unusually rich in its characterization, never letting the spectacle overpower the relationships. Tom Dunson is no hero but neither is he a simple tyrant. He has a far-reaching vision—the sort of vision that

settled the West—but he cannot admit its limitations. He is deeply affected when one of his men is killed in the stampede, yet he is eager to hang the few that leave the drive. His love for his adopted son cannot withstand the ignominy of being humiliated and powerless, and he pursues him vengefully, vowing to kill him on sight. His unrelenting pride promises to destroy him in the end, and we expect to witness the downfall of a tragic figure. Instead, in an ending of almost embarrassing foolishness, Matt's girl (Joanne Dru) intervenes, scolding Tom and Matt like a pouting schoolmarm and forcing them to make peace. (Scenarist Borden Chase, to his credit, bitterly opposed this ending, which violates not only our rightful expectations but the rules of sound dramaturgy as well.) Except for this unfortunate closing, *Red River* is a splendid achievement in the genre.

Although John Ford continued to offer his romanticized view of the West into the fifties, a new strain was evident in the genre by the start of the decade. The keynote was realism, or specifically, a more objective and blunter approach to subject matter, as evidenced in other genres as well: the "socially aware" films on anti-Semitism and alcoholism, the *films noirs* with their nighttime world of crime and corruption. In the Western, the new approach took the form of demythologizing longstanding concepts concerning people and events of America's pioneer period. The cowboys and gunfighters of legend were shown to be weary, indecisive, and all-too-human figures in a gray, often hostile world.

This sober view of the old West first became evident in 1950 with the release of Fox's *The Gunfighter*. Here a celebrated but tired gunfighter named Jimmy Ringo (Gregory Peck) arrives at a Western town to make one last effort to come to terms with his wife and child, and to settle down to a peaceful life. Instead, his reputation as "the fastest gun who ever lived" prompts the town bully to challenge him to what becomes his last shootout. Ringo's old friend (Millard Mitchell), now the sheriff, orders the bully to leave town ("Get killed

Left: Red River *(Monterey/United Artists, 1948). In Howard Hawks's gritty Western film, cattle baron Tom Dunson (John Wayne) and his adopted son Matt (Montgomery Clift) face a conflict of wills that will ultimately destroy their relationship.*
Right: The Gunfighter *(Fox, 1950). Famed but weary gunfighter Jimmy Ringo (Gregory Peck) is challenged by town bully Hunt Bromley (Skip Homeier). At the bar in the background: Karl Malden.*

somewhere else!"), and Ringo's wife proudly identifies herself as his widow at the funeral.

Spare in its details, starkly photographed in black-and-white, *The Gunfighter* has been regarded as a turgid anti-Western by some critics. Ringo may lack the intended stature of a genuinely tragic figure, yet his plight and his pathetic last attempt to turn his life around give the character and the film a poignant quality rare for the genre. Ringo's scene with his alienated wife (Helen Westcott) expertly conveys the gunfighter's longing for an oasis of peace in another part of the country ("We would be safe out there the rest of our lives"), and his last words to his killer are edged with muted anger and bitterness: "I want you to go on being a big tough gunman. I want you to see how it is to live like a big tough gunnie!" Gregory Peck's understated (to some, colorless) style of acting seems appropriate for Ringo, and Henry King's direction, although not in a class with his lively handling of *Jesse James* (another gunman shot down in his prime), is competent if uninspired.

The theme of the footloose, gunslinging Westerner as an anachronistic figure in a changing world received its fullest treatment in Paramount's 1953 film *Shane*. In contrast to the bleak, gray style of *The Gunfighter*, however, *Shane* was afforded a lavish production in which sweeping Western vistas, photographed in stunning color by Loyal Griggs, gave the film at least the look of a John Ford Western. (There the resemblance ends—George Stevens's direction lacks the vigor and pace that Ford would have given it, and Alan Ladd, unlike John Wayne, gives the impression of walking through rather than inhabiting the title role.) This time the gunfighter was neither worn nor aging but a mysterious blond stranger (Ladd) who rides out of nowhere to help besieged homesteaders in their fight against the cattlemen. Shane is welcomed into the home of the most outspoken homesteader (Van Heflin), where he becomes an object of muted attraction for the man's wife (Jean Arthur) and the idol of his young son (Brandon de Wilde). Reluctant at first to wield his gun, Shane

finally resorts to violence and then, knowing that he is a man out of his time, he rides away forever.

Although the story is familiar, it takes on the quality of a legend by being related from the viewpoint of Joey, the ten-year-old boy who worships Shane. There are other obvious attempts to achieve that legendary quality, especially in Shane's blond handsomeness and buckskin garb set against Jack Palance's cold, sneering countenance and jet-black clothing. But Joey is the central figure: as he runs across the fields against a background of majestic mountain peaks, or observes the rituals that are part of life on the frontier—a funeral, a gunfight—the film becomes the visualization of a myth concerning America's West as a place of unspoiled beauty and heroic endurance, marred by bursts of violence. *Shane* is perhaps the last great statement of that myth before the Western genre became eccentric, "adult," or self-mocking. (John Ford's *The Searchers*, a greater film, is not intent on creating a myth—its leading character is no knight on horseback like Shane, no grave and honorable man with a gun, but a driven and secretive loner with a wide streak of bigotry in his makeup. Nor is his departure orchestrated to childish pleas to return—"Come back, Shane!"—a door is simply closed on him, and he goes on his way.)

One Western film of the early fifties was both unusual and unusually successful, winning an Academy Award for its star, its editing, its

Left: Shane *(Paramount, 1953). Homesteader Van Heflin and his wife (Jean Arthur) stand solemnly beside the grave of a neighbor. Watching them are son Brandon de Wilde and Alan Ladd, the mysterious gunman who will help them in their struggle against the cattlemen. Right:* High Noon *(Stanley Kramer/United Artists, 1952). Gary Cooper in his Academy Award–winning role as sheriff Will Kane. The film was an allegory disguised as a Western, but it still offered some traditional Western excitement.*

musical score, and its title song. *High Noon* (1952) veered from the traditional concept of the Western, but in a way different from *The Gunfighter* or *Shane*. The central figure was not a worn, battle-scarred anachronism but a proud and sensitive lawman who finds himself trapped in a desperate situation. As Marshal Will Kane of Hadleyville, Gary Cooper learns, on the last day of his job, that desperadoes he has sent to jail are returning to town to kill him. Though newly married, he accepts their challenge out of a deep sense of duty, and tries to organize help. To his bitter chagrin, he discovers that he is utterly alone—the cowardly, irresponsible towns-people have turned their backs on him. After a climactic shootout, he grinds his marshal's badge in the dirt and rides away with his bride (Grace Kelly).

Fred Zinnemann's tightly controlled direction and Gary Cooper's solid, austere performance, which made excellent use of his masklike countenance and repressed personality, drew praise from the critics. But it was Carl Foreman's screenplay that won not only admiring notices but also heavy analysis and interpretation. Foreman was a victim of the McCarthy purge in Hollywood, and it was generally agreed that his script was both a taut Western melodrama and a cry of protest at the cowardice and vacillation with which most Americans met McCarthy's savage onslaught. To a great extent, *High Noon* was the first "message" Western, barely concealing its true theme in the traditional barrage of gunfire.

As such, the film has met with contempt over the years from purists who believe that messages have no place in the Western genre, especially when the nobility of the Western myth is distorted to accommodate them. Others have complained about the movie's overly schematic structure and its popular but slightly absurd theme song performed by Tex Ritter at regular intervals. Yet the film has substantial merit on its own, building tension as the fateful day progresses with repeated shots of a clock and of the deserted railway station where the killers will arrive. In one memorable shot, the camera moves away from Cooper's face to show him standing alone in the town's deserted main street: the man of honor knowing that he has been betrayed, yet facing possible death with dignity.

During this period of "meaningful" Westerns, melancholy and parabolic, the masters of the genre continued working in their own vein, Howard Hawks with *The Big Sky* (1952) and *Rio Bravo* (1959), and John Ford with *Wagonmaster* (1950), *Rio Grande* (1950), and *The Searchers* (1956). The latter film was by far the best, bringing a new richness and subtlety to the genre. In *The Searchers*, Ford deepened John Wayne's familiar persona of the ambling, reticent, but quick-drawing cowboy by starring the actor in perhaps his greatest role. Wayne gave a surprisingly rounded performance as Ethan Edwards, a bitter, intensely private man who spends five years relentlessly searching for the niece who was kidnapped by Indians after her family (including his brother and sister-in-law) was murdered. During the course of Frank S. Nugent's dense and complex screenplay, many relationships emerge, but ultimately Edwards discovers that his beloved niece has become a white-hating squaw. In

a moment of anguish, he moves to kill her, but he relents and carries her off to a home of safety and comfort he can never share.

The Searchers is a remarkable film, considered by many to be the greatest in the genre, and John Ford's finest achievement. Discounting hyperbole and allowing for a number of faults (mainly some sluggish sections and too much footage to a romance between Jeffrey Hunter and Vera Miles), the film comes close to deserving its reputation. Throughout, Ford never loses his sense of spectacle—the Western scenery has never looked more breathtakingly beautiful as photographed by Winton Hoch—and the action scenes, especially the climactic battle between Rangers and Comanches, have the director's usual pace and excitement. *The Searchers* is not a stark or bleakly photographed film in the style of "serious" Westerns of the period. Yet it cuts deeper than Ford's sentimental cavalry Westerns of the forties. In Ethan Edwards it offers a character whose inner conflict and contradictions not only serve to humanize him but, at the same time, increase his stature as a tragic figure.

Much has been written about the film's opening and closing scenes: Ethan, at the beginning, riding alone to join his brother's beloved and welcoming family, and Ethan, at the end, equally alone as the door shuts him out of all human companionship. At the heart of his severe and remorseless code is a hatred of Indians: he shoots out the eyes of a dead Comanche so that his soul will wander forever, he refuses to allow the Indians to bury their dead, and when he comes upon young white girls who have lost their wits in Indian captivity, he says bluntly, "They're not white anymore." Yet during the course of his long search (actually inward as well as outward), he is able to soften his stance enough to make an heir of his young traveling

Above: The Searchers *(Warner Bros., 1956). Ethan Edwards (John Wayne) manhandles Martin Pawley (Jeffrey Hunter), the young man with Cherokee blood who accompanies Ethan on his long search for his niece Debbie.*
Opposite: The Wild Bunch *(Warner Bros.-Seven Arts, 1969). The bunch arrives in town. Left to right: Ben Johnson, Warren Oates, William Holden, and Ernest Borgnine. Sam Peckinpah's Western was a shockingly violent but gripping film.*

partner, Martin (Jeffrey Hunter), who has Cherokee blood. And, most movingly, he can accept his niece (Natalie Wood), now a fierce Indian maiden, back into the world (or at least the civilized world as he knows it) with a simple, "Let's go home, Debbie." John Wayne's performance as this dour, obsessed, contradictory man refutes all those who would dismiss him as a one-note actor.

The Searchers also contains moments of truth that are rare in the Western genre. Early in the film, Ward Bond, as a clergyman who also happens to be a captain in the Rangers, sees Ethan's sister-in-law stroking Ethan's coat, and he turns his head away discreetly at the sight of this loving gesture. Ethan meets the Indian chieftain Scar (Henry Brandon) in a Comanche village, and as they sit between rows of scalps, the look that passes between them summarizes many years of deep-rooted hostility and a wary groping toward understanding. Without undue emphasis, Ford even manages a few moments of visual poetry: the funeral of the massacred family, the group huddled around the pitiful graves; the bowed figures of Ethan and Martin as they move through a raging snowstorm; the Indians in full war regalia, riding on either side of the Rangers, ominously silent before their attack.

Ford continued making Westerns into the sixties—strong, often effective films with a deepening sense of pessimism. These are autumnal films—one of his last movies was *Cheyenne Autumn* (1964)—and they deal with somber subjects: a black soldier falsely accused of rape (*Sergeant Rutledge*, 1960); the grim consequences of long captivity by Indians (*Two Rode Together*, 1961); the betrayal of Indians and their desperate trek homeward (*Cheyenne Autumn*). Ford was not alone in this twilight mood. This decade of Westerns was framed by two melancholy films, both directed by Sam Peckinpah. His *Ride the High Country* (1962) concerned two tired, aging gunfighters (Joel McCrea and Randolph Scott, themselves venerable artifacts of the genre) who are reunited for one last battle in which McCrea is fatally wounded. As he succumbs, Scott tells him, "I'll see ya later." This poignant scene capped an unusual film that was lyrical at times and earthy at others, and also more convincing than the sincere but somewhat studied films of the fifties on the fading gunfighter.

Peckinpah's *The Wild Bunch* was quite a different matter. A savage and extraordinarily violent Western drama, it burst on the film scene in mid-1969, causing more intense controversy than any other film in years. Here was the bitter culmination of America's Western saga, the flip side of John Ford, the dark side of *Shane*. The leading

Overleaf, left: Butch Cassidy and the Sundance Kid *(Fox, 1969). Teacher Etta Place (Katharine Ross) enjoys a merry bicycle ride with outlaw Butch Cassidy (Paul Newman). Below: Posing as if for a Western tintype are (left to right) the Sundance Kid (Robert Redford), Etta Place, and Butch Cassidy.*
Overleaf, right: Little Big Man *(Cinema Center Films/National General, 1970). Young Jack Crabb (Dustin Hoffman) is given a bath by the preacher's wife, Mrs. Pendrake (Faye Dunaway). Below: Jack Crabb practices to become the fastest gun in the West.*

characters are not men of honor and integrity but members of a motley band of filthy, hopelessly corrupt, doomed outlaws. Their desperate flight into Mexico, led by the steely eyed, laconic Pike Bishop (William Holden), brings them the destruction they have courted for years. Pursued by bounty hunters and Deke Thornton (Robert Ryan), a former colleague, on one side, and by a sadistic general and his men on the other, they are finally wiped out in a bloody battle.

Despite Lucien Ballard's beautiful photography, *The Wild Bunch* is no lyrical tribute to Western tradition, but a harsh, uncompromising view of the burned-out end of the frontier period in American history. (Significantly, the film is set in 1913 and not in the mid-to-late 1800s, as are most Westerns.) The tone is set in the very first sequence, in which the bunch, disguised as soldiers, rides into a town while young boys gleefully watch red ants devouring a scorpion. A bloody battle erupts, killing not only some of the fighters but innocent bystanders as well. This grim, despairing note never falters as the outlaws are cut down one by one in a cross fire not only of bullets but of greedy intentions. There are no moral distinctions in this world—even the children are amoral and ruthless.

It should be noted that *The Wild Bunch* is a bleak film that despairs of humanity's bloodlust and corruption, but it is not a totally nihilistic one. The bunch may be killers hell bound for extinction, but they still retain a vestige of the creed that informed the old Westerners. The bunch (or at least Pike) even has professional pride. Before robbing a train, Pike states, "This is our last time round. This time we do it right." When there is a suggestion of splitting up, Pike protests, saying, "When you ride with a man, you stay with him. Otherwise, you're an animal!" He insists, "We started together—we'll end together!" When they attempt to rescue the

young Mexican they befriended earlier, they move like mythic figures through the village shouting, "We want Angel!" For their efforts, they are rewarded with murderous gunfire in one of the most explicitly violent scenes ever filmed. In the end, their lives have been not tragic, but bitter jokes on themselves and the world—quite a distance from the lives of the ennobled outlaws of past movie legend. In fact, the film ends with the ironic laughter of the gnarled old man (Edmond O'Brien) who is the only member of the bunch to survive the mayhem. His laughter is echoed by the ghostly laughing images of Pike and his crony Dutch (Ernest Borgnine), mocking the world in which they could never find a place. Like those other (and much more lovable) outlaws, Butch Cassidy and the Sundance Kid, they live and die on their own terms. The fact that both films were released in 1969, two years after *Bonnie and Clyde*, suggests that the concept of the antiestablishment rebel had become deeply ingrained in the consciousness of filmmakers and the viewing public.

No discussion of *The Wild Bunch* can avoid dealing with its violence. Peckinpah has written that his intention was to show how utterly gruesome violence really was, yet he betrays an ambivalence that has disturbed many viewers. A number of his images are truly hideous, but they are also perversely beautiful. For example, when a bridge blows up and men and horses fall into the water, their descent is shown in slow motion so that it becomes both graceful and horrifying. The violence is somehow softened and does not get the reaction intended by Peckinpah. The frequent gory deaths are recorded in a near-balletic style that is reminiscent of the famous "blood bath" at the end of *Bonnie and Clyde*. They have an oddly voluptuous feeling about them that mixes revulsion with fascination. (Since the late sixties, films have become increasingly involved in the pornography of violence.)

If *The Wild Bunch* marked the collapse of the myth of the old West, what of those who survived the collapse and lived on in bitterness and bewilderment? Several sixties films attempted to find the answer, setting their stories in the contemporary West. The 1963 film *Hud* was a harsh and acrid movie set in present-day west Texas, in which the strong, solid virtues of the old West, represented by a cantankerous old rancher (Melvyn Douglas), clashed with the cynicism, opportunism, and corruption of the new West, embodied by his son Hud (Paul Newman). Douglas was the last gasp of a legend, the culmination of every leathery, straight-talking cowpoke Walter Brennan or Henry Fonda had ever played. Here was a man who would sooner shoot all of his diseased cattle than have them affect other herds. Hud was an avaricious, womanizing rotter who disillusions his nephew (Brandon de Wilde), tries to rape the ranch's housekeeper (Patricia Neal), and bitterly opposes his father until the old man lies dead.

Although some critics deplored the film's dubious romanticizing of the old virtues and its facile attack on present-day greed and hedonism, there were many others who responded to the strong performances (especially by Douglas and Neal), Martin Ritt's capable direction, and James Wong Howe's brilliantly sharp photography.

The Wild Bunch *(Warner Bros.-Seven Arts, 1969). In the brutal opening sequence of
this film, a gun battle breaks out between outlaws and bounty hunters, catching many innocent
townspeople in the crossfire.*

There were scenes that throbbed with dramatic intensity. The killing of the diseased cattle is difficult to forget, a lifetime of working and caring destroyed by the very men who had lived it. When De Wilde remarks that the shooting "didn't take long," the old man responds, "It don't take long to kill things, not like it does to grow." His pride, his suffering, and his memory of a vanished world are all etched in his face, and in his words.

From the late sixties to the present, there have been a number of Western films of considerable merit if not special distinction, although the number produced has declined drastically. Familiar patterns of other years have remained in evidence: we still have the aging cowboy at the end of his trail, visible in Tom Gries's *Will Penny* (1968) and in Henry Hathaway's *True Grit* (1969). Other films continued the demythification of what might be called the Fordian West; unvarnished views of cow country could be found in Robert Altman's eccentric *McCabe and Mrs. Miller* (1971), *Dirty Little Billy* (1972), a grubby view of Billy the Kid, and Arthur Penn's outrageous *The Missouri Breaks* (1976), which featured non-stop violence and a ludicrous performance by Marlon Brando as an obese, Irish-brogued hired gun.

This period also witnessed a revival of the comic Western. Almost every great film comedian had used the old West as a setting for high jinks, and in 1939 *Destry Rides Again* had thumbed its nose at Western movie conventions. Now the keynote was not satire but a brash, sportive, good-humored approach to the genre, laced with moments of conventional action and occasional seriousness. The prototype for this sort of film was *Butch Cassidy and the Sundance Kid* (1969), a basically comic Western adventure concerning the rise and fall of two amiable outlaws at the turn of the century. Loosely based on fact, the movie cast Paul Newman and Robert Redford in the title roles and had them scramble about Western settings, mocking the heroics of the old Westerns in scenes that mixed slapstick and adventure in felicitous proportions. They leap off a cliff to escape a posse, although Sundance can't swim; when they rob a bank in Bolivia, they can't remember the Spanish for such basic phrases as "This is a robbery"; and in the closing minutes, finally trapped by an army regiment, they face the end with cheery bravado, although the film wisely ends with a freeze frame before their deaths. Even the heroine, a schoolteacher named Etta Place (Katharine Ross), is not the virginal damsel of the old Westerns but Sundance's mistress who, up to a point, accompanies both men in their wanderings. The film may be distractingly anachronistic (this is the West filmed through a sixties viewpoint), but it entertains.

Arthur Penn's production of *Little Big Man*, an unusual 1970 Western, was both comic and serious. Based on Thomas Berger's sprawling, picaresque novel, this quite remarkable film purported to be the autobiographical account of a 120-year-old man named Jack Crabb (Dustin Hoffman), the sole white survivor of Custer's Last Stand, whose adventures from childhood to age thirty-five reveal the old West as it really was. Varying wildly in its approach from slapstick comedy to grim, near-documentary realism, the film was many things (perhaps too many): a jaundiced, satirical view of Western American history, a scalding diatribe against the brutal slaughter of Indian tribes (really the beating heart of the movie), and a comic tall tale related by an old man who had lived as an Indian brave, a con man, and a hermit, and had survived several marriages and a bout with alcoholism. This heady brew alternated scenes of lyrical beauty with sequences of almost unbearable carnage. It was as if Penn were trying to crowd into one 150-minute film all the disparate elements that had gone into the making of Westerns since the days of *The Great Train Robbery*. The result was both exhilarating and distracting.

Today, the Western is virtually nonexistent. The erosion of the genre that began in the fifties with the popularity of Western series on television has deepened with every decade. Audiences have apparently rejected the realistic view of the old West that discards or mocks its myths and legends; they do not wish to see the brutality and ugliness that tarnish their once proudly held view of the West as a place where courage and endurance thrived. They have not appreciated their loss of innocence.

Was John Ford correct in asking us to "print the legend"? Perhaps, if one wishes to accept the dangers inherent in the lie. Nevertheless, the Western as it once existed in the films of Ford and Howard Hawks may not be gone forever. Somewhere there's a cowboy ready and eager to ride the trail again.

Hud (Paramount, 1963). An amoral, arrogant loner in the new West, Hud Bannon (Paul Newman) comes into conflict with his father, Homer (Melvyn Douglas). Douglas won an Academy Award for Best Supporting Actor.

CAUTION TO THE WINDS
Great Adventure Movies

As mature adults, we like to believe that we are knowledgeable about the world. We understand fully, of course, life's responsibilities, rewards, vagaries, and disappointments.

Yet there is one part of us (or many of us) that wants to consciously retain at least a fragment of our lost innocence, to preserve one small corner of our minds that can still enjoy the sense of wonder and discovery we knew as children. Those of us who share this feeling will deny emphatically that it suggests an evasion of reality or a deep-seated longing to return to the womb. We would rather think of it as the need to take an occasional journey back to places that now exist largely in our imaginations.

Over the years, the best adventure films have taken us on many such journeys. On the sails of full-rigged ships, through the perilous African jungle, in the gilded halls of British or Ruritanian castles, we have followed intrepid heroes from Robin Hood to Indiana Jones as they hurtle through breathtaking adventures and escapades. Rooted in fantasy, yet moored to earth, the adventure films flourished in the thirties, when people needed to escape periodically from an intolerable present into a never-never past. They suggested that, contrary to all existing evidence, good could triumph over evil, and that heroism, chivalry, and romance were not gone forever.

Rarely, however, does an adventure film of the old swashbuckling or derring-do school turn up on today's screens. Adventure in the 1980s lies in the far reaches of space and time, not on earth. The challenges of uncharted sea courses, rampaging native hordes, and impenetrable jungles have been replaced by the limitless possibilities of worlds beyond our own. Perhaps that is why we welcome a film such as *Raiders of the Lost Ark*, which for two hours reminds us, joyfully and with no pretense to art, of what we once cherished. Of course there are other reminders: revivals of adventure films that stir old memories and recall old dreams. In our computerized age, it is pleasant to remember these films, which are an authentic part of our movie heritage.

The acknowledged master of the silent adventure film was the high-spirited and extraordinarily agile Douglas Fairbanks. In 1915, an established stage star, Fairbanks was lured to Hollywood to make his first movie for Triangle Films. The studio's leading director, D. W. Griffith, was puzzled and irritated by this exuberant actor who would carry his physical stunts far beyond the expected limits. But actor-director John Emerson and young writer Anita Loos (later Emerson's wife) knew what to do with him: they starred him in a series of breezy modern comedies that made him one of the first major film stars. In 1919 he formed the prestigious United Artists with Mary Pickford (whom he married), Charlie Chaplin, and D. W. Griffith.

In his first adventure film, *The Mark of Zorro* (1920), he was cast as the dashing outlaw in Spanish California who disguises himself as an aristocratic fop while opposing his country's tyrannical rulers. This was followed by a strenuous new version of *The Three Musketeers* (1921), and then by his most lavish film to date, *Robin Hood* (1922). Fairbanks played the Earl of Huntington, who becomes the legendary Robin Hood when his beloved King Richard is imprisoned and Richard's evil brother John takes the throne. Leaping and cavorting through sets that rivaled those of *Intolerance* in size, he made a most convincing hero: ardent, brave, and uncommonly athletic. Of his subsequent adventure films, the best was *The Black Pirate* (1926), which was notable as a major advance in color—it used the continually improving Technicolor process with restraint and imagination. The movie

Opposite: A poster for The Adventures of Robin Hood *(Warner Bros., 1938).*
Above: The Black Pirate *(Elton Corp./United Artists, 1926). Douglas Fairbanks in one of his best roles: the nobleman who turns pirate leader to avenge his father's death. Apparently, Fairbanks's film and real-life images were similar; he reveled in his fame, delighted that everything he did or said was fascinating to the public.*

also included Fairbanks's most astonishing single stunt—he inserts a dagger into the top of a sail and clings to it as it cuts rapidly down the canvas.

By the late twenties his popularity was fading. His last movie, *The Private Life of Don Juan* (1934), was a pale echo of his triumphs as a silent star. That same year, however, saw the release of a film that, along with MGM's *Mutiny on the Bounty*, helped to launch a revival of the adventure film, which continued to thrive until the end of the decade. Alexandre Dumas's *The Count of Monte Cristo* was filmed for the third time in a lavish production that made the plight of Edmond Dantes as harrowing as ever. Robert Donat, in his first American film, starred as the hapless Dantes who, against a background of political upheaval in nineteenth-century France, exacts revenge for the long years of unjustified imprisonment. His grim period of life-in-death within the impregnable fortress is especially well realized, as is his intricate plotting to destroy his tormenters.

The Count of Monte Cristo enjoyed wide popularity, but no adventure film of the period had more enthusiastic audiences than MGM's spectacular production of *Mutiny on the Bounty* (1935). Under Frank Lloyd's direction, the best-selling novel by Charles Nordhoff and James Norman Hall became a long but flavorsome movie with all the ingredients to keep willing viewers enthralled: rebellion at sea against a monstrously cruel captain (based on a true incident); romance on a languorous South Sea island; and the sensational trial of the mutineers. All this heady material enjoyed the benefits of superb photography by Arthur Edeson, a nautically flavored score by Herbert Stothart, and, above all, a glittering and marvelously hammy performance by Charles Laughton as the infamous Captain Bligh.

Clark Gable is the film's nominal star, playing the tenacious ship's officer Fletcher Christian, who finally leads the mutiny against the captain. Although unconvincing as a Briton, and uneasy in his eighteenth-century garb, he plays the role commendably. Franchot Tone is

also earnest as Byam, the foppish but brave officer who finally speaks out against the brutal conditions of life in the British Navy. But it is Laughton's film, not only because of the actor's formidable presence but also because Bligh is by far the most complex figure in the story. (In most swashbucklers, the villain is more interesting than the hero, and is played by a better actor.) At first he is purely villainous, a grim-faced martinet who believes that his men only respect "the law of fear." Yet after the mutiny, we see an entirely new aspect of his character. As he leaves the *Bounty* to take his place in a small open boat among the loyal remnant of his crew, he shouts, "I'll live to see all of you hanged from the highest yardarm in England!"—an appropriate parting volley for Bligh. But then he succeeds in saving the lives of his crew during the grueling voyage by virtue of his courage and indomitability. He is clearly a born leader, and the band of mutineers aboard the *Bounty* suddenly becomes less sympathetic. Dauntless, Bligh survives the ordeal at sea to become yet another character: an obsessed Ahab relentlessly searching for Christian and the mutineers, a man so driven that he wrecks the ship in his command by leading it into perilous waters. At the trial of Byam and the mutineers, he reverts to the remorseless, bitter Bligh of the beginning. Laughton's performance rings every change in this character with ripe (and sometimes overripe) assurance.

Left: The Count of Monte Cristo *(Reliance/United Artists, 1934). In his American film debut, Robert Donat played Edmond Dantes, with Elissa Landi as his beloved Mercedes. The film was a first-rate version of Alexandre Dumas's classic story of imprisonment and revenge. Right:* Mutiny on the Bounty *(MGM, 1935). An explosive confrontation between Fletcher Christian (Clark Gable), head of the mutineers, and Captain Bligh (Charles Laughton), sadistic master of the* Bounty.

Both *The Count of Monte Cristo* and *Mutiny on the Bounty* were first-rate adventure films, but neither Robert Donat, a fine actor but quintessentially British, nor Clark Gable, rarely at ease in period costume, could hope to inherit the mantle of Douglas Fairbanks. That honor was reserved for one actor alone: the epitome of cinematic dash and daring, Errol Flynn. (Tyrone Power was a later contender, but he lacked humor and style.) Flynn had been a peripatetic jack-of-all-trades for a number of years until he signed a contract with Warners, which was at a loss as to how to use this startlingly handsome, faintly disreputable young actor.

After small roles in three films (he played a corpse in the second), Flynn at age twenty-six was awarded his first starring role in a movie that indelibly established his swashbuckling image. Rafael Sabatini's novel *Captain Blood* had been filmed before in 1924, and now it was trotted out again as a vehicle for Flynn after Robert Donat bowed out in a contractual dispute. In keeping with the pattern Warners established in many of its films into the forties, the film's central issue was the triumph of brave men over the forces of tyranny. Flynn played the wronged hero who must endure severe trials, including slavery and banishment, before defeating his oppressors and winning the hand of the heroine (Olivia de Havilland).

The 1935 production is not as lavish as later Flynn films, nor is

Flynn anywhere near a polished actor. But from his very first scene we can clearly recognize the special charisma of a potential film star. Apart from his good looks, he exhibits the proper amount of gallantry, bravado, and romantic ardor, mixed with a generous dose of swagger and impudence. He moves with dexterity and grace, and, being an expert fencer, he is able to carry off a duel with Basil Rathbone as the duplicitous Captain Levasseur. (The actors clashed swords twice more, and at greater length, in upcoming films.) In his scenes with De Havilland he displayed the sort of unforced charm and lighthearted flirtatiousness that had made Douglas Fairbanks a major star of the twenties. Flynn dominates the film throughout, and director Michael Curtiz gives him so many close-ups that the studio's decision to create a new star is already evident in the first reel.

In *Captain Blood*, Errol Flynn played an Irish doctor who takes over a Spanish pirate ship to oppose the navy of an English ruler. Yet by the end of the film, he is made English governor of Port Royal, eager to serve his country and his new king. This resolution holds no surprise whatever, since during the mid-to-late thirties virtually every major Hollywood studio, and especially Warner Bros., was enthusiastically Anglophilic. Easily duplicated English settings, studio wardrobes packed with period costumes, and many resident players of English birth made it possible for filmmakers to indulge the audience's fondness for elaborate, fast-moving adventure films with a British accent. And by the end of the decade, as a new war appeared imminent, extolling British steadfastness and courage under an ordeal of fire seemed a laudable undertaking.

There was also an aspect that was somewhat less than laudable. Admiration for English fortitude also carried with it the germ of acceptance for that nation's condescending and blatantly racist attitude toward the native "heathens" of India and other farflung outposts. Occasionally the weight of the "white man's burden" threatens to topple the enterprise entirely, but usually the vigor and pace of the action sequences and the direct, hearty innocence of the playing soften the implied ugly message of these Anglophilic adventure films.

Such a film was Errol Flynn's next venture after *Captain Blood*: a large-scale spectacle suggested by Alfred Lord Tennyson's narrative poem, *The Charge of the Light Brigade* (1936). Again under Michael Curtiz's direction, Flynn was cast as Geoffrey Vickers, captain in the Twenty-seventh British Lancers, who, on the Crimean frontier in the mid-nineteenth century, ultimately leads the troops in a bold but suicidal charge against the native forces of the villainous Surat Khan. (The Khan is allied with Russia in the Crimean War, which is nasty enough, but all his followers are portrayed as swarthy, sinister primitives, much like our American Indians in most Western films until the fifties.) Geoffrey's personal motive for the futile endeavor is sacrificial: his certain death will free his fiancée Elsa (Olivia de Havilland) to marry his younger brother Perry (Patric Knowles), whom she has always loved.

The first reel of *The Charge of the Light Brigade* is sluggish and static, with indifferent performances by the three leading players. But once the action gets under way, director Curtiz's skill with this

Captain Blood (Warner Bros., 1935). A doctor wrongly enslaved on a Caribbean island, young Peter Blood (Errol Flynn) meets and falls in love with Arabella Bishop (Olivia de Havilland), niece of the plantation owner on the island. This was the first of many teamings of Flynn and De Havilland.

sort of material helps to spring the film into life. A lavish sequence depicting the attack of the Khan's hordes on a poorly defended fort at Chukoti is exceptionally well handled. The desperate struggle of the outnumbered British as ladders are thrown against the walls of the fort, the roar of cannon fire mixing with shouts and screams, the daring if improbable escape by boat of Geoffrey and Elsa—these combine to create a vivid battle scene.

The celebrated charge, staged by second-unit director B. Reeves Eason, is one of the great action sequences in motion pictures. Set against excerpts from Tennyson's poem, the scene begins with a stirring view of the mounted soldiers as they prepare to face the enemy at Balaklava. When Geoffrey shouts, "Onward, men! Onward," the Lancers move out with sabers forward through the fire of rifles and cannons. Amid clouds of dust, British and enemy soldiers topple from their horses, fatally wounded. Finally, Geoffrey and archvillain Surat Khan kill each other, and the Lancers plunge their swords into the Khan's body. The episode is, of course, light-years removed from the truth, but it is memorable, nevertheless. Afterward, officers speak about the "conspicuous gallantry" of the Lancers, but a question goes unanswered: By what right, except the assumed (and in this case, unlawfully seized) right of command, did Geoffrey Vickers lead six hundred men to their inevitable deaths? And wasn't his

"magnificent blunder" motivated more by personal reasons than by patriotic fervor? Over a decade later, the same questions are raised by the actions of Henry Fonda's martinet colonel in John Ford's Western *Fort Apache*.

In 1938, Flynn starred in the movie that assured his screen immortality: *The Adventures of Robin Hood*. As the legendary Saxon outlaw whose band of Merrie Men stole from the rich to give to the poor, Flynn cut a dashingly handsome figure, virile and stalwart. His lighthearted insouciance suggested that he was not taking the role with the utmost seriousness, and neither should the audience. In *Captain Blood*, when Flynn swaggered about the deck of his pirate ship, a viewer could sense the birth of a film star. But when he first appears as Robin Hood, swinging on a rope to land on the branch of a tree in Sherwood Forest, his stardom was fully confirmed.

Yet Flynn is only one strong element in a film that after more than four decades is still one of Hollywood's finest adventure films. *The Adventures of Robin Hood* fairly vibrates with the energy, exhilarating pace, and confidence that turn people of all ages into devout movie buffs. Photographed in radiant three-strip Technicolor by Warners's most skilled cameramen, headed by Sol Polito and Tony Gaudio, the film tells a simple story of (once again) tyranny opposed and virtue triumphant, as Robin Hood and his band of Merrie Men, loyal to

The Charge of the Light Brigade (Warner Bros., 1936). Captain Geoffrey Vickers (Errol Flynn) leads the charge of his men against the forces of the Surat Khan. Brilliantly staged by director Michael Curtiz, the charge was one of the most exciting action sequences ever filmed.

King Richard, set things right for England. Writers Norman Reilly Raine and Seton Miller manage to crowd a satisfying number of well-remembered incidents into their screenplay: Robin's first encounters with followers Little John (Alan Hale) and Friar Tuck (Eugene Pallette); a beautifully filmed archery tournament; and the rousing climax in which Robin and King Richard invade Prince John's false "coronation." These scenes bear the stamp of Michael Curtiz, who replaced William Keighley as director during production.

The Adventures of Robin Hood is a triumph of talented professionals who are not reaching for art but who are perfectly content to offer ripe entertainment. The cast could not be bettered (somehow, Eugene Pallette's Friar Tuck, a bellowing, gluttonous mountain of a man, lingers most in memory), the settings of art director Carl Jules Weyl are properly lavish, and Erich Wolfgang Korngold's Academy Award–winning score quickens the pulse. In the tradition of Warner Bros., the film even contains a smattering of the studio's penchant for making social and political points in its films. Anticipating the heroes who would later defy the Nazis and other authoritarian types on screen, Robin tells Marian, "It's injustice I hate, not the Normans." He asks his men to "fight to the death against the oppressors," and when he shows Marian the pitiful condition of the Saxons under Prince John's heel, she is converted to his cause. Robin, she insists, is "the one man who protected the helpless." Other references also suggest that the authors' minds were not entirely on days of yore.

The parallel between past and present history was even more apparent in Flynn's 1940 swashbuckler, *The Sea Hawk*. Filmed before in a 1924 silent version, the movie focused on the lusty pirate captain Geoffrey Thorpe (Flynn) who, with the tacit approval of Queen Elizabeth (Flora Robson), defends England from the treachery and ambitions of the Spaniards. Although the film's historical credentials were highly dubious, its intentions were clear. In a year when England was being assaulted by the enemy, *The Sea Hawk* was patently demonstrating that force must be met with force—that appeasing any nation bent on destruction was futile and dangerous. Perfidious members of the court urge such appeasement, but wiser heads and stronger wills prevail. As the forties began, Anglophilic fervor would soon be directed toward England's courage under siege by Germany, but in *The Sea Hawk* it was expressed in terms of sixteenth-century history.

Aside from its contemporary parallel, *The Sea Hawk* is an impressively staged if somewhat cumbersome and talky film of its genre. Once the story leaves Elizabeth's court, where intrigue lurks in every corner, the movie gains momentum with action sequences that move swiftly under Michael Curtiz's direction. A sea battle in which Thorpe and his men swarm aboard a Spanish ship carrying the villainous Don Jose Alvarez (Claude Rains) and his niece Maria (Brenda Marshall) is exciting to watch, and there is a magnificent

Left: The Adventures of Robin Hood *(Warner Bros., 1938). Robin Hood (Errol Flynn, center) and his band of Merrie Men gather in Sherwood Forest. Behind Robin is the fierce and hearty Friar Tuck (Eugene Pallette).*
Right: The Sea Hawk *(Warner Bros., 1940). Queen Elizabeth (Flora Robson) knights Geoffrey Thorpe (Errol Flynn), the pirate captain who has helped her defeat the Spanish Armada. At right is the queen's advisor Sir John Burleson (Donald Crisp).*

climactic duel between Thorpe and the wicked Lord Wolfingham (Henry Daniell). Their shadows loom large on the walls as they leap across corridors and down staircases. The acting is capable (and why not, with so many seasoned Warners veterans on hand), but Flora Robson leads the way in a sturdy and not excessive portrayal of Queen Elizabeth.

Before the vogue for period adventure films ended with the advent of World War II, only one movie could qualify as equal or possibly superior to the Flynn swashbucklers. This was David O. Selznick's superb 1937 production of *The Prisoner of Zenda*. For this first sound version of Anthony Hope's popular 1894 novel, Selznick assembled all the ingredients for a crackling adventure movie: a dramatic story of deception, betrayal, and romance; a fine cast headed by Ronald Colman; John Cromwell's alert, smoothly flowing direction, and James Wong Howe's black-and-white photography, which bathed the entire film in a romantic glow. The fanciful tale involved Colman in a dual role as Rudolf, the hard-drinking, irresponsible ruler of Strelsau, and as his distant English relative Rudolph Rassendyll, who is asked to pose as Rudolf at his coronation when the king-to-be is kidnapped. The villains who plunge Rassendyll into danger and intrigue include Rudolf's envious half-brother Black Michael (Raymond Massey) and wily young Rupert of Hentzau (Douglas Fairbanks, Jr.). On the sidelines is Rudolf's beautiful bride-to-be, Princess Flavia (Madeleine Carroll).

Even without color, this *Prisoner of Zenda* is an ideal adventure film. The story is related with reasonable seriousness, but, without once edging over into parody, the screenplay frequently hints that it is all a storybook diversion, an evening's blithe entertainment. Nor

Swordplay from the best adventure films, mostly involving the duplicitous Basil Rathbone.
He duels with Errol Flynn in Captain Blood *(Warner Bros., 1935), below; again with Flynn in*
The Adventures of Robin Hood *(Warner Bros., 1938), above; and with Tyrone Power in*
The Mark of Zorro *(Fox, 1940), opposite, right. Douglas Fairbanks, Jr., locks swords with hero*
Ronald Colman in The Prisoner of Zenda *(Selznick International/United Artists,*
1937), opposite, left.

endearing pet, not to be taken seriously until he proves his mettle under fire. Still, it all works so beautifully that a viewer is inclined to forgive its suggestion of white supremacy and concentrate on the many rousing action sequences, beautifully photographed by Joseph H. August and directed with surprising vigor by George Stevens. (A capable director, Stevens was not noted for his pacing, which was inclined to be poky.) No filmgoer of a certain age is likely to forget the climactic section in which the soldiers and Gunga Din move stealthily about the temple of the Thugs as the Thugs, incited by their guru (Eduardo Ciannelli, looking like a demented Gandhi in his awesomely awful makeup), chant, "Kill! Kill for the love of killing!" Discounting its "white man's burden" attitude, *Gunga Din* is likely to survive into the next century as a prime example of the Hollywood adventure film.

does it ever neglect the essential action sequences that keep viewers alert and happy. Both aspects—the slightly tongue-in-cheek approach, and the straightforward melodrama—converge in the climactic duel between Rassendyll and Rupert. (Fairbanks was an excellent swordsman but Colman had to be heavily doubled.) As they duel, they exchange quips. Rupert tells Rassendyll, "Your golden-haired goddess will look well in black. I'll console her for you, kiss away her tears," but Rassendyll is not intimidated. When Rupert, who knows Rassendyll's true identity, dashes away from the duel, shouting, "This is getting too hot for me! *Au revoir,* play-actor," we recognize that *The Prisoner of Zenda* is an adventure film that dares to be amusing without also laughing at itself.

Another adventure film at the end of the thirties has achieved a special niche in movie annals since its release. In fact, few films of the period are as well remembered or well loved as RKO's production of *Gunga Din* (1939). For young moviegoers, it represented the peak of adventure: an exciting tribute to the foolhardy courage and boisterous bravado of the British soldiers who fought for the Empire in nineteenth-century India. Scenarists Ben Hecht and Charles MacArthur (William Faulkner also worked on the script) took Rudyard Kipling's famous poem and his novel *Soldiers Three* and reworked them into a full-bodied story concerning soldiers Cary Grant, Douglas Fairbanks, Jr., and Victor McLaglen, whose escapades finally make them the prisoners of murderous fanatics called the Thugs. These overgrown Rover Boys are helped by their devoted native water boy Gunga Din (Sam Jaffe), who succeeds in warning the oncoming regiment with his trumpet just before he expires of his wounds.

The film is arrant nonsense and also not a little racist in its condescending attitude toward the natives, both friendly and hostile. The three heroes are childlike, yet they treat Gunga Din as a sort of

Overleaf, above: The Prisoner of Zenda *(Selznick International/United Artists, 1937).*
Rudolph Rassendyll (Ronald Colman) is unable to reveal his true identity to Princess Flavia
(Madeleine Carroll).
Overleaf, below: Trader Horn *(MGM, 1931). Through darkest Africa with Antonio Moreno,*
Edwina Booth, and Harry Carey. This pioneer African adventure film included some startling
on-location photography.

During the forties, Hollywood's adventure films were largely linked to the war, with fearless heroes (usually military) venturing into enemy territory or single-handedly routing the enemy. There were occasional forays into the old escapist fare of costumed swashbucklers, and for a time Douglas Fairbanks, Jr., imitated his father's style with limited success in such films as *The Corsican Brothers* (1941) and *Sinbad the Sailor* (1947). However, an actor closer to the mold of Fairbanks, Sr., was Fox's handsome Tyrone Power, who cut a reasonably dashing figure in *The Mark of Zorro* (1940), *Son of Fury* (1942), and *The Black Swan* (1942). Veteran director Cecil B. DeMille, when he was not immersed in the Bible, contributed several lavish, straightforward adventure films during the decade, notably a seafaring epic called *Reap the Wild Wind* (1942), complete with John Wayne and a giant marauding squid.

The revival of the genre began in the fifties, when the studios could drop their wartime involvement and concentrate on providing large-scale entertainment. (The wide-screen processes were launched in the early fifties as a means of luring audiences away from television and back to the movie theaters.) In the first few postwar years, the emphasis had been on a new "realism," a concern with America's social problems. "Responsible" films such as *Gentlemen's Agreement* and *The Snake Pit* were considered long overdue. But now moviegoers wanted (or studio moguls *believed* that they wanted) elaborate adventure films in the Fairbanks and Flynn tradition: lusty tales that could take advantage of improved cinematic techniques, on-location settings whenever economically feasible, and glorious Technicolor.

In the first half of the decade, virtually every major studio conscientiously dusted off its most lavish costumes of other eras and turned to new and old friends in the heroic mold. With the most prodigious resources on hand, Metro-Goldwyn-Mayer led the pack, turning out an almost word-for-word remake of *The Prisoner of Zenda* (1952); a spectacular adaptation of Sir Walter Scott's *Ivanhoe* (1952); and other chivalric adventures such as *Knights of the Round Table* (1953) and *Quentin Durward* (1955). Warner Bros. offered C. S. Forester's *Captain Horatio Hornblower* (1951) and *King Richard and the Crusaders* (1954); Fox went to the comic strips for *Prince Valiant* (1954).

Although these films were handsomely produced with exquisite attention to detail, they were not, on the whole, as popular or as well received as their predecessors. The reasons are elusive but they can be surmised. Aside from a public that had weathered a terrible war and was perhaps not so ready to return to a long-vanished world of panoplied knights and swooning maidens, it may be that the fault lay in the films themselves. Few of the films had directors who could match Michael Curtiz or Frank Lloyd in their skill at pacing a narrative and at handling action sequences. Often the sets seemed to overwhelm the action; the actors were dwarfed amid all the splendor. Even more importantly, the films lacked male stars who had the panache or romantic appeal of Douglas Fairbanks, Ronald Colman, or Errol Flynn; such actors as Robert Taylor, Gregory Peck, and Robert Wagner never appeared fully at ease in their

Opposite, above: King Solomon's Mines *(MGM, 1950). Travelers Richard Carlson, Deborah Kerr, and Stewart Granger encounter the extremely tall members of Africa's Watusi tribe. The imposing Watusis, with the jungle animals in firm support, were the true stars of the film.*
Opposite, below: Mogambo *(MGM, 1953). A triangle takes shape in the African jungle as Ava Gardner and Grace Kelly vie for the attention of hunter Clark Gable. The film was a colorful remake of* Red Dust, *which Gable had starred in twenty years earlier.*

costumes, and their bravado was more lethargic than lusty. Burt Lancaster came closest to fitting the mold, starring in two colorful tongue-in-cheek adventure films from Warners, *The Flame and the Arrow* (1950) and *The Crimson Pirate* (1952). Teeth flashing, sword at the ready, he made a convincing hero, part-swashbuckler, part-acrobat.

In addition to the costume sagas, the early fifties saw the modest return of the African adventure film. In the early years of sound, the "Dark Continent" had been an obvious source of new material, replete with animal noises, the beating of native drums, and the earsplitting yell of that ever-popular tree-swinger, Tarzan. Even then, MGM had led the way, with such films as *Trader Horn* (1931), *Tarzan the Ape Man* (1932), and *Red Dust* (1932). *Trader Horn* was the most effective, not for its standard story but for its extraordinary on-location animal photography. The sequences showing a leopard attacking a defenseless hyena and two angry rhinos in deadly combat are startling even today. Harry Carey was convincing as easygoing trader Aloysius Horn, who, though given to talking about the "beauty and terror" of Africa, remains unaffected by its brutality. ("Well, that's Africa for you" is his favorite remark.) Horn is not above a bit of racism—he shouts to the natives, "Hey, one of you monkeys, bring a blanket." His friend and traveling companion Peru (Duncan Renaldo) goes him one better, telling "white goddess" Edwina Booth, "White people must help each other." Yet *Trader Horn* remains an early sound classic, rarely seen but worth the viewing.

MGM's first full-scale return to the African adventure, after years of producing popular but modest *Tarzan* movies, was the 1950 remake of H. Rider Haggard's novel *King Solomon's Mines*. Filmed largely on location in Nairobi, the movie was a superior example of the subgenre. It revolved around Allan Quartermain (Stewart Granger in his first American film), a famous but world-weary big-game hunter who shares his adventures in the jungle with a well-bred English lady (Deborah Kerr) searching for her lost husband and the lady's brother (Richard Carlson). Robert Surtees's camera captured stunning views of the jungle landscapes and won him a well-deserved Academy Award. The scenes filmed around the imposing Murchison Falls were especially impressive.

As every adventure-film lover will attest, the fun lies in the increasingly colorful and dangerous dilemmas into which the hero and heroine are propelled. *King Solomon's Mines* is no exception. Codirectors Compton Bennett and Andrew Marton (Marton filmed the final scenes of the movie after Bennett collapsed of exhaustion) succeed in generating excitement from the sights and the events that confront the trio of explorers, including a massive animal stampede—thousands of terrified giraffes, zebras, gazelles leaping and galloping to safety—and the exotic tribal rites and dances of the Watusi warriors. The Watusis are, in fact, the true stars of the film: imposing and improbably tall, they command attention with their fierce dignity. The film's highlight is the hand-to-hand combat between two contenders for the Watusi throne, while the assembled natives watch.

Several years after *King Solomon's Mines*, MGM returned to Africa for a new version of the 1932 movie *Red Dust*, retitled *Mogambo* (1953). This time, the actors were more important than the animals or the scenery, but since the principal players were Clark Gable, Ava Gardner, and Grace Kelly, and their dialogue was lively and amusingly suggestive, this was no serious loss. Looking amazingly fit for his years, Gable repeated his *Red Dust* role as a big-game hunter who has as much trouble with two women—Gardner and Kelly—as he does with the jungle inhabitants. Director John Ford gave the best footage—and scriptwriter John Lee Mahin gave the funniest and most risqué lines—to Ava Gardner, who excelled as "Honey Bear" Kelly, a softened version of the tough, sluttish girl played by Jean Harlow in *Red Dust*. Unaccountably trapped in the jungle, she looks upon all kinds of animal life, including human, with wry skepticism.

The most unlikely—and also the most popular—African adventure film of the period was shot largely on location in the Congo, under the most grueling conditions. Forty intrepid people, headed by director John Huston and stars Humphrey Bogart and Katharine Hepburn, spent nine weeks in the jungle, battling heat, insects, disease, and exhaustion, to film Huston and James Agee's adaptation of C. S. Forester's novel *The African Queen* (1952). This tale of two wildly mismatched people who share romance and a grand adventure in German East Africa of 1914 teamed Bogart and Hepburn for the first time in roles that were drastically different from any they had ever played: Hepburn as Rose Sayer, the prim, highly moral sister of a British missionary, and Bogart as Charlie Allnut, the disreputable, gin-soaked captain of a broken-down launch called *The African Queen*. Against all reasonable odds, they take the *Queen* on a dan-

The African Queen (Horizon-Romulus/United Artists, 1952). Before being executed, Rose Sayer (Katharine Hepburn) and Charlie Allnut (Humphrey Bogart) ask to be married. Page 104, above: A classic meeting of opposites: Katharine Hepburn as prim spinster Rose Sayer and Humphrey Bogart as gin-swilling Charlie Allnut. About his two leads, John Huston said, "The spontaneity, the instinctive subtle interplay between them, the way they climbed inside of the people they were supposed to be—all of this made it better than we had written it" (Thomas, The Great Adventure Films, p. 65).

gerous journey to a lake dominated by the German warship *Louisa*. The odds are even greater against their sinking the ship, but they succeed. By this time, they have also fallen in love.

None of this is really believable, especially the notion that these two people would ever become romantically attached. But viewers looking for logic would have to look elsewhere. *The African Queen* is a romp, a tongue-in-cheek adventure that never takes itself too seriously and is all the more enjoyable because of that. Undoubtedly the film has its share of exciting sequences: Charlie, dragging the *Queen* through the jungle swamp, is suddenly covered with leeches; Rose and Charlie miraculously survive the *Queen's* perilous ride over a waterfall; married by the German ship's captain and about to be executed, Charlie and Rose hear a joyful noise—the good old *Queen* has fulfilled its destiny and blown up the *Louisa!*

Yet it is the unexpected chemistry between the two stars that makes *The African Queen* a special joy. They had never met, but, apparently, respect for each other's professionalism and tolerance for each other's eccentricities (especially Hepburn's) resulted in mutual admiration and an on-screen rapport. We watch their quirky, bristling relationship evolve into an unblushing devotion. The early scene in which Charlie and his growling stomach take tea with Rose and her brother Samuel (Robert Morley) provokes many laughs. And after Rose and Charlie begin their great adventure, the action scenes are brightened with their humorous exchanges. When temperance-minded Rose throws Charlie's liquor overboard, he accuses her of being a "crazy, psalm-singing, skinny old maid!" Even when they fall in love, Rose retains a certain reticence. "Mr. Allnut, dear," she says. "There's something I must know. What's your first name?" Grinning, he replies, "Charlie!" and she repeats his name over and over, lovingly and almost girlishly. Bogart's ingratiating and expert performance won him an Oscar.

The past few decades have seen relatively few adventure films in the sense we have defined them in this chapter. With innocence trampled in the years of assassinations and unwanted wars, an old-style adventure movie seemed an unnecessary throwback to a storybook age created for children. The handful of films that surfaced, especially in the sixties, substituted size for pace or narrative excitement. An elaborate but cumbersome remake of *Mutiny on the Bounty* (1963) failed to come within hailing distance of MGM's old film, and such adventure-spectacles as *55 Days at Peking* (1963) and *Khartoum* (1966) were heavy-handed and dull.

One highly touted adventure film of the sixties did have substantial merit. There was genuine scope, breathtaking photography (by F. A. Young), and a charismatic performance by Peter O'Toole in David Lean's award-winning production of *Lawrence of Arabia* (1962), a biography of the soldier-adventurer T. E. Lawrence, but the film was ultimately defeated by Robert Bolt's muddled and turgid screenplay and by its excessive, 220-minute length. Concentrating on the "Arabian" period in Lawrence's life, when he went from minor government official to obsessed, tortured leader of the Arabs in conflict with the Turks, the movie featured some of the finest battle scenes

ever filmed, particularly the storming of a military installation at Aqaba and the Arab army's bloody attack on a Turkish train, one boxcar of which contains magnificent horses. Yet we never are given a clear sense of Lawrence as a human being—he is merely a cipher who is excessively vulnerable to changing winds. We never understand why he moves from visionary to collapsed wreck to bloodthirsty monster and finally to a man defeated by duplicitous people, both Arab and English.

It was not until 1981 that an adventure film caught the public fancy again and reestablished the genre as a viable commercial offering. The extraordinarily astute Steven Spielberg joined with producer-director George Lucas *(Star Wars)* and others to create a film that deliberately harked back to the old matinee adventure serials of the thirties and forties. With Spielberg as director and Lucas as one of the executive producers, *Raiders of the Lost Ark* came to the screen as one of the most adroit and entertaining fantasy-adventure films in many years. If it tested our willing suspension of disbelief to the limit, if its giddy screenplay by Lawrence Kasdan consisted of one outrageous climax tumbling after another, the result was a film that moved with a swiftness and an assurance that startled and exhilarated filmgoers at every age level.

The story of *Raiders of the Lost Ark* is not exactly sensible: in 1936, a resourceful professor of archaeology, improbably named Indiana Jones (Harrison Ford), joins with Marion (Karen Allen), the daughter of a celebrated archaeologist, to locate the lost Ark of the Covenant before a team of Nazi scientists can seize it. Before they succeed in winning the day (is there ever any doubt?), they are subjected to numerous attempts on their lives by means of asps and cobras, poisoned darts, violent explosions, torture with a red-hot poker, and other more traditional methods. Very little fazes our intrepid hero and feisty heroine as they experience one jolting or gruesome surprise after another, only to emerge unscathed. (As in *Star Wars*, the heroine is no shrinking damsel in distress but a hard-drinking, tough-talking woman—another nod in the direction of women's liberation.)

Filmed in various parts of the world, *Raiders of the Lost Ark* succeeds because it does not call undue attention to its spectacular backgrounds, nor does it pause for expository dialogue, logic, or underlying significance. Its only message seems to be: do not meddle with God's ordinances. Except for a religiously oriented climax, which is unduly solemn for the rest of the film, and a few unnecessarily gory moments, it never veers from its intention of reconstructing the old cliffhangers on a lavish scale.

The enormous success of *Raiders of the Lost Ark* guaranteed more of the same, and indeed television made several feeble and obvious attempts to capture that movie's ambiance. It may be, however, that films have seen the last of earthbound adventurers, and that pirates, soldiers-of-fortune, jungle explorers, and knights-in-armor have joined the screen's endangered species. If so, we can still enjoy the memorable adventure films of other years, in which the bold champions of honor and justice fought for us all in a simpler world.

Overleaf, left, below: Lawrence of Arabia *(Columbia, 1962). The visionary T. E. Lawrence (Peter O'Toole) leads the Arab army against the Turks. Robert Bolt's screenplay did not entirely clarify this enigmatic figure, but the film had some spectacular action sequences.*
Overleaf, right: Raiders of the Lost Ark *(Lucasfilm Ltd., 1981). Intrepid Indiana Jones (Harrison Ford) flees through a cave from a giant boulder that threatens to crush him to death.*
Below: Indiana fights his way out of another tight spot in Steven Spielberg's entertaining fantasy-adventure.

BATTLEGROUNDS
Great War Movies

War has many faces: tragic, painfully absurd, brave, and heartbreaking, and all of them have appeared in films across the years. Since the first flickering images, war's heroes and lunatics, its warriors and despots have furnished the stuff of drama and often comedy, and battlefields have provided natural settings for spectacle on the largest of scales. Whatever their feelings about war's savagery and hopelessness, audiences have responded to its unavoidable melodrama, its strong emotional content. In re-creating some of the darkest moments in human history, war films have aroused pride, revulsion, grief, and despair.

Since World War I, there has been an unmistakable—and probably inevitable—cycle in Hollywood's handling of war films. While the war is being waged, the uppermost goal of the films is to exhort civilians and the armed forces to patriotic action. The keynote is not art but persuasion; audiences must be cajoled into believing that their cause is just, their fighting men courageous, their enemies vile and inhuman. Following a time of revulsion and indifference after the end of the conflict, there is the period that can produce distinctive war films—a period of examination and introspection in which the romantic myths about war are tempered by realism. War is no longer a glorious enterprise but a sobering, embittering experience.

This pattern of alternate glorification and debunking continued until the mid-sixties, when protests against America's role in Vietnam began to spiral. A decade earlier, the shadow of world annihilation resulting from nuclear war between the superpowers had altered the audience's attitude toward war and war movies. But now the concept of America as a peace-loving nation that would fight to uphold its democratic ideals began slowly to unravel. War—any war—became anathema, an unthinkable possibility to a generation of troubled, angry young people. *The Longest Day* (1962) turned out to be the last major film for a long time to portray war combat in the old heroic mold. (It was also the last film for many years to receive the full cooperation of the military establishment, a fact that also soured filmmakers on producing war movies.) By the seventies, war films were few and far between. Only by the end of the decade could producers find the perspective and the insights to attempt important films on the Vietnam experience. And when they did, their films *(The Deer Hunter, Apocalypse Now)* had an audacity and a blistering frankness that set them apart from previous war movies.

The subject of war was not unknown to American filmmakers in the early years—*The Birth of a Nation* and *Intolerance* drew much of their sweep and scope from depictions of battle and bloody conflict —but World War I turned film, for the first time, into a powerful and effective propaganda tool. Even before America entered the war, there were films that called (or more often screamed) for preparedness or

vengeance. Prowar films became abundant, often starring popular favorites such as Mary Pickford. In *The Little American* (1917), "our Mary" played an American relief worker whom the Germans accuse of being a spy and threaten with rape and murder. During America's participation in the war, the tone of these films became even more hysterical and overwrought. Although D. W. Griffith's *Hearts of the World* (1918), concerning a beleaguered French peasant girl (Lillian Gish), had a degree of restraint, more often than not the movies were blatantly jingoistic. Not surprisingly, the end of the war brought a rapidly diminished interest in war movies and a reluctance to discuss the lessons or the meaning of the conflict.

It was not until 1925 that the first important film about World War I, King Vidor's epic *The Big Parade*, came out. No film until that time had attempted to capture the awesome sweep of battle, the sense of ordinary men caught up in an extraordinary experience that could mean their sudden and violent death. These scenes were framed with a romance, the story of a passionate attachment between an American doughboy and a French peasant girl. The extent of King Vidor's success can be judged by the fact that immediately after the release of *The Big Parade*, he became the most sought-after and widely discussed director in America. Over a half-century later, his film remains one of the finest ever made about World War I.

The first part of the film is fairly conventional, as Vidor sets up the ordinary routines of army life, in deliberate contrast to the inferno that lies ahead. Three men—irresponsible rich boy Jim Apperson (John Gilbert), bartender Bull O'Hara (Tom O'Brien), and happy-go-

Opposite: The Big Parade *(MGM, 1925). In this classic scene, Melisande (Renee Adoree) bids farewell to American doughboy Jim Apperson (John Gilbert). Above: World War I doughboys Tom O'Brien, John Gilbert, and Karl Dane take a welcome pause from action in one of the trenches. Some of the film's large-scale battle scenes were added after the film was completed to give it a more "epic" scope.*

lucky riveter Slim (Karl Dane)—are caught up in the patriotic fervor surrounding America's entry into the war. Sent to a small French village after their training, they engage in horseplay while carrying out their soldier's duties. Although engaged to a girl back home, Jim falls in love with peasant girl Melisande (Renee Adoree), and she returns the feeling. They communicate in pidgin English, and he teaches her how to chew gum.

When the troops move up to the front, Jim and Melisande have a tearful, wrenching separation. (Their farewell, with Melisande cling-ing frantically to his leg, then being dragged by the truck taking him away from her, is one of the classic scenes in film history.) In the fighting, both Bull and Slim are killed, while Jim loses a leg and comes to recognize the terrible futility and pointlessness of war. He returns home, but cannot forget the simple peasant girl he loved. Finally, he returns to France, and in a much-imitated ending, he hobbles across a field to the waiting arms of Melisande.

The romance of Jim Apperson and Melisande is sweetly touching,

but the fame of *The Big Parade* rests squarely and deservedly on its incomparable battle scenes. The first baptism of fire is viewed as a terrifying, bewildering experience; the camera tracks along with the soldiers as they move in attack formation through the woods, their guns in readiness against invisible snipers. Men fall in an almost rhythmic pattern, while others keep marching until grenades blow up the enemy machine-gunners. In another battle, the camera turns and gives us a marvelous shot from the vantage point of the Germans, as rows of soldiers caught in the light of the flares take on a nightmarish intensity. In one especially harrowing scene, Jim is trapped in a trench with a dying German soldier. Deeply stricken, he is unable to look at the young man's pain-wracked face. The man (more of a boy, really) dies with Jim's cigarette clenched in his mouth.

The implications of this scene are very clear, but *The Big Parade* is not really an antiwar film in the truest sense. Distraught after the death of his friend Slim, Jim does express his bitterness and despair: "Who the hell is fighting this war—men or orders? Cheers when we

What Price Glory *(Fox, 1926). American troops are welcomed into a French town. This film adaptation of the Maxwell Anderson–Lawrence Stallings stage play contained some salty dialogue for expert lipreaders.*

left—and when we get back. But who the hell cares after this?" Vidor's view, however, is more romantic than polemical: he looks on war as an overwhelming force that separates lovers. The sense of war as a terrible waste of promising young men, as a deadly game played by madmen that pervades *All Quiet on the Western Front* is not as strong in *The Big Parade*. In Vidor's film, the shots of snaking troops and strafing planes, of battlefields overrun with soldiers, may be realistic and unglamorous, but they do not carry the foreboding or disorienting terror of Milestone's film. War is a big parade, not a monstrous event followed by the endless "quiet" of the grave.

The famous war films that followed *The Big Parade* were also fundamentally romantic in their outlook, although they never concealed the pain or violent death that came with war. The film version of the Maxwell Anderson–Laurence Stallings play *What Price Glory* (1926) had its share of grim battle scenes, but on the whole it made war seem like a giant game for overgrown boys, a springboard for boisterous bickering. A romantic, even glamorous view of wartime combat, specifically combat in the air, was offered the following year in William Wellman's production of *Wings* (1927). This film, a lavish and heartfelt tribute to the courage of America's flyers during the war, garnered praise in its own time and is still regarded, rightfully, as a classic. With the full assistance and cooperation of the War Department and the Army Air Corps, Wellman, a tough, rambunctious direc-

Wings (Paramount, 1927). The tall young actor (at right) making his film debut in this scene with Richard Arlen went on to enjoy a long career in films. His name is Gary Cooper. Below: Low-flying planes strafe the soldiers on the battlefield in one of the most impressive battle scenes in William Wellman's epic air drama. The scenes of air combat, filmed mostly near San Antonio, Texas, are astonishing even today.

tor who had actually fought with the famed Lafayette Escadrille, created an air spectacle that set the standard for all future films of this type.

The plot of *Wings*, concerning two aviator friends (Richard Arlen and Charles "Buddy" Rogers) who love the same girl (Clara Bow), was standard, but it came to a tragic end when Arlen, flying back from enemy lines in a captured German Fokker, is shot down by Rogers. Their mournful farewell, with a dying Arlen forgiving his grief-stricken friend, is a moment of rare and unforgettable poignancy in an action-filled movie. And the appearance of a gangly youth as an ill-fated flyer who takes his plane up for "a flock of figure eights before chow" caused a stir; the film debut of Gary Cooper did not go unnoticed.

But the excitement of *Wings*, and the aspect for which it will always be remembered, comes from its truly remarkable aerial photography. Intricate and breathtaking, this photography captures, to an astonishing degree, the exhilaration and danger of flying under a wartime alert, with all the nose dives, tailspins, crash landings, and near-collisions in midair. Phenomenal, death-defying stuntwork was required to carry out the many dogfights, which have a kind of terrible beauty on screen. It is amazing to realize that no trick photography was used—the photographers flew along with the pilots. Many a youngster dreamed of glory in the skies after seeing *Wings*, and many another film followed in its path, most notably Howard Hughes's *Hell's Angels* (1930).

Some months before *Hell's Angels*, Universal released its landmark film version of Erich Maria Remarque's 1929 novel, *All Quiet on the Western Front* (1930). A grim and unsparing view of war's futility and brutality, the film followed a group of naïve German schoolboys as they discover that the battlefield holds not glory, but disillusion, pain, and death. Largely through the eyes of young Paul Baumer (Lew Ayres), we learn that there is no humanity in war, no honor in winning, no elation in killing—only the cold, merciless sting of quick oblivion. Bitterly, Paul tells the eager schoolboys of his town, "Our bodies are earth. Our thoughts are clay. And we sleep and eat with death."

More than five decades after its release, *All Quiet on the Western Front* is still the most powerful of antiwar films. Despite the awkward-

ness of much of the acting and dialogue, the film continues to make its point with simple eloquence. In contrast with *The Big Parade*, it also demonstrates the value of sound in a war film. The terrifying noise of bursting bombs and machine-gun fire, the wrenching screams of the wounded and dying, the young voices registering fear and despair —these cannot help but add to the impact of the film.

The film is actually a series of incidents in which Paul and his fellow schoolmates move ever deeper into the maelstrom, experiencing the death of friends, the terrible ferocity of battle. Their first taste of action at the front is depicted in an unforgettable scene: enemy soldiers race across an open field like avenging demons; the camera moves rapidly down the trench, catching the exhausted, terrified faces of the boys; bodies clash in hand-to-hand combat. For the boys, the only note of sanity is the presence of the resourceful, generous, and practical Katczinsky ("Kat"), played with hearty directness by Louis Wolheim. Kat knows the score; he is contemptuous of the boy who rushes away to bring back the body of his mortally wounded friend— "He's a corpse, whoever he is!"

Paul Baumer's wartime odyssey takes him from one anguished moment to another. He prays over the body of a dying friend, to no avail. ("I saw him die. I didn't know what it was to die before!") In a famous scene, he lies in a trench with a dying French soldier (Raymond Griffith), listening to the man's intolerable groaning. Movingly, he

All Quiet on the Western Front (Universal, 1930). In the course of Lewis Milestone's film version of the Erich Maria Remarque novel, young Paul Baumer (Lew Ayres, at left) discovers that war is not a glorious adventure. Right: The experienced, resourceful soldier "Kat" (Louis Wolheim) consoles the dejected Baumer. Lewis Milestone's film is still a powerful statement of war's horror and futility.

pleads for forgiveness: "You're just a man like me and I killed you. Forgive me, comrade. Oh, God, why do they do this? We only wanted to live, you and I. . . . You *have* to forgive me, comrade!" His cries echo piteously through No Man's Land. Ironically, when he goes home on leave, he is branded a coward for telling the ugly truth about war.

Returning to combat, a disillusioned Paul is reunited with the reliable Kat, who represents one last link to sanity and common sense. But then Kat is wounded, and when Paul carries him to an aid station, he learns that his friend is already dead. There is no escape, not for Kat, and not for Paul. In the celebrated last scene, Paul is alone in a trench, listening to the sound of a harmonica. He sees a butterfly and, heedless of the danger, he reaches out to touch it. A French sniper draws his gun on him and fires. Paul's fingers go slack, and he is dead. In a brief epilogue, we see a line of marching soldiers, like ghosts of the dead, their eyes deeply mournful and accusing.

All Quiet on the Western Front remains unexcelled as a portrait of war as a horrifying and harrowing charnel house. Whereas other war films permit its characters a few haranguing speeches against the conflict, this film is steeped in an atmosphere of gray and dank hopelessness. Although the dialogue occasionally turns maudlin, director Lewis Milestone keeps reasonably firm control of the emotional content, often allowing the camera or the soundtrack (he uses sound well) to convey the feeling of a waking nightmare for the bewildered young men.

The strongly antiwar feeling persisted in films until the late thirties, when events in Europe made war seem inevitable once again. With the invasions of Poland and Czechoslovakia, with sinister tales of "Fifth Column" activities in American cities, a combative tone returned to films, and there were unmistakable efforts to use the persuasive power of movies to prepare the nation for a new world conflagration. Always ready for the fray, Warner Bros. geared for action with such films as *The Fighting 69th* (1940) and *Sergeant York* (1941), which recalled the bravery of American doughboys in World War I.

Occasionally a major film would touch on the most serious concern of all: the growing threat of totalitarianism in Europe and the fearful disruption of family life under the menacing shadow of Nazi Germany. The subject lent itself to overwrought melodrama, and many films succumbed, but a few were forceful in their depiction of a crumbling world. One of the most successful was MGM's *The Mortal Storm* (1940). Although it evasively used the word "non-Aryan" instead of "Jew," the film was a moving account of the destruction of the Roth family within Germany itself during the early years of Hitler. The father (Frank Morgan), a renowned professor, is sent to a concentration camp; his two stepsons become Nazis, and the rest of the family is cruelly dispersed. Opposing the Nazis, daughter Freya (Margaret Sullavan) flees with Martin Breitner (James Stewart), the young man she loves, but she is shot just before they cross the border to freedom and dies in his arms.

Under Frank Borzage's sympathetic direction (his unabashed romanticism is often unfairly accused of being sentimentality), *The Mortal Storm* is a passionate film that rarely slips from pathos to bathos. True, it is superficial and overstated in the style of this period, but it

also brings off a number of affecting scenes. Significantly, these scenes do not involve overt enemy violence but quiet, privileged moments of love and pride. As troubles increase, Professor Roth is urged to flee but refuses, saying, "I've never prized safety in myself or my children. I've prized courage." Later, when Freya and Martin are reunited at Martin's home in the mountains, they join in a lovely "wedding" ceremony performed by his mother (Maria Ouspenskaya), drinking from the same bridal glass containing apple wine made from the apples on Martin's special tree. The camera focuses on the mother's shaking hand as she says, "This is the moment of your wedding." Freya's death, ironically at the hand of her former friend (Robert Young), is played with the sensitivity and poignancy that Margaret Sullavan brought to all her roles.

Inevitably, films made during World War II included many that paid tribute to the courage and resilience of America's allies. In the context of their time, they stirred audiences and critics to emotional responses with their trampled but defiant peasants, their suddenly noble merchants, teachers, and doctors, facing slavery and death without flinching. Today, most of these films look like highly theatrical melodramas, well-intentioned certainly but unconvincing and heavyhanded. Occasionally a film succeeded moderately well by exercising a measure of restraint—*The Moon Is Down* (1943) was an often moving version of John Steinbeck's novel and play about an occupied Norwegian town. On the whole, however, these films were shrill diatribes intended to strengthen our ties with the Allied and occupied nations.

The plight and indomitability of the British during the war years were conveyed with true feeling and only occasional lapses into sentimentality in MGM's highly popular film *Mrs. Miniver* (1942), based on Jan Struther's novel. Here the victim of the war was not any one

The Mortal Storm (MGM, 1940). In a German tavern during the early days of Adolf Hitler, James Stewart and Margaret Sullavan refuse to join in the Nazi salute. They played ill-fated lovers who are forced to flee from Nazi oppression.

After December 1941, the American people began to face many of the same problems that confronted Mrs. Miniver. There were no bombings at home (although the threat was real enough) and, for civilians at least, no face-to-face contact with the enemy, but it was the same war compounded of anxiety, hope, pride, and deep commitment. Perhaps the most memorable film to deal with the impact of the war on civilian life was contributed by David Selznick. *Since You Went Away* (1944) was not memorable because of any intrinsic qualities—its sweetness could cause tooth decay and its physical production is glossy and distractingly unreal—but because it presented, like *Mrs. Miniver*, a dramatized guide to suitable behavior on the home front. In a sense, it was as instructional as any army training film; in the face of wartime crises both overpowering (the death of a loved one) and trivial (shortages), this is how Americans were expected to react.

What did it matter that the Hiltons of *Since You Went Away* lived in a home that seemed conspicuously beyond their means, or that the mother of the family took the glamorous, stylishly attired form of Claudette Colbert? Mrs. Hilton, buttressed by two pretty daughters (Shirley Temple and Jennifer Jones), had to cope with having a husband away at war and ultimately missing in action; the combat deaths of one daughter's boyfriend (Robert Walker) and other boys of the town; the indignity of people who are selfish and callous about the war; and other tribulations. John Cromwell's direction of this long film extracted the last ounce from every emotion.

Although the effect of the war on civilians received ample coverage from the filmmakers, the majority of war films concentrated on the battlefields where men were fighting and dying. During the nearly four years of America's involvement in the war, the combat films fulfilled their purpose of glorifying the heroic efforts of our servicemen, but for the most part, although competently made, they were crudely written and devoid of cinematic interest. Often the dialogue consisted of hysterical invective against the enemy ("Degenerate moral

person but an entire way of life. The serene and gracious existence of English upper-class countryfolk, epitomized by serene and gracious Kay Miniver (Greer Garson), is suddenly shattered by war. In place of genteel teas and prize-winning roses, there are terrifying bombings, unforeseen dangers, and the always-present imminence of death. Kay's devoted husband, Clem (Walter Pidgeon), assists in the evacuation of Dunkirk. Kay herself captures a wounded German flyer in her garden. And their lovely young daughter-in-law (Teresa Wright) is killed in an air raid.

Mrs. Miniver was roundly mocked by the British themselves, but most Americans respected its vision of an idealized England under intolerable siege by the enemy. More important, the film offered a kind of blueprint for how to behave gallantly and responsibly in wartime—the sort of behavior that might well be called for from Americans just entering the fray. *Mrs. Miniver* is really not a superior film, despite its nostalgic reputation, but it has moments that are touching not for themselves but for what they represent. Director William Wyler took some pains to establish the leisurely life of the Minivers and their neighbors—many moviegoers will remember the gentle stationmaster Mr. Ballard (Henry Travers) and his Miniver Rose—and then plunged the characters into the war. In perhaps the best-remembered scene, the Minivers huddle in the cellar with their children as the area is bombed. Their efforts to keep the small talk going while the children cower in terror are eloquent in their restraint.

Left: Mrs. Miniver (MGM, 1942). Kay and Clem Miniver (Greer Garson and Walter Pidgeon) examine the damage after a German air raid. Although the British scoffed at the movie, Americans found it a stirring view of English courage and gallantry in wartime.
Right: Since You Went Away (David O. Selznick/United Artists, 1945). This home front gathering during World War II includes (left to right) Monty Woolley, Joseph Cotten, Jennifer Jones, and Claudette Colbert.

idiots! Wipe them off the face of the earth!") or of fist-waving calls
to action ("We're going to play 'The Star-Spangled Banner' with
two-ton bombs!"). The battle scenes were expertly photographed,
but the men who fought them usually seemed dull stereotypes, too-
carefully assembled representatives of social or ethnic groups.

As the war continued, the films showing men in battle acquired
some restraint and a more documentary-like quality. In the last year
of conflict, there were even several war films that attempted, with
considerable success, to suggest the true nature of battle—the terror,
the disorientation, the endless weariness, the desperate courage—or
to examine the special relationships between men whose lives may
be forfeit at any moment. William Wellman's *The Story of G.I. Joe*
(1945) was an exceptional film: a study of war, based on the writ-
ings of popular journalist Ernie Pyle (Burgess Meredith), that followed
a platoon of infantrymen through an ordeal that ended with the
death of their captain (Robert Mitchum). The men's farewell to the
captain was one of the most touching in any war film, a simple
utterance of reverence and deep admiration. *A Walk in the Sun*

Above: The Story of G.I. Joe *(Lester Cowan/United Artists, 1945). An evocative scene of men
poised for battle, from a film that paid homage to the American infantryman as seen
through the eyes of journalist Ernie Pyle.*
Below: A Walk in the Sun *(Fox, 1946). War-weary men take a badly needed pause in the
fighting. At right: Dana Andrews as the sensitive sergeant who leads the men into combat.*

(1945) was also the story of one group of infantrymen, but it veered from the usual in the stream-of-consciousness soliloquies spoken by the men as they march along. Lewis Milestone's direction was somewhat self-consciously arty, but the film managed to penetrate the façade of soldiers in battle and to express their true feelings of fear, pride, and despair.

In the immediate postwar years, until 1950, the films dealing with the war reflected the national mood: joy in the end of the conflict but also the need for introspective questioning of its motives, its goals, and especially its wounds. It was a time not only for healing but also for reexamining American values and for readdressing the social problems that lay fallow during the war. The war and war-oriented films, as well as those in other genres, were more realistic, more uncompromising, less rose-colored than they had been since the beginning of the forties. They hardly plumbed the depths, but the best of them were thoughtful and sober.

A true reflection of the postwar mood came in Samuel Goldwyn's *The Best Years of Our Lives* (1946). The first major film to deal with the problems of servicemen returning to civilian life, this emotional drama probed the bewilderment, bitterness, and pain of these men with compassion and understanding. Robert E. Sherwood's screenplay, based on MacKinlay Kantor's novel *Glory for Me*, presented a cross section of all those who had served bravely and came home to encounter trials of a different nature: a captain (Fredric March) returning to a loving wife (Myrna Loy) and the bank where he was an officer; a sergeant (Dana Andrews) with no real job prospects and a bored, sluttish wife (Virginia Mayo); and a sailor (Harold Russell) who has lost his hands and is afraid of the reactions of his family and girlfriend (Cathy O'Donnell).

The film does not totally avoid clichés or predictable conclusions, but it is so deeply felt, so marvelously expressive of its time and place, that its flaws can be discounted. The early scene in which the three men talk together in the plane carrying them home to Boone City is emblematic of the film. Their happiness is tempered with worry—Al Stephenson (the banker) says, "The thing that scares me most is that everyone will want to rehabilitate me." And the troubled shadows that pass over the face of handicapped sailor Homer Parrish speak more than volumes.

As their stories separate and converge, the film manages a number of subtly expressive moments, some of them without the need for words: the awkward, sorrowful embrace of Homer's father; the stiffening back of Al's wife, Millie, when she senses he has just arrived home; ex-sergeant Fred Derry's poignant walk through the graveyard of abandoned planes. (The latter scene is generally regarded as the best in the film—as Fred climbs into the cockpit of one of the mute and useless planes and hears the roar of its engine, he feels pride in having performed an important job well, and sadness that such a feeling will now be irretrievably lost.) The tensions increase and become almost intolerable: uneasy with his wife and children, Al drinks himself into a blissful stupor (the gentle forbearance of his wife is suggested largely with looks and glances in Myrna Loy's best

performance). Homer explodes with anger and frustration—he asks his girl, "You wanna see how the hooks work? You wanna see the freak?" Fred has terrible nightmares and finds solace with Al's daughter Peggy (Teresa Wright).

At its best, *The Best Years of Our Lives* offers several piercing truths about the returning veteran. At a dinner in his honor, Al,

The Best Years of Our Lives (Samuel Goldwyn/RKO, 1946). In the plane carrying them home, Dana Andrews, Fredric March, and Harold Russell reflect on the reception they can expect to receive. Russell, a nonactor who had actually lost his hands in battle, won an Oscar for his credible, touching performance. Below: Milly Stephenson (Myrna Loy) warmly embraces her husband, Al (Fredric March), just home from the war. Few films of the postwar period took a more incisive look at the problems of America's returning veterans.

drinking too much again, makes a speech calling on his fellow bankers to have some human feeling for the plight of veterans, to give them the loans they need badly. ("We'll be gambling on the future of this country!") Most moving of all is the scene in which Homer, wanting his girlfriend to be free of her commitment to him, forces her to see how dependent he is on others. But when she tells him, "I love you, and I'm never going to leave you," he breaks down with tears of relief and gratitude.

During the same period, films were searching out new insights into the nature of wartime combat, especially the stresses and responsibilities of leadership. MGM's *Command Decision* (1948) starred Clark Gable as a flight commander who must endure the agony of sending his men out on near-suicidal raids over Germany. Fox's *Twelve O'Clock High* (1950) touched on the same subject more effectively. Most of the film took place in the offices of General

Savage (Gregory Peck) who, in the fall of 1942, inherits command of the 918th Air Force Group from a colonel (Gary Merrill) who has become dangerously involved with his men. Deliberately harsh and relentless, Savage badgers and humiliates those who fall short of their responsibilities and forces his pilots to face the terrible reality of their situation. ("Stop worrying about fear. Think of yourself as already dead.") He is thoroughly despised, but a sympathetic officer (Dean Jagger in an Academy Award–winning performance) recognizes the signs of strain. Finally, General Savage collapses completely into a catatonic state, no longer able to function. The questions raised by *Twelve O'Clock High*—What does it take to be a combat leader? How can you subdue human instincts? What is the breaking point?—were hardly new (*The Dawn Patrol* had examined the same questions back in 1930), but the film was a cogent and sobering study of the pressures unique to war.

By the 1950s, with our involvement in Korea, the screen's attitude toward war took a new and deeper turn. The postwar films may have had a more clear-eyed view of military battles and of conflict among nations, but now the concept of war itself was seen as an aberration perpetuated by fools, lunatics, or self-serving monsters. At the end of *The Bridge on the River Kwai* (1957), the observant doctor cries, "Madness! Madness! Madness!" as the clash of military minds leads to devastation. In *Attack!* (1956), a hysterically incompetent officer causes the death of many men, until he is killed by another officer. In *Paths of Glory* (1957), set in World War I, three innocent soldiers are tried and shot for "cowardice" only to placate the high command. Conversely, and also curiously, such movies as *The Desert Fox* (1951) and *The Enemy Below* (1957) depicted German officers in a highly sympathetic light.

By far the most prestigious war film of the fifties was David Lean's production of *The Bridge on the River Kwai*. Pierre Boulle (with uncredited help from blacklisted writers Carl Foreman and Michael Wilson) adapted his novel into a multilayered screenplay set largely in a Japanese prison camp in the Burmese jungle during 1943. Although William Holden was nominally starred as a tough, resilient American prisoner named Shears, the film's central conflict was actually between Colonel Saito (Sessue Hayakawa), the harsh, intelligent camp commander, and the British Colonel Nicholson (Alec Guinness), the very essence of the military man: imperious, brave, and dangerously blind to the truth of his situation. Ordered to build a strategic bridge for the Japanese, Nicholson, out of misguided pride and military rectitude, drives his men to build the *best* bridge possible. The bridge is completed but a team of commandoes, headed by Shears and Major Warden (Jack Hawkins), arrives on a mission to destroy it. In the violent climax, with Shears and Colonel Saito among the dead, Nicholson belatedly realizes the extent of his folly and, dying, he falls on the detonator that explodes the bridge, taking a Japanese train with it. The question of whether his fall is deliberate or accidental has never been resolved satisfactorily, which may have been the intention.

The Bridge on the River Kwai contains action scenes as vivid as in any major war film, but its core of interest lies in the complex, fascinating characters of Nicholson and Saito: two detailed portraits of the military mind. At first Saito regards Nicholson with utter contempt ("What do you know of codes? A coward's code!") and when Nicholson refuses to have his officers work along with the enlisted men, Saito explodes in a furious tirade: "You are prisoners but you have no shame! I hate the British!" Nicholson's stubbornness, his insistence on Saito's observing the letter of the military law, is a kind of madness under the circumstances, but a madness Saito cannot overcome, and in one of the film's most unforgettable moments, he sobs with abandon in his room. The victor in their clash of wills, Nicholson sets about building a "proper" bridge. When the doctor suggests that he may be aiding the enemy, Nicholson is aghast: "You're a fine doctor but you've got a lot to learn about the army!" The irony reaches massive proportions when Nicholson congratulates his men on a job well done: "You're going to feel very proud of what you have achieved here. . . . Here in the wilderness you have turned defeat into victory!"

Twelve O'Clock High (Fox, 1950). In this war drama on the burdens and strains of command, General Savage (Gregory Peck) shares a pensive moment with the sympathetic Major Stovall (Dean Jagger). Jagger won an Oscar as Best Supporting Actor.

In the late forties, films had examined the agony of command, but *The Bridge on the River Kwai* offers little sentiment about military leadership, only glancing praise for its ability to come through any ordeal. (Nicholson survives Saito's heartless torture, but Shears says he has "the guts of a maniac.") Nicholson and Saito hold many lives in their hands, but their concern is for saving face, or for instilling regimental pride, or for merely being one-up in a deadly battle of strong wills. Trapped in a world gone mad, they blindly demand observance of the only principles they have ever known —honor, authority, discipline, and a sense of order—regardless of the cost. In a sense, both men are monstrous products of the military machine. *The Bridge on the River Kwai* is a subtle and impressive antiwar film; its powerful statement reverberates over a quarter-century later.

Released at the same time as *The Bridge on the River Kwai*, Stanley Kubrick's *Paths of Glory* (1957) was another important anti-war film, flawed but disturbing. Here the cynicism, duplicity, and corruption of command was attacked in a blistering screenplay derived from Humphrey Cobb's controversial 1935 novel. Based on a true World War I incident, the film centered on the trial and execution of three French soldiers on the charge of cowardice. In reality they are the innocent victims of the ambitions and the vanity of top-ranking officers who need scapegoats. Kirk Douglas starred as the outraged colonel who tries futilely to defend the men.

Written without evasion or compromise, and played with brooding intensity, *Paths of Glory* was clearly a film produced out of conviction rather than with an eye on the box office. The issue is presented as somewhat too cut and dried: the moral monsters in charge vs. the pathetic innocents and their high-minded defender. The deck is unmistakably stacked against the men on trial. Also, the film fails to convince us that this wretched incident can be applied to a larger canvas on the cruel pointlessness of war. (Films of recent years with similar stories on the sacrifice of men to the pitiless war machine—*King and Country, Breaker Morant*, for example—have been more successful in this regard.) But the movie has several strong scenes, especially the brilliantly designed execution scene, which captures the true horror of the situation.

Another important film to explore the military life was Columbia's 1953 adaptation of James Jones's best-selling novel *From Here to Eternity*. Like the book, Daniel Taradash's screenplay focused on the fortunes of a group of people living in or around Hawaii's Schofield Barracks in 1941. The principal characters were Prewitt (Montgomery Clift), a strange, withdrawn loner from Kentucky, whose greatest pleasure is playing his bugle; Sergeant Warden (Burt Lancaster), tough and knowing; Karen Holmes (Deborah Kerr), the restless wife of the camp's captain; a prostitute named Lorene (Donna Reed); and Prewitt's easygoing friend Maggio (Frank Sinatra). By the end of this strong and fascinating if somewhat melodramatic film, both Prewitt and Maggio are dead.

Fred Zinnemann's direction captured Jones's harsh and cynical

view of the military system, stripping his cumbersome prose down to a lean visual narrative. The army is depicted as a regimented world of casual cruelty that someone as sensitive as Prewitt must ultimately reject, despite his love for its rituals, represented by his heartfelt playing of the bugle. The sequences showing the dehumanizing of individuals by the military machine were by far the best: the abusive "treatment" given Prewitt when he refuses to box for his company (he confesses to Lorene that he killed a boxer in the ring); the brutalizing and killing of Maggio (a surprisingly vivid, award-winning performance by Sinatra) by the sadistic "Fatso" (Ernest Borgnine), especially his poignant death in Prewitt's arms; and the brilliantly staged climactic bombing of Pearl Harbor, ending with Warden's eulogy over Prewitt's body: "He loved the army more than any other soldier I ever saw." There is no irony intended in his statement; the bitter irony comes with the army's insistence on denying the humanity of a man who cared deeply about its way of life.

Like other films of the fifties, *From Here to Eternity* took a more penetrating look at the nature of military command and the military mind than could ever have been possible in the embattled forties. (It ran into considerable trouble on this score from government sources.) As the decade wore on, the concept of the noble but deeply troubled military leader in such films as *Twelve O'Clock High* was

Opposite: The Bridge on the River Kwai *(Columbia, 1957). Broken but not destroyed by his long sojourn in the torture chamber called the "box," Colonel Nicholson (Alec Guinness) is returned to his men in the Japanese prison camp. Below: Colonel Nicholson and Colonel Saito (Sessue Hayakawa) find evidence that the bridge has been wired for destruction. The conflict between these two military men forms the core of this outstanding war film.*
Above: Paths of Glory *(Bryna/United Artists, 1957). Kirk Douglas starred as a colonel who must defend three soldiers unjustly singled out for execution during World War I.*

*From Here to Eternity (Columbia, 1953). Sergeant Warden (Burt Lancaster) tries to break up
a dangerous fight between Maggio (Frank Sinatra) and the sadistic Fatso (Ernest Borgnine).
Sinatra won an Academy Award for Best Supporting Actor. Below: The famous amorous
beach encounter between Sergeant Warden and Karen Holmes (Deborah Kerr), wife of the
captain in charge of Schofield Barracks in Hawaii just before the attack on Pearl Harbor.*

replaced by that of the arrogant, blindly rigid officer: the vindictive Captain Holmes of *From Here to Eternity*, the despised captain of *Mister Roberts* (1955), Colonel Nicholson of *The Bridge on the River Kwai*, the cowardly captain of *Attack!* Increasing distance from World War II, public puzzlement over our involvement in the Korean "police action," coupled with the longstanding American irreverence for authority, resulted, for a while, in a jaundiced view of the military.

In the sixties, our controversial entanglement in Vietnam and the fierce protests against it precluded any strong inclination on the part of filmmakers toward movies about wartime combat. Most of the war films that were made, with the conspicuous exception of the outrageous *Green Berets* (1968), found it safer to continue dealing with the "acceptable" war, World War II. The increased realism, gritty and explicitly violent, was still evident in such films as *The Dirty Dozen* (1967) and *The Devil's Brigade* (1968).

The most outstanding and certainly the most ambitious war film of the sixties (and also the most expensive war movie to that time) was Darryl Zanuck's production of *The Longest Day* (1962), based on Cornelius Ryan's book. An awesomely detailed account of the Allied invasion of Normandy, the movie brought together no fewer than three directors (Ken Annakin, Andrew Marton, and Bernhard Wicki) and a cast of international players to re-create the momentous event. As in most star-studded epics on a grand theme, there are

almost inevitable flaws: too many personal stories of little interest or impact, the distraction of spotting well-known actors (some of them in inappropriate roles), and too many high-flown pronouncements ("We're on the threshold of the most crucial event of our time—the big stepoff").

Still, the viewer cannot help but be impressed by the vivid and overwhelming battle scenes, particularly the landing at Omaha Beach, with the camera sweeping across row after row of soldiers as they come ashore. The taking of a strategic bridge is also a sequence of high drama and excitement, as is the scene in which waves of American paratroopers descend on a French village to engage in battle in the streets. As the conflict spreads into other French towns, there are individual acts of heroism and sacrifice, but the emphasis is on conveying the staggering scope of the enterprise.

Most interesting of all is the film's attitude toward military leadership and toward war itself. In a throwback to the forties, *The Longest Day* offers a consistent view of officers as rugged, courageous, smugly defiant, and usually right. Similarly, the idea of war expressed in other movies as a deadly game for fools and opportunists is minimized in the stirring displays of courage under fire. True, there is a glancing swipe at the end when a wounded British pilot (Richard Burton) talks with an American private (Richard Beymer) while a dead German soldier lies nearby. The pilot remarks, "He's dead. I'm crippled. You're lost. I guess it's always like that. I mean

The Longest Day *(Fox, 1962). Brigadier General Norman Cota (Robert Mitchum) leads his men in a scene from Darryl F. Zanuck's epic re-creation of the Allied invasion of Normandy in World War II.*

Overleaf: Patton *(Fox, 1970). In Franklin J. Schaffner's superb war film, George C. Scott gave a compelling performance as the controversial general who loved war and loathed cowardice.*

war." On the whole, however, *The Longest Day* is a "machismo" war movie that suggested the patriotic bravado of the World War II years, but with an obligatory tinge of the cynicism and skepticism of the war films that both preceded and followed it.

By the end of the sixties, with the uneasiness, confusion, and anger surrounding the Vietnam War, there was no way that a war film could hope to succeed by offering a conventionally heroic, straightforward view of that conflict or, for that matter, of anything military. *The Green Berets* (1968) attempted a full-scale justification of America's presence in Vietnam and was largely received with scorn and derision. Even in such a prestigious and imposing war film as Franklin Schaffner's *Patton* (1970), it was found necessary to present a deliberately ambivalent portrait of the controversial World War II general.

Dominated by George C. Scott's charismatic, commanding per-

formance in the title role, *Patton* offered the most conspicuous blending to date of the two prevalent cinematic attitudes toward war during the previous three decades: war as a refuge for deluded, insensitive lunatics with the power of life and death over many men, or war as one of the last outposts for bold and venturesome heroes. On the one hand, General George C. Patton was portrayed as a self-important, war-loving tyrant whose contempt for cowards and incompetents extended to physical violence. On the other hand, he was shown as a forceful military leader with the audacity and imagination to win great battles. The inevitable questions were raised: Was *Patton* a dishonest evasion of the truth that hoped to please both hawks and doves? Or was it the truth itself: the biography of a military man who was a tragically flawed but still noble warrior? Scott's brilliant performance and his own rugged charm seemed to tip the scales in favor of the latter approach, but critical voices

The Longest Day (Fox, 1962). One of the large-scale battle scenes from Darryl F. Zanuck's detailed reconstruction of the D-Day invasion of Europe.

condemning the film as a deliberate compromise were vociferous.

Valid arguments can be made for both points of view, but on the whole *Patton* was attacked unfairly for not being the kind of ferocious attack on the military mind that events of the time possibly supported. Unlike a purported biography such as *Lawrence of Arabia*, which offered no coherent view of its hero and which asked its audience to do more work than it did itself, *Patton* equitably balances both major facets of a complex man, and it provides the audience with all the material it needs to draw its own conclusion. The Patton who says about war, "I love it. God help me, I do love it so," is not far removed from the mad Lieutenant Colonel Kilgore of *Apocalypse Now*, who cries, "I love the smell of napalm in the morning. It smells like . . . victory." But Patton is also a warrior who inspires respect and allegiance when he leads his men into battle.

Whether *Patton* is distorted or equitable, it is also an impressively made war film. Patton is the overwhelming presence—the film opens with the general, placed against an enormous American flag, addressing the troops, and it closes with him walking away from the army with his white dog, while the wheels of a giant (and clearly symbolic) windmill turn slowly behind him. But often the movie expands its personal portrait to include battle scenes of scope and grandeur. Cinematographer Fred Koenekamp conveys the awesome quality of military operations but never lets his camera wander too far from the craggy face or formidable presence of George C. Scott's Patton. (Despite its enormous cast, *Patton* comes close to being the most lavish one-man movie ever made.)

Nearly a decade later, there was no ambiguity possible concerning Francis Ford Coppola's epic war film, *Apocalypse Now* (1979). Produced, written (with John Milius), and directed by Coppola at a staggering cost of $31 million, the film used the Vietnam War as a central metaphor for his vision of war as a demonic voyage into the deepest pit of hell, from which no man can emerge unchanged or unscourged. Drawing on Joseph Conrad's story "Heart of Darkness," the film concerned Captain Willard (Martin Sheen), a battle-weary officer who is sent by the army on a secret mission into the Cambodian jungle to "terminate with extreme prejudice" (that is, assassinate) a once-heroic but now dangerously demented Green Beret officer named Kurtz (Marlon Brando). His journey by patrol boat into the war-plagued jungle is also a journey into his inner self: in one terrible, violent, grotesquely comic incident after another, Willard comes to share and understand the "madness" that infests the world and that has turned Kurtz into an obsessed lunatic fighting his own wars. In the end, Willard's identification with Kurtz is almost complete. ("There is no way to tell his story without telling my own.")

From the time Willard, accompanied by a group of easygoing eccentrics, begins his down-river trip, there is a sense of disorientation, of war as a monstrous joke. For relaxation the men go surfing to the tune of "I Can't Get No Satisfaction." The dementia increases abruptly when they meet Lieutenant Colonel Kilgore (Robert Duvall in a splendid performance), a maniacal, tough, brutally insensitive officer who wears his cavalry hat as he orders his helicopters to attack a serene Vietnamese village. He revels in the destruction: "Let's bomb the shit out of them. These people never give up!" The scene of the attack—set to the music of Wagner—is astounding. While horrifying, it is also, like many of the film's combat scenes, perversely beautiful as photographed by Vittorio Storaro.

The "madness" continues: a stunning sequence in which USO entertainers come to the troops and inadvertently precipitate an all-out riot is followed by the cold-blooded massacre of natives in a dugout. A magnificently staged scene that takes the audience into the nightmarish and disorienting heart of battle ("Where's your commanding officer here?" "Ain't *you?*") alternates with a lyrical and touching scene in which the dead body of Chief (Albert Hall), killed in a skirmish, is tenderly placed on the water by Lance (Sam Bottoms), the increasingly spaced-out California surfer. As Willard goes deeper into hallucinatory country, he learns more about the man he has been ordered to kill. He wonders what the military has against Kurtz—"it wasn't just insanity or murder. There was enough of that to go around."

When he finally meets Kurtz, he finds a bloated, demented man, a monstrous guru who has penetrated into the innermost reaches of evil and has madly justified his use of violence. ("I have seen the horror. . . . Horror has a face and you must make a friend of horror.") As played by Marlon Brando in half-shadow, his voice out of the depths mumbling fragmented thoughts, Kurtz is a character that threatens to send a singularly fine film crashing to disaster. By the time Kurtz appears, he is something of an anticlimax: through Willard we have come to know him well enough, and it is not Kurtz's disintegration but Willard's journey to the end of the river, which "smelled like slow death . . . malaria . . . nightmare," that constitutes the heart of the film. Willard has seen the "horror" long before Kurtz verbalizes it, so that Kurtz's weighty presence (in more ways than one) at the end of the film becomes distracting, incoherent, an almost unnecessary addendum.

If films like *Apocalypse Now* or *The Deer Hunter*, Michael Cimino's flawed but interesting 1978 drama of the Vietnam War's impact on three Pennsylvania steel workers, suggested that the war film had changed its face forever, or at least for a very long time (conventional war films like *MacArthur* and *Midway* failed at the box office), there was no evidence that the genre itself would also disappear. For many filmgoers, the war film has the same appeal as the adventure or Western film: the sense of men and women confronting danger and imminent death; occasions for unselfish heroism and reckless daring; people joined together in a common cause (the routing of a tyrant, the taking of a bridge, the defeat of marauding Indians). In spite of all the antiwar films, in spite of all the newsreels, the documents, and the firsthand accounts, war, to many, will continue to be the great adventure, the Big Parade.

Once war is viewed without self-righteousness or self-justification, without a trace of glamour or patriotic zeal, the parade may slow to a halt. Unfortunately, it can probably never stop.

Overleaf: Apocalypse Now *(Omni-Zoetrope/United Artists, 1979). Francis Ford Coppola's drama of the Vietnam War was a vision of hell-on-earth that propelled viewers into the disorientation and terror of combat. Right: In the foreground: Martin Sheen as Captain Willard, the Special Services officer sent deep into the Cambodian jungle to locate the mad Colonel Kurtz and to "terminate him with extreme prejudice."*

STRANGE WORLDS,
DISTANT WORLDS

MAYHEM IN THE DARK
Great Movies of Mystery and Detection

I f it is true that everyone loves a mystery, then the American moviegoer has been able to indulge that love in happy proportion for many years. Since the twenties, the mystery film in its many variations has baffled, intrigued, and titillated audiences, most notably during the thirties and forties. Detectives have stalked killers in the fogbound streets of London and San Francisco or in the mean streets of New York City. Heroes and heroines have been plunged unwittingly into maelstroms of murder and deception. Nefarious schemes spawned by avarice and greed have been hatched in the darkness. And occasionally the mix of mystery and detection has resulted in films that last the decades.

Inevitably, the detective has been the mainstay of the mystery film. Whether turning up as that eccentric master Sherlock Holmes, the urbane Nick Charles, or those tough private eyes Sam Spade and Philip Marlowe, the detective has been one of the last surviving bastions of honor and integrity in an increasingly corrupt world. He may not be above an occasional bending of the rules, he may even be harsh and brutal, but in general the movie detective has adhered to a code of behavior in times when self-serving anarchy rules the day. Not surprisingly, the only thing that can penetrate his armor is an alluring but dangerous female.

When a detective is not around—and sometimes even when he is—the characters in mystery films are on their own, trapped in a hostile environment and confronted with forces bent on destroying them. They may even discover, to their horror, that some of these forces are within their own nature; their own seeds of evil are ready to sprout. Over many years, these characters-in-jeopardy found their most accomplished creator in the complex and irresistible films of Alfred Hitchcock. But other directors have found in mystery films the inspiration to do their most professional work.

The film detectives of the thirties, usually lifted from the pages of popular fiction (Philo Vance, Ellery Queen, Sherlock Holmes, Mr. Moto), went about their business with dispatch, and were usually to be found at the bottom of double features. The notable exception was Dashiell Hammett's debonair Nick Charles, the detective-hero of *The Thin Man* (1934), the first in a series of diverting comedy-mysteries (actually more comic than mysterious, and memorable for the sophisticated exchanges between Nick and his comely wife, Nora, played by Myrna Loy). Apart from *The Thin Man*, the mystery film had to wait until 1941 for its first bona fide classic. This was John Huston's legendary *The Maltese Falcon*, also derived from a novel by Dashiell Hammett.

There were no high hopes for the property, which had been filmed twice before. Huston, a screenwriter at Warners, was permitted to

direct his first film, and he chose to remake Hammett's tale of treachery and murder in San Francisco. He prepared a detailed plan of the production before shooting, then completed the film in only two months. The result surprised not only Warners's executives but the critics and the paying public. Over four decades later, it remains a model mystery-drama, graced with compact, incisive dialogue, sharp black-and-white photography by Arthur Edeson, and a beautifully matched set of performances.

The Maltese Falcon continues to fascinate, not so much for its plot as for the subtle interplay of its principal characters: detective Sam Spade (Humphrey Bogart), the beautiful but deceitful Brigid O'Shaughnessy (Mary Astor), the fat, falsely jovial Casper Gutman (Sydney Greenstreet in his film debut), and the effeminate Joel Cairo (Peter Lorre). These people are an unsavory lot, given to murder and double-crossings as they compete for possession of a priceless, jewel-encrusted black falcon. What compels our interest is not their quest for the bird (which turns out to be a phony, after all), but their relationships, in which mistrust, treachery, and greed guide every thought, every action. They are night people—dawn would only expose their empty dreams.

Humphrey Bogart's Sam Spade is the film's most complex figure. Hard, cynical, and unsentimental even about his partner's death, he

Preceding pages: Psycho *(Paramount, 1960). Hitchcockian atmosphere prevails as Norman Bates (Anthony Perkins), concealing a deadly and terrible secret, stands in front of the house near the Bates Motel.*
Opposite: Klute *(Warner Bros., 1971). Bree Daniel (Jane Fonda) strolls down a New York street. Fonda's performance as the tough, knowing, vulnerable call girl won her an Oscar.*
Above: The Thin Man *(MGM, 1934). As detective Nick Charles and his wife, Nora, William Powell and Myrna Loy played a couple who actually enjoy being married to each other.*

between Spade and Brigid. From the very first he doesn't trust her, but he admires her style and her audacity. (He tells her, "You're good. You're very good.") He reacts with a smile that is halfway to a sneer as he observes her changing stories, her tearful confessions of a bad life, her stinging confrontations with Gutman and Cairo. At the end he seals her fate in a scene that reverberates with sexual tension and bitter regret. Brigid pleads with him to let her escape, but he is adamant. "I hope they don't hang you, precious, by that sweet neck," he admits. Bogart beautifully delivers the speech that crystallizes Spade's belief that in a life without illusions, we must cling to a private code of honor and decency.

Surly and incorruptible, Bogart's Sam Spade took his place in film history, to be joined five years later by another memorable fictional detective, Raymond Chandler's Philip Marlowe. In *The Big Sleep* (1946), Bogart gave the definitive performance of this dour, hardened, but fundamentally decent detective. (Other actors, from Dick Powell and Robert Montgomery to Elliott Gould, have tried their hand at the role, with middling success.) Whereas Spade had to contend with vipers whose main intent was thievery, Marlowe's nasty group casts a wider net of vices that includes blackmail, nymphomania, pornography, and murder. He also becomes romantically entangled with a sultry widow (Lauren Bacall) whose motives are as complex as their relationship.

Directed by Howard Hawks with his usual professional aplomb, *The Big Sleep* is celebrated not only for its tough, allusive, racy dialogue but also for the complexity and impenetrability of its plot (even Raymond Chandler was alleged to have been baffled by it). There are those who profess to find it perfectly clear and can offer rational explanations for its tortuous series of events. Yet the plot hardly looms as the largest factor in the film's longstanding fame. More striking is the atmosphere of covert evil and depravity, from Marlowe's strange first meeting in a hothouse with the dying General Sternwood to the violent climax, after a number of persons, both seen and unseen, have been killed. Even more important to the film's overall impact is the performance of Humphrey Bogart, perfectly attuned to the movie's hard-boiled mood. It is a pleasure to watch him exchange suggestive banter with Bacall or with Dorothy Malone (playing a sexy bookstore clerk), or to see him threading his cool and knowing way through a hornet's nest of killers, henchmen, and pimps, with occasional time-out for some sharp verbal sparring with the police.

nonetheless adheres to a code that demands justice for that death —although he only hints this to the other characters ("Don't be too sure I'm as crooked as I'm supposed to be," he tells Brigid). Brigid O'Shaughnessy, as played with breathless femininity by Mary Astor, alternates between girlish helplessness and the steely determination of an unregenerate murderess. And Sydney Greenstreet's formidable bulk, stentorian voice, and pompous aphorisms make him a villain both sinister and comic. But the core of the movie is the relationship

In both *The Maltese Falcon* and *The Big Sleep*, Bogart had limned private detectives whose tough and ruthless behavior concealed a creed that called for the implacable pursuit of justice. Sex was a pleasant byproduct of that pursuit, but romantic love could not exist when sullied with deception or marred by suspicion. Bogart's Sam Spade and Philip Marlowe were at ease in the sort of hard-edged and tawdry nighttime world Warners had created in its melodramas. Twentieth Century-Fox's attempts to emulate this world, in such films as *I Wake Up Screaming* (1941), *Fallen Angel* (1945), and *The Dark Corner* (1946), were not successful—the players lacked the brash, power-driven conviction of the Warners players, and the suggestion of decadence in low places was not very persuasive. Fox's style, as in most of

Above: The Maltese Falcon *(Warner Bros., 1941). Detective Sam Spade (Humphrey Bogart) is clearly not too threatened by the effete Joel Cairo (Peter Lorre).*
Below: The Big Sleep *(Warner Bros., 1946). In this scene from Howard Hawks's complex detective mystery, Lauren Bacall converses with a tied-up Humphrey Bogart.*
Opposite, above: A lobby card for The Maltese Falcon *(Warner Bros., 1941).*
Opposite, below: Klute *(Warner Bros., 1971). In the last scene from Alan J. Pakula's thriller, call girl Bree Daniel (Jane Fonda) vacates her apartment to go off with detective Klute.*

HUMPHREY **BOGART** · MARY **ASTOR**

A
WARNER BROS
FIRST NATIONAL
PICTURE

the *Maltese Falcon*

its genre films, was smoother, softer, and shinier than Warners's—blue velvet to Warners's rough brown burlap. Murders were plotted and carried out in glistening penthouses where the whiff of decadence could be masked by expensive perfume.

That whiff was certainly strong in Fox's classic mystery melodrama, *Laura* (1944). Derived from Vera Caspary's novel and directed by Otto Preminger with firm assurance, *Laura* had a detective who, like Spade and Marlowe, becomes more emotionally involved with his case than he had ever intended. Almost hypnotically, detective Mark McPherson (Dana Andrews) is drawn into the dark underside of a murder case that unravels in the swank setting of New York's penthouse society. A beautiful girl named Laura Hunt (Gene Tierney) is apparently killed, and the suspects who swirl around her death include radio commentator Waldo Lydecker (Clifton Webb), her sarcastic, snobbish mentor and would-be lover; Shelby Carpenter (Vincent Price), her weak, shallow would-be fiancé; and her wealthy aunt Ann Treadwell (Judith Anderson).

By the time McPherson has solved the case, he has uncovered the private demons that can claw away at a sophisticated veneer, he has revealed the tangled relationships that affluence cannot mask, and he has fallen in love.

Laura is sleek, silken entertainment, with a screenplay that manages a degree of wit and maturity quite rare in mystery films, and with glistening photography by Joseph La Shelle that perfectly conveys Hollywood's idea of high life in Manhattan. From Waldo Lydecker's memorable first line, "I shall never forget the weekend Laura died," to a final, fatal confrontation in Laura's apartment, the film tells a gripping story of obsession and murder. But its principal fascination lies in the many perverse and distasteful implications that are concealed beneath its surface. As played by Clifton Webb, Waldo Lydecker is a vicious egomaniac whose all-consuming passion for Laura seems more than a little unhealthy. (Mark McPherson tells Laura, "He's infatuated with you—in some peculiar way.") Yet Waldo also seems highly effete,

Laura (Fox, 1944). The peerless moment in which detective Mark McPherson (Dana Andrews) discovers that the supposed murder victim, Laura Hunt (Gene Tierney), is actually very much alive. Otto Preminger's silken mystery drama was one of the best of the decade.

an unlikely lover for Laura, and his bitchy exchanges with the equally effete Shelby Carpenter sound more like the sniping of aging dowagers than the wrangling of rival suitors. This aspect, coupled with the decidedly masculine manner of Ann Treadwell, gives the film a disturbing subtext. McPherson's growing infatuation with the "dead" Laura (he is repeatedly photographed in the same frame as her portrait, often shown staring at it with lover's eyes) is also rather strange. Waldo senses Mark's feelings and suggests that he visit a psychiatrist: he would be the "first patient who fell in love with a corpse!" Laura herself gives off odd vibrations in spite of her blandly beautiful appearance. We wonder about her motive in ever considering marriage to an unscrupulous paid escort like Shelby Carpenter, or how she can so easily make the quantum leap from Carpenter to the tough, virile Mark McPherson.

The detective or policeman's relationship with his female client or leading suspect has surfaced in so many films over the years that it could be considered a subgenre. Lately, it has been depicted with such frankness and complexity that it often surpasses in interest the pure thriller aspects of the story. In Alan J. Pakula's *Klute* (1971), for example, the rapport that develops between call girl Bree Daniel (Jane Fonda) and the title character, private detective John Klute (Donald Sutherland), is actually more intriguing than the story. The plot is fairly conventional material, laced with the increased permissiveness of the sixties and seventies. Klute's investigation of the disappearance of a friend leads him to Bree, who, as it turns out, is being stalked as the latest victim of a homicidal sadist. This leads to the inevitable killer-stalking-victim scenes and ultimately to a suspenseful if rather contrived climax in a deserted garment factory.

But in Bree Daniel, as played by Jane Fonda in an Academy Award–winning performance, scriptwriters Andy and Dave Lewis created an exceptionally well-rounded character, a tough, cynical, intelligent, coolly professional call girl who also possesses a streak of vulnerability and compassion. Brilliantly, Fonda fleshes out a girl who can justify her sordid life ("It made me feel that I wasn't alone") but who also seeks a kind of oblivion ("I'd like to be faceless and bodyless and be left alone"). Then John Klute enters her life, and this strange, silent man arouses hidden, complex feelings in her. As he falls in love with her, she is moved by his acceptance of what she is, yet she is compelled by the need to destroy their relationship. She *feels* something for the first time, yet longs for "the comfort of being numb again." Fonda's Bree Daniel is one of that splendid actress's finest characterizations.

From Brigid O'Shaughnessy to Mrs. Mulwray of Roman Polanski's *Chinatown* (1974), a thriller that filtered the *Maltese Falcon* tradition through a seventies sensibility of sex and violence, the women in detective films have been a resourceful lot: self-reliant, resolute, and often duplicitous. Frequently, they have set the events in motion, inadvertently or even deliberately triggering chaos and mayhem. Most often, however, the ladies of the mystery films have been victims rather than victimizers, caught in a web of treachery and deceit. Sometimes the victims have been men or children, innocently caught

up in perilous adventures, their lives endangered. All fiction, on the screen and elsewhere, has thrived on the concept of characters-in-jeopardy. Once in a while the concept has resulted in memorable films that cause *frissons* of pleasure and suspense at every viewing.

This was indisputably the case with MGM's 1944 production of *Gaslight*. Adapted from the long-running play *Angel Street* by Patrick Hamilton (filmed once before in England under its original title), the movie is really little more than an artful contrivance—a Victorian melodrama complete with dastardly villain and swooning damsel-in-distress. Ingrid Bergman played the hapless heroine, the niece of a murdered opera singer who marries an amorous musician (Charles Boyer) in Italy and returns with him to her aunt's house in

Gaslight (MGM, 1944). Terror lurks in the house on Thornton Square. As the wicked Gregory Anton (Charles Boyer) descends from the attic, where he has been searching desperately for hidden jewels, his tormented wife, Paula (Ingrid Bergman), waits below.

London's Thornton Square. Little does she know (as the saying goes) that her husband is actually her aunt's murderer, who married her to find the jewels hidden in the house. His diabolical scheme to drive her insane is finally thwarted by a sympathetic Scotland Yard detective (Joseph Cotten).

Under George Cukor's direction, *Gaslight* works beautifully, amply fulfilling its intention of providing two hours of suspense. Cukor is well served by art directors Cedric Gibbons and William Ferrari's plush Victorian town house with its overstuffed furniture and clutter of bric-a-brac, and by Joseph Ruttenberg's photography, which fills the house with ominous shadows, conveying a sense of ever-lurking menace. Above all, the director has the advantage of first-rate performances by his small cast. As the bedeviled wife, Ingrid Bergman moves in well-controlled stages from nervousness to terror to rampant hysteria, winning her first Academy Award in the process. In the closing scene, when she regales her trapped husband with bitter loathing ("Without a shred of pity, without a shred of regret, I watch you go with glory in my heart!"), she is a fierce avenging angel who has discovered hidden strength. As the cunning villain, that often underrated actor Charles Boyer manages the shift from seductiveness to menace very persuasively.

Many directors have tried their hand at the melodrama-of-jeopardy, but the indisputable master of this popular subgenre is Alfred Hitchcock. Before and since his death in 1980, the corpulent Englishman with the gifts of a true artist, the skills of a craftsman, and the sense of humor of a particularly wicked child has been analyzed and evaluated *ad infinitum*. His films have been probed relentlessly, and sometimes foolishly, for cosmic themes, his techniques have been aped by lesser directors, and his shortcomings have been submerged in torrents of praise. Yet there is no diminishing of Hitchcock's stature as one of the towering figures in the history of films in saying that he is, above all, a supreme entertainer whose mesmerizing tales take his characters—and his audiences, too, of course—into the most intricate labyrinths of fear and terror. This is

Rebecca (Selznick International/United Artists, 1940). A nervous Joan Fontaine, standing with her new husband (Laurence Olivier), is welcomed by the staff of her new home, Manderley. Foremost among the household staff is the sinister Mrs. Danvers (Judith Anderson). Alfred Hitchcock's Gothic mystery received that year's Academy Award for Best Picture.

not to deny the larger meaning in his films. During the course of their travails, Hitchcock's innocents-in-jeopardy usually discover that they are not so innocent after all; they come face to face with evil and sometimes it is their own reflection. Time and again Hitchcock has shown himself to be a grimly smiling moralist with a cynical view of mankind. But on the whole, he remains the screen's most accomplished spinner of mystery stories.

Hitchcock's first American film, *Rebecca* (1940), is one of his best-remembered "woman-in-danger" tales, although critics have tended to downgrade it over the years, and the director himself remarked that "it's not a Hitchcock picture." Based on Daphne du Maurier's popular Gothic novel, the film may lack the patterns of meaning that Hitchcock would often weave lightly into the fabric of his mysteries. Yet it retains its fascination as the darkly romantic tale of a painfully shy and naïve young girl (Joan Fontaine) who marries Maxim de Winter (Laurence Olivier), the brooding master of Manderley, and gets caught up in the buried secrets of the past. Sinister implications swirl about the memory of Maxim's beautiful deceased wife, Rebecca, until all is revealed and Manderley goes up in flames.

Aided by Robert E. Sherwood and Joan Harrison's screenplay and George Barnes's photography, Hitchcock manages to extract every ounce of menace from the situation. Best of all, he succeeds in making Manderley itself a central character in the story; its shadowed rooms and corridors are as ominous as Mrs. Danvers (Judith Anderson), the malevolent housekeeper who guards the house's secrets from outsiders. Hitchcock also manages to bring out the considerable talents of young Joan Fontaine, whose performance as the terrified heroine is beautifully shaded and controlled. As the mysterious Maxim de Winter, Laurence Olivier glowers in his most impressive Heathcliff style.

Unquestionably, the film's most interesting character is Mrs. Danvers. As played by Judith Anderson with barely repressed rage and malice, she brings an unmistakable suggestion of perversion into the novelettish story. Her obsession with the dead Rebecca seems more of a lesbian attachment than the devotion of servant to mistress, and her psychopathic personality surfaces when she tries to goad the heroine into suicide. Mrs. Danvers believes in death as a release from torment and, like Rebecca, she finally rushes into its welcoming arms. Anderson's performance never varies as she stalks the halls of Manderley almost soundlessly, but she somehow makes the one note seem like a complex musical passage.

Young Charlie Newton (Teresa Wright), the heroine of Hitchcock's *Shadow of a Doubt* (1943), is another girl-in-peril, but she is light-years removed from the Gothic trappings and dark-shadowed world of *Rebecca*. She is, in fact, the sunny, high-spirited all-American girl in Hitchcock's first truly American mystery film. Living in the placid California town of Santa Rosa, secure in herself and in her warm bonds with her family, Charlie comes face to face with the monstrous side of humanity in the person of her beloved but homicidal Uncle Charlie (Joseph Cotten). Although in the process of discovery she is almost killed by her uncle, she allows the myth of his goodness and generosity to live on when he dies instead. Yet the shadow of evil will never leave her now, like the dense black smoke of the train that hovers in the sky when Uncle Charlie first arrives in town. In a sense, the film is a parable of paradise lost and innocence destroyed.

Shadow of a Doubt is a complex and disturbing film that perhaps more than any other Hitchcock movie delineates his central theme of the dual nature within every human being: the boundless capacity for good and evil in each of us. His heroine, bored and restless at the beginning, is overjoyed when she learns that dear Uncle Charlie, for whom she was named, is paying her family a long-delayed visit. Her identification with her uncle is complete, not only in name but emotionally and even telepathically ("When I think of myself, I think of Uncle Charlie")—she is linked with him in numerous ways throughout the film. But gradually she learns that he is a deranged murderer of wealthy widows, and that to him the world is "a foul sty . . . a hell" in which houses are "filled with swine." Her discov-

ery is ours as well—as usual, Hitchcock insidiously draws his audience into the film so that we share young Charlie's painfully ambivalent feelings toward the man she once worshiped: a shining image turned blackly evil.

Shadow of a Doubt is a dazzling suspense film with bravura sequences that are all the more shocking for being set in such a cozy environment—an environment familiar to most of us. We recall with admiration the dinner scene at which Uncle Charlie speaks of his loathing for the widows he has killed ("smelling of money . . . faded, fat, greedy women"), the camera moving in closely to a profile

Shadow of a Doubt *(Universal, 1943). Young Charlie (Teresa Wright) is beginning to suspect that her beloved uncle and namesake (Joseph Cotten) may not be all he seems. One of Alfred Hitchcock's personal favorites among his films, the movie adeptly suggests the evil that may lurk beneath the surface of a placid small town.*

of his face as an image of waltzing couples fills the screen, or the scene in which young Charlie races to the library at night to read an incriminating newspaper article about her uncle, with each word looming large on the screen with triphammer impact. Yet even more impressive than the expected scenes of melodramatic suspense are the artful touches that are deftly executed by Hitchcock: the ironic palaver about fictional murder by the father (Henry Travers) and his mother-fixated neighbor (Hume Cronyn); young Charlie talking about Uncle Charlie and instinctively clutching the wrist he had twisted earlier in a moment of blind anger. Cumulatively, these touches and many others instill a sense of disorder and irrationality, triggered by the very presence of Uncle Charlie. Somewhere between the idyllic Santa Rosa of the beginning and Uncle Charlie's "foul sty" lies the approximate truth as voiced by the young detective (Macdonald Carey) who falls in love with young Charlie: "The world needs watching. . . . It seems to go a little crazy now and then."

Three years later, Alicia Huberman, a Hitchcock heroine-in-

distress much less innocent than Charlie Newton, turned up in a film that François Truffaut has called "the quintessence of the director's art." A deceptively simple espionage melodrama, *Notorious* (1946) actually touched on such matters as redemption for a parent's sin, overpowering mother love, and love vs. duty. Alicia (Ingrid Bergman at her most alluring), the alcoholic, promiscuous daughter of a convicted Nazi, agrees—out of deep guilt—to infiltrate and expose a spy ring of Nazi refugees living in Brazil. She even agrees to marry their mother-dominated leader, Sebastian (Claude Rains), although she has fallen in love with Devlin (Cary Grant), the American agent assigned to help her. Cold and hostile at first, he comes to reciprocate the feeling.

Backed up by Ben Hecht's taut and evocative screenplay (on which Hitchcock collaborated) and Ted Tetzlaff's deep-focus black-and-white photography, *Notorious* represents Hitchcock at his glittering best. As always, the principal objects involved in the plot, or what Hitchcock called the "McGuffins" (here, the key to a wine cellar

Notorious (RKO, 1946). One of many tense moments in Alfred Hitchcock's adroit thriller: caught by Claude Rains in their visit to the wine cellar to uncover evidence, Ingrid Bergman and Cary Grant move into an embrace to disguise their real intention.

and fake wine bottles filled with uranium), are of less consequence than the romantic interplay of the principals, the strange triangle formed by Alicia, Devlin, and Sebastian, and Alicia's dire peril when her true identity becomes known. These situations result in scenes and moments that are among the best-remembered in Hitchcock's films: an erotic encounter between Alicia and Devlin, the camera circling around them as they kiss repeatedly; a lavish dinner party at which Alicia must pass the wine cellar key to Devlin (the single tracking shot from the top of a staircase to the key clutched in her hand is justly famous); and the chilling scene in which the humiliated Sebastian must tell his mother the truth about his wife. "Mother," he says without flinching, "I am married to an American agent." The formidable lady digests this information and then quietly lights a cigarette as she plots Alicia's murder.

The relationship between Alicia and Devlin is complex: although he loves her, he permits her to marry Sebastian to carry out the mission. When he believes that she has returned to drinking heavily (actually, she is ill from being poisoned), he returns to the cold, contemptuous attitude toward her and all women he demonstrated earlier in the film. A dismayed Alicia can only suffer in her predicament—yet she believes that she *must* suffer to atone for her father's sins. In the end, both find redemption from lovelessness (Devlin) and guilt (Alicia). Interesting as these characters are, they are almost surpassed by that of Sebastian, played with his usual finesse by Claude Rains. Although controlled by a ruthless mother, he can still express his ardor for Alicia so openly and honestly that at times he becomes more sympathetic than Devlin.

After *Notorious*, Hitchcock did not hit his stride again until *Strangers on a Train* (1951), a film that he did not find satisfying but which has gained in reputation over the years. This time a man rather than a woman is in jeopardy, but for decidedly peculiar reasons. Guy (Farley Granger), a top-ranking tennis player, enters into a strange relationship with Bruno (Robert Walker), a wealthy, psychopathic young man. Bruno proposes a pact of mutual killings: he

Strangers on a Train *(Warner Bros., 1951). In the hair-raising climax on an out-of-control carrousel, Guy Haines (Farley Granger) grapples with his nemesis, Bruno Anthony (Robert Walker). Walker's death scene in this film was used again in his last movie,* My Son John, *when he died unexpectedly before the end of production.*

will murder Guy's unpleasant and unwanted wife if Guy will kill Bruno's domineering father. In this way, nobody will be suspected of apparently motiveless killings. Although Guy refuses indignantly, Bruno proceeds with his end of the pact and strangles Guy's wife. Many complications ensue (Guy becomes the chief suspect in the crime) until a breathtaking climax aboard a wildly runaway carrousel brings the story to a violent end.

Hitchcock thought that the final screenplay was weak—Raymond Chandler's original version was completely reworked by Czenzi Ormonde—yet *Strangers on a Train* contains many scenes of riveting suspense, as well as, in Bruno, a character of reptilian fascination. As usual, even when his plot is less than watertight (and this one has a number of holes), Hitchcock manages to divert his willing audiences with set pieces of astonishing virtuosity: the murder of Guy's wife in an amusement park, with the killing reflected in the lens of her dropped eyeglasses; the brilliantly edited double race against time, with cross-cutting between Guy frantically hurrying to win a championship tennis match and Bruno desperately attempting to lift Guy's incriminating lighter out of the manhole into which it has fallen; and, of course, the climax on the out-of-control carrousel, the customers' shrieks of pleasure turning into screams of terror as the horses move at breakneck speed and the protagonists engage in a life-and-death struggle.

As played by Robert Walker in an interesting change of persona (Walker was usually the shy, awkward boy-next-door), Bruno projects an air of depravity and viciousness from behind his veneer of the cultured, pampered young man of affluence. His soft, insinuating voice as he insists on Guy's carrying out his part of the bargain suggests a man for whom murder is only an idle pastime. Many critics have remarked on the homosexual undercurrent of his relationship with Guy, although they did not discuss it very openly at the time the film appeared in 1951. Bruno's impotent nature ("I never seem to do anything") suggests that he finds a kind of sexual release in his dealings with Guy. What is more interesting, however, is the recurrence of the Hitchcockian theme of the potential for evildoing in everyone. Like young Charlie in *Shadow of a Doubt*, as well as characters in later Hitchcock films, Guy comes into terrifying contact with the dark side of human nature, unleashing private demons he had once suppressed. As in *Shadow of a Doubt*, Hitchcock wickedly wants us to identify as much with the villain as with his victim. (Isn't Bruno actually an extension of Guy's most secret thoughts?)

The theme of the person who must share at least some of the guilt for events that have placed him in jeopardy surfaced again in Hitchcock's *Rear Window* (1954). The film is one of the director's most intriguing works: a crackling suspense story, a bold cinematic experiment, and a reflection on the dangers of prying too deeply into the private lives of others. This latter point is driven home all too vividly when the central character, free-lance photographer L. B. Jeffries (James Stewart) comes to believe that one of his neighbors is a murderer. Confined to a wheelchair after breaking his leg in an accident, Jeffries uses binoculars to spy on his neighbors. To his mounting horror, he suspects that the man (Raymond Burr) in an apartment opposite may have strangled his wife. His suspicions prove to be horribly right, and very nearly fatal for him.

Hitchcock's experiment of photographing the events entirely from the view seen from Jeffries's rear window is another of the director's occasional forays into new cinematic techniques (as in *Lifeboat* and *Rope*), and it has the deliberate effect of making voyeurs of the audience as well as of Jeffries. Hitchcock is making certain that we understand the consequences (in this case, extremely dangerous) of being a dispassionate observer of humanity rather than one who participates in the mainstream of life. He forces us to look, with Jeffries, at the pathetic and comical specimens eking out their meager existences. There is no such thing, he suggests, as an "innocent" voyeur (the nurse Stella, played by Thelma Ritter, says, "We've all become Peeping Toms"), and Jeffries almost pays for that information with his life. What's more, he comes to realize that his own inner life and even his relationship with his fiancée (Grace Kelly) are not unrelated to the lives of those he has viewed from his window. In the end, as he sits in his chair with *both* legs in a cast, he has made another of Alfred Hitchcock's perilous journeys from darkness into light.

Despite its subtext of meaning, *Rear Window* is fundamentally a diverting thriller with sharp and often witty dialogue by John Michael Hayes. Skillfully, Hitchcock manages to capture the insignificant lives of the neighbors Jeffries watches through his binoculars while gradually building tension toward Jeffries's grisly realization about the wife-murderer in his view. The director suggests cleverly that Jeffries *may* be wrong about the killer—the man's suspicious story possibly could be true, and this, of course, would make his voyeurism even more reprehensible. The fact that Jeffries is right does not, as some critics have maintained, make his voyeurism acceptable. His catching of a killer does not excuse or mitigate his prying into the lives of others.

Another journey of self-discovery was taken by advertising executive Roger Thornhill in Hitchcock's 1959 comedy-thriller, *North by Northwest*. Cross-country rather than stationary, the trip involves Thornhill in a frantic chase to affirm his true identity, to prove his innocence of murder, and, ultimately, to apprehend enemy agents at the risk of his life. As played by Cary Grant, that deftest and most debonair of film actors, Roger Thornhill begins the film as a flippant, hard-drinking man-about-town and ends it, after many sobering and harrowing experiences, as a responsible, caring adult.

It would be highly misleading, however, to suggest that *North by Northwest* is weighty with meaning. In fact, it is one of Alfred Hitchcock's most amusing diversions, a breathtaking adventure that hurls its frantic hero from one unlikely situation to another, ending on the distinguished American visages carved into Mount Rushmore. Written for the screen by Ernest Lehman, its story actually makes as little sense as the film's title. We can only be sure that it involves Thornhill in a case of mistaken identity as enemy agents and FBI

Psycho (Paramount, 1960). Norman Bates (Anthony Perkins) is horrified to discover what his "mother" has done. Norman is one more in the line of mother-dominated characters found in Hitchcock's films.

men swarm around him, trying either to kill or arrest him. He also becomes amorously entwined with a beautiful blonde named Eve Kendall (Eva Marie Saint), who may or may not be working for the enemy.

North by Northwest is Hitchcock's roller coaster—so swift as it hurtles from climax to climax that it is almost over before the viewer realizes he has been taken for a ride. But it is quite a ride, a veritable anthology of Hitchcockian set pieces that both amuse and unnerve audiences: Thornhill's car drive down a treacherous mountain road after he has been forced to drink an entire bottle of liquor; a murder at the United Nations, with Thornhill left holding the incriminating knife while visitors gasp in horror; the famous sequence in which a crop-dusting plane tries to kill him as he rushes through open cornfields (why, one wonders, must the enemy resort to such an elaborate plan when they could simply drive up to him in the deserted fields and plug him full of holes?); and the pursuit of

Thornhill and Eve across the face of Mount Rushmore. Nor should we ignore the suggestive banter that passes between Thornhill and Eve on their cross-country train ride.

North by Northwest is an amusing, suspenseful thriller, but the Hitchcock film that followed it, *Psycho* (1960), is something else, despite the director's possibly tongue-in-cheek assertion that it was intended as black humor. If it is not a dark comedy (and only the most ghoulish mind could laugh at its violent shocks and bloodletting), neither is it, as some critics have stated, "one of the great works of modern art" (Spoto, *The Art of Alfred Hitchcock*) or "one of the key works of our age" (Wood, *Hitchcock's Films*). These are absurdly inflated claims, although the film may well be the director's most audacious work.

Psycho contains situations that have appeared in previous Hitchcock films and in many other thrillers, and their familiarity leads to certain audience expectations as to how they will turn out. Boldly

Opposite: North by Northwest *(MGM, 1959). Fleeing from the villains, Cary Grant and Eva Marie Saint make a perilous climb across Mount Rushmore. Above: In a restaurant near Mount Rushmore, Eva Marie Saint fires at Cary Grant—but there is more going on than meets the eye. The film is one of Alfred Hitchcock's most diverting entertainments, as amusing as it is exciting.*

and outrageously, Hitchcock shatters these expectations, leaving his viewers thoroughly unsettled. It begins with a lady in a kind of distress, although her true jeopardy isn't revealed until it is much too late for her. Marion Crane (Janet Leigh), involved in a clandestine love affair with Sam Loomis (John Gavin), steals forty thousand dollars from her boss and flees Phoenix—but soon regrets her impulsive act. Ostensibly, she is the film's heroine, flawed but sympathetic. But then in her flight she stops for a night at the rundown Bates Motel, whose manager, Norman Bates (Anthony Perkins), is a strange, shy young man. Suddenly, in her shower, she is brutally, violently stabbed to death by a person who appears to be Norman's mother. In one of Hitchcock's most celebrated scenes, we are stunned into shifting our attention and sympathies from the ostensible heroine to hapless Norman Bates, distraught at his mother's senseless act.

Immediately, we are plunged into Norman's disordered world, and even though we may sense the ghastly truth behind his shame and terror, we are asked to identify with his frantic efforts to wipe away all evidence of the crime. So completely does Hitchcock force this identification on us that we are even asked to accept a *second* shocking reversal of our expectations in the genre. Just as Marion was unexpectedly murdered before our eyes, so are we witness to the sudden fatal stabbing of Arbogast (Martin Balsam), the detective who comes to the Bates's house in search of information or evidence. The detective, normally the person who solves the crime in the usual thriller, has become another victim of Norman's derangement. (The detective's murder is one of Hitchcock's most memorable scenes—it is hard to forget the shrill, birdlike noises on the soundtrack as the killer lunges at the startled Arbogast, who tumbles backward down the stairs.)

The mystery unfolds as Sam and Marion's sister Lila (Vera Miles) investigate Marion's disappearance, but neither character is as interesting as Norman Bates (actually, they are rather thinly characterized), so that our interest wavers temporarily when Norman is out of focus. Hitchcock, however, brings us back to Norman for a jolting climax. Almost maliciously, he has transferred our concern to this ultimate mama's boy and his hideous secrets, so that when Lila moves intrepidly into the Bates house, we are less concerned with *whether* she will be discovered than *what* she will discover. After the monstrous revelation in the cellar, the film moves to a perfunctory ending with a psychiatrist (Simon Oakland) offering a glib explanation for Norman's homicidal behavior. Wisely, Hitchcock closes with the face of the deranged Norman, the demonic creation of unbearable guilt and repressed sexuality.

Hitchcock's influence over the years has been far too deep and extensive to be covered in these pages. Most recently, this influence has been clearly evident in the films of Brian DePalma, who has apparently mastered some of Hitchcock's trickery, spicing it with a smattering of latter-day permissiveness, but who has sorely missed the wit, cinematic panache, and larger vision of Hitchcock's best films. Occasionally a homage to Hitchcock has come markedly close to duplicating the master's blueprint. Stanley Donen's *Charade* (1963)

comes to mind as an example: a stylish and hugely entertaining thriller of the woman-in-jeopardy school, with Audrey Hepburn as a young widow who becomes dangerously embroiled in the nefarious events surrounding her husband's death. She is assisted (and also loved, of course) by a mysterious man (Cary Grant) who assumes various identities over the course of the film.

Charade emulates Hitchcock in the swiftness of its pace, its ingenious and sometimes bizarre way of disposing of characters, and its use of multiple identities to baffle the audience. There are similarities to *North by Northwest*, not only in the same leading man, Cary Grant, but also in the character's relationship with the heroine, now ardent and romantic, now apparently duplicitous. With Paris for a backdrop and a lush Henry Mancini score on the soundtrack, *Charade* manages occasionally to evoke a romantic feeling, despite all the mayhem, particularly in a moonlit boat ride on the Seine. The film is an enjoyable dip into the Hitchcock pool.

The great films of mystery and deduction, highlighted by the wickedly entertaining creations of Alfred Hitchcock, are a sturdy part of cinematic tradition. They are different from *films noirs* and from the gangster films, which trade in fatally thwarted passions and brutal gang violence. In the mystery films, the tone is lighter, not as grimly apocalyptic as in the films of crime and punishment. Murder is no less real or punishable, but it is essentially one part of a game with fixed rules that only Hitchcock would dare to violate.

In a nation that thrives on game-playing, we can be sure that films of mystery and deduction will continue to attract audiences for years to come.

Opposite: Charade *(Universal-International, 1963). Reggie Lampert (Audrey Hepburn) is clearly in danger—but she knows not why. Above: Stanley Donen's entertaining thriller in the Hitchcock style starred Audrey Hepburn as a lady in jeopardy and Cary Grant as a mysterious man who assumes various identities.*

CREATURES WALK AMONG US
Great Horror Movies

Steeped in the graphic gore, the incessant bloodletting of today's horror films, we tend to forget that the genre has a long and honorable history. Since the days of the silents, audiences (or at least a large part of their members) have enjoyed movies in which they experience vicarious terror at the sight of some depraved, otherworldly night creature bent on mayhem. Seeing imagined terrors given form and substance on the screen perhaps allows us to cope with them better in our minds, where they tend to assume outsize—or monstrous —proportions. Watching a horror film, we can sublimate or exorcise our most deeply rooted fears: loss of identity (man-into-wolf), loss of control (rampaging beast), or loss of sanity (the mad scientist). The doomed, obsessed characters become our surrogates for a suffering we hope never to experience.

It is true that the horror film has rarely approached the realm of art. With all its overreaching scientists, pathetically confused monsters, and fatally driven dreamers, there has been no character of tragic stature in the genre. Horror films have not altered the way we look at the world, except to make us avoid cobwebbed castles in Transylvania. Even the greatest horror films have not been influential, merely spawning more (and usually lesser) films of the same ilk (or should we say blood type), until repetition breeds parody. In the forties, a producer named Val Lewton showed that less could be more in generating fright, but usually the horror genre has eschewed subtlety for florid dialogue and lurid special effects. Today, it is splattered with blood, even in relatively "serious" horror films like *The Shining*.

Yet why quibble? Many filmgoers delight in being frightened out of their wits by lumbering creatures in the darkness. And there may be a stronger reason than the sublimation or exorcism of their fears. The horror film may, in fact, act as a moral corrective for willing audiences, demonstrating for them the terrible, even fatal effects of excess. Over and over again, the horror film offers the same moral message: you may pursue unlimited power, you may indulge in unbridled sexuality, but in the end you will be utterly destroyed by your lusts. The puritanical instinct that has informed the horror film from its beginnings to the present has perhaps become obscured in recent years by a greater emphasis on the crime than the punishment, but it still exists in the fate that befalls those who choose to defy nature and reason.

Even during the silent era, the horror films out of Hollywood often drew on the themes of out-of-control power and sexual obsession. In many cases, they were influenced by the early German cinema, where these themes were embedded in the dark, centuries-old legends of Teutonic lore. In 1915, for example, famed German stage actor Paul Wegener starred in and codirected *The Golem*, based on the ancient Jewish legend of a stone figure summoned to life by a rabbi to protect

the ghetto. Obviously related to the Frankenstein monster, this golem falls in love with the rabbi's daughter and goes on a murderous rampage when she rejects him. Both the rabbi's excessive pride in animating a stone figure and the golem's rampant sexuality bring disaster.

The horror tales out of Germany took on new significance in the years immediately after World War I, when Expressionism had its greatest impact on the arts. With its intensely subjective, distorted view of reality, its emphasis on effect above content, and its pantomimic approach to acting, Expressionism was eminently suitable for films, and its influence was soon apparent on the screen. *The Cabinet of Dr. Caligari* (1919), directed by Robert Wiene when Fritz Lang was unavailable, was an expressionistic fantasy best remembered for its strange, stylized sets representing the landscape of a madman's mind. Although the film was generally received with a mixture of scorn and admiration, it sparked a series of German movies emphasizing fantasy and terror. One of the most notable of these films was F. W. Murnau's *Nosferatu* (1922), very loosely adapted from Bram Stoker's *Dracula*. A basically absurd but occasionally terrifying version of the vampire legend, it had an actor appropriately named Max Schreck playing the celebrated count (here named Orlock) as a grotesque, cadaverous fiend.

These and other German horror films, with their odd camera angles, brooding atmosphere, and moments of jolting terror, were hardly lost on American filmmakers, who filtered the Expressionistic style through their own less idiosyncratic, less hallucinatory approach, in which

Opposite: Frankenstein *(Universal, 1931). Boris Karloff in his immortal role of the pathetic monster who inspires terror and revulsion in everyone who sees him. The first release prints of this film were tinted green, but this proved too horrifying, and black-and-white prints were substituted.*

Above: Dr. Jekyll and Mr. Hyde *(Paramount, 1920). Dr. Jekyll (John Barrymore), transformed into Mr. Hyde, attacks Brandon Hurst in a fury. Barrymore played Hyde as a hideous old man with a grotesque, leering face.*

horrific and realistic elements were juxtaposed. An early example of German influence was John S. Robertson's 1920 version of Robert Louis Stevenson's *Dr. Jekyll and Mr. Hyde*, starring John Barrymore as the overweening scientist who unleashes the dark side of his nature and transforms himself into a demonic killer. Not the first but certainly the most celebrated silent adaptation of Stevenson's cautionary tale, the film added two characters who were carried over to later versions: an aristocratic fiancée for Dr. Jekyll and a lower-class female victim for Mr. Hyde. Barrymore made the transformation from driven Jekyll to repulsive Hyde without the aid of trick photography, distorting his features to suggest utter depravity. His sinister figure scurrying through the stylized London streets at night had unmistakable echoes of the German horror films.

The undisputed master of Gothic horror in American silent films was Lon Chaney. By 1925, the year of his triumph in *The Phantom of the Opera*, Chaney had established a reputation for his remarkably detailed portraits of physically repugnant but still human characters. Like Boris Karloff in his earliest horror roles, he recognized the humanity that could exist in even the most deformed of creatures, and, concurrently, the covert evil that could lurk in the most outwardly perfect form. His characterization of Eric, the demented organist in *The Phantom of the Opera*, was his greatest achievement: a tour-de-force performance mixing pity and terror in almost equal proportions. (Inevitably, terror holds the edge—the character is too repellent to command our total sympathy.)

Living in his private purgatory beneath the Paris Opera House—an intricate maze of cellars that were once used as dungeons—this masked Phantom terrorizes everyone, strangling a stagehand who has seen him and at one point bringing the theater's immense chandelier crashing onto the heads of the audience. He succeeds in kidnapping Christine (Mary Philbin), the young singer he adores, and he hypnotizes her and takes her to his gloom-ridden "home." There the terrified girl makes the supreme mistake of tearing away his mask. In one of the classic moments in horror films, Eric exposes a face described by one character as "leprous parchment": skull-like, with deathly white skin, gaping nostrils, and rotting teeth. In rage and despair, he cries, "Feast your eyes, glut your soul on my accursed ugliness!" Eventually, Christine is rescued by her lover and the chief of the Secret Police, and Eric is beaten to death by a vengeful mob and thrown into the Seine.

If *The Phantom of the Opera* can be numbered among the great films of the genre, it is largely due to Lon Chaney's performance. Except for the unmasking sequence, there are virtually no moments of true horror (even the scene of the toppling chandelier is handled perfunctorily), and most of the other performances are either routine or worse. But Chaney has a towering presence that is all the more effective for being kept off the screen for periods at a time, and he invests his baleful Phantom with a poignancy that goes beyond his horrific features. He tells his captive, "If I am the Phantom, it is because man's hatred has made me so. . . . Your love will redeem me." Whether making his appearance at the Bal Masqué as a spectral figure robed in red (key scenes were filmed in early Technicolor), or

guiding his boat through the fetid waters of the underground canals, Chaney creates a pathetic monster of unforgettable impact. He is yet another in the horror film's line of outcasts who turn with murderous vengeance on a society that deprives them of love and companionship.

With the coming of sound, the horror film could take on an added and important dimension. Willing audiences could be subjected to the creaking doors, the sudden shrieks in the night, the sepulchral voices forecasting or threatening doom—all the aural trappings of the genre we now take for granted. The visual shocks continued to be the most essential, but sound gave them a new stimulus.

The first major sound horror film remains the most famous—if not the best—of the genre. *Frankenstein* (1931), released by Universal to admiring reviews by the critics and an enthusiastic reception by the public, was based on a novel that had fascinated writers and filmmakers for many years with its haunting story of a scientist who defies the natural laws of the universe by creating a living monster from the bodies of the dead. Mary Shelley's novel had been the basis for several early silent films, and a stage adaptation by Peggy Webling had starred the well-known actor Hamilton Deane as the Monster.

Directed by an Englishman named James Whale, Universal's *Frankenstein* set the standard for future horror films. Although it now creaks with age and its rhetorical dialogue may induce laughter, it retains a large measure of its original power. From the opening sequence, in which Dr. Henry Frankenstein (Colin Clive) and his assistant Fritz (Dwight Frye) stalk a graveyard in search of bodies, the film emanates a forbidding chill. Nowhere is this more evident than in the classic scene in which the Monster is brought to life. In an immense expressionistic laboratory cluttered with crackling machinery, the creature is lifted to an opening in the roof as an electrical storm rages. Lowered to the ground, the body quivers with the first signs of life as Frankenstein shouts, "It's alive!" Our first view of the Monster is truly shocking: the cross-stitched temples, the dark-socketed eyes, the scarred brow, the wide-slit mouth—all convey the uneasy sense of a living corpse.

James Whale's sympathetic direction and Arthur Edeson's stark, atmospheric photography help to offset the film's deficiencies: the awkward acting in the romantic sequences, the obviously fake settings outside of the laboratory, the tediousness of some portions (even in the brief running time of seventy-one minutes). But what sets *Frankenstein* apart from all its successors is the performance of Boris Karloff as the Monster. A gentle, cultivated actor, Karloff turned this poor, confused creature into a figure of pity as well as revulsion. From the first, when his misshapen hands grope toward the light with a sense of wonder and bafflement, then move supplicatingly toward his creator, we are equally moved and horrified. His scene with the little girl at the lake (cut from the original release) is a memorable highlight of the film. His delight in playing with her, his dawning despair when he realizes he has drowned her (he had thought she would float like the flowers) are expressed by Karloff with a delicacy astonishing for so grotesque a character. The Monster's final terror and anguish as the windmill burns down around him cannot help but evoke compassion for this

Opposite: The Phantom of the Opera *(Universal, 1925). Opera singer Christine (Mary Philbin)
receives a rude shock as Eric (Lon Chaney), the Phantom of the Paris Opera, is unmasked to
reveal his horribly deformed face. During production the director was changed, and
Chaney directed some of his own scenes.*

CARL LAEMMLE Presents THE MONSTER THRILLER KARLOFF in

The BRIDE of FRANKENSTEIN

A UNIVERSAL Picture

wretched creature. Henry Frankenstein's cosmic tirades give the film its theme (defy the laws of nature at your own risk), but, ironically, it is the unhuman monster who gives the film its humanity.

Four years later, with James Whale repeating as director, and with Boris Karloff and Colin Clive again playing the Monster and his creator, a sequel to *Frankenstein* was released. Although it also reveals the influence of the German silents, *The Bride of Frankenstein* (1935) is unlike the original version in most ways. Indeed, it is unlike any other horror film: more amusing and poignant than frightening, it is a quite remarkable combination of "scientific" mumbo jumbo, baroque comedy, and standard horror-film trappings, overlaid with the theme of the monster as martyr. If this sounds like a decidedly odd combination, so be it. *The Bride of Frankenstein* is one of the oddest—and, despite its lapses, one of the best—American horror films.

In this version, Mary Shelley's original story is forgotten, although the lady herself (played by Elsa Lanchester), along with husband Percy and their friend Lord Byron, appears in a curious prologue. On a stormy evening, she relates the tale of Dr. Henry Frankenstein's reluctant new involvement with his monstrous creation, forced on him by the mad scientist Dr. Praetorius, who has found the Monster and now wants to build him a mate. As expected when such unnatural experiments are undertaken, the result is not a durable contribution to scientific achievement.

In addition to the expected Gothic atmosphere carried over from the earlier film, *The Bride of Frankenstein* also contains the usual tedious "comic" relief, provided by an incessantly shrieking Una O'Connor. However, the humor here takes a bizarre turn from the first appearance of Dr. Praetorius, played with flamboyant skill by Ernest Thesiger. A genuine original, the redoubtable doctor has managed to reduce people to homunculi, miniature figures he keeps in bottles for his amusement. His tiny people include a ballerina, a devil, an archbishop, and a king who lusts for the queen in the next bottle. "Normal size has been my difficulty," he tells Frankenstein. When he is not expounding on matters of life and death, Dr. Praetorius is given to making such remarks as "Gin. It is my only weakness, you know."

As in *Frankenstein*, it is Boris Karloff who gives the film its most memorable quality, portraying a pitiable creature who strikes out only because of his uncomprehending terror. Captured after being pursued by vengeful villagers, he is bound to boards and then chained to a chair in a dungeon, all the while suggesting the figure of Christ. When he breaks loose, he stumbles through the woods until he is befriended by a lonely blind hermit (O. P. Heggie). This well-remembered sequence, so easily parodied, becomes deeply touching when the Monster smiles at the sound of the hermit's violin music, or when he holds out his burned hand to the hermit like a frightened child. These two afflicted souls join in a brief, curious friendship ("Alone bad. Friend good") that ends with the fiery destruction of the hermit's hut. By now, even the Monster understands what he is, and he knows that he can expect nothing but torment: "I love dead! Hate living!"

The creation of the Monster's mate is splendidly handled, pho-

tographed in expressionistic style and climaxed by the extraordinary moment in which the "bride" (also played by Elsa Lanchester) is first revealed. Resembling Egypt's Queen Nefertiti and also the robot played by Brigitte Helm in the classic German film *Metropolis*, this fantastic creature, with her white-streaked hair, startled eyes, and quick, darting movements, is horrified at the sight of the Monster. "We belong dead!" the despairing Monster cries, and as the bride emits a hideous hissing noise, he blows up the laboratory, ending his "life" until the next reincarnation.

The scientist who is cursed for delving into the so-called "mysteries of life" has made frequent appearances over the history of the horror film, his scientific equipment squawking, gurgling, and sputtering, and his test tubes overflowing with noxious materials. In the end he is usually destroyed for his presumption, or, as in Henry Frankenstein's case, brought back for further ordeals. Only a year after *Frankenstein*, and no doubt spurred by its success, Rouben Mamoulian directed a new version of *Dr. Jekyll and Mr. Hyde* (1932), in which Fredric March undertook the role of the doctor whose secret experiments unleash the demon inside him.

Following the lead of John Barrymore's 1920 version, this *Jekyll and Hyde* gave Dr. Jekyll and his alter ego Mr. Hyde the opportunity to dally with two women: one pure (Rose Hobart) and one impure (Miriam Hopkins as the dissolute café singer called "Champagne Ivy"). Unlike Barrymore, however, March chose to rely on makeup for his transformation, turning Hyde into an extremely hirsute creature somewhat more repulsive than frightening. Yet his on-camera transformation from Jekyll to Hyde, combining clever trick photography and a specially prepared cacophonic soundtrack, was the film's most impressive scene.

Except for March's performance, too bland as Jekyll, too apelike as Hyde, this version of the Stevenson story excels in all ways, from the first extraordinary sequence: everything is shown from Jekyll's point of view until the moment he begins a university lecture to his students, and then we see his face for the first time. Mamoulian's direction works wonders in making visual and even boldly explicit Jekyll's dual nature and the repressed sexuality that emerges hideously in Hyde. It becomes clear that Jekyll's experiments are prompted less by his scientific zeal than by his desire to release the sexual drive he must conceal from his demure fiancée and which has been aroused by the promiscuous Ivy. Even early in the film, we see Jekyll's importunate haste to marry, his barely suppressed physicality.

At about the same time that Dr. Frankenstein was electrifying his creature into life, another night monster was about to be set loose on the moviegoing public by the same studio. The vampire, that most eminent resident of the realm of the undead, had enjoyed a long history in legend and nightmare, and there was even evidence of a real-life Dracula, a sadistic fifteenth-century prince named Vlad II. The family coat of arms was a dragon, or *dracul* in Rumanian, and this became the nickname of Vlad's father; passed on to Prince Vlad, it was altered to *dracula*, or "little dragon." In 1896, Bram Stoker wrote a novel called *Dracula*, which created a sensation when

Opposite: A lobby card for The Bride of Frankenstein (Universal, 1935). *Below: In this film, Dr. Praetorius (Ernest Thesiger) gazes on his unusual collection of homunculi, miniature living figures the doctor keeps in bottles for his enjoyment. James Whale's film contained many such delightfully bizarre touches.*

never fails to shock us. Even after repeated viewings, we can take pleasure in Dracula's falsely cordial reception to Renfield ("I am . . . Dracula . . . I bid you welcome . . .") and in his sly refusal to join his guest in a toast ("I never drink . . . wine . . ."). Lugosi's baleful stare and thickly accented, insinuating voice may be the stuff of parody, but there is no denying the aura of depravity that hovers over this demonic figure, or the chill we feel as he stalks the corridors of the castle.

Yet too much of the film is static and stagebound, and despite Karl Freund's eerily effective, expressionistic photography, there are far too many abrupt cuts and ellipses that leave the viewer bewildered and unsatisfied. Even the crucial scene of the destruction of Dracula is staged in a surprisingly offhand manner. (Actually, all we hear is an offscreen groan as a stake is driven into his heart.) The film's other principal characters, especially the ostensible hero (David Manners) and his endangered fiancée (Helen Chandler), are much too vapid. Still, there is a great deal to remember, and much that is haunting in its primitive power to turn dreams into nightmares. Some of us may long for eternal life, but when Dracula, doomed to a life-in-death, proclaims, "To die . . . to be really dead . . . that must be glorious!" we see the terrible curse implicit in living forever. Others may hope for undiminished sexual feelings, but Dracula's insatiable thirst for blood (obviously bloodlust is being equated with sexual lust) makes him a creature who will never know peace or fulfillment. The message is crude but clear: refusing to accept the finiteness of life, or the limitations of sexual desire, is tantamount to self-destruction, the path to damnation. The battle between Dracula and the vampire hunter Professor Van Helsing (Edward Van Sloan) for the soul of Mina is a classic confrontation of good and evil, highlighted by the scene in which the count simply uses his magnetic stare to draw the professor into his power.

After photographing *Dracula*, Karl Freund turned to directing for a brief period, making his debut with one of the best horror films of the early thirties, *The Mummy* (1932). His background in German cinema of the twenties is evident in virtually every frame of this macabre film concerning a mummified ancient Egyptian high priest named Im-Ho-Tep (Boris Karloff), brought back to life when the inscription on a scroll found with his body is intoned despite a dire warning to leave the scroll untouched. (Once again the natural order has been dangerously disturbed.) Taking the form of a sinister Egyptian named Ardath Bey, Im-Ho-Tep battles the forces of British science for possession of his beloved Princess Anck-es-en-Amon, reincarnated as a beautiful modern-day woman (Zita Johann) of part-English, part-Egyptian extraction. Of course Im-Ho-Tep is finally returned to his mummified state, but not before some nasty doings, directed in striking but heavily Teutonic fashion by Freund. In the eeriest scene, Im-Ho-Tep spirits away his reincarnated princess and shows her their past lives reflected in a pool.

One of Tod Browning's first films after directing *Dracula* was a grim and highly controversial melodrama called *Freaks* (1932). To relate the story of a group of circus freaks who inflict a terrible

it was published the following year. Inevitably, the story of the evil count continued to fascinate writers over the years, with F. W. Murnau's silent film version *Nosferatu* and a twenties stage version by Hamilton Deane and John F. Balderston attracting the most attention. It was from this stage version that the most famous adaptation was drawn: Tod Browning's 1931 film, *Dracula*. The film's star was a Hungarian actor named Bela Lugosi who had appeared in the 1927 Broadway production of the play.

For all of its legendary reputation, *Dracula* is far from a superior movie, and its ancient bones creak more noticeably than *Frankenstein*'s. It begins well, with an unnerving sequence in which the heedless Renfield (Dwight Frye) takes a mysterious coach ride to Dracula's ruined castle in the Carpathian Mountains (the coachman's transformation into a bat is a startling moment), and our first view of Dracula rising out of his coffin to join his bloodthirsty concubines

Above: Dr. Jekyll and Mr. Hyde (Paramount, 1932). Dr. Jekyll (Fredric March) is welcomed by the dissolute "Champagne Ivy" (Miriam Hopkins). Below: The evil Mr. Hyde looks in on Dr. Jekyll's distraught fiancée (Rose Hobart). March's remarkable transformation into Hyde was achieved with colored filters, changed to reveal different layers of makeup. Opposite: Dracula (Universal, 1931). At home with Count Dracula (Bela Lugosi) in Tod Browning's classic horror film. No doubt the coffins the Count is surveying contain a few of his vampire concubines.

she denied the humanness of the freaks and ended up subhuman. The film was greeted with outraged charges of exploitation and sensationalism on its release, and it was removed from circulation for many years. It remains a unique and disturbing classic of the genre.

No night creature of the horror film could approach the vampire in deathless popularity, but the movie werewolf had its share of howling success. Like vampirism, lycanthropy has had its serious scholars; they have uncovered evidence of wolflike creatures who stalk human prey when in that aberrant condition. Films, of course, have tended to exploit the subject as a source of hair-bristling terror.

One film that did show a certain amount of skill was Universal's *The Wolf Man* (1941). Despite a limited budget, it managed to serve up the requisite number of frightening moments for the popcorn trade while suggesting a larger meaning: the deep-seated fear of losing one's identity, one's individual will to act and behave. (The classic science-fiction film *Invasion of the Body Snatchers* centers on this fear.) Lon Chaney, Jr., son of the eminent twenties actor, played Larry Talbot, who returns to his Welsh home only to be attacked by a werewolf (our old friend Bela Lugosi) and is thereby doomed to a life of misery and mayhem as a man who keeps turning into a murderous, wolflike creature against his will. He is finally slain by his father (Claude Rains) with a silver-tipped cane.

Despite improbabilities and some absurd casting (Rains as Chaney's father is difficult to believe, as is Lugosi as the son of gypsy fortuneteller Maria Ouspenskaya), George Waggner's direction, aided by atmospheric if hardly authentic scenery and arresting music, keeps suspense and interest relatively high. Perhaps the film's most exemplary feature is Chaney's wolf-man makeup, which took many

revenge on Cleopatra (Olga Baclanova), the beautiful aerial artist who betrayed and nearly killed one of their own, the midget Hans (Harry Earles), Browning brought together people of virtually every kind of deformity to play leading roles. Evidently, Browning intended to use the freaks in a discreet and sympathetic manner, exposing us to their everyday lives. In ironic contrast to their grotesque appearance, they behave naturally and are warmly protective toward each other. Even more ironically, it is the normally proportioned people—Cleopatra and her lover—who are truly ugly. (In this the film harks back to many of the deformed creations of Lon Chaney, such as the misshapen but caring bell ringer Quasimodo, at odds with the regally attired but cruel members of Church and state.)

Yet whatever Browning's sincere intentions, there is little doubt that his freaks are used purely for shock purposes in the film's horrifying climax. At the wedding banquet of Cleopatra and Hans, the Goya-like revelry, scored to the music of an ocarina, is undercut by a sense of foreboding until Cleopatra finally reveals her contempt and revulsion for her groom and his friends. Her insults become more brutal until the guests are disillusioned and angry. Soon the freaks are plotting their revenge, and on a stormy evening we see them crawl, hop, and slide from wagon to wagon in search of their victim. The driving rain, the figures moving quickly through the darkness, the flashes of knives—all conspire to create a mood of mesmerizing terror. Later, we see that they have somehow changed Cleopatra into a freak attraction: half-woman, half-chicken. Ironically,

Left: The Mummy *(Universal, 1932). The mysterious Ardath Bey (Boris Karloff) is actually the reincarnation of an ancient Egyptian high priest named Im-Ho-Tep.*
Right: Freaks *(MGM, 1932). The circus freaks gather to celebrate the marriage of aerial artist Cleopatra to one of their own, the midget Hans—possibly the most bizarre wedding feast in film history.*
Opposite: A lobby card for The Wolf Man *(Universal, 1941). Below: In this film, Larry Talbot (Lon Chaney, Jr.), transformed into a murderous werewolf, stalks the night. The movie was the best of many lycanthropic horror stories.*

hours to apply and which resembled no wolf that ever lived. Created by Jack Pierce, who had designed the Frankenstein monster, it included a black shirt and trousers for the actor, so that he could avoid the ordeal of body makeup. Some critics objected to making the wolf-man so visible, claiming that it diminished the horror.

At RKO-Radio, a producer named Val Lewton was apparently in accord with those critics. The series of notable horror films he created in the early forties no doubt owed some of their reticence and restraint to the studio's constricted budgets, but there was also Lewton's conviction that the mind could imagine horrors greater than any that the screen could make visible. By using low-key lighting, unusual camera angles, and spare but allusive dialogue, and especially by staging macabre events in recognizable settings, Lewton's films terrified moviegoers more readily than any explicitly gory horror film.

The Russian-born Lewton, a nephew of famed actress Alla Nazimova and former story editor to David O. Selznick, had been put in charge of the special unit organized by RKO to turn out these low-budget horror films. Besides assembling the best people he could find for the lowest feasible salaries, he also participated in all aspects of his films. His first, *Cat People* (1942), was one of the best: a chilling fable concerning a young Serbian girl (Simone Simon) haunted by an ancient curse that turns her into a huge, murderous cat when her passions are aroused. (The implicit fear of sexual feelings out of control was made hideously explicit in the 1982 remake.) The story was patently nonsense, the production was obviously skimpy, and much of the acting was indifferent. Yet under Jacques Tourneur's direction (with Lewton's close supervision), the film had more than its share of frightening moments, and one scene that has become a classic in horror-film annals.

Much of the film's early part cleverly depends on the indication of something feline and deadly in the nature of Irena, the cat-woman. She responds to the sound of lions from the zoo ("natural and soothing") and sends the birds in a pet shop into wild panic. When she feels threatened by Alice (Jane Randolph), a coworker of her husband (Kent Smith) who has loved him for years, the film offers sequences of stalking terror that work by suggestion rather than the usual visual shocks. Alice becomes an intended victim: first in Central Park at night and then, memorably, in an indoor swimming pool. In the park, Alice is suddenly terrified by the knowledge that she is being followed. We see nothing, and hear only the sound of clacking heels, rustling leaves, and possibly a low hiss. Abruptly, the hiss becomes unnervingly loud, but it is only caused by a bus stopping to pick her up. The pool sequence is masterly: alone in the darkened area, Alice hears a low growl above the lapping of the water and jumps into the pool. The growl soon becomes the screech of an angered animal. Alice screams in terror, and when the lights come on, her nemesis is standing there, smiling slightly—but Alice's robe has been torn to shreds. In all ways except cost, this *Cat People* is superior to the gory 1982 remake.

Lewton's next film, *I Walked with a Zombie* (1943), was also surprisingly effective, despite its lurid title, and in many ways it is

superior to *Cat People*. Jacques Tourneur directed this bizarre tale, deliberately reminiscent of *Jane Eyre*, in which Betsy (Frances Dee), a young Canadian nurse, comes to a West Indian island dominated by voodoo to attend the seriously ill wife of plantation owner Paul Holland (Tom Conway). Betsy falls in love with Paul, only to discover that his wife Jessica is a zombie, one of the "walking dead" who inhabit the island. Also involved are Paul's alcoholic half-brother Wesley (James Ellison), who loves Jessica and blames Paul for her condition, and Mrs. Rand (Edith Barrett), mother of Paul and Wesley, who finally admits to being responsible. (When Jessica wanted to run off with Wesley, Mrs. Rand asked the villagers to turn her into a zombie.) Ultimately, Wesley kills Jessica to free her from her living death and drowns himself. Paul, who loves Betsy, is now free to marry her. From Paul Holland's description of the island as a place of "death and decay," we come at last to the prayer of the villagers, "Give peace and happiness to the living."

Within its stringent budget, *I Walked with a Zombie* manages a convincing atmosphere of supernatural dread. As expected in a Lewton film, the terror is always implied rather than explicit: a cumulative buildup of evocative details. The film's best-remembered scene occurs when Betsy takes the somnolent Jessica through the cane fields to the meeting place of the zombies, where she hopes to have her cured by voodoo. As they pass a series of strange objects, the symphony of noises on the soundtrack induces a feeling of unease in the audience so that when a tall zombie with dead, staring eyes suddenly looms out of the darkness, the effect is terrifying.

Of Lewton's subsequent films, the most successful was *The Body Snatcher* (released in 1945 but made two years earlier), a tightly knit and atmospheric costume melodrama that indicated how much could be accomplished with judicious editing, low-key lighting, and

Above: Cat People *(RKO, 1942). A deceptively quiet moment in the life of Oliver Reed (Kent Smith) and his bride, Irena (Simone Simon). Here crouched catlike at his side, Irena will later turn into a predatory cat.*
Opposite: The Body Snatcher *(RKO, 1945). Gray (Boris Karloff), an Edinburgh coachman and part-time graverobber, has finally killed his blackmailing nemesis, Joseph (Bela Lugosi). The movie was one of the best of the series of modest but atmospheric thrillers produced by Val Lewton in the forties.*

an eye for authentic period detail. *The Body Snatcher*, based on Robert Louis Stevenson's story, featured an impressive performance by Henry Daniell as Dr. MacFarlane, an Edinburgh doctor in 1832 who is in thrall to a sinister coachman and part-time graverobber named Gray (Boris Karloff). It seems that Gray, who has long supplied the doctor with bodies for surgical experiments, once served a prison term for MacFarlane's crimes, and now continually threatens to expose him. Robert Wise's direction reached heights of Gothic terror in two scenes: Gray's murder of a street singer (he has run out of graveyard bodies), in which the girl's sweet song ends abruptly as he strangles her offscreen; and the film's stunning climax, in which Dr. MacFarlane drives a coach with the body of a recently buried woman beside him. As a storm rages, the corpse keeps bumping against him. Irritated, he finally pulls back the shroud, only to see the body of Gray, whom he has recently killed, and not that of the woman. To MacFarlane's horror, Gray's dead arms grasp at his neck until he loses control of the coach, which shatters, sending him screaming to his death.

In a sense, the end of Lewton's horror films for RKO marked the end of the "golden" period for the genre. By the 1950s, the movie-spawned monsters were a vastly different breed from the night-stalking creatures of old. Many of them emerged from newly hatched fears of outer space: the idea that beings from other planets were actually plotting to destroy the earth. A prevalent view that irresponsible testing of the atom bomb had somehow unsettled the balance of nature in the universe gave rise to numerous low-budget horror films inhabited by marauding giant creatures. The mass paranoia that saw Communist infiltration at every turn and produced such films as *I Was a Communist for the F.B.I.* extended to witnessing

invasions by outer-space beings in such movies as *The War of the Worlds* (1953) and *It Came from Outer Space* (1953). With so much danger from without, who could be frightened by monsters within our own walls?

If most movie monsters of the fifties came in swarms, there were still individualists among them. Most of them betrayed the zealous efforts of the studio's makeup department, but one, coming early in the decade, succeeded in generating fright through suggestion rather than globs of rubber cement. RKO's *The Thing from Another World* (1951), directed by Christian Nyby but rumored to have been worked on by its producer, Howard Hawks, was a modest, talky, but intermittently terrifying film that stressed its horrific elements over those from science fiction. It concerned a massive, unidentifiable creature that arrives at a remote scientific outpost in Alaska in some sort of spaceship. Encased in ice, it proceeds to defrost and wreaks havoc until it is demolished. The creature turns out to be made entirely of vegetable matter, giving rise to the memorable line, "An intellectual carrot! The mind boggles." It also feeds on an exclusive diet of blood, which it obtains from the Eskimo huskies at the station.

All this familiar nonsense would be easily dismissed were it not for the ingenious ways in which the film avoids showing the "thing" with any clarity until the climax, where even then it appears as a looming mass without sharp definition. When the creature (played by James Arness in his pre-*Gunsmoke* days) finally thaws (a room heater melts the ice), we hear only an unearthly roar and see the hysteria of the soldier who was guarding it. A scary moment occurs when a door is opened and the creature's arm suddenly appears, only to be lopped off when the door is shut. Even more frightening in a way is the scene in which the scientists watch planted portions of the "thing" begin to sprout with amazing speed when nourished with plasma, making sounds "like the wail of a newborn child." The film, incidentally, betrays an antiscientific bias common to the period. One of the scientists pleads to spare the creature for experimentation ("Knowledge is more important than life!"), hinting at the excessive zeal that many people felt had led us to the terrors of the atom bomb.

The fifties produced few noteworthy examples of the horror film, but in 1960, a producer-director named Roger Corman, working at American International Pictures from the mid-fifties, released the first of a series of horror films suggested by the stories of Edgar Allan Poe. *The House of Usher* shortened the title but extended the plot of Poe's story, creating a mood of foreboding largely through the judicious use of one principal set, a huge, gloomy mansion, and through color photography that emphasized vivid hues. The best of the Poe adaptations was the British-made *The Masque of the Red Death* (1964), stunningly photographed by Nicholas Roeg, with moments of horror that reach a peak when the masked figure of the Red Death passes among the terrified party guests.

The steady diet of Corman horror films during the sixties appeared to satisfy the appetites of horror-film buffs, leaving little room for main courses from the major studios. Occasionally, a horror film of substance or substantial merit surfaced during the period.

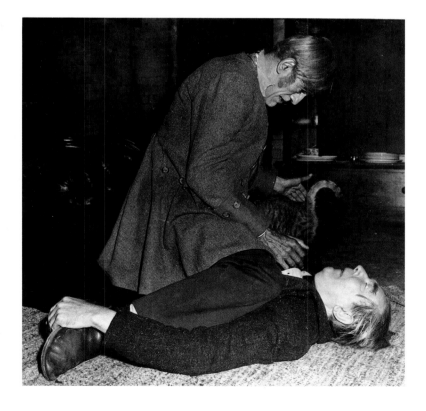

Overleaf, left: A one-sheet poster for I Walked with a Zombie *(RKO, 1943). Below: In this movie, nurse Frances Dee, on her way to a voodoo ceremony with her patient, confronts a fearful sight. Overleaf, right, above:* The Thing from Another World *(Winchester Pictures/RKO, 1951). Scientists in a remote Alaskan outpost determine the measurements of the spaceship that crash-landed in the ice. The surprise is inside: a homicidal creature of unknown origin. Overleaf, right, below:* Rosemary's Baby *(Paramount, 1968). A horrified Rosemary (Mia Farrow) prepares to destroy the infant she has conceived with the Devil.*

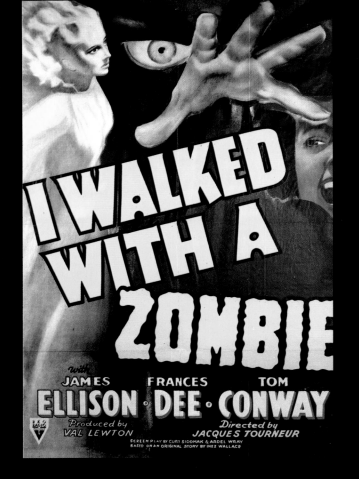

The Birds (Universal, 1963). A flock of vicious birds attacks Tippi Hedren, Rod Taylor, and
Jessica Tandy. Many critics found a parabolic meaning in the story of birds on a sudden
rampage, but Alfred Hitchcock said that he intended it only as speculative fantasy.

One was Alfred Hitchcock's *The Birds* (1963), the director's only excursion into the realm of pure horror (as opposed to films, such as *Psycho*, that are studded with horrifying moments). Here, as in many science-fiction films of the fifties, the terror descends from the skies without warning, except now the evil creatures are not oddly-shaped spacemen bent on inhabiting our planet or giant lizards created by atomic fallout but our everyday feathered friends. Suddenly, in a California town, birds turn vicious and deadly for no apparent reason, leaving death and destruction in their wake.

In spite of flaws (an opening section that takes too long to establish the realistic structure of the story, and some flabby acting, especially by the leading lady), *The Birds* has more than its share of dazzling Hitchcockian scenes, as well as remarkable technical virtuosity. One recalls the crows gathering ominously behind heroine Melanie Daniels (Tippi Hedren) as she waits outside a school; the soundless scream of the hero's mother (Jessica Tandy) when she comes upon the body of a murdered farmer, his eyes gouged out by the birds; the relentless attack of the birds on Melanie as she cowers in a telephone booth; and the climactic assault on the house, with the bird shrieks and the flapping of wings causing the terror to mount almost intolerably. Melanie's last ordeal with the rampaging birds, as they descend upon her en masse in the attic, is as brilliantly staged as the shower scene in *Psycho*. Hitchcock's mordant view of people as pawns in an indifferent world, or the butts of a cosmic joke, is nowhere expressed more vividly than in the final scene, in which the besieged survivors leave the bird-controlled area to face possibly greater terrors ahead.

The last few decades have produced only a handful of distinctive horror films, although several achieved great popularity. Roman Polanski's *Rosemary's Baby* (1968), based on Ira Levin's novel, took too long to get under way, but the story of a hapless young wife impregnated by Satan in modern-day New York City succeeded in frightening audiences by cleverly juxtaposing the dark, sinister images of ancient diabolism with the bright, colorful images of a bustling metropolis. More effective than the scenes in which Rosemary (Mia Farrow) falls into the clutches of the devil's conclave were those in which everyday objects—an empty closet, for example —took on ominous coloration and became part of a waking nightmare. Another tale of demonic horror, William Peter Blatty's novel *The Exorcist* (1973), was made into a lurid melodrama concerning a young girl (Linda Blair) possessed by the devil. Here, whatever shocking moments the movie may have had were offset by long stretches of stomach-churning special effects.

Explicitness became the rule in horror films of the seventies and eighties, targeted for audiences apparently unsatiated by countless views of blood and gore. Where films were not extending popular themes—for example, the demonically possessed child of *The Exorcist* was followed by the literal personification of the Antichrist in *The Omen* (1976)—they were grafting explicit horror onto familiar genres and subgenres: the haunted house story took on new depths

of revulsion with *The Amityville Horror* (1979) and *The Shining* (1980), and no film of space exploration had ever remotely contained scenes as gruesome as those that assaulted moviegoers unlucky enough to see *Alien* (1979).

As all these sanguinary shockers continue unabated, we cannot reflect on the future direction of the horror film with much hope. Nor can there be much hope for members of the human race who revel in watching their fellow humans dismembered, disemboweled, or otherwise destroyed out of some atavistic need to see violence enacted. To say that "it's only a movie" is no longer an acceptable retort. We cannot claim that human life is sacred while at the same time gloating over the many ways in which it can be profaned.

There is no bloodshed in the 1931 *Frankenstein*, and although blood is, of course, the life source for *Dracula* of that same year, the camera moves away discreetly whenever the count goes for the jugular. A decade later, Val Lewton's films showed some regard for human imagination by allowing viewers to conjure for themselves the horrors he was only suggesting. We must not mistake these films for cinematic art or, in some cases, even cinematic competence. But in their comparative restraint, they showed that no horror is as great as those we can invent in our own minds. They also showed that a touch of pathos or a hint of humanity is not only essential in the horror film but may also be its core. We have come a long way from Frankenstein's monster holding out his burned hand to the blind hermit to the seemingly endless parade of monstrous homicidal humans hacking their way, on camera, through scores of pubescent youngsters. Maybe it is not too late to find our way back.

Rosemary's Baby (Paramount, 1968). Rosemary (Mia Farrow) registers horror at the thought that her husband (John Cassavetes) might be in league with the Devil. Ira Levin's novel of ancient diabolism in modern-day New York City was made into a terrifying film by Roman Polanski.

ANYBODY OUT THERE?
Great Science-Fiction and Fantasy Movies

A rocket is fired from a huge gun loaded by a group of girls and lands in the eye of the Man in the Moon. The space travelers come upon strange lunar inhabitants called Selenites, who explode when tapped with an umbrella. Due to the pull of Earth's gravity, the spacemen manage to escape back to their own planet, where they are rewarded with a statue in their honor.

Such is the "plot" of the sixteen-minute film, made by Frenchman Georges Méliès in 1902, called *A Trip to the Moon (La Voyage dans la Lune)*. Loosely derived from Jules Verne's *From Earth to the Moon* and H. G. Wells's *The First Men in the Moon*, the film was presumably the first effort in the area of cinematic science fiction, a genre that has continued to please and excite vast numbers of moviegoers to this day. In its concern with the limitless possibilities of scientific exploration, both on Earth and on worlds far beyond our own, in its reflections on the hidden wonders of the universe, science fiction has stimulated the imaginations of filmmakers who seek to extend the technical resources of motion pictures. No genre has witnessed a greater number of advances in cinematography, special effects, set design, and new musical forms. It may be only three-quarters of a century from the cardboard Selenites of *A Trip to the Moon* to the ethereal aliens of *Close Encounters of the Third Kind*—a fleeting second in the span of time—but over that period, science-fiction film has made giant strides in production techniques.

It has not, however, made equal strides in sophistication of content. Until the late sixties, when a note of reverence and even mysticism entered scientific speculation in such films as *2001: A Space Odyssey*, science had not fared well in the genre. In fact, many films from the twenties on reflect the general public's fear and mistrust of scientists, a belief that their overweening pride and arrogance is at least partially responsible for the troubles of the human race. This antiscientific, anti-intellectual bias can be seen in movies as different and as separated in time as *Frankenstein* (1931), in which the obsessed doctor defies the laws of nature by creating life in the laboratory, and *Forbidden Planet* (1956), in which brilliant scientist Dr. Morbius, isolated on a distant planet in the last decade of the twenty-first century, unleashes a demonic force from his own destructive id. In film after film, scientists have been depicted as well-intentioned but woolly-minded at best and tyrannical or purely evil at worst.

In the early years of the science-fiction film, the most notable advances came from Germany, where the flourishing of Expressionism gave impetus to many bizarre but striking fantasy movies by such directors as Paul Leni and Fritz Lang. By the thirties, however, the Expressionistic mode was fading, while science-fiction films, or, more accurately, fantasy films laced with aspects of science fiction, were diminishing in quality. Like many films both before and after them, they were much more fictional than scientific. Most were designed to appeal to imaginative teenagers who devoured the pulp magazines and who longed to soar in spaceships with Flash Gordon and Buck Rogers. Even back on Earth, they (and a great many adults as well) saw science as merely an opportunity to dabble heavily in the fantastic; movie scientists were often not scientists at all but magicians, alchemists, and sorcerers bent on nefarious deeds. Dr. Jekyll and Fritz Lang's Dr. Mabuse had their inheritors in the thirties: other madmen with scientific obsessions, a passion for secrecy, and an unbounded loathing for humanity.

The genre deteriorated even further in the forties; with few exceptions, the films were third-rate efforts that perpetuated the "mad scientist" theme, occasionally mixing in references to World War II. (Naturally, the scientist was in league with the enemy, or at least had a highly suspicious accent.) But the fifties brought a surge of renewed interest in science fiction and, along with it, a veritable deluge of movies on the themes of space exploration and invasion from outer space.

There were several reasons for the boom in science fiction. The war years had witnessed a prodigious growth in scientific advances. The race for supremacy between the superpowers spurred giant strides in technological sophistication, especially in the production of new weaponry. People were both intrigued and baffled by the unlimited potential of science; for the first time it seemed possible that the fantasy of Flash Gordon and Buck Rogers might someday become a reality.

But scientific development had a double edge, and that other edge was represented by the atom bomb. The awesome explosions at Hiroshima and Nagasaki not only unleashed a new scientific age, they also brought a deeply rooted fear of world annihilation. Coupled with the very real anxiety induced by America's cold war with the Soviet Union, this fear took root and finally sprouted in the science-fiction movies of the fifties. In the minds of many, Communist subversion from within was somehow related to alien invasion from without. Basic themes began to appear regularly in movies produced from 1950 to 1955: the possibly dire effects of atomic power and atomic radiation; invasion of the Earth by alien forces; the imminent end of the world.

One of the earliest and most interesting of these films was Fox's *The Day the Earth Stood Still* (1951). Directed by Robert Wise, the movie had a clever idea that survived its rather clumsy execution: the visitor from outer space is not a fire-breathing monster but a reasonable,

Filmed in Technicolor and directed by Byron Haskin, *The War of the Worlds* was most ingenious in its creation of the Martian spaceships, menacing copper-colored vehicles with cobra-like arms that protruded from the top and went about their destructive work with terrifying efficiency. A representative of the Martian invaders themselves was seen only briefly in the form of a mushroom-like, not very frightening creature who wanders into the farmhouse where the hero and heroine are hiding, and also as a hand emerging from beneath a crushed Martian war machine.

By the mid-fifties, the interest in science-fiction films was waning. However, one movie released by MGM in 1956 proved to be not only the decade's most unusual contribution to the genre but also a perennial favorite among science-fiction aficionadoes. Directed by Fred McLeod Wilcox, *Forbidden Planet* has a basic plot line not unlike that of many other outer-space dramas: in the final decade of the twenty-first century, a spaceship (United Planet Cruiser C-57D) ventures into the planetary system of the star Altair in search of an expedition that vanished twenty years earlier. It lands on a planet called Altair 4, occupied only by a scientist named Morbius (Walter Pidgeon), his young daughter Altaira (Anne Francis), and a robot named Robby. We are prepared for the unraveling of the mystery: Why are they the only survivors? What are the buried secrets of Morbius and Altair 4? And what adventures lie in wait for the space explorers?

To its credit, *Forbidden Planet* offers intriguing surprises rather than conventional answers. For one thing, it becomes apparent after a while that the story is based, however loosely, on William Shakespeare's

gentlemanly person whose urgent mission is to keep the embattled planet Earth from destroying itself and every other planet in the solar system. His warning: leave us in peace or Earth will be obliterated. With the help of a young Washington widow (Patricia Neal) and her small son (Billy Gray), the ultimate disaster is averted.

For all its stretches of absurdity and its amateurish staging—the crowd scenes are especially awkward—*The Day the Earth Stood Still* manages to carry off enough odd, intriguing moments to make it a superior example of the genre. The first appearance of Klaatu (Michael Rennie) in his disguise as an ordinary mortal is striking: at the boardinghouse where he has come to live, he appears as a looming shadow, then emerges into the light as a kind of apparition. The title sequence, in which the world's electricity is cut off for thirty minutes to demonstrate Klaatu's power, has some amusing effects as the public reacts with bewilderment. Best of all is the climactic scene in which Patricia Neal saves the Earth from destruction by uttering the crucial words—"Klaatu barada nikto!"—given to her by Klaatu.

More conventional and much less benign invaders from outer space than Klaatu turned up in the profusion of science-fiction films of the fifties. Many of them were lurid, cheaply made efforts designed to keep special-effects departments active, but some displayed an admirable amount of imagination and ingenuity. One of these was George Pal's *The War of the Worlds* (1953), loosely adapted by Barre Lyndon from H. G. Wells's book. In the film, narrated in appropriately portentous tones by Sir Cedric Hardwicke, hostile Martians invade California (not England, as in the book). Their oddly shaped war machines emit rays that indiscriminately destroy everything in their path, including a company of soldiers and a priest. (So much for the power of the military and religion.) After some impressively staged scenes of carnage and interplanetary battle, the Martians are defeated by—surprise!—their lack of immunity to common, earthly bacteria.

Left: The Day the Earth Stood Still *(Fox, 1951). To prevent the robot Gort (Lock Martin) from destroying Earth, Helen Benson (Patricia Neal) is about to utter the crucial words "Klaatu barada nikto!" This phrase has long held a special cachet for science-fiction fans.*
Right: The War of the Worlds *(Paramount, 1953). A Martian spaceship wreaks destruction on the city. The scenes of the devastation of Los Angeles, with crowds of people fleeing the city in panic, had more conviction than the usual scene of this kind.*

The Tempest, with the magician Prospero turned into Dr. Morbius, Miranda into Altaira, Ariel into Robby the Robot, and Caliban into a monster whose presence triggers the suspense and terror. Much more fascinating, however, than the film's Shakespearean source is its central concept, which provides an explanation for the mystery and precipitates the ultimate resolution. The astronauts learn that Altair 4 was once inhabited by a superhuman but now extinct race called the Krel. Many centuries ago, they had been destroyed by "some dark, terrible, incomprehensible force" that turned out to be the embodiment of the evil desires hidden in their subconscious minds. This hideous creature of the id still exists in Morbius's mind, against his will, and, taking the form of a fiery red electrical charge, it is determined to destroy the astronauts. (Daughter Altaira and the leader of the space mission have fallen in love, setting off the creature's reaction.) In the end, the surviving men escape with Altaira, and Morbius perishes in the explosion that destroys Altair 4.

No doubt this was the first (and possibly the last) science-fiction film to create a destructive monster from the depths of the human mind rather than a subterranean laboratory, and as such it represents the purest statement of the prevalent fifties idea that the man of science and intellect was the source of much of the evil unleashed on the world. The scores of movies in which hideous creatures spawned by atomic radiation rampaged across entire cities had suggested that science's indiscriminate tinkering with the universe was more dangerous than helpful. It was the old "mad scientist" theme of the thirties brought to a new level of fear by the presence of the atom bomb. *Forbidden Planet* went one step further, implying that the superior mind was a breeding ground for vicious and murderous impulses that cannot be suppressed, no matter how highly civilized it may be. (Neither the astronauts nor Altaira are infected with the subconscious desires that destroy Morbius and the Krel.)

One of the best-remembered outer-space films of the fifties was *Invasion of the Body Snatchers* (1956), directed by Don Siegel. The screenplay by Daniel Mainwaring and Sam Peckinpah (uncredited) was derived from Jack Finney's novel. Clearly produced on a small budget, the film had no need for elaborate special effects; it had a genuinely frightening idea instead. Miles Bennell (Kevin McCarthy), a doctor in a small California town, discovers that an alien invasion is under way in which pods take on the exact appearance of people, then replace them when their victims are sleeping. Eventually, Miles is the only surviving human in a town of pod-people without feelings and without individual personalities—the first wave of alien invaders bent on taking over the world. He finally escapes and manages to convince the authorities that he is not insane, that the Earth is facing a terrible danger.

Within its limitations, *Invasion of the Body Snatchers* does well with the disturbing idea that the people whose appearance and behavior are as familiar to us as our own might be concealing another and totally different identity. The ordinary look of the aliens shatters our security: in the film's most frightening sequence, Miles and his fiancée Becky (Dana Wynter) move stealthily through streets

Above: Forbidden Planet *(MGM, 1956). On the planet called Altair 4, Commander Adams (Leslie Nielsen) tries to restrain Dr. Morbius (Walter Pidgeon), while the doctor's daughter, Altaira (Anne Francis), looks on.*
Below: Invasion of the Body Snatchers *(Allied Artists, 1956). Dana Wynter and Kevin McCarthy flee in terror from the "body snatchers"—the pod-people who have assumed the familiar forms of ordinary people. In the film's original ending, an unheeded McCarthy desperately tries to warn people about the alien invasion.*

filled with pod-people until Becky screams when a dog is nearly run over, an emotional reaction that clearly labels them as humans. The sight of scores of townspeople—housewives, policemen, shopkeepers, and others—chasing the couple relentlessly, their faces emotionless masks, is truly disquieting.

Invasion of the Body Snatchers has been given interpretations that turn it from science-fiction horror to allegory. The pods have been said to represent the people of the fifties, the men and women of the "button-down" generation: conventional-minded, regimented, and resentful of anyone who is "different." Sometimes the film is cited as a political allegory, a disguised message on the dangers of non-conformity in the age of Senator Joseph McCarthy. Whatever the original intentions of its creators, *Invasion of the Body Snatchers* has come to be regarded as a warning against any further erosion of our humanity, and an implied plea for each of us to retain his or her stamp of individuality. All this may be a heavy burden for such a small film to carry, but it seems to have managed it with ease.

By the sixties, interest in scientifically spawned monsters was fading, and filmmakers were turning back to classic science-fiction stories for material; there were new versions of works by Jules Verne, H. G. Wells, Conan Doyle, and others. The arrogant scientist had not disappeared altogether, but there was greater concern with the threat of world annihilation through a clash of the superpowers. The screen's apocalyptic vision was treated either satirically, as in Stanley Kubrick's *Dr. Strangelove* (1964), or with complete serious-ness, as in *Panic in the Year Zero* (1962) and *Fail-Safe* (1964).

By the second half of the decade, it seemed to be time for varia-tions of familiar science-fiction themes, and for further expansion of the possibilities of special effects. Two fascinating and expensive films in the genre came from Twentieth Century-Fox. *Fantastic Voyage*, directed by Richard Fleischer in 1966, amusingly reversed the usual course by dealing with "inner" rather than outer space. To remove a blood clot from the brain of a defecting Czechoslovakian scientist, a surgical team is miniaturized and injected into the scientist's bloodstream—we see the liquid pouring from a hypo-dermic needle carry a tiny nuclear-powered submarine into one of the arteries. Although the screenplay is ludicrous from a scientific viewpoint, the special effects are ingeniously contrived and rea-sonably authentic, taking the viewer into huge facsimiles of the heart, lungs, and brain.

Planet of the Apes (1968) was another clever variation on the usual space exploration story. Michael Wilson and Rod Serling adapted Pierre Boulle's novel *Monkey Planet* into an entertaining science-fiction adventure concerning an astronaut on a space mis-sion two thousand years into the future. Arrogant and misanthropic, George Taylor (Charlton Heston) finds himself trapped on a planet run entirely by intelligent apes who regard human beings as inferior beasts fit only for slavery. Taylor finally manages to escape with the help of two sympathetic apes, Dr. Zira (Kim Hunter) and her ar-chaeologist fiancé Cornelius (Roddy McDowall). He ventures into the mysterious Forbidden Zone, where, to his horror and disgust, he

discovers that the Planet of the Apes was once the planet Earth, destroyed by man's violence. Coming upon a remnant of the Statue of Liberty, he cries, "So you finally really did it! You maniacs! God damn you all to hell!"

Although the touch of allegory at the end is predictable, *Planet of the Apes* manages to keep an even keel as it veers from fantasy to adventure to satire and back again, sometimes within the same sequence. The first view of the apes on horseback, rounding up their mute human slaves, is genuinely startling, and the switching of gorilla and human aphorisms and attitudes is amusing for a time: "Human see, human do," "I never met an ape I didn't like." The film also cuts a little deeper than other movies in the genre in its sharply satirical characterization of the most eminent and learned apes as men with closed minds who refuse to believe the evidence of their own eyes. Their snobbish contempt for what they regard as the lower order of animals is complete and unshakable; their self-declared superiority has made them bigoted—when they call humans "natural-born thieves," or declare that "a man has no rights under ape law," the implication of racism is very clear.

In the same year as *Planet of the Apes*, MGM released one of the most ambitious science-fiction films to date, Stanley Kubrick's pro-duction of *2001: A Space Odyssey* (1968). Written by Kubrick and British science-fiction author Arthur C. Clarke (from Clarke's story "The Sentinel"), the film was a bold attempt to lift the genre into the more rarefied realms of theology, philosophy, and abstract science. At its core, the movie was squarely in the tradition of many other futuristic melodramas of much lesser pretensions: in the year 2001, a spaceship called *Discovery I*, carrying five astronauts and an unusually intelligent computer known affectionately as HAL, is head-ing for Jupiter to investigate why a mysterious slab discovered on the moon is beaming its communications at that planet. Fearful that it will be dismantled for making an error in its calculations, com-puter HAL disrupts the mission and causes the death of four of the astronauts. The surviving astronaut, Bowman (Keir Dullea), is hurled into an astonishing vision of the future, a phantasmagoria of sight and sound that ends with his death from old age and his rebirth into a new millennium of mankind.

It is clear from the outset, however, that Stanley Kubrick has much more grandiose intentions in mind: he is attempting to por-tray no less than the cosmic evolution of mankind over the centu-ries and into the future. With the help of cinematographer Geoffrey Unsworth and an imaginative team of production designers and special-effects people, Kubrick framed the story of the space mis-sion with images of human progress across the ages. These images are often stunning: in the prologue set at the dawn of time, an ape-man flings the stick he has used as a destructive weapon high into the air and it immediately becomes the spaceship *Discovery I;* a quantum leap of time is joined to an even greater leap in man's progress. Frequently, however, the images offer less than meets our astonished eyes. The final section of Bowman's journey into his own life has many dazzling moments, especially his moving encounter

Opposite, above: Forbidden Planet *(MGM, 1956). Dr. Morbius (Walter Pidgeon), accompanied by Robby the Robot, welcomes visiting astronauts to the distant planet Altair 4.*
Opposite, center: Fantastic Voyage *(Fox, 1966). A miniaturized submarine enters the bloodstream of a scientist, carrying passengers who are equipped to remove a blood clot from his brain.*
Opposite, below: Planet of the Apes *(Fox, 1968). Astronaut Taylor (Charlton Heston) is interrogated by the apes in charge while sympathetic chimpanzees Drs. Zira (Kim Hunter) and Cornelius (Roddy McDowall) look on. John Chambers's makeup cost a million dollars.*

with his aged self, but it is also essentially hollow at heart. The fact that life renews itself can hardly be regarded as profound, nor are we plumbing any true depths in the idea that man's pursuit of knowledge is a never-ending circle in the endless reaches of time.

Filmed in England at a cost of $10.5 million, *2001: A Space Odyssey* looks expensive but it also tends to be turgid—the countless shots of *Discovery I* moving languidly through space become wearying after a while. The settings, while impressively designed, are so cold and antiseptic that they cast an emotional chill on the characters who inhabit them. On the other hand, the computer HAL, for all its sinister intentions, arouses more of our concern than the imperiled spacemen. Soft-spoken and all-knowing, HAL begins to disintegrate when its error is discovered, and its demise is actually touching in a way. There is, of course, a comment being made here on the increasing dehumanization of man—a machine has more feelings than those who created it—but the effect is to leave the viewer aloof from the events that overtake the spaceship.

The element of mysticism that appeared in *2001: A Space Odyssey* could be found again years later in two major but vastly different outer-space films. In *Star Wars* (1977) and *Close Encounters of the Third Kind* (1977), the primary goal was certainly to entertain audiences with fanciful concepts of distant worlds and faraway galaxies, yet these films also felt the need to add at least a smattering of mystical belief in a powerful force that dominated not only Earth but beyond. In *Star Wars*, it was literally known as the Force; in *Close Encounters of the Third Kind*, it permeated the actions of virtually all the characters, drawing them into a close communion with each other and with otherworldly beings. These films reflected a new

attitude: the fears of the fifties, as we stood poised at the threshold of space, had changed into the awe and wonder of the seventies, as we penetrated deeper into the outer reaches of the universe.

The Force aside, *Star Wars* is a phenomenon in itself: to date the second largest-grossing film ever produced, as well as a vastly entertaining outer-space spectacular. For George Lucas, in his first film since *American Graffiti*, it was a deliberate attempt to recapture the heady atmosphere of the comic books and movie adventure serials that millions of viewers had cherished in their youth. For good measure, it also mixed in aspects of the popular Westerns, swashbucklers, and war films of past decades. Lucas's screenplay wasted no time; it plunged immediately into the action as young Luke Skywalker (Mark Hamill) rallies the forces of rebellion against the evil Galactic Empire and its most sinister figure, the black-clad, hollow-voiced giant named Darth Vader (David Prowse). His mission is personal: many years ago the Empire had murdered his father, one of the brave Jedi knights. Their recent killing of the aunt and uncle with whom he lived rouses him to seek retribution. With the help of wise old warrior Ben Kenobi (Alec Guinness), a mercenary space pilot named Han Solo (Harrison Ford), Solo's copilot Chewbacca, a hairy creature known as a Wookie, and two adorable robots provided for comedy relief, Luke leads the attack against the Empire's armored space station, the Death Star, and also rescues Princess Leia (Carrie Fisher).

The dialogue may be grade-school level and the acting mediocre (with the exception of Alec Guinness's performance), but *Star Wars* offers nonstop enjoyment for audiences willing to surrender to its giddy mood. There is high adventure, especially in the dazzling

Above: 2001: A Space Odyssey *(MGM, 1968). A futuristic airport lounge, one of the many imaginative sets in Stanley Kubrick's ambitious space extravaganza. In the long run, the movie may evoke more admiration than enthusiasm, but it remains a fascinating plunge into the deeper waters of science fiction.*
Opposite: Star Wars *(Lucasfilm Ltd./Fox, 1977). Luke Skywalker (Mark Hamill) is attacked by a Tusken Raider, a vicious desert bandit.*

climactic bombing raid across the surface of the Death Star, as well as low comedy in the antics of the robots R2D2 ("Artoo") and C3PO ("Threepio"). There is a touch of horror in the grotesque Sand People, and more than a touch of wit in the intergalactic nightclub swarming with bizarre creatures. *Star Wars* has been criticized for its excessive violence (scores of extras are blown up without bloodshed) and for the vacuity of its mystical concept of the Force. It has even been charged that the Force is an expression of a basically totalitarian idea—a mysterious bond between those who must justify their violence. (Ben Kenobi tells Luke, "The Force can have a strong influence on the weak-minded.") All these cavils had less than no effect on the film's overwhelming popularity. A 1980 sequel, *The Empire Strikes Back*, proved almost as popular; it was an equally enjoyable film that related the continuing adventures of Luke Skywalker and his friends.

Close Encounters of the Third Kind resembled *Star Wars* only in

the element of mysticism that skimmed along the surface of the story. Whereas *Star Wars* was a calculated throwback to the past, *Close Encounters* looked ahead to the future, examining with utmost seriousness and even awe the possibility of a face-to-face encounter (the "third kind") with beings from a distant planet. Written and directed by Steven Spielberg, the film centered on a group of people in a small Indiana town who experience a strange manifestation. One, an electrical-power company worker named Roy Neary (Richard Dreyfuss), becomes obsessed with learning the meaning of his experience, especially of the vision of a mountain-like shape that has become implanted in his mind. At the same time, scientists are investigating mysterious worldwide phenomena. Finally, everyone converges at a mountain in Wyoming, where the encounter takes place between humans and the alien creatures. To bursts of electronic music, a vast spaceship lands, bringing with it the alien beings: oddly shaped, glowing, androgynous humanoids with friendly

Overleaf, left, above: Star Wars *(Lucasfilm Ltd./Fox, 1977). A gathering of the film's heroic figures (left to right): Ben Kenobi (Alec Guinness), Han Solo (Harrison Ford), the robots R2D2 and C3PO, Chewbacca, and Luke Skywalker (Mark Hamill).*
Overleaf, left, below: The Empire Strikes Back *(Lucasfilm Ltd./Fox, 1980). The villainous Darth Vader (David Prowse) plots another nefarious scheme. The voice belonged to James Earl Jones.*

intentions. (Only afterward do we wonder about the difference between these benign beings and the mischievous and destructive invisible creatures at the film's beginning.)

This last sequence is by far the most impressive in a film that tends to vacillate between the familiar mumbo jumbo of movie science fiction and solemn scientific speculation on the possibility of life on other planets. The early scenes in which the alien presence disrupts ordinary lives are both amusing and frightening in the style of earlier "space invasion" movies—driving alone at night, Roy Neary is badly shaken by a bizarre experience in which his truck seems to come apart by itself and even move about on its own, while the house of Jillian Guiler (Melinda Dillon) and her small son (Cary Guffey) is subject to weird phenomena in which electrical gadgets run wild and the boy's toys come to life. (The boy's delight in the phenomena and his unquestioning acceptance of the alien beings reflect a frequent Spielberg theme: the pure understanding of childhood.) While all this is happening, scientific and military experts, headed by a French scientist named Lacombe (French director François Truffaut), are trying to decipher musical signals recorded from various UFOs.

The long section of the film in which Roy frantically tries to learn the meaning of his vision tends to become tedious and repetitious, but when the climactic sequence takes place, it proves to be worth the waiting. A phalanx of brilliantly lit UFOs is followed by the landing of the mother ship, an immense circular object with hundreds of illuminated windows. The appearance of the ethereal alien children, the awe and wonder of the onlookers, including Roy and Jillian, the majestic ship glittering in the night sky as it leaves Earth, the soaring music—all converge to make this sequence one of the most beautiful and most moving ever conceived for the genre. Evidently it can be—and frequently has been—interpreted as the cinematic equivalent of a religious experience, a hoped-for manifestation of God on Earth.

Apart from the spaceships and alien invaders, fantasy has flourished in earthbound films. It has taken the form of musicals such as *The Wizard of Oz* and *Mary Poppins*, or materialized as horror films such as *Frankenstein*. It has surfaced in virtually every genre from comedy to mystery, and it is, of course, the mainstay and guiding principle of science-fiction movies. And why not? In art and in literature, the element of fantasy has always excited people's imaginations, giving wing to their most extravagant flights of fancy. In our own time, the increasing ingenuity of film and the remarkable techniques developed by special-effects experts have made any illusion possible, from the conjuring of otherworldly spirits to the creation of an entire futuristic civilization. Moviegoers want to be moved and provoked; they enjoy being challenged. But they also crave the undemanding exhilaration that fantasy offers, and they treasure the films that offer it to them in heaping portions.

Of all the films that have blended fantasy with adventure, none has captured the imagination or retained the affection of the public

as has *King Kong* (1933). For half a century, the giant ape destroyed by his love for a woman has stirred pity and terror in audiences who are surely aware by this time that he was only eighteen inches high, the end product of an ingenious process combining animation, miniatures, and trick photography. Imitations have come and gone (including a ponderous 1976 remake), but the original *King Kong*, for all its crudity, remains a classic example of cinematic folklore.

The origins and sources of *King Kong* have been often recorded. Basically, the film was a longstanding dream of Merian C. Cooper, new head of production at RKO Studios, who envisioned a modern version of "Beauty and the Beast" in which a huge gorilla, transported from his jungle home, would wreak havoc on Manhattan. The dream became reality with the help of director (and Cooper's former partner) Ernest B. Schoedsack and special-effects wizard Willis O'Brien, whose "stop-motion" process could bring inanimate objects to life on the screen. Innovative techniques were combined with the then-current vogues for adventure films with on-location footage and stories of marauding beasts. After all these years, the result remains an occasion for wonder and amazement.

Codirected by Merian Cooper and Ernest Schoedsack, *King Kong* has many memorable scenes, but it never rises above the routine in its early portions. The dialogue is either bland or overemphatic as an expedition, headed by movie producer Carl Denham (Robert Armstrong), sails uncharted waters to mysterious Skull Island to seek out the legend known as Kong. But once Kong makes his appearance (to the relentless sound of Max Steiner's celebrated score), the adventure moves into high gear. A towering creature, Kong is lost the moment he sees Ann Darrow (Fay Wray); his attacks on the invaders and his raging battles with other creatures are precipitated by his adoration of Ann.

The best scenes in *King Kong* evoke admiration not only for their technical skill—the sudden emergence of a prehistoric sea monster and its fierce pursuit and destruction of members of the ship's crew is a small miracle of model animation—but also for their ability to excite the viewer even after repeated screenings. When Kong crashes through the massive doors that have kept him safely from the natives, he seems like some demonic force of nature, crushing everything in its path. Yet, cleverly, the film implants a residue of sympathy in the audience's mind. Kong is a terrifying beast, but he is also a creature wronged—his domain invaded, his life threatened, his toy-woman spirited away. Once Kong is bombed into submission, our sympathy increases, and when he is chained up and put on display in a New York theater, he has earned our compassion.

Kong breaks loose to terrorize the city, and our ambivalent attitude toward him—should he be pitied or destroyed?—creates a tension and an excitement that have seldom been matched, even in far more polished movies. His rampage through the streets has moments of genuine fright (who can forget Kong's huge eye appearing at the window of an elevated train?); when he is atop the Empire State Building, besieged by airplanes, he becomes a kind of heroic

---

Preceding page: Close Encounters of the Third Kind *(Columbia, 1977). Little Cary Guffey played the boy who responds innocently to the mischievous visitors from outer space. Steven Spielberg's film is the screen's most vivid expression to date of man's hopeful belief in the presence of benign, intelligent life on other planets.*
Opposite: King Kong *(RKO, 1933). The mighty Kong attempts to dislodge the ship's crew from a log over a ravine. Below: Master of all he surveys in his jungle domain (but not for long), Kong defies the men who have come to take him. In the end, Kong inspired more pity than revulsion.*

figure. Although his demise is hardly the stuff of tragedy, when he topples to his death, we feel a pang of sorrow and regret for the Beast killed by Beauty.

Like many mythic films over the years, *King Kong* has been weighted down with a variety of allegorical meanings. It has been interpreted in Marxist terms: the enslavement of the powerful but ignorant masses, straining to break their bonds. It has been called a diatribe against the brutality of civilized man. Some have called it a demonstration of the dire things that occur when natural sexual impulses are thwarted. Occasionally the movie has been viewed from both sides of the racist coin. On one side, it is seen as proof positive that unfettered blacks will surely run roughshod over fair-skinned women. On the other, it has been said to show that blacks have a formidable strength that will overwhelm and destroy their oppressors. No doubt these views would shock and dismay Messrs. Cooper, Schoedsack, and O'Brien. All they do is indicate that a legendary film such as *King Kong* can be anything one wants it to be.

In addition to *King Kong*, the year 1933 also saw the release of a film adapted from a novel by H. G. Wells. *The Invisible Man* was fantasy tinged with horror and a clever variation of the "mad scientist" theme: a scientist named Jack Griffin (Claude Rains in his film debut) discovers a drug that renders him invisible, but the side effects turn him into a raving megalomaniac plotting to conquer the world. Playwright R. C. Sherriff's screenplay combines black humor and genuine terror in almost equal proportions; Griffin's bizarre appearance when he tries to hide his invisibility, especially the huge dark glasses that dominate his completely bandaged face, generates fright as well as a few laughs at the expense of the bewildered police and townspeople. Director James Whale gives the film the stylish, expressionistic touches he had brought to *Frankenstein* and would later bring to *The Bride of Frankenstein*. Claude Rains is heard but not seen for most of the film, yet he succeeds in giving a

fine performance; his mellifluous voice projects every change in his obsessed character.

Giant apes and demented scientists aside, one name towers above all others in the area of film fantasy—that of Walt Disney. Early in 1928, Disney conceived of an amiable mouse named Mickey, small in stature but enormous in his relation to film history. Mickey was followed by cartoons that advanced the art of animation and delighted audiences with their clever effects and infectious good cheer. With painstaking care, Disney and his artists strove for perfection in an area that was only starting to develop.

Throughout the thirties, Disney's Mickey Mouse and "Silly Symphony" cartoons were popular diversions. But Disney was ambitious, and by the mid-thirties, with the aid of a revolutionary machine called the multiplane camera, which made it possible to achieve a sense of deep perspective in animation, he ventured into feature-length movies. The first, *Snow White and the Seven Dwarfs* (1937), marked a turning point in his career.

In later films, the Disney animators were able to refine and improve their techniques, but the sweet, simple story of Snow White and the seven little men who befriend her retains an appeal to which unsophisticated audiences can still respond. Mostly, *Snow White* introduced in a feature-length film the style and the approach that would evolve into Disney trademarks: the blending of fantasy figures with realistically drawn backgrounds; the graceful movement and artful touches of characterization given to the animal characters; and especially the knockabout slapstick used as comic relief to the main story. In *Snow White* the comic relief virtually stole the show: there is little doubt that the adorable dwarfs, each with his own distinct personality, were the film's funniest and most memorable creations. At the same time, the movie betrayed the weaknesses that would become familiar in criticisms of Disney films, particularly the insipid look of the hero and heroine and scenes that could easily terrify small children, such as Snow White's flight through the forest and the transformation of the wicked Queen into a haggard, poison-dispensing crone. (The latter sequence, however, was brilliantly animated.)

Pinocchio (1940) was a decided improvement over *Snow White*, and one of Disney's best feature films. Animated with remarkable attention to detail, this version of Collodi's celebrated story of a wooden puppet's adventures had all the ingredients for a first-rate Disney entertainment: a group of colorful characters; a series of events that test Pinocchio's worthiness to become a real boy (including a frightening trip to Pleasure Island and a fierce encounter with Monstro the Whale); and a batch of cheerful songs, including "An Actor's Life for Me" and "When You Wish Upon a Star." Here the shortcomings—a flatness in the human characters (even Pinocchio is not as amusing as his animal friends and enemies) and a penchant for frightening the audience (the scene on Pleasure Island, especially the transformation of Pinocchio's friend Lampwick into a donkey, is disturbing in its horror)—are far outweighed by the many virtues.

Above: The Invisible Man *(Universal, 1933). The mysteriously shrouded figure of scientist Jack Griffin (Claude Rains) gives Una O'Connor a turn.*
Opposite, above: Snow White and the Seven Dwarfs *(Disney, 1937). A tranquil scene in the forest with Snow White, the dwarfs, and her animal friends.*
Opposite, center: Pinocchio *(Disney, 1940). Pinocchio and Jiminy Crickett share a reflective moment. Right: Pinocchio is introduced by the cruel puppetmaster, Stromboli.*
Opposite, below: Bambi *(Disney, 1942). Bambi with his friends Thumper (rabbit) and Flower (skunk).*

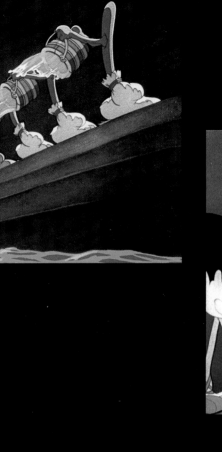

One of Disney's most popular animated features after *Pinocchio* was *Bambi* (1942). Derived from Felix Salten's children's classic, it was a beautifully animated film about the forest adventures of a princely fawn, particularly his encounters with that deadliest of enemies, Man. Although some scenes were excessively sticky and the death of Bambi's mother upset many children, *Bambi* had more than its share of effective scenes, especially the grown hero's battle with another buck for the attentions of the doe Faline.

No Disney film of the early forties was as ambitious or as controversial as his production of *Fantasia* (1940). It began as a cartoon in which Mickey Mouse cavorted to the music of Paul Dukas's *The Sorcerer's Apprentice*, conducted by no less a personage than Leopold Stokowski. The great conductor suggested to Disney that they expand the idea to include a wide range of musical compositions that would be visually interpreted by Disney's artists. Intrigued by the concept, Disney began work on *Fantasia*, bringing in the popular composer and musicologist Deems Taylor to be on-screen commentator (and to lighten the heavy aura of cultural uplift that hovered over the project). Predictably, the finished film drew an outraged response from many critics, especially those who felt that great music was not meant to be visualized, but many others were delighted by its beauty and imagination.

Although every viewer has a favorite section, there are those that are almost universally admired. Most of Tchaikovsky's *Nutcracker Suite* is exquisitely or amusingly animated; one recalls with pleasure the "Chinese Dance" performed by mushrooms or the lovely underwater setting for the "Arabian Dance." The original segment, *The Sorcerer's Apprentice*, in which Mickey Mouse unwisely assumes the powers of his master, is cleverly executed, and Igor Stravinsky's *The Rite of Spring* becomes an astonishing visualization of the creation of the Earth and the dawn of history. This segment contains a number of memorable moments, none more so than one in which prehistoric animals, dying in the blazing heat, raise their huge, majestic heads to the pitiless sun. The film's most delightful section, however, is a ballet to Ponchielli's "Dance of the Hours," hilariously performed by a corps of ostriches, hippos, elephants, and crocodiles. (The sight of the hippo ballerina emerging daintily from a lily pool is delightfully comic.) The film ends with Mussorgsky's *Night on Bald Mountain* followed by Schubert's "Ave Maria," demonstrating the continuing battle between the sacred and the profane. *Fantasia* has had its detractors over the years, but at its best it is an entrancing example of the animator's art.

Four decades after Disney's best animated features, the magic they evoked was combined with the perennial wonder of outer space to create the unforgettable adventure-fantasy of *E.T.: The Extra-Terrestrial* (1982). As of this writing, Steven Spielberg's film has become the highest grossing in film history, assuring the endearing little alien a permanent place in movie annals. Clearly, *E.T.* has appealed to all groups of moviegoers; with the kind of deep-rooted pleasure that eventually lifts film into legend, they have responded to the fable-like story of the frail, ugly, but intelligent creature from another planet who is inadvertently left behind by his spaceship. E.T.'s adventures on Earth—his befriending by a boy named Elliott (Henry Thomas), and the strong ties that develop between them as Elliott seeks to hide E.T. from the authorities—make up the heart of Melissa Mathison's screenplay.

The film weaves its spell from the very beginning: as seen from E.T.'s point of view, we are lost on an alien planet where the tall trees and noisy automobiles are terrifying, and where flashlights seem like alien creatures. Actually, we are in a California community where young Elliott lives with his divorced mother (Dee Wallace), his older brother Mike (Robert Macnaughton), and his little sister Gert (Drew Barrymore). (One of the movie's many diverting features is the convincing family dialogue.) After their initial fright and awe, the children accept E.T. with the unquestioning warmth and understanding only they can muster, and they prevent the adults—seen only as dark, ominous beings without much form or substance—from discovering their alien friend. They also learn more about E.T.—that he can learn to speak their language, that he has the power to heal and other magical gifts, and that he is a shy, frightened being in a bewildering world. It also becomes apparent that E.T. can transmit his feelings to Elliott and, most seriously, that he is slowly dying in Earth's atmosphere.

The first part of the film is funny and charming as E.T. and the children come to understand one another and a curious E.T. explores his new environment. The Halloween adventure of E.T. and the children is a delightful sequence, especially when E.T. makes Elliott's bicycle soar into the air with joyful ease. But once E.T.'s presence is discovered, a deeper response is called for. The adults become truly frightening—the men in spacesuits seem sinister and grotesque—and a dying E.T. evokes genuine pathos, especially when Elliott, linked to E.T. in feeling, appears to be expiring as well. Elliott's farewell to E.T., manipulative of the audience as it may be, is infinitely touching: "You must be dead because I don't know how to feel. I'll believe in you all my life, every day. . . . E.T., I love you." But E.T. is reborn, and the film returns to cheerful adventure as Elliott and his friends, pursued by the authorities, take E.T. to his spaceship. (When all the boys take wing on their bicycles, it is an exhilarating moment.) A bittersweet but satisfying ending has E.T. leaving Earth for his home planet.

Like many mythic films, *E.T.* is subject to various interpretations. Clearly, it is meant as a reflection of the instinctive generosity and understanding of children versus the obtuseness of adults. (The only understanding adult is the scientist who can relate to Elliott's feelings and who tells him, "I've been waiting for this since I was ten years old.") This lofty view of childhood has surfaced in films and literature over the years, and the fact that it is fallacious and possibly harmful has not kept it down. More specifically, *E.T.* relates to well-loved films of the past. There is more than one indication that its links to *The Wizard of Oz* were intentional. E.T., in a sense, is the Dorothy of the 1980s, lost in a threatening, topsy-turvy world he cannot fathom and helped by a group of friends. He, like Dorothy,

Opposite: Fantasia *(Disney, 1940). Above and center, left: "The Sorcerer's Apprentice," otherwise known as Mickey Mouse, dreams of taking his master's place. He finds, however, that he is unable to control his magic, and the brooms get out of hand. Center, right, and below: An ostrich ballerina prances merrily through a double chorus line, and a pair of hippos dance gracefully in two moments from Ponchielli's "Dance of the Hours."*

Preceding pages and above: E.T.: The Extra-Terrestrial *(Universal, 1982). Elliott (Henry Thomas) peers apprehensively at E.T., his lovable friend from outer space, who is languishing in Earth's foreign atmosphere. Above: E.T.'s spaceship soars into the night sky. Steven Spielberg's film was an enchanting fantasy that fully deserved its extraordinary popularity.*

only wants to get "home," and the last scene, in which he bids everyone a tearful, painful farewell, closely resembles Dorothy's departure from the land of Oz. There is also more than a passing resemblance to Walt Disney's animated features—like the protagonists of *Snow White and the Seven Dwarfs* and *Pinocchio*, E.T. revives from a deathlike state just in time for a happy ending.

E.T. has also been given religious connotations. Much has been written about E.T.'s Christlike characteristics: his gift of healing with a simple touch, his ability to enter the minds and hearts of those who love him, his very presence on a planet where many are not willing to accept him. Elliott's parting statement to E.T., "I'll believe in you all my life," can be interpreted as a testimony of faith, and E.T.'s last words, "I'll be right here," could well be a paraphrase of Christ's "I am with you alway." As E.T.'s spaceship

lifts into the air to John Williams's stirring music, Elliott's mother kneels in awe and reverence. The concept may be valid or far-fetched, but it is only one possible way of looking at this enchanting movie.

E.T. soars home, but no doubt other extraterrestrials will come along to replace him. As long as we reflect on the possibility of life on distant planets, or project civilization eons into the future, or invent creatures of our imagination, filmmakers will venture into the realms of science fiction and fantasy. The results may be more fanciful than factual in the case of scientific speculation, and the films may provide more exercise for the eyes than for the mind. But those we have considered at least tell us what scientists have always told us: no limit can be placed on the possibilities of tomorrow.

Above: E.T.: The Extra-Terrestrial *(Universal, 1982). A moment of pure movie magic as Elliott (Henry Thomas) and his friend from outer space soar into the air.*
Overleaf: Our Town *(Sol Lesser/United Artists, 1940). Emily Webb (Martha Scott) and George Gibbs (William Holden) are married in a scene from the film version of the Thornton Wilder play. The story of Grovers Corners was tender and nostalgic, with intimations of sadness. The lovely but unobtrusive score was by Aaron Copland.*

FACES OF
A NATION

THE WAY WE ARE
Great Movies on American Life

For decades, the movies have been a mirror reflecting what we are, how we behave, and especially how we see ourselves—as people and as Americans. If the images are often colored or distorted, if they frequently conceal harsh truths or suggest false values, they have also shaped and affected how we perceive the many threads that make up the fabric of America. In darkened theaters, we have been asked to consider the nature of the American family—is it a bulwark against trouble, or itself the rooted source of the trouble? We have visited American small towns where we may be greeted either by a hearty welcome and a warming cup of tea, or by the mindless brutality of a vengeful mob. We have stood in farmlands both flourishing and arid, or stalked the streets of our cities at night, disoriented by our loss of identity in the faceless crowd.

In dealing with American life over the years, the movies have clearly tried to show us both sides of the coin; they have presented contrasts in light and dark. Whether we interpret this as evasiveness or as an attempt to be evenhanded, the result has been a number of worthy films on the changing face of America.

During the formative years of motion pictures, and well into the decades beyond, the heart of American life resided in its small towns. In the modest but neat, comfortable, tree-shaded houses of David Harum's Homeville or Andy Hardy's Carvel, families lived in general harmony and contentment, loving, steadfast, and devoted to each other's needs. Main Street harbored friendly shopkeepers, town hall was the setting for clamorous community meetings, and the church offered sheltering peace. If there were problems to resolve or sorrows to share (*something* had to happen), all difficult matters were happily settled by the final frame. In scores of movies, this idyllic view prevailed, and yet serenity and sweetness does not generate high drama. Although audiences appreciated and attended the many homespun movies, the more durable films attempted to penetrate the shiny façade, to look beyond the friendliness, the gentility, and the puritanical morality.

Sometimes the approach was lightly tongue-in-cheek or satirical—Frank Capra's gangly hero of *Mr. Deeds Goes to Town* (1936) was called "pixilated" by two elderly spinsters from his home town who were clearly much more "pixilated" than he was. In Preston Sturges's *Hail the Conquering Hero* (1944), the townspeople who whoop it up for "hero" Woodrow Truesmith were characterized as a pack of fools and louts. Even *Alice Adams* (1935), RKO's adaptation of Booth Tarkington's novel about a socially ambitious young wallflower, took several well-aimed swipes at small-town snobbery.

Alice Adams, played by Katharine Hepburn with the odd mixture of charm and eccentricity that characterized a number of her early performances, is not exactly the belle of South Renford. Pathetic,

wistful, and vulnerable, she is also affected, preening, and obsessed with the need to be accepted in the town's social circle. She bears the burden of an obtuse and vulgar family; at the same time, she encourages her own isolation from those she would impress by refusing to modify her offbeat ways. In short, Alice Adams is her own person and a rather unusual movie heroine for the period. During the course of the film, she finally manages to win Arthur Mitchell (Fred MacMurray), the town "catch" and the man of her dreams.

Under George Stevens's direction, Katharine Hepburn somehow avoids all the pitfalls and succeeds in making Alice more entrancing than irritating. Entering a society party down a flight of stairs, she brings a breath of fresh air into a stale and pompous environment; in her simple gown, she makes the overdressed society girls look foolish. Afterward, humiliated by her brother's obnoxious behavior, she stands sobbing at her rain-swept window in an image of hopelessness that Hepburn makes convincing and touching. Elation followed by despair keeps Alice on an emotional roller coaster: deliriously happy when Arthur becomes her suitor—he recognizes class when he sees it—she is distraught when, after keeping him away from her family (she has lied about their social status), she is forced to invite him to dinner, where the truth about them is finally exposed. This dinner scene is one of the highlights of thirties films: damaged beyond repair by Hattie McDaniel as the world's most slovenly maid, the dinner becomes a tragicomic nightmare as one thing after another goes dreadfully wrong. Unconvincingly, the movie opts for a happy ending, with Arthur confessing his love for her despite everything and Alice responding with an inadequate "Gee whiz!"

Opposite: Ordinary People *(Paramount, 1980). The wrenching estrangement of mother and son is suggested in this scene with Mary Tyler Moore and Timothy Hutton. Hutton's award-winning performance was a stunningly true portrait of a teenager in torment. Above:* Alice Adams *(RKO, 1935). The classic dinner scene from George Stevens's version of the Booth Tarkington novel. The participants (left to right): Ann Shoemaker, Fred MacMurray, Katharine Hepburn, and Fred Stone. The wonderfully slovenly maid is Hattie McDaniel.*

Alice Adams took a lightly jaundiced view of small-town snobbery, but most films were generally inclined to treat the residents of Main Street with kindness. Their essential warmth and decency cast a glow over the 1940 adaptation of Thornton Wilder's Pulitzer Prize–winning play *Our Town*, and yet nostalgia for a vanished time was hardly the sole intention of this haunting film. The 1938 play had been in the nature of an experiment; without the use of scenery, it had transported the audience to three different periods in the life of Grovers Corners, New Hampshire. By stripping away the familiar trappings of the theater, it had attempted to reveal the universal or the cosmic within simple, everyday events.

With Sam Wood as director, the film version modified the play's stylization but retained the basic stage device in which the omniscient Stage Manager (played, as in the theater, by Frank Craven) takes the viewer into Grovers Corners, offering basic information on the town's history and politics, interrupting the action at will, and introducing the small but crucial episodes in the lives of the principal characters: the discovery of first love, a wedding, and a funeral. Largely through the eyes of next-door neighbors Emily Webb (Martha Scott) and George Gibbs (William Holden), whose romance and marriage form the core of the story, we come to see the larger pattern within the innumerable small details that make up the fabric of life. The rituals of our existence, the stages by which we all move from birth to death, are made clear and immutable in the homely conversation of ordinary people.

For the most part, *Our Town* manages to steer an even course without stumbling into mawkishness, although its ultimate message—that we should live every moment of every day—is not exactly profound. Frank Craven's Stage Manager provides a steadying influence as he amiably and wryly allows us to eavesdrop on the people of Grovers Corners. In one of the most memorable scenes, George and Emily exchange teenage confidences at night from their respective bedrooms, and the effect is ineffably touching. ("The moonlight's so *terrible*," Emily tells George in one of Wilder's many apt and evocative lines.) Before his wedding, George has an awkward but loving conversation with his father, and at the ceremony, each person expresses his private thoughts; we are moved by the depth of feeling in simple folk. In the last sequence, Emily is allowed to relive one day of her life (presumably she has died in childbirth), and she chooses her sixteenth birthday. As she moves unseen among the members of her family, all heedless of their fates, her mixture of joy and despair leads to the film's most lyrical moment, in which Emily cries, "Oh, earth, you're too wonderful for anybody to realize you!" By this time, Wilder has made it evident that "our town" really refers to our "wonderful earth." His play—and its film version—is not merely an ode to small-town life, shadowed as it is by sadness, but to life itself.

Not even *Our Town* was all sweetness and light—the characters included an alcoholic choirmaster who commits suicide—but its view of small-town life was virtually rose-colored compared with that of several other films of the period. Occasionally, a studio was bold enough to expose the small town as a repository of bigotry,

criminality, and aberrant behavior, revealing the evil that lurked behind drawn shades, or confronting the submerged hatred that suddenly turned quiet small-town folks into a violent mob. One such film was MGM's blistering drama *Fury* (1936).

Produced by the studio with considerable trepidation and caution, *Fury* was the first American film directed by Fritz Lang after two years of frustrating inactivity in Hollywood. It offered a bleak, unsparing vision of a small midwestern town—carefully unidentified —that is deeply stained with the bloodlust of its citizens. The film's hero, Joe Wilson (Spencer Tracy), while driving to see his fiancée, Katherine (Sylvia Sidney), is falsely arrested on a charge of kidnapping. A mob, whipped into hysteria by a local rabble-rouser, burns down the jail in which Joe is sequestered. Somehow, he escapes the fire, but the mob leaders are brought to trial and convicted for his "murder." Now a grim angel of vengeance, Joe would allow the sentence to stand, but a change of heart leaves the defendants punished only by their own guilt and mortification.

Fury offers another of Fritz Lang's fate-hounded heroes, but it is an angrier, much more straightforward indictment of society than

Fury *(MGM, 1936). A mob attempts to break down the jail in which an innocent Spencer Tracy is being held on suspicion of kidnapping. Below: Joe Wilson (Spencer Tracy) returns from the dead to confront the man (Bruce Cabot) who led the hate-crazed mob that almost destroyed him. Fritz Lang's first American movie was a corrosive study of mob violence.*

his subsequent film, *You Only Live Once*. In *You Only Live Once*, escaped convict Henry Fonda and his young wife (Sylvia Sidney again) are pursued by the police and die in a hail of bullets. Yet they never really confront their true enemy, which is a cold, hostile society that will not let them live in peace. In *Fury*, however, Joe Wilson's enemy is brutally visible: a mob of revenge-minded people, their faces contorted with rage as they scream for a lynching. Lang gives this key scene a primal force: he takes us into the mob and shows us the frantic plight of the victim and the helpless terror of the girl who loves him. The cold, unpitying Joe Wilson who emerges from the ashes of the jail resembles another Joe—the despairing fugitive who cries, "I steal!" at the close of Mervyn LeRoy's *I Am a Fugitive from a Chain Gang* (1932).

Fury may cool down at the end, but it raises a few blisters along the way. Lang's grim view of American justice occasionally leads to melodramatic excess, but Spencer Tracy succeeds in keeping the

events moored to reality with one of the strongest and most persuasive of his thirties performances. Starting as a man baffled by the accusation against him ("Am I the only guy in the world that eats peanuts?"), he ends as a ravaged, embittered figure; his speech to his brothers justifying his refusal to stop the murder trial of the mob leaders is one of Tracy's finest moments. With savage irony he argues that if the law was mocked in an attempt to murder him, so can the law now be used to condemn his murderers. He changes his mind, however, and later, in a stunned courtroom, he says he was obliged to return to save the lives of the defendants. But the damage is permanent; no longer can he believe in justice or civilized man, or, especially, in his country. To Joe, all the Grovers Corners have vanished, and violence exists next door to small-town tranquillity.

The idea that America's small towns were hotbeds of hostility and secret vices continued to surface occasionally in other decades. In the forties, Warners's *Kings Row* (1942) depicted a town in which sadism,

To Kill a Mockingbird *(Universal, 1963). Atticus Finch (Gregory Peck) defends Tom Robinson*
(Brock Peters) on a charge of attempted rape in the courtroom scene from this sensitive drama
based on Harper Lee's novel. Gregory Peck's stolid, understated acting style suited his role
perfectly; his Academy Award was well deserved.

insanity, and sexual hysteria seemed almost as common as quilting and church socials. In the fifties, the most corrupt community in the nation was evidently *Peyton Place* (1957), which Fox fashioned out of Grace Metalious's best-selling novel. In this overheated drama, exquisite color photography of New England could hardly gloss over the sordid events that rocked the town, which included suicide, rape, murder, and incest. By contrast, the sleepy Southern town in *To Kill a Mockingbird* (1963) seemed almost tame; its main concern, during a hot summer in the early thirties, was the sensational trial of a black man accused of raping a white girl.

Adapted by Horton Foote from Harper Lee's popular novel, *To Kill a Mockingbird* offered a sensitive and atmospheric view of small-town life in the Depression years, but actually it was more interested in evoking the unseen, unknown terrors of childhood, and in a child's first perception of bigotry. The young son and daughter of Atticus Finch (Gregory Peck), the lawyer defending the black man, come to understand how justice can be thwarted and perverted, how familiar surroundings can suddenly turn inexplicably frightening, and how love and caring can finally heal all wounds.

Directed effectively by Robert Mulligan, although at somewhat too leisurely a pace, and beautifully photographed in black-and-white by Russell Harlan, *To Kill a Mockingbird* is narrated by Atticus's daughter, Scout, who recalls that crucial summer when she was six and her brother Jem was ten. There are the familiar small joys and tribulations of childhood, as well as the fears. But the event that looms largest is the trial and conviction of Tom Robinson (Brock Peters), falsely accused of attacking sluttish Mayella Ewell (Collin Wilcox). Through the children's eyes, we witness the rabid racism of many townspeople, set against the honesty, compassion, and warmth of their father.

Although *To Kill a Mockingbird* runs too long, many of its sequences adeptly convey the curiosity and bafflement of children caught up in events too large for them to grasp. At an attempted lynching of Tom Robinson, Scout (Mary Badham) innocently greets one of the men in the mob and shames them all into leaving, and at the trial, no comment is made when she and Jem (Philip Alford) quietly seat themselves in the black section of the courtroom. The film's finest moment comes when Atticus makes his eloquent summation to the jury, speaking in measured but passionate tones about the quest for truth in the face of prejudice.

By the late sixties and early seventies, Hollywood's idea of small-town life was far from Andy Hardy's Carvel, but no audience was likely to believe that every town was Peyton Place. The prevalent attitude seemed to be that the changing mores of the fifties, followed by the social and political upheavals of the sixties, had drastically affected the lives of Americans, especially the young people, and that the most telling and devastating impact could be felt in the small towns that had once taken pride in their traditions and their sense of continuity.

One of the most impressive and widely discussed films in this vein was Peter Bogdanovich's *The Last Picture Show*, released by

Columbia in 1971 to enthusiastic reviews. Adapted by Bogdanovich and Larry McMurty from McMurty's novel, the film was an attempt to crystallize the ways of life and attitudes of the fifties; in particular, it focused on the forces that were eroding the small oil town of Anarene, Texas, altering its face forever. Part nostalgia, part social commentary, the movie centered on the misadventures (mainly sexual) of Sonny Crawford (Timothy Bottoms) and Duane Jackson (Jeff Bridges), high school seniors without purpose or direction whose aimlessness mirrors the town's own drift toward oblivion. Sonny's dalliance with the frustrated middle-aged wife (Cloris Leachman) of the school coach and Duane's affair with the spoiled, social-climbing Jacy Farrow (Cybill Shepherd) end in bitterness and regret.

The Last Picture Show accurately re-creates the look and sounds of the fifties (songs of the period play continually on the soundtrack), and Robert Surtees's black-and-white photography of gray landscapes, shabby stores, and desolate prairie streets does an outstanding job of conveying a sense of the town's nearly terminal bleakness. But the movie's intention is not merely verisimilitude. Its overall tone is one of sadness: sadness for the dissatisfied, roaming youths who cannot get themselves to break the chains that bind them to the town, and for the older people whose frustrations have deepened over the years as they watch their hopes wither and die in the increasingly torpid atmosphere. Young or old, these people are both confused and propelled by their sexual drives and torn between restlessness and lethargy. The young people seem perched uneasily between the war-committed generation of the forties and the upcoming protest generation of the sixties. Bogdanovich observes them in retrospect with compassion rather than satire, providing a rueful but honest portrait of small-town America at low ebb.

While *The Last Picture Show* was touted as a youth film, it is actually more adept at dealing with its middle-aged characters. Cloris Leachman's Ruth Popper is a touching portrait of loneliness

Above: The Last Picture Show *(Columbia, 1971). Sonny Crawford (Timothy Bottoms) talks with the coach's lonely wife, Ruth Popper (Cloris Leachman), in a scene from Peter Bogdanovich's observant, moving account of life in Anarene, Texas, in the fifties. Opposite:* American Graffiti *(Universal, 1973). In George Lucas's evocative film of small-town life in the early sixties, Candy Clark and Charlie Martin Smith take a pause in their nocturnal ramblings. Below: Candy Clark and Charlie Martin Smith stop to share a beer with Ronny Howard.*

and self-hatred, and Ellen Burstyn is fine as Jacy's mother, Lois. The film's best performance is given by Ben Johnson as Sam the Lion, a former cowboy and the owner of the local pool hall, café, and movie theater. Sam's death clearly represents the death of the pioneer spirit and the passing of a gentler, more serene way of life, just as the closing of the movie house marks a major step in the transition of Anarene from bustling community to ghost town.

Another reflection of recent American small-town life appeared in George Lucas's second feature film, *American Graffiti* (1973). The time was 1962, the place was a small town in California, and the film evoked the teenagers' mores and attitudes of the period: the pranks, the sexual rituals, the boredom, the restlessness, and, above all, the sudden sense of change. More of a summation of the complacent, acquisitive fifties than a comment on the turbulent sixties, the original screenplay by Lucas, Gloria Katz, and Willard Huyck covered twelve hours—evening to the following morning—in the lives of four friends: Curt (Richard Dreyfuss), the town "intellectual" who is about to leave for college; Steve (Ronny Howard), also college-bound but emotionally tied to the town and his girlfriend, Laurie (Cindy Williams); Terry (Charlie Martin Smith), known affectionately as "Toad," bumbling but amiable, and John (Paul Le Mat), a strutting hot rodder. During the one night, the four experience mishaps and misadventures, mostly comic; at the same time, decisions are made and lives are changed, all to the sounds of rock music and interminably "cruising" cars.

American Graffiti is a sunnier film than *The Last Picture Show*—its town is not heading toward the dusty end of oblivion, and if there are any frustrated or defeated adults around, they are invisible. Much of the movie is very funny, especially when Toad, wanting to impress his none-too-bright pickup for the evening (Candy Clark), tries to buy liquor. Yet the film also has a residue of unsentimental toughness in its view of restricted young lives and the passing of youth. As Curt experiences his last night in town, he is actually bidding a rueful farewell to childhood. We see him moving through the school locker room, a smile of remembrance on his face, or paying a visit to the disc jockey "Wolfman Jack," whose music is ubiquitous throughout the film. In one quiet but revealing scene, he and Steve discuss the virtues and disadvantages of leaving home, their voices tinged with fear and false bravado, and it is here that we see the difference between *American Graffiti* and previous films on small-town life. While the rites of passage have hardly changed over the years, *American Graffiti* probed, more deeply than other movies, the ambiguous feelings they engendered: love for the place called home vs. the sense of being stifled by its smallness; the need to be embraced by the community vs. the fear of being held too tightly.

If the movies saw small-town life as both cheerful and depressing, there was usually little ambivalence about their attitude toward life in America's cities. In the abstract, cities were glamorous, exciting places that held the promise of adventure and fulfillment—romance

could be found in a penthouse apartment, backstage at a theater, or even in Pennsylvania Station. In scores of glittering films, the city was meant to be "conquered" by talent; its impressive skyline was a challenge, an invitation, a thrilling recurrent dream.

But this wasn't reality—this wasn't true "city life." The swank penthouses occupied by Joan Crawford and Norma Shearer were only symbols representing their upward mobility—they could look out over the river with John Garfield or Clark Gable and see how far they had come. When films moved into the city streets, it was a different matter. The puritan ethic took over and the cinematic cities became places of violence and sin, inhabited by gangsters, thieves, schemers, hopeless dreamers, and greedy, seductive women. Lust, vengeance, and sudden death lurked in the shadows cast by the tall buildings; the luckier people merely had their hearts broken or their wallets stolen.

In the twenties, the city was either a snare that swallowed up unwary farm folk, as in F. W. Murnau's *Sunrise*, or a heartless entity oblivious to suffering, as in King Vidor's *The Crowd*. One of the finest films of the late silent period, this was a simple but affecting tale of a young couple, John and Mary Sims (James Murray and Eleanor Boardman), who experience small triumphs and overwhelming tragedy as they strive to eke out an existence in a cold, indifferent city. The movie traces their courtship and marriage, John's inability to get ahead despite his high hopes, and the accidental death of their daughter, which nearly destroys their lives. Vidor filmed no fewer than seven different endings, finally giving exhibitors a choice of two: one in which John becomes successful, and another in which John, Mary, and their surviving child attend a vaudeville show. As they laugh at a clown, the camera pans back to show them lost in the crowd.

Despite its air of sober realism (the exteriors were filmed on location in New York City, Buffalo, and Niagara Falls), *The Crowd*

The Crowd (MGM, 1927). James Murray and Eleanor Boardman mourn the death of their child in King Vidor's superb drama of an ordinary American couple. Murray, an unknown actor chosen by Vidor for this role, came to his own tragic end. His career suffered a steady decline, and in 1936 his body was found floating in the Hudson River.

has a number of expressionistic touches influenced by the German cinema. When John as a boy climbs a tenement staircase to learn of his father's death, he moves toward the camera, his eyes wide with fear, until his face fills the screen. To dramatize the hero's anonymity in the crowd, the camera glides up a huge office building and through the window of an enormous room, then over the tops of many identical desks to discover John at work, one small figure out of many. The film's most moving scene occurs when John's child lies dying, and a distraught John rushes into the noisy street, pleading for quiet. The din continues, however, and a callous policeman says, "Get inside! The world can't stop because your baby's sick!" John has become a cipher in the city that is indifferent to pain and

suffering—a view of urban life that would be reflected many times over in future films.

In films of the thirties, cities continued to breed the desperate, the lonely, the criminally minded. Occasionally, the implied social comment of *The Crowd* became more overt, as in the film adaptation of Sidney Kingsley's play *Dead End* (1937). The imposing set that Norman Bel Geddes designed for the 1935 stage production, although obviously artificial, was transposed to the screen. It made a clear point of showing the split that existed between classes in the teeming streets of New York City—the towering skyscrapers of the rich on one side, and the shabby riverfront slums on the other. As directed by William Wyler, the filmic *Dead End* was no social tract,

Dead End (Samuel Goldwyn/United Artists, 1937). Some of the "Dead End Kids" assemble at the pier in their slum neighborhood. Left to right: Leo Gorcey, Huntz Hall, Bobby Jordan, and Gabriel Dell.

but it dramatized the dangerous inequities of city life, revealing the seeds of crime that can sprout so easily in the soil of poverty and neglect.

Basically, *Dead End* was melodrama (Lillian Hellman wrote the screenplay, and her forte was always melodrama, despite the "meaningful" underpinnings in her work): Baby Face Martin (Humphrey Bogart), a big-time gangster wanted by the police, returns to his old slum neighborhood where he is ultimately routed by his childhood friend Dave (Joel McCrea), now a poor, struggling architect. At the same time, a gang of rowdy young toughs swaggers through the streets until one boy (Billy Halop) gets into serious trouble. Although the film includes a romantic triangle, it is mostly concerned with contrasting the brash, potentially criminal activities of the street gang with the sinister presence of Baby Face Martin, a grim product of these very slums, whom the gang admires. Aided by the usual expertise of cameraman Gregg Toland, Wyler keeps events churning as Martin, rebuffed by the people he has come to see or disillusioned when his old happy memories turn rancid, smothers his bitter resentment by plotting to kidnap a local rich boy.

The film's nominal stars do competent work, but *Dead End* derives much of its pungency from supporting players, who were each given a brief but bravura acting turn. Repeating her stage role as Mrs. Martin, Marjorie Main spews venom at her son with a ferocity that makes a viewer cringe, and Claire Trevor as Martin's childhood sweetheart Francie suggests a sordid life in only a few minutes of screen time—there is a stunning moment in which her face, hidden in shadow, moves under the light to reveal the painted features of an experienced hooker. The gang members, forever enshrined as the "Dead End Kids" from this point on, play with such assurance that many viewers thought they had been lifted from the city streets to appear in the play and film.

After a decade of *films noirs*, the city remained a permanent setting for both skulduggery-in-darkness and the abuse of downtrodden "little people." In 1954, a gray, unyielding, and threatening New York City, an environment that would not be unfamiliar to the trouble-plagued characters of *The Crowd* and *Dead End*, loomed large in Elia Kazan's production of *On the Waterfront*. Superficially, the film dealt with labor racketeering on the city's docks—one of the few films to deal with the problems of the working man—but Budd Schulberg's screenplay was more concerned with the personal drama of a slightly punchy ex-boxer named Terry Malloy (Marlon Brando). A lackey to dock boss Johnny Friendly (Lee J. Cobb), Terry turns informer when he learns the extent of Friendly's exploitative and murderous power. He is supported by a feisty priest (Karl Malden) and by Edie Doyle (Eva Marie Saint), a girl whose brother is killed by the mob. Terry's brother, Charlie (Rod Steiger), a lawyer in Friendly's pocket, is also murdered. Terry himself is nearly broken, but he survives with his defiance intact.

Although *On the Waterfront* has undeniable flaws, it is a trenchant and expertly made film, with many scenes that have become part of movie legend. In his first scene with Edie, Brando reveals much more than his words can express; his dawning love for her is reflected in his eyes. When he must tell Edie that he was involved in her brother's murder, the wrenching moment is played with dramatic force; his words are drowned out by a boat whistle but we see her anguished reaction. His taxicab scene with his brother is justly celebrated; it reverberates with feelings of loss and regret. "You was my brother," he tells Charlie. "You should have looked out for me a little. I could have had class. I could have been a contender."

With strong material, Elia Kazan is usually able to draw fine performances from his cast, and *On the Waterfront* offers a generally first-rate example of ensemble acting. In her film debut, Eva Marie

Above: On the Waterfront *(Columbia, 1954). In the famous taxicab scene, Terry Malloy (Marlon Brando, right) faces the bitter truth about his life with brother Charlie (Rod Steiger).*
Right: A badly beaten Marlon Brando is helped by Karl Malden and Eva Marie Saint. Boris Kaufman's photography and Leonard Bernstein's score contributed to the film's impact.
Opposite: A lobby card for The Grapes of Wrath *(Fox, 1940). Below: During their trek to California, the Joad family halts to attend to dying Grandpa (Charley Grapewin). Crouching around him are Jane Darwell, Russell Simpson, and Henry Fonda.*

Saint is lovely and touching as Edie—she won an Oscar as Best Supporting Actress—and Lee J. Cobb is forceful if rather strident as Johnny Friendly. Also making his film debut, Rod Steiger trots out his now-familiar vocal mannerisms for the first time; nonetheless, his Charlie is an effective portrait of a decent man destroyed by his willing proximity to corruption. But Marlon Brando dominates the movie, never losing Terry Malloy's inarticulate quality while developing his awareness and sensitivity. From his first disturbed reaction to Joey Doyle's death ("I thought they was goin' to *talk* to him") to the final assertion of his own value ("They always tell me I'm a bum. Well, I ain't a bum!"), Brando makes the character believable and affecting.

In general, rural American life has been depicted in films as a mixed blessing. On the one hand, the farm has been shown as an oasis of quiet and serenity, where crops are abundant and pleasures are homemade; on the other, it has often been perceived as a burden, cursed with unyielding soil, disasters of nature, and threats of foreclosure. Frequently both aspects are in the same film. In such movies as *State Fair* (1933 and 1945) and *Our Vines Have Tender Grapes* (1945), there are occurrences that disturb the placid lives—a prize hog behaves erratically during the fair, children playing in a bathtub are swept into a raging river—but on the whole, events are associated with simple rewards: the winning of a mincemeat competition, the birth of a calf, rituals of love and sharing.

During the Depression years, a few films touched frankly on the farmer's increasing plight. One of these, King Vidor's *Our Daily Bread* (1934), made a simplistic but heartfelt plea for action against the nation's agrarian ills. Subtitled "A Story of Today's Headlines," the film concerned an embattled young man (Tom Keene) who organizes a farming commune and fights to keep it working. Although the movie carefully avoided advocating any one form of government—it seemed more humanistic than communistic—its most famous sequence, the all-out effort to irrigate the land, clearly echoed the use of montage in the Soviet cinema. There were other influences in the film, including suggestions of D. W. Griffith's style, and the subplot, involving the hero's seduction by a brazen woman (Barbara Pepper) and his remorseful return to his wife (Karen Morley), seemed to have been lifted out of F. W. Murnau's *Sunrise*. Yet for all of its derivative qualities, *Our Daily Bread* was a striking example of social-minded filmmaking.

No film has ever expressed the terrible plight of the rural poor in

Our Daily Bread *(King Vidor/United Artists, 1934). Mary Sims (Karen Morley) rings the dinner bell in King Vidor's social drama about America's rural troubles during the Depression years.*

the depressed thirties with greater power than Fox's 1940 adaptation of John Steinbeck's novel *The Grapes of Wrath*. Published to wide acclaim the year before, the novel told the moving story of the Joad family, impoverished Oklahoma Dust Bowl farmers ("Okies") who were forced to flee their drought-plagued land and headed for a new and presumably better life in the "promised land" of California. It combined harsh social commentary on the collapse of an entire class of agrarian people with a near-poetic view of the family's strength in the face of adversity. Nunnally Johnson's screenplay, however, deemphasized the social aspects (except for a few plugs for the New Deal) and concentrated instead on the tribulations of the Joads on their long journey. Henry Fonda starred as Tom Joad, newly released from prison, who rejoins his family, headed by indestructible Ma (Jane Darwell). They move from one transient camp to another until Tom, in deep trouble with the police, must leave them again. But now he has been fortified by his experiences; he has learned to rely on his own resources, to stand firm against injustice.

John Ford's direction brings eloquence and force to every scene, whether it involves a bitter clash between the Okies and those who scorn them or the few quiet moments in the course of their wanderings. The deaths of the weary, bewildered Joad grandparents, the moving speech of a grieving man telling about the death by starvation of his children, or the lovely moment in which Tom and Ma dance together at a camp social are as powerful as any scene showing violent encounters. Ford is helped immeasurably by Gregg Toland's photography, which burns the image of the parched and arid land in our memories. The refrain of "Red River Valley" haunts the soundtrack as we watch the Joads confront hostility and hunger. They are people without a home, without rights, and without a sense of an American heritage. Ironically, it is only the senile grandfather (Charley Grapewin) who retains a vestige of his privileges as an American. "This is my country," he tells the others, "and I belong here."

Ultimately, Tom Joad achieves a new awareness, a commitment to social action, and in his last unforgettable scene with Ma, he summarizes his new resolve with a mystical fervor: ". . . I'll be all around in the dark. I'll be everywhere. . . . Wherever there's a fight so hungry people can eat, I'll be there. Wherever there's a cop beatin' up a guy I'll be there. . . . And when people are eatin' the stuff they raise and livin' in the houses they build, I'll be there too."

The beleaguered, resilient men and women created by John Steinbeck have become emblematic of the Depression poor; these were the people who suffered the death of the American dream in the harshest years of the thirties. All the golden promises of pioneer days had withered in the dust of their ruined land. In the film, these characters are played with exemplary skill. Surely Tom Joad is the finest of Henry Fonda's early performances; his loping gait, steady gaze, and flat midwestern inflections never seemed so appropriate, nor did the innate decency and honesty of his persona ever serve him as well. As John Casy, Tom's friend who was an evangelistic preacher until he "lost the spirit," John Carradine manages to survive the heavy hand of symbolism that rests on his shoulder in

almost every scene; his performance is persuasive despite the obvious Christ references, from the character's initials to Tom Joad's remark after his martyred death, "He was a lantern. He helped me to see things clear."

The film's greatest strength, however, lies in the towering, award-winning performance of Jane Darwell as Ma Joad. A lifetime of sorrow, pain, and disappointment is etched in her face, and in her scenes with Tom, she conveys compassion and heartbreak with few words. Nor does she need rhetorical dialogue to express what she is feeling when she pores over her mementoes just before they leave the farm. When she tries on a pair of earrings, smiling slightly at a memory of when she was young, we are watching one of the screen's most indelible moments.

Another and vastly more idealized view of rural life in the Depression years was offered many years later in the 1972 production of *Sounder*. A moving and perceptive story of a black sharecropper and his family in the Deep South of the 1930s, this film gave a somewhat romantic gloss to the meager existence of the Morgans, although it handled honestly their bewilderment and anguish when Nathan Morgan is sent to prison. Cicely Tyson starred as Rebecca Morgan, still young but careworn, whose strength and innate dignity help to carry her husband and three children through their troubles. *Sounder* is also the story of the Morgans' older son David (Kevin Hooks), whose journey to see his father in prison becomes a voyage of self-discovery in which he learns resilience and self-pride.

Directed sensitively by Martin Ritt, *Sounder* is one of the great films on the American family in general and the black experience in particular. Its portrait of a family forced by deprivation and suffering to become strong and resourceful has the power of conviction, and the film even gains force as it moves to its touching conclusion. There are moments as true and beautiful as any in films of the seventies, and many of them are as simple as an afternoon's baseball game between two black teams or an unfruitful hunting trip by Nathan, David, and the family hound, Sounder. (This dog, maimed but loyal, is intended to be symbolic of the family's perseverance, but the movie doesn't press the point.) When strong emotion is called for, *Sounder* succeeds in avoiding histrionics; a climactic scene in which Nathan urges the boy to follow his dreams, even if it means leaving his family, is genuinely affecting.

The entire cast is fine, but Cicely Tyson is the film's heart and sinew. Gaunt and inexpressibly weary, she registers intelligence, sorrow, and fleeting hope with her eyes; her Rebecca Morgan is a woman to be reckoned with, inspiring and radiant. An extraordinary actress, Tyson makes casual scenes memorable, as when she must deal with white people and we watch a subtle mixture of cunning, cynicism, and subservience pass across her face. When she sees her husband returning from prison and runs toward him down the road, her cry of elation is one of the unforgettable moments in films. Paul Winfield is also impressive as Nathan, overflowing with devotion to his family and trying to restrain his desperation and bitterness.

Just as small-town life was idealized in films of the thirties and forties, so the family was usually depicted as the wellspring of the nation's decency, honesty, and all-around goodness. In the shiny midwestern town of Carvel, Andy Hardy spent most of his time in loving communion with his family: an extraordinarily wise and patient father (a judge, no less), an adoring mother, a noncompetitive sister, and an understanding maiden aunt. Reality intruded occasionally—a near-fatal illness, serious financial setbacks—but life in the American movie family was mostly serene.

In fact, films on the American family during this period tended to be so idealized that a movie such as Paramount's *Make Way for Tomorrow* (1937), with its frank view of helpless old age, could hardly expect to attract a wide audience. It was, however, an unusually fine and honest little film that refused to shy away from an ongoing family problem. Derived by Viña Delmar from a novel by Josephine Lawrence and a play by Helen and Nolan Leary, *Make Way for Tomorrow* (an ironic title considering the central situation) concerned the plight of Barkley and Lucy Cooper (Victor Moore and Beulah Bondi), an elderly couple forced to sell their home and separate. Lucy goes to live with her son George (Thomas Mitchell) —there is only room for her—but she becomes a well-meaning nuisance and finally agrees to move into an old folks' home. Bark and Lucy have one last meeting before they are parted.

With a plot line that could easily descend into bathos or a polemic against the abuse of oldsters, *Make Way for Tomorrow* manages to keep its balance, beautifully and sensibly, under Leo McCarey's direction (his first attempt at drama). Although some of the Cooper children are broadly characterized, their impatience and irritation with their parents is often justified: father is something of a crotchety pest; mother can be obtrusive and distracting. George and his wife Anita (Fay Bainter), troubled by a conflict between their responsibilities to their parents and their own needs, are not treated unsympathetically. Yet the dilemma of the old folks is made painfully moving: in one especially touching scene, Bark and Lucy converse affectionately on the telephone as the members of Anita's bridge club listen with sadness and embarrassment. When Lucy agrees to go to the home for the aged, her dialogue with George has a core of truth rare in American films of the thirties.

As Bark and Lucy, Victor Moore and Beulah Bondi give luminous performances (amazingly, Bondi was only in her mid-forties, and Moore was noted for his roles as a comic bumbler), and their final sequence is one of the loveliest in thirties movies. They walk in the park, musing on their fate ("I figure that everyone is entitled to just so much happiness in life") and trying to assess their years as husband and wife. They go to the New York hotel where they spent their honeymoon and are received royally. When they must say goodbye at the train depot, their parting is transcendent, sentimental without being at all mawkish. Bark says to Lucy, "In case I don't see you again, it's been very nice knowing you, Miss Breckenridge," and she replies, "It's been lovely, every bit of it, the whole fifty years. . . . I'd rather have been your wife than anything

else on earth." *Make Way for Tomorrow* is a warmly remembered film, and yet it sounds an early warning to a problem that has become critical in America of the eighties: the plight of the elderly, lost and unwanted in a society they helped to create.

During the forties, especially during the years of World War II, it seemed more important than ever for films to emphasize the enduring values of family life in America. *Since You Went Away* designated the home as a "fortress," indomitable and impregnable, and films such as *I'll Be Seeing You* (1945) saw it as a shelter against adversity, a place for healing. In the fifties, the idyllic view persisted, but there were notes of dissension, especially in a series of "rebellious youth" stories that saw the family as a disruptive, insensitive force. In *Rebel Without a Cause* (1955), the troubled young people suffered or turned incorrigible because of weak, uncaring, or absentee parents. For every warm-hearted *Father of the Bride* (1950), there were more who seemed to destroy their children. There was little concern for the serious complexities of family life in the films of the sixties and seventies, although the subject received some satirical treatment in *Goodbye Columbus* (1969), *Little Murders* (1971), and other movies.

In recent years, sparked by an introspective and realistic generation that has tended to destroy its sacred cows, films have come to grips with the problems of the family, have sought to examine the small tensions and conflicts that can explode almost imperceptibly into open warfare. If few movies have managed to cut into the heart of family strife—perhaps *Shoot the Moon* (1982) has come the closest —several have taken family drama far beyond the blandness and

Opposite: Sounder *(Fox, 1972). One of the most memorable film performances in recent years: Cicely Tyson as Rebecca Morgan, the strong, resourceful woman who holds her sharecropper family together during the Depression years in Louisiana.*
Above: Make Way for Tomorrow *(Paramount, 1937). Elderly Lucy and Barkley Cooper (Beulah Bondi and Victor Moore) spend their last day together before parting, probably forever. Leo McCarey's film was a poignant look at a rare movie topic: the tribulations of old age.*

vacuity of other decades. One was Columbia's *Kramer vs. Kramer* (1979), which dealt with the nearly overwhelming problems of divorce and child custody. Written and directed by Robert Benton (from Avery Corman's novel), this perceptive and moving film focused on Ted Kramer (Dustin Hoffman), an advertising man whose life is torn apart when his wife Joanna (Meryl Streep) leaves him to "find" herself, and he is obliged to raise his small son, Billy (Justin Henry), by himself.

Kramer vs. Kramer has scenes of emotional turmoil, but it is at its very best—observant, funny, and touching—in its view of a suddenly single father forced to deal with the needs and demands of a puzzled child. Played by Hoffman with the right blend of exasperation and tenderness, Ted Kramer is a man trying desperately to cope: making a disastrous breakfast for two ("We're having a *great* time!"), struggling with daily rituals while holding on precariously to his job, dealing with an unexpected crisis (Billy is injured falling off a jungle gym). In one sensitively written scene, he tries to explain to a troubled Billy why his mother has left him (the boy thinks it was because he was bad), and father and son embrace in a moment of sorrow and mutual need that wrenches the heart.

The custody trial has inevitable moments of high drama, and also one quietly eloquent moment when Joanna, on the stand, is asked by Ted's attorney if she believes that she was a failure in the one most important relationship in her life—as wife and mother—and her eyes meet Ted's. Shaking his head to indicate "no," Ted reaffirms a once-loving relationship. Under questioning, Ted asserts his rights as a father ("Why is a woman a better parent by virtue of her sex?"), and he describes the life he and Billy have built together. "If you destroy that," he tells the court, "it may be irreparable." It is, of course, a surefire scene for any actor, but Hoffman never plays for the grandstand; he speaks in a flat style that scores its emotional points. When he must part with Billy, the scene wrings honest tears from the audience. The look of anguish on Ted's face, Billy's brave little smile, and Joanna's distraught state when she comes to get Billy amply suggest the pain caused by a shattered family.

The year after *Kramer vs. Kramer*, another drama concerning family upheaval won enthusiastic reviews. *Ordinary People* (1980), adapted by Alvin Sargent from Judith Guest's novel, involved quite a different family, however. The Jarretts, who live in an affluent Chicago suburb, share a terrible burden, the death by drowning of an older son, which brings to the surface deeply rooted antagonism and resentment that tears them apart. Mother Beth (Mary Tyler Moore) is a frosty patrician who smothers her feelings in propriety. Father Alvin (Donald Sutherland) is well-meaning but baffled and weak. And son Conrad (Timothy Hutton) feels the greatest anguish; blaming himself for his brother's death, he is wracked with guilt and tormented by the belief that his mother hates him. By the film's end, Conrad, with the help of a kindly psychiatrist (Judd Hirsch) has worked his way toward a new beginning, but Calvin and Beth separate.

Ordinary People was actor Robert Redford's first assignment as a director, and he does a commendable job of conveying the private demons that lurk in the shadows of well-ordered lives. At the very beginning of the film, we see the split between sunny reality and the dark psyche where peace of mind seems impossible: a church choir singing on a bright, serene Sunday morning is interrupted by Conrad's terrifying nightmare about his brother Bucky's drowning. It is moving to watch Conrad groping painfully to get control of his life, to deal with his submerged feelings, while the schism between his parents grows wider. An altercation at Christmas leads to Conrad's explosion of rage and sorrow at his mother's attitude toward him. "I can't talk to her!" he cries. "The way she looks at me! She hates me!" In a climactic scene in Dr. Berger's office he finally expresses all the anger at himself and his dead brother, all the self-flagellation that has brought him to attempt suicide. At the same time, Beth and Calvin are locked in their own battle of guilt and recrimination; when they finally talk about Bucky's funeral, there is no release from pain, and a quarrel on a golf course only deepens the wounds.

Ordinary People is most effective in moments that crystallize a character, a situation, or a point of view with little more than a

Above, left, and opposite, above: Kramer vs. Kramer *(Columbia, 1979). Divorced parents Dustin Hoffman and Meryl Streep confront each other over custody of their young son. Opposite: Single father Ted Kramer (Dustin Hoffman) sees his young son, Billy (Justin Henry), off to school. Above, right:* Ordinary People *(Paramount, 1980). Alvin and Beth Jarrett (Donald Sutherland and Mary Tyler Moore) share a deeply troubled relationship with each other and with their son. Opposite, below:* Nashville *(Paramount, 1975). Country singing stars Barbara Jean (Ronee Blakley) and Haven Hamilton (Henry Gibson) greet their enthusiastic fans. At Gibson's side is Barbara Baxley.*

single carefully constructed shot, a few offhand remarks, or a glance. Early in the film, a view of the family silently at dinner emphasizes their separateness. (Beth sits rigidly in her chair, her face a mask.) Later, the camera roams over Bucky's room as seen through Beth's eyes, and her conversation with Conrad as they stand amid Bucky's trophies and banners is tense and awkward for all its seeming triviality. Most expressive of all are the silent looks that tell everything: Conrad's flicker of pain when their car passes the graveyard, or Beth's surprised face when Conrad goes to hug her and she can only react by turning away.

Ordinary People is especially interesting as a reflection of film's changing approach to family life among the American well-to-do. In previous years, affluent youth troubled by the neglect or lovelessness of their parents turned to dangerously antisocial actions. In *Rebel Without a Cause* (1955), their private torment leads to public rage and spurs them to risk their lives in switchblade fights and nighttime drag-racing. The problem is seen in purely social terms: help our misunderstood children. But a quarter-century later, the problem has been internalized—while Conrad's guilt and anguish trigger antisocial behavior, it is not violent (except toward himself), and it leads him to the psychiatrist's couch. The age of the sociologist has apparently been replaced by the age of the psychiatrist.

Away from home and hearth, Americans have enjoyed playing and watching games. By common agreement, one of the country's most popular spectator sports is politics. On the whole, politics has not been a favorite subject in films, and only in recent years has it been afforded realistic treatment. In previous decades, the politician was depicted either as an *enfant naïf*, innocently opposing the forces of evil and routing them by total goodness or by innate political knowhow, or as a blustering fraud. Inevitably, colorful chicanery held the edge; for every high-minded aspirant to political office (Spencer Tracy in *State of the Union*, 1948), there were many more charlatans, fools, and opportunists already *in* office: William Powell's bumbling Melvin Ashton in *The Senator Was Indiscreet* (1947), or Charles Laughton's bombastic Senator Cooley in *Advise and Consent* (1962).

By the sixties, there was a certain balance in the portrayal of politicians. *The Best Man* (1964), the film version of Gore Vidal's play, characterized politics as an exhilarating game, pitting a not-exactly-pure liberal (Henry Fonda) against a far-from-pure conservative (Cliff Robertson). Movies of the seventies, such as *The Candidate* (1972) and *The Seduction of Joe Tynan* (1979), saw the up-and-coming politician as neither saint nor ogre but as a decent, even idealistic person confounded by personal problems and the need to compromise. The heroes of both of these films, adept, knowing, and eager to play at politics, make an interesting contrast to fledgling Senator Jefferson Smith, the naïve protagonist of Frank Capra's *Mr. Smith Goes to Washington* (1939).

If any director could be counted on to offer a rosy view of American politics, it was Capra, an Italian-born citizen with an abiding

love for his adopted country. His movie had all the familiar Capra ingredients: the "lamb-bites-wolf" concept in which the good-hearted, unworldly underdog defeats the rich and the mighty; the populist belief that people of good will can join together to effect a change for the better. In *Mr. Smith Goes to Washington*, he offered a simplistic approach to politics: young Jefferson Smith (James Stewart), fairly bursting with patriotic zeal, is appointed to a seat in the U.S. Senate, unaware that he is merely a pawn of his state's corrupt and powerful forces, headed by political boss Jim Taylor (Edward Arnold). When he opposes these forces, he is nearly destroyed, but with the help of Saunders (Jean Arthur), his cynical but ultimately admiring secretary, he finally triumphs.

There is every reason why *Mr. Smith Goes to Washington* should not work. The character of Jeff Smith, though played by James Stewart with gangling charm, is perilously close to simple-minded; in his awe at Washington's landmarks, his dithering over a pretty girl, and his homespun belief in everyone's good intentions, he seems more like an overage Boy Scout than a Scout leader or a potential senator. And Capra's sentimentality can become painful—we wince when a boy reads from the Gettysburg Address inscribed on the wall of the Lincoln Memorial while Jeff watches reverently. Yet, as we are stirred by the film's unabashed assault on our feelings, a sophisticated response becomes pointless.

Sidney Buchman's screenplay reaches its apogee of emotion in the rousing climax, in which Jeff Smith stages a filibuster to keep himself in the Senate and the forces of evil at bay. The sequence is corny, manipulative, and enormously gripping. Virtually overwhelmed by Taylor's vicious campaign against him, Jeff gasps out his creed: "... there's no compromising with human liberty. Graft, lies, self-seeking—and that kind of man scrambling for money and power no

Mr. Smith Goes to Washington (Columbia, 1939). At the end of his tether, a filibustering Senator Jefferson Smith (James Stewart) reacts to the thousands of hostile telegrams demanding his resignation.

matter who or how many he grinds on the way—*all* those things— they can't live here if this democracy is going to live too!" He finally collapses, but a Capra hero is never really alone; as his friends rally around him, chicanery has no chance to survive. James Stewart gives Jeff a disarming warmth and conviction, and that delicious comedienne Jean Arthur successfully leavens the sweetness with her wry and lightly caustic manner.

The other side of the movies'-eye view of politics was perhaps one that more Americans (especially in the last few decades) were likely to believe. In this view, the politician is someone whose ideals have been corrupted by greed, self-interest, and an insatiable thirst for power. To achieve his political goals, he is willing to lie, cheat, or curry favor. The movies in which he figures usually arrange his downfall, although in actuality he often survives and prospers.

A rough-hewn but dangerously persuasive politician of this stripe dominated the screen in Robert Rossen's *All the King's Men* (1949). As adapted by Rossen from Robert Penn Warren's novel, the film is a blistering view of political demagoguery, strongly suggested by the career of Huey P. Long, the notorious and bigoted senator from Louisiana who was shot to death in 1935. In the best role of his career, Broderick Crawford played Willie Stark, a crude, ambitious grass-roots politician who stomps and kicks his way to becoming governor of the state. He rules by terror and intimidation, and his nefarious ways lead to impeachment. He wins by mustering his army of supporters, only to be assassinated by one of his victims.

All the King's Men has something to say about the ways in which the democratic process can be perverted by a demagogue disguised as a populist, but it works best as churning melodrama. The film's fascination rests largely with the character of Willie Stark, enacted with open-throttle power and authority by Crawford in his Oscar-winning performance. We see Willie's first taste of power in a vivid shot: surrounded by admirers, he basks in their praise, grinning

and sweating. His most effective moment comes at a barbecue where his bare-knuckled, honest speech rouses the crowd to fever pitch. "Listen, you hicks! I'm out for blood!" he cries, and he soon begins to believe his own pitches. "I don't need money," he tells his supporters. "People give me things because they believe in me." He seems indestructible, but as he lies dying, his last words bear a curious resemblance to those of Tony Camonte, Rico Bandello, or any of the overweening gangsters of the thirties. "Could have had the whole world," he groans. "Why did he do it to me? Why?" Willie Stark, like the gangsters, cannot understand that he himself is the source of his corrupted dream. *All the King's Men* sags in its middle section, with some unconvincing and vaguely handled business concerning Willie's adopted son, but it is a gripping film.

Americans had long regarded the Willie Starks of the world —the bold, scheming power brokers—with a mixture of moral disapproval and grudging admiration. But with the shock of Watergate in the seventies, at least some of the nation's political naïveté vanished in the spectacle of men at the highest reaches of government impeding justice and engaging in other criminal acts to retain their seats of power. It was a dismaying spectacle that would have made Jefferson Smith distraught and heartsick.

The screen's single attempt to deal with the Watergate phenomenon was Alan J. Pakula's film version of *All the President's Men* (1976), the best-selling book by investigative reporters Bob Woodward and Carl Bernstein. Their story of how they had doggedly and painstakingly uncovered what lay behind the Watergate break-in and its shattering ramifications seemed an unlikely candidate for filming, but with the persistence of Robert Redford, who recognized its value and costarred as Woodward, it paid off in an absorbing movie that combined aspects of the newspaper drama, the political exposé, and the detective mystery. With few cinematic flourishes, *All the President's Men* traces the events that began with the break-in at the Watergate Office Building and the capture of the burglars, and ended two years later with the resignation of President Nixon. Without benefit of big emotional scenes, the drama emerges from the step-by-step unraveling of the mystery by Woodward and Bernstein (Dustin Hoffman).

William Goldman's adroit, Oscar-winning screenplay maintains steady interest as the people encountered by the reporters react in varying ways to their probing questions. From an interview with a shocked Howard Hunt, who gasps, "Good God! No comment!," to a secret meeting with "Deep Throat" in a dark garage, these encounters are dramatic and unpredictable. A nervous secretary with the Committee to Re-elect the President ("CREEP"), expertly played by Jane Alexander, conveys a mixture of fear ("a lot of people are watching me") and hidden antipathy. As more information is uncovered, there are on-camera responses of suppressed anxiety, indignation, and denial. The moment when the reporters learn that Haldeman is conducting a criminal conspiracy from inside the White House has all the exhilaration of a long-awaited breakthrough in detective fiction.

All the King's Men (Columbia, 1949). Politician-on-the-rise Willie Stark (Broderick Crawford) is exhorted by his acid-tongued aide Sadie Burke (Mercedes McCambridge). Looking on: John Ireland. McCambridge won that year's Oscar for Best Supporting Actress.

One of the most brilliant dissections of American life—combining scathing social satire, implied political commentary, and a basically unattractive view of the nation's mores—was the 1975 production of *Nashville*. Director Robert Altman's most masterly achievement to date, *Nashville* was a stunning mosaic made up of many parts, some dark, some light, but all carefully organized to create a detailed portrait of a hedonistic, vulgarized America. Written by Joan Tewksbury, with added contributions by Altman and the actors, the film brought twenty-four diverse people to "the country music capital of the world," where their lives intertwine in a mad mélange that begins with a rendition of a patriotic song ("We Must Be Doin' Somethin' Right to Last Two Hundred Years") and ends with the onstage assassination of Barbara Jean (Ronee Blakley), a popular country singer. In between the music and the violence, we are subjected to the loudspeaker rantings of one Hal Phillip Walker, an unseen ultra-conservative candidate for the presidency, and we witness the antics of prodigiously untalented people who are reaching for fame but who will settle for a night's comfort. This *Nashville* is populated with country music stars and their sycophants, frustrated dreamers unwilling to discard their obsessions, and drifters groping for their identity in the chaos of a combined circus, musical concert, and political rally. The climate is ripe for exhibitionism, lunatic behavior—and violence.

Nashville's picture of mid-seventies America may be unflattering, but it is also funny and sometimes touching. The smirking self-satisfaction of singing star Haven Hamilton (Henry Gibson) as he offers his optimistic and emotional tunes ("It Don't Worry Me," "For the Sake of the Children") recalls every entertainer who has confused popularity with power, and Geraldine Chaplin offers a hilarious characterization of an inane BBC reporter who is trying to bring perspective to the proceedings. (In an uproarious scene, she reports solemnly from a car graveyard.) There is eccentric humor, as well, in the would-be singer (Barbara Harris) whose determination to be heard knows no bounds. When Barbara Jean is shot in the climactic sequence, Harris leaps to the microphone to fill the gap. But humor spills over into poignancy in the characters of the waitress (Gwen Welles), at best a hopeless amateur, who is forced to perform a humiliating striptease at a smoker for presidential candidate Walker, and the gospel singer (Lily Tomlin), the only white member of the group, who agrees to a one-night stand with a guitar-strumming womanizer (Keith Carradine).

Nashville is not a film to cheer devout believers in the American way. It presents an appalling spectacle in which politics, country music, and fried chicken are offered on the same level by hucksters whose only goal is to sell the product. Perhaps the film's most revealing scene occurs when the airport reception for Barbara Jean becomes chaotically enmeshed with the Walker campaign—at one point, a reporter gushes into his microphone about Barbara Jean while, in the background, a Walker supporter carrying a sign manipulates herself into camera range, smiling fetchingly. At the end,

when Barbara Jean is killed by a crazed fan, Haven Hamilton shouts into the microphone, "This isn't Dallas! This is Nashville!" Amid the hysteria and confusion, after two-and-a-half hours in which we have seen traditional American values vulgarized or aborted, Hamilton's words echo ironically. In a world where everything is worth the same, nothing, including human life, can be worth very much. The movie suggests that it may be a shorter distance from Dallas to Nashville than we could have ever believed.

Can we believe what the movies have shown us about American life? To an extent, we can, if we think of it as a single view seen from opposite ends of a telescope. Films have shown us the best we can be—and also the worst. If most Americans are not paragons of all the virtues, if they are not Judge Hardys dispensing wisdom and compassion or Atticus Finches pleading for justice, neither are they the hatemongers of *Fury* or, for that matter, the crass fame-seekers of *Nashville*.

We grope for reason and understanding. Luckily, every once in a while, the movies will take us a step further toward understanding the source and meaning of the American dream.

Opposite, above: A lobby card for Mr. Smith Goes to Washington *(Columbia, 1939).*
Opposite, below: All the President's Men *(Warner Bros., 1976). Dustin Hoffman as Carl Bernstein and Robert Redford as Bob Woodward, the investigative reporters whose best-selling account of the events that led to the Watergate scandal was adapted skillfully to the screen.*
Above: Nashville *(Paramount, 1975). Lily Tomlin, the only white member of a group of gospel singers, leads them in a rousing song. She was one of many characters who figured importantly in Robert Altman's funny and acerbic look at American life.*

GUILTY PARTIES
Great Crime Movies

Despite admonitions to the contrary, crime pays—at least at the box office. As early as 1912, in his Biograph feature film *Musketeers of Pig Alley*, D. W. Griffith had included a hard-bitten gangster as a central character, and in every decade since, audiences have been fascinated by underworld activities and criminal behavior. It may be simplistic to suggest that people enjoy watching others enact the violence that lurks in the most remote corners of their minds, but there is certainly a core of underlying truth in the idea. The dapper crook who defies the law, the underworld rajah who plots mass murder, the cold-blooded vixen who schemes to kill her husband may be morally reprehensible, but they compel our interest, and they are the stuff of which melodramas have been made for over seventy years.

Certainly the figure looming the largest in crime movies has been the gangster, a ruthless man driven by a lust for power or a thirst for social acceptance—money is merely a necessary means of achieving either goal. The movie gangster, although indifferent to human life, is still guided by a private code of honor that rewards unswerving loyalty and exacts punishment for betrayal. In the early years of the century, many gangsters came from the swelling ranks of the immigrants (like "godfather" Vito Corleone); provoked by bitter poverty and a hostile society to act outside the law, and later given momentum and a kind of furtive charisma by Prohibition, the gangsters built empires that no amount of effort could topple. In subsequent years, when their children inherited the mantle of leadership, they retained their parents' cold brutality and harsh code of reprisal.

The gangster as a viable film subject did not really emerge until the mid-twenties, although Lon Chaney had included several underworld types among his grotesque characterizations. Gradually, filmmakers began to realize that Prohibition had created a new breed of powerful men who represented a kind of American success story—the gangster with his expensive accouterments, including an elaborately furnished apartment and a decorative dame, was, after all, a distorted version of the American dream. Bootlegging had made him rich, and his riches bought him a degree of respectability. He had politicians in his pocket, and he hobnobbed with society. By the late twenties, however, there was a groundswell of reaction against the rampant lawlessness that had taken hold in America. A warning note was introduced into the crime film, making it clear that behind all the bluster of the underworld was an urgent danger to society.

The first important gangster film to topple the kingpin criminal from his throne was Josef von Sternberg's *Underworld* (1927). Sternberg had come to Paramount after gaining a reputation as a difficult but innovative director. He applied his bold use of light and shadow and his emphasis on pictorial composition over plot or characteriza-

tion to the tale of an arrogant gangster who acquires integrity too late to save himself from an inevitable fate. Derived from an original story by Ben Hecht (which won the first Academy Award in that category), the film took the now-conventional "crime-doesn't-pay" approach, but Sternberg used the camera in such striking ways that *Underworld* appeared to reinvent the milieu of vicious gangsters and relentless cops.

The film begins with a robbery and a title that set the mood for this and scores of subsequent gangster movies: "a great city in the dead of night, streets lonely, moon-flooded . . . " The thief is blustering Bull Weed (George Bancroft), confident of the faithfulness of his girl Feathers McCoy (Evelyn Brent) and of the loyalty of "Rolls Royce" (Clive Brook), the alcoholic, disbarred lawyer who witnessed the robbery ("I am a Rolls Royce for silence"). Betrayed by the clandestine love affair of Feathers and Rolls Royce, Bull goes down to defeat, but not before saving the couple from arrest.

Underworld lacks the unnerving clatter of gunfire and the harsh banter of hoods that sound would bring to the gangster film. But it has the requisite number of action scenes and an unusually sensual heroine, played with forthright sexiness by Evelyn Brent. (She asks Rolls Royce, "How long since you had the body washed and polished?") The movie also contains a remarkable sequence in which gangsters gather for their annual ball, an orgy of drinking and carousing at which guests are asked to check their "gats" at the door. But above all, *Underworld* is replete with Sternbergian touches: close-ups of faces that reveal more than dialogue; heavy shadows that suggest impending doom, used especially well to indicate Bull's flight from the law; and a faintly exotic aura that infiltrates the film's dingy nightclubs and cramped apartments. Bull's final shootout with the police almost edges into

Opposite: The Godfather *(Paramount, 1972). Marlon Brando as the aging Don of the Corleone family in Francis Ford Coppola's adaptation of Mario Puzo's popular novel. Brando won the Academy Award for Best Actor for his self-conscious performance.*
Above: Underworld *(Paramount, 1927). Mobster Bull Weed (George Bancroft) is trapped with his one-time moll, Feathers McCoy (Evelyn Brent), in the climax of Josef von Sternberg's gangster melodrama.*

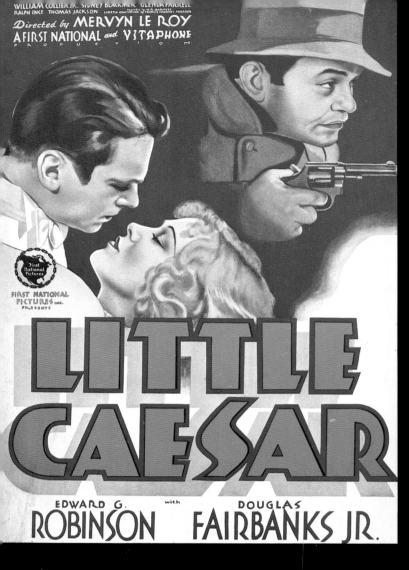

LITTLE CAESAR

EDWARD G. ROBINSON with DOUGLAS FAIRBANKS JR.

surrealism: the police firing indiscriminately at his hideout, people rushing from their homes in their nightclothes, a raging Bull attempting to strangle his once-beloved Feathers. The ending, however, is improbable: a suddenly reformed Bull surrenders meekly to the police.

With the success of *Underworld*, a flurry of gangster films with such titles as *Romance of the Underworld* and *The Racket* followed, but with the onset of the Depression, the gangster began to lose much of his glamour. His profits, mainly from illegal liquor, were still enormous, and his murderous exploits still warranted banner headlines, but now the price he had to pay was all too evident in tabloid photographs of his blood-splattered body or lurid accounts of his execution by a rival or the law. If the American public retained a sneaking fondness for the gangster, occasionally turning him into a latter-day Robin Hood or robber baron, it was not the fault of the filmmakers, who plastered their movies with invective against crime and issued clarion calls to action. Could they help it if James Cagney and Edward G. Robinson had a cock-of-the-walk swagger, a masculine self-assurance that made them more attractive than anyone on the side of the law? And didn't they come to a bad end? Despite these disclaimers, there was an unmistakable ambivalence in the extremely popular gangster films of the early thirties—their bold central figures were both repellent and undeniably fascinating. And no two film figures embodied the new breed of gangsters with more compelling flair than Caesar Enrico Bandello of *Little Caesar* and Tom Powers of *The Public Enemy*.

By no means the first but certainly one of the most potent of the early sound gangster films, *Little Caesar* (1930) was released by Warners to audiences stunned by its harshness and brutality. Adapted by Francis E. Faragoh (and anonymous writers) from W. R. Burnett's novel, the film depicted the rise and fall of a mobster whose ruthlessness takes him to the top of the Chicago underworld, and whose arrogance and pride send him plummeting to defeat and death. The goal of Caesar Enrico Bandello ("Little Caesar") is not wealth but total power, and he achieves it partly because of his utter contempt for morality (he will destroy anyone in his path) and partly because his colleagues refuse to take him seriously until it is too late (he is short and comically pugnacious, with delusions of grandeur). Rico is an obsessive killing machine who cares for neither liquor nor women; he has only two soft spots of humanity: his love for his old Italian immigrant mother, and his possibly homosexual attachment to Joe (Douglas Fairbanks, Jr.), a would-be dancer whose desire to leave the mob triggers Rico's murderous rage.

As directed by Mervyn LeRoy, *Little Caesar* has the crude forcefulness and primitive, unadorned style of many pioneer sound movies. It manages the obligatory scenes of the genre with reasonable efficiency, but it is Edward G. Robinson's performance that makes the film memorable. His glowering face and snarling voice were like no other actor's, and his very presence was riveting. Mouthing such lines as "Shoot first and argue afterwards" or "This game ain't for guys that's soft," he cut a convincing, terrifying figure. In a climactic scene, he moves to shoot Joe and his girlfriend Olga (Glenda Farrell), striding toward the camera

until his face is in frightening close-up. By the time of his famous death scene, he is no longer imposing. A small, shabby ghost whose bravado cannot be squelched, he is fatally shot by the cop who has been his nemesis for years. "Mother of God," he cries, "is this the end of Rico?"

As Warners's head of production, Darryl F. Zanuck had been instrumental in launching the cycle of gangster films of which *Little Caesar* was an auspicious part. By the time *Little Caesar* was released, he was already producing another crime drama with a by-now familiar pattern. *The Public Enemy* (1931) was yet another cautionary tale concerning the life and death of a gangster, but there were important differences. For one, its story was more fully rounded than usual; it gave the central character an existence before crime, however lightly sketched. For another, this character was played by an actor of individual style and striking self-assurance. James Cagney's vicious, smiling Tom Powers was more frightening than Rico Bandello because his ruthlessness was cloaked by a disarming personality—brash and extroverted, like a salesman on the rise.

Although *The Public Enemy* has its crudities, it is superior to *Little Caesar*, and not only because of Cagney's electrifying presence. Its screenplay by Kubec Glasmon and John Bright is more compact, more attentive to character and the revealing detail, and William Wellman's direction is also livelier and more tightly controlled than Mervyn LeRoy's in *Little Caesar*. The film begins by tracing the boyhood careers in petty crime of Tom Powers and his friend Matt (Edward Woods), then moves swiftly to show Tom's rise in the underworld during Prohibition. In scenes pared to the bone, we see Tom's brutality: his murder of the fence Putty-Nose, for example, is a model of economical filmmaking—Putty-Nose sings and plays the piano; the camera cuts to Tom's smiling face as he fires; Putty-Nose's song changes abruptly to a scream, and we hear the sickening thump as his body hits the floor. Tom is also nasty to women: in one of the iconic moments in thirties films, he pushes a grapefruit into the face of his whining mistress (Mae Clarke). And yet for all

his vicious behavior, he seems brighter and more likable than any of his criminal associates, and even smarter than his honest but stolid brother Mike (Donald Cook).

Tom's downfall is much swifter than his rise; finally shot by a rival gang, he mutters, "I ain't so tough!" as he staggers, wounded, down the street. The ending is grisly: kidnapped from the hospital and murdered (we never see this), Tom is wrapped in a shroud and his body is propped against the doorbell of his house. When his brother opens the door, the body topples to the floor. The scene demonstrates the virtues of implication and understatement; instead of explicit gore, we are given its aftermath, and the effect is doubly shocking. (This is true of the entire film—there is surprisingly little violence, considering the subject matter.)

As strong as *The Public Enemy* and *Little Caesar* were, they seemed almost tame in comparison with Howard Hawks's uncompromising gangster classic, *Scarface* (1932). Produced by an eccentric young millionaire named Howard Hughes, *Scarface* transformed the disreputable career of "Scarface" Al Capone into a savage fiction that mixed organized 'murder and assorted mayhem with a bold suggestion of incest. The film offended many civic leaders, who clamored for its removal from theaters and for reform of Hollywood's immorality. On its home ground, *Scarface* ran into trouble: the Hays Office insisted on many cuts and changes, including the addition of

a subtitle—"The Shame of a Nation." (This was a compromise; the censors originally wanted the title changed to *The Menace*.)

Adapted by Ben Hecht from a novel by Armitage Trail, with dialogue and continuity later added by others, *Scarface* retains a primitive power that can still be felt more than five decades after its release. Under Howard Hawks's direction, it veers from the naturalistically portrayed criminal world of *The Public Enemy* and *Little Caesar* into feverish expressionistic melodrama in which murder occurs at regular intervals (there are at least fifteen killings in the screenplay). Gangland executions become symbolic rituals (an "x" motif is used in various ways throughout the film, even in the credits, to indicate the "wiping out" of a victim), and the rain-slashed city streets are photographed like visions of hell—traps from which the only escape is violent death. The unrelenting harshness and ugliness has the curious effect of offsetting the realism and turning the film into a hallucinatory nightmare that ends only with the last frame.

There are superficial similarities between Al Capone and Paul Muni's Tony Camonte: the facial scar, the coarse Italian immigrant's manner, the love of Italian opera. Muni, playing, as he often did, with all stops out, makes Camonte a swaggering, simian-like hood who resembles an entrepreneur turned vicious—his creed could be that of any ruthless businessman: "Do it first. Do it yourself. And keep on doing it!" But Camonte's business is the seizing of power through violence, and the film traces his rise to the top with a raw ferocity. His killings are swift, brutal, and brilliantly staged, often in shadow or silhouette; they reach a dramatic peak in the shooting of a rival gangster (Boris Karloff) in a bowling alley—the dying man makes a strike, with the last pin spinning and then toppling over in a manner that suggests the victim himself.

Camonte's incestuous feelings for his sister Cesca (Ann Dvorak) are so overt, despite the cuts, that a viewer must wonder how the Hays Office approved even this trimmed version. In their last scene

Left: The Public Enemy *(Warner Bros., 1931). The famous but grisly ending: the body of murdered gangster Tom Powers (James Cagney) topples in at the feet of his brother (Donald Cook). Cagney created a new kind of gangster—a man whose pugnacious charm barely concealed the instincts of a killer.*
Right: Scarface *(Howard Hughes/United Artists, 1932). Paul Muni (center) gave a compelling performance as Tony Camonte, the vicious gangland boss modeled on Al Capone.*

together, besieged by the police, the two behave like Cesare and Lucrezia Borgia, which is not so coincidental since Hecht had originally conceived of the film as "the Borgias in Chicago." "You're me, and I'm you," she insists. "It's always been that way!" And although she cries out the name of her new husband (George Raft, in his famous coin-flipping performance) before she dies, her brother knows the truth. He surrenders pathetically—"Don't shoot. I got nobody. I'm all alone"—and we see him finally brought to the gallows. Despite the obvious insertions of moralizing policemen, *Scarface* is the harshest and most compelling of crime films.

By the mid-thirties, the pure and simple screen gangster, as embodied by James Cagney, was already fading into legend, weakened by a repelled (or possibly just satiated) public and a stronger Production Code. A growing spirit of optimism prompted filmmakers to abandon the grim and cynical attitude of the early thirties. Even Cagney himself moved to the right side of the law for *G-Men* (1935), and *The Roaring Twenties* (1939), in which he starred, was virtually a sentimental elegy to the American gangster. Under Raoul Walsh's direction, he played a World War I veteran who turns to crime but finally gives up his ruined life to save others. (It was a noble gesture that would have revolted Tom Powers of *The Public Enemy*.) In *High Sierra* (1941), an even better "gangster-at-the-end-of-the-line" melodrama, Walsh directed Humphrey Bogart in a bravura death scene. As Roy ("Mad Dog") Earle, a burned-out gangster trapped by police on a mountaintop, Bogart exposes himself to gunfire when he calls to his pet dog. (Little Caesar would have shot the dog.) He falls from High Sierra and his loyal girl Marie (Ida Lupino) speaks his epitaph: "He's free! He's free!" The screenplay, which John Huston and W. R. Burnett fashioned from Burnett's novel, portrayed him as a lonely, even sensitive man out of his time. By the war years, gangsters were turning patriotic, helping the government capture German or Japanese spies.

In the postwar years of the forties, as crime once again became

domestic, a new type of hard-bitten melodrama came to the fore, given the name *film noir* by French critics (and accepted by that name in America only in the late sixties). There had been early suggestions of the genre in the first years of the decade in such films as *I Wake Up Screaming* (1941) and *This Gun for Hire* (1942), but its characteristics and conventions were not firmly set until the end of the war. There was a clearly defined *noir* world, peopled by vicious gangsters and desperate, frightened losers, guilty men and seductive women. Theirs was essentially an urban nighttime existence, delirious and dangerous; deserted, rain-swept streets, dimly lit hotel rooms, sleazy nightclubs, and impersonal police stations were their natural habitats. They fed obsessively off each other, caught in a trap constructed by their own malevolence and corruption. They had long abandoned the eternal verities: love was replaced by carnal desire, friendship by treachery, dreams of happiness by nightmares of revenge. *Film noir* absorbed many strands from the past—German expressionism, the blunt crime films of the thirties, even a touch of postwar Italian neorealism—but basically it developed its own recognizable style.

Perhaps the purest *film noir* of the forties was Billy Wilder's adaptation of James M. Cain's novel *Double Indemnity* (1944). It starred Barbara Stanwyck, the high priestess of the genre, whose deep, nasal, insinuating voice and unadorned acting style made her ideal for melodramas involving crimes of passion or treachery. As icy, deceitful Phyllis Dietrichson, she is the definitive *noir* heroine; from the first view of the jangling bracelet decorating her shapely ankle to her final look of surprise as she is shot dead by her lover, we are given a chilling portrait of a hollow woman, unfeeling, unrepentant, and thoroughly dangerous.

Stanwyck's performance is the cold, hard center of a film that moves its protagonists to their grim fate—"the end of the line," as Phyllis Dietrichson puts it—with few wasted moments. Its plot is strictly pulpish: in a California community in 1938, illicit lovers murder the lady's husband to collect on the double indemnity clause in his insurance, then trap themselves in a web of deceit that spells their doom. Yet the screenplay by Billy Wilder (with an assist by Raymond Chandler) generates a surprising amount of sexual heat for a film of its day, its requisite scenes of suspense (notably one involving a stalled car during the killing) have a cutting tension that keeps the viewer enthralled, and it is played with hypnotic skill by actors in perfect tune with the film's intention. As Walter Neff, the gullible insurance agent lured into crime by Mrs. Dietrichson, Fred MacMurray plays convincingly against his usual affable type, and Edward G. Robinson brings his familiar intensity to the more conventional role of Walter Keyes, a suspicious insurance investigator working on the Dietrichson case.

Directing his own screenplay, Billy Wilder followed Cain's novel closely, but he gives the film his own sense of inexorable fate, of people destined to destroy each other. He allows no sentiment to intrude (as he would in later films) in putting the murderous duo through their paces. Their suggestive banter when they first meet

High Sierra (Warner Bros., 1941). Gangster Roy Earle (Humphrey Bogart, right) makes a point to his cronies, played by Arthur Kennedy and Alan Curtis, while Roy's girlfriend, Marie (Ida Lupino), watches. This was one of the best films to sound the death knell for the tough, violent underworld figures of the thirties.

FRED MacMURRAY   BARBARA STANWYCK
EDWARD G. ROBINSON

DOUBLE INDEMNITY

A Paramount Picture

PORTER HALL • JEAN HEATHER • BYRON BARR • RICHARD GAINES • JOHN PHILLIBER

Directed by BILLY WILDER

Screenplay by Billy Wilder and Raymond Chandler

(He: "How fast was I going?" She: "About ninety miles an hour") turns hectic and feverish when they become lovers; often photographed in half-shadow, she becomes soft, pliant, irresistible as she seduces him into killing her unpleasant husband (Tom Powers). But when their plot is hatched, they can no longer hide in the shadows: in a tense scene in a brightly lit supermarket, they whisper among the neat shelves of food. Wearing dark glasses and a tight white sweater, Stanwyck resembles a bored, slightly tawdry housewife doing routine chores.

The murder sequence is an example of film craftsmanship, tightly edited and unnerving. (As Walter kills Phyllis's husband, the camera rests on her stony face.) It is also the irretrievable act that starts them on the way to their own destruction. The climax in Phyllis's house may lend itself to parody four decades later, but it has a scorching impact. Phyllis and Walter meet in a darkened room while a distant radio plays "Tangerine." Accusing words fly back and forth until she shoots and wounds him. Suddenly remorseful, she admits that she never loved him, only used him—until now. It is all too late: a look of wonder and surprise crosses her face as he presses the gun against her, says, "Goodbye, baby," and fires. The music, the half-light, the hygienic room without character or personality, the voices confessing everything—these combine to create a scene that is the essence of *film noir*.

Inevitably, the underworld frequently provided settings for the *film noir*; it offered all the prerequisites for dark and brooding tales of violence and vengeance. One of the definitive films in this vein was *The Killers* (1946), directed by Robert Siodmak in the somewhat Germanic style he often brought to his films, and adapted by Anthony Veiller (with an uncredited assist by John Huston) from Ernest Hemingway's short story. The film is essentially an intelligent extension of the story, explaining in a complex series of flashbacks why Swede (Burt Lancaster in his film debut) felt obliged to await his executioners rather than attempting to flee. The beginning of the film is taken up with a superb visual replica of the story, complete with cryptic Hemingway dialogue ("Bright boy wants to know what it's all about." "We're gonna kill a Swede. We're killing him for a friend") and his understated sense of inexorable fate. The investigation of Swede's murder by Reardon (Edmond O'Brien), a determined insurance man, leads to a variety of devious and corrupt people, especially a kingpin crook named Big Jim Colfax (Albert Dekker) and a duplicitous vixen, Kitty Collins (Ava Gardner).

The Killers exemplifies the world of *film noir*: its dark and downbeat tone seldom varies as Reardon pursues the truth with a zeal over and above the call of duty. (His obsession with unraveling a mystery is not uncommon in the genre.) As one person after another reveals a piece of Swede's past, the puzzle begins to take shape, and it makes an ugly picture. It is clear that the nemesis in Swede's short life was Kitty, played by Ava Gardner as the epitome of the forties *femme fatale*, alluring, treacherous, and amoral. ("I'm poison—to myself and everybody around me!") In typically *noir*

settings—a grubby Atlantic City hotel room, a gang hideout, a cheap rooming house, a gaudy nightclub ("The Green Cat"), we see Kitty lie to Swede, cheat on him, and ultimately desert him, all in secret collusion with Jim Colfax. Ironically, the only character with any integrity is the Swede, a man proud of his boxing prowess who holds on to a semblance of honor and self-worth in a corrupt world—he takes the rap for Kitty when she is accused of wearing stolen jewelry, and he goes to jail; loving her, he believes her lies.

The *film noir* attitude toward organized crime—implacable, nonjudgmental, and coolly observant—achieved a peak with *The Killers* and persisted for a number of years in such films as *Johnny O'Clock* (1947), *Force of Evil* (1948), and *Criss Cross* (1949). Within the framework, however, there were interesting variations, and several crime films that were only marginally *noir*. These were the work of directors who really lacked the temperament for the brooding milieu of *film noir* and were more inclined to create movies that were uncluttered and naturalistic, relating more to the straightforward crime dramas of the thirties and early forties than to the later, somber mood pieces.

One of these was Raoul Walsh's *White Heat* (1949), a churning melodrama that restored James Cagney to the sort of explosive gangster role that had made him a star back in 1931. However, the changing times brought a significant difference in the character he played here—Cagney's Cody Jarrett was Tom Powers of *The Public Enemy* without the undeniable charm and charisma, but with the added burden of a severe mother-fixation, blinding headaches, and a psychotic personality. He was Tom Powers for the psychiatric age, a self-created demon who would kill anyone except his sainted mother. Finally trapped in an oil refinery, Jarrett climbs to the top of a tank, fires a bullet into it, and cries, "Made it, Ma! Top of the world!" as the tank explodes in flames.

Opposite: A lobby card for Double Indemnity *(Paramount, 1944). Below: A tense moment from Billy Wilder's definitive film noir: scheming lovers Barbara Stanwyck and Fred MacMurray receive a surprise visit from insurance investigator Edward G. Robinson.*
Above: The Killers *(Universal, 1946). Some devious scheme is surely being discussed by (left to right) Jeff Corey, Burt Lancaster, Albert Dekker, and Ava Gardner. Ernest Hemingway's famous short story became the springboard for an excellent, early film noir.*

White Heat was Raoul Walsh's first crime film since *High Sierra*, and it makes an interesting contrast to the earlier film. *High Sierra* concerned the twilight of the gangster after years of dominance; it ended almost elegiacally, with an anachronistic Roy Earle tumbling off a mountaintop to his death—in a sense, "crashing out" to freedom. But *White Heat* holds not an ounce of sentiment for its homicidal protagonist. After years of violent conflict on the battlefields, there could be no glorification of a violent killer. In one of his most audacious, unrestrained performances, Cagney makes Jarrett a monster who kills with cold-blooded indifference, but who collapses into unbridled hysteria in the prison mess hall when he learns of his mother's death. Cagney was never more daring than in this scene; his animal moans and flailing arms convey a man whose rage and grief cannot be contained. He is well served by Walsh's direction,

forceful and unobtrusive as usual, and by Ivan Goff and Ben Roberts's crackling screenplay.

John Huston's *The Asphalt Jungle* (1950), adapted by Huston and Ben Maddow from W. R. Burnett's novel, was another film with strong elements of the *film noir* but with an approach and an attitude all its own. It had the requisite collection of criminals—plug-uglies, hoods, and high-level schemers—caught up in an environment of double-crosses and violence. In *noir* fashion, they were spiders trapped in a web of their own devising, doomed to failure or an ignominious death.

But *The Asphalt Jungle* was directed and cowritten by John Huston, and as such it veers from *film noir* in interesting ways. Like Huston's *The Maltese Falcon*, it is essentially a caper movie that draws its special strength from the interplay of characters whose aspirations

White Heat (Warner Bros., 1949). Cody Jarrett (James Cagney) cries, "Made it, Ma! Top of the world!" as an oil tank explodes into flames. Jarrett—a psychotic kingpin gangster with a mother fixation and a propensity for cold-blooded murder—was one of Cagney's most audacious and memorable characterizations.

are greater than their ability to achieve them, and whose weaknesses finally do them in. The principal figures, involved in an ingenious attempt to steal a million dollars worth of diamonds, are linked to previous characters in Huston films: small-time hood Dix Handley (Sterling Hayden) shares the dream of *High Sierra*'s Roy Earle to find an elusive freedom in the great outdoors (Huston coauthored the screenplay of *High Sierra* from another W. R. Burnett novel). Dix's girl (Jean Hagen) is as doggedly loyal to him as Marie was to Earle. Like Howard of *The Treasure of the Sierra Madre*, Doc Reidenschneider (Sam Jaffe) dreams of living like a king in Mexico, surrounded by compliant females, and the apparently well-heeled lawyer Emmerich (Louis Calhern) resembles Caspar Gutman of *The Maltese Falcon*, desperately concealing his corruption behind a suave and urbane exterior. In a sense, these men and women are like everyone else, and that is the film's point. When Emmerich's wife complains about the people he must deal with, he replies, "There's nothing so different about them. After all, crime is only a left-handed form of human endeavor." Huston strengthens this point by making the minions of the law, especially a vindictive police commissioner, seem nastier than any of the crooks.

The Asphalt Jungle is a first-rate example of crime melodrama, bristling with taut and expertly staged scenes. The sequence of the jewel heist is justly famous. Prepared, according to Huston, with the advice of safecracking experts, it generates breathtaking suspense without resorting to tricky editing and camera placement. Throughout the movie, the exchanges of accusations and recriminations among the thieves are convincingly tense and forceful. Yet the film's characters are its most fascinating aspect. A proud man who has had seven years in prison to perfect his robbery plan, Doc Reidenschneider is uneasy with those who are less professional than he, but he also has a deep sense of reality. "One way or another,

we all pay for our vices," he tells a colleague prophetically, and he is caught when he pauses too long to watch a young girl dancing to the music of a jukebox. Dix Handley longs to return home to his Kentucky farm to live among the horses he loves, and the film's closing finds him fulfilling that dream in the last few minutes of his life. Emmerich can find release only in suicide; as superbly played by Louis Calhern, he is a man with no more illusions about himself or his status.

The scrounging and desperate criminals who inhabit *The Asphalt Jungle* seem mild in comparison with the nest of vipers assembled for Fritz Lang's melodrama *The Big Heat* (1953). Written by Sydney Boehm (from William P. McGivern's story), the film is a blistering tale of revenge in a world without moral order. A policeman's young wife is murdered by the mob (he was the intended victim), and his relentless obsession to avenge her death takes him beyond the law and explodes into further mayhem. Among those who become involved with the policeman Bannion (Glenn Ford) are Mike Laguna

(Alexander Scourby), a smooth, wealthy criminal kingpin, a sadistic hood named Vince (Lee Marvin), and Debbie (Gloria Grahame), Vince's tough but basically decent girlfriend.

In his customary fashion, Lang never permits a shred of pity, remorse, or compassion to soften his characters, all of whom he observes with cool detachment. Even the brutally widowed hero eventually becomes abrasive in his single-minded goal of revenge, permitting himself a few tender memories of his dead wife only after the body count has ended. *The Big Heat* bristles with unusually savage moments, none more so than the scene in which Lee Marvin, suspecting Gloria Grahame of informing, throws a cup of scalding coffee in her face. (It makes Cagney's grapefruit scene in *The Public Enemy* seem like a loving gesture.) Marvin gives his role a snarling intensity, and Gloria Grahame, by this time a specialist at pouting,

Left: The Asphalt Jungle *(MGM, 1950). A jewel robbery is being planned by (left to right) Sam Jaffe, Sterling Hayden, Anthony Caruso, and James Whitmore. John Huston's caper melodrama was one of the best: tough, well-written, and with an unusually complex group of outside-the-law characters.*
Right: The Big Heat *(Columbia, 1953). Policeman Dave Bannion (Glenn Ford), obsessed with avenging his wife's murder, roughs up hood Vince Stone (Lee Marvin).*

seductive women, makes Debbie a genuinely touching figure. (This is rare in crime films, in which the attitude toward women, more often than not, is misogynistic.) Exacting her own revenge by flinging hot coffee into Lee Marvin's face, she dominates this hard and gripping film.

Side by side with the *films noirs* that flourished from the mid-forties to the early fifties were crime dramas, many from Twentieth Century-Fox, that assumed a semidocumentary style, complete with laconic narration, frequent use of on-location settings, and straightforward stories based on true incidents. The best of these films was *Kiss of Death* (1947), a hard-edged melodrama directed by Henry Hathaway, with a taut screenplay by Ben Hecht and Charles Lederer from a story by Eleazar Lipsky. There was nothing extraordinary about the plot, concerning an ex-convict and gang member, Nick Bianco (a subdued, effective Victor Mature), who turns informer for the sake of his motherless children. Yet several new factors combined

to make *Kiss of Death* an uncommonly fascinating and successful film in its genre. One was Norbert Brodine's on-location photography in New York City, which used, to maximum advantage, such settings as the Criminal Courts Building, the Tombs, and a house in Queens. Another was the star-making performance of Richard Widmark, a stage and radio actor in his film debut as psychotic hood Tommy Udo, who becomes Nick Bianco's nemesis. Widmark startled audiences with his maniacal laugh and falsely jocular manner ("You're a big man!"), and his bursts of sudden violence were truly frightening. His Tommy Udo entered the ranks of film's most sadistic villains by pushing a wheelchair-bound old lady (Mildred Dunnock) down a flight of stairs to her death.

Most interesting of all, however, was the film's ambiguous attitude toward the morality of informers and those who spur them to inform. Since any "snitch" or "squealer" is bound to be regarded by audiences with some distaste, the screenplay bends over back-

Above: Kiss of Death *(Fox, 1947). Nick Bianco (Victor Mature, right) meets with Tommy Udo (Richard Widmark). In his first movie, Widmark created a sensation as the sadistic crook who becomes Nick's deadliest enemy.*
Opposite: In Cold Blood *(Columbia, 1967). Perry Smith (Robert Blake) and Dick Hickok (Scott Wilson) break into the Cutter farm in Kansas, where they will commit murder. Richard Brooks's film probed the reasons behind the actual killings that had taken place in 1959.*

ward to make Nick a *reluctant* informer; he agonizes over his decision and bitterly resents the badgering efforts of the assistant district attorney (Brian Donlevy) to get his cooperation. He is also a kind father, and a loving husband to the faithful girl (Coleen Gray) he marries when out of prison. Still, there are disturbing gray areas that the film cannot erase; in fact, he is indirectly responsible for the old lady's death—he falsely names her son as the informer, triggering Tommy Udo's brutal act. There are also questionable aspects to the behavior of the police officials who urge Nick to inform. Although their laudable goal is to put a crazed killer out of circulation, they feel no compunction about distorting the facts to Nick, or placing both him and his family in jeopardy to get their man. They are, in fact, ruthless.

Dramas involving crime, both organized and independent, continued to appear throughout the fifties, but few of them had any distinction. (Director Stanley Kubrick had a *succès d'estime* with *The Killing*, 1956, an efficiently made melodrama concerning a failed racetrack robbery.) The early sixties saw few crime films being produced; in addition to the familiar genres, audiences seemed to prefer large-scale spectacles, shiny comedies (often starring a sunny Doris Day), and James Bond adventures.

It was not until 1967 that renewed interest in stories involving violence and gunplay was sparked by two films, each drastically different from the other in style and approach. Richard Brooks's *In Cold Blood* was a stark, chilling adaptation of Truman Capote's book concerning the actual murder of a Kansas family by two ex-convicts, and the pursuit, capture, and execution of the killers. Photographed in austere black-and-white by Conrad Hall and written by Brooks with a deliberately fragmented continuity, the movie gave more emphasis to the background of the murderers than did Capote's "nonfiction novel." Although its lingering view of the death house execution seemed to violate the attempt at documentary-like objectivity, the sum total was a harrowing portrait of evil.

The second film, Arthur Penn's production of *Bonnie and Clyde*, was one of the most controversial and outstanding of the decade. The story of Bonnie Parker and Clyde Barrow, two small-time thieves and murderers who had achieved notoriety and a kind of legendary status in Depression-era Kansas, had served as the basis for previ-

Overleaf: Bonnie and Clyde *(Warner Bros., 1967). The fateful meeting of Clyde Barrow (Warren Beatty) and Bonnie Parker (Faye Dunaway) that will propel them into crime and violent death in America's Depression years. Right:* Bonnie and C. W. Moss *(Michael J. Pollard), her none-too-bright partner in crime, stand before a bank they no doubt intend to rob. The movie shocked many viewers with its juxtaposition of raucous comedy and explicit violence.*

ous films reflecting their particular periods: Fritz Lang's *You Only Live Once* (1937); *They Live by Night* (1949), Nicholas Ray's first film; and *The Bonnie Parker Story* (1958). But Penn's *Bonnie and Clyde* offered a startlingly original approach to the crime film that precipitated a veritable flood of both outraged and admiring criticism. Although there was generally high praise for the production, especially for its brilliant re-creation of the look of thirties America, the original screenplay by David Newman and Robert Benton was often harshly attacked for its shocking juxtaposition of boisterous comedy and explicit violence, and for its glamorization of Bonnie and Clyde as folk heroes not unlike the beleaguered antiestablishment rebels of the sixties. (Much, perhaps too much, was made of the fact that the title roles were played by Warren Beatty and Faye Dunaway, two attractive, charismatic movie stars who in no way resembled the actual couple.)

Viewed some fifteen years after the furor, *Bonnie and Clyde* no longer shocks, but it remains a stunning film. It begins as a raucous folk tale complete with twanging country music and ends as a nightmare in broad daylight with the bullet-riddled bodies of its protagonists. Contrary to the prevalent view that the movie is an antiestablishment, counterculture defense of the sixties' protesting youth, it can be argued persuasively that the ill-fated Bonnie and Clyde demonstrate the danger of coming to believe in one's self-created myth. Bonnie and Clyde are characterized as resolutely ordinary people: he is a good-looking but impotent drifter with a middle-class attitude despite the vainglory (talking with Bonnie's mother, he sounds like an accountant—"We'll settle down," but you know "how uncertain times are"), and she is a bored, restless girl sexually aroused by Clyde's bravado. Their companions in crime are even more ordinary: Clyde's brother Buck (Gene Hackman) is just a "good ol' country boy"; Buck's wife Blanche (Estelle Parsons in an Academy Award–winning performance) is a hysterical drab; and C. W. Moss (Michael J. Pollard) is close to imbecility.

But the film shows how easily this motley group becomes "the Barrow gang," robbing out of impulse and killing almost as an afterthought. Clyde gives them a catchy slogan, "We rob banks"; Bonnie writes doggerel poetry about their exploits as if they were Robin Hood and his Merrie Men; when they humiliate a Texas ranger, they insist on having their picture taken with him, to send to the newspapers. They appeal to the public because, in spite of their celebrity, they insist that they are "just folks." But once they kill their first innocent victim—and the camera shows us his startled, blood-splattered face—they take their myth to a new level of madness that deliberately jolts viewers and throws them off balance. They may continue to delude themselves into believing that they are still "just folks," but the first fatal step to their destruction has been taken. The film seems to be saying that seeds of evil can sprout in any soil, casually and imperceptibly, and that they can flower quickly.

Despite flaws—a somewhat mannered performance by Faye Dunaway and too-obvious Freudian symbolism in the use of guns—*Bonnie and Clyde* is a superbly made film in which settings, costumes, music, screenplay, direction, and performances merge into an effective unit. (Dede Allen's editing and Burnett Guffey's award-winning photography are especially fine.) Inevitably, the scene that provoked the most outrage was the climactic "ballet of death" in which Bonnie and Clyde are brutally mowed down by the police. It has been interpreted in several ways: as a comment on the perverse beauty of violence (two years later, Sam Peckinpah would make this a major theme of *The Wild Bunch*); as the ironic final orgasmic communion of Bonnie and Clyde (their bodies leap and twitch in almost sexual positions); or as a case of overkill—the bloody out-of-control retribution of the ranger who had been humiliated by Bonnie and Clyde. Whatever the interpretation, it marks the unforgettable ending of a landmark film.

The face of crime that *Bonnie and Clyde* showed us looked not much different from any other; these were down-home folks who just happened to rob banks and kill people. Many years earlier, in *The Asphalt Jungle*, corrupt lawyer Louis Calhern had told his wife that there was "nothing so different" about criminals. This concept—that the most evil of men have basically the same dreams, drives, and ambitions as the most innocent (what Hannah Arendt had called "the banality of evil")—never received more elaborate attention than in the 1972 film adaptation of Mario Puzo's novel *The Godfather*. At its core, this extraordinary movie may have harked back to the gangster melodramas of the thirties, but it dramatized an idea that would never have occurred to that tyrannical loner Caesar Enrico Bandello—that organized crime thrived on, indeed, depended on "the family." The family was all—and not just the gang members but their wives, their children, their friends in the community. This was the central metaphor of *The Godfather*; one could lie, steal, cheat, and kill for the family, but the strictest code of honor, fidelity, and respect must be maintained.

The Corleones, the principal family of *The Godfather*, live in a protected fortress that we see in the film's opening sequence: the wedding day of Vito Corleone's daughter Connie. Even on this festive occasion, Vito Corleone (Marlon Brando), the Godfather, the revered head of the family, is receiving those who need his help. Proud of his Italian heritage, proud of his children, he is the stern but benign patriarch. He worships his adopted country—he tells his first visitor, "You found paradise in America." But during the course of this extremely violent movie, we see the consequences of Vito Corleone's criminal empire. His sons are drawn into the network of murder and vengeance: Sonny (James Caan) is brutally murdered by a rival family, and Michael (Al Pacino), the family "scholar" and the one who had stood outside the nefarious activities, proves to be the most ruthless of all when he inherits his father's mantle. Carlo (Gianni Russo), the treacherous son-in-law married in the opening scene, is strangled by Corleone musclemen. Within this tightly knit, intensely loyal family, lives are lost or wrecked—in

Opposite: The Godfather: Part II *(Paramount, 1974). The young Vito Corleone (Robert De Niro, crouching at left) is involved in a shootout in Sicily as he settles a longtime vendetta against an enemy.*

this private club, the price of membership is high.

The Godfather is the gangster film carried to a new level of bravura and theatrical intensity. The screenplay, credited to Mario Puzo and director Francis Ford Coppola, is punctuated with scenes of explicit violence that earlier crime movies could only hint at; in these scenes death is ugly, grotesque, horrifying—it lacks the "aesthetic" quality suggested in *Bonnie and Clyde*. Essentially, the film is concerned with events that drastically change the makeup of the Corleone family, and especially with the emergence of Michael as the new Don. His transformation from a dutiful but withdrawn son into an all-powerful Godfather is traced in Al Pacino's strong, vivid performance. When he commits his first act of murder, killing a corrupt police chief and a rival family head, his eyes turn cold and his face hardens. A series of revenge killings—his brother Sonny and Michael's young Italian wife—draws him closer to the family, and his father's death confirms his position. When he is finally addressed as Don Corleone, his face half-hidden in darkness, the

effect is disquieting. In the film's most brilliant sequence, Michael's power is consolidated at the same time that the continuity and indestructibility of the family is demonstrated: scenes of the baptism of Connie's baby alternate with others showing the extermination of the heads of opposing families.

Francis Ford Coppola keeps events flowing smoothly, and he manages a large cast with skill, extracting noteworthy performances from everyone but his star, Marlon Brando. Elaborately made-up and speaking in a hoarse voice, Brando appears to be acting in a different film from anyone else. True, it is a showy role, but he seems to be overly aware of the weight and bearing he must bring to it. Despite the Academy Award Brando won—and refused—it is a self-conscious performance. Yet his death scene is both poignant and chilling; he expires in the garden while playing with his little grandson, and as he lies dead, his grandson "guns him down" with a spray can, a reminder of the boy's inheritance and probable destiny.

As good as *The Godfather* was, *The Godfather: Part II* (1974) was

Overleaf, left: The Godfather *(Paramount, 1972). In Sicily, where he has gone to hide, young
Michael Corleone (Al Pacino) is married to a local girl. She will later become a victim of the
violence surrounding the Corleone family.*
Overleaf, right: The Godfather: Part II *(Paramount, 1974). In an ironic flashback near the
end of the film, the Corleone family gathers soon after the attack on Pearl Harbor in December
1941. Ahead for the Corleones are years of power, marked by violent death.*

even better: a film of staggering dimensions and near-operatic power that deepened the story of the Corleone family. Sweeping both backward and forward in time from the period of *The Godfather*, it begins in Sicily in 1901, with nine-year-old Vito Corleone as the only survivor of a bloody vendetta against his family, and ends in Lake Tahoe in 1958, with Michael Corleone as the undisputed Don, feared and alone. Between the frightened immigrant boy and the Mafia leader isolated in his fortress lay the corruption of the American dream, a subject large enough to embrace the epic style employed by Francis Ford Coppola. Few movies of the seventies made such eloquent use of the medium or crowded such an array of stunning images into a running time of three hours and twenty minutes.

Part of the film was devoted to the early years of Vito Corleone and the steps by which he became a force in New York City's impoverished immigrant community. These scenes have a verisimilitude and a conviction due in large measure to Dean Tavoularis's production design (the views of slum life in 1917 New York are astonishing) and to Robert De Niro's superb performance as young Corleone. (He won that year's Oscar for Best Supporting Actor.) But the film centered on the concept of crime as big business and not, as in *The Godfather*, as a family affair of which business was only one important part. Here was the true corruption of the dream: during the course of the movie, Michael Corleone, as he ruthlessly seizes control, must deal with a venal United States senator, a powerful deported American gangster, a Cuban dictator allied to American business, and assorted thugs and opportunists. By the time the film ends, we have seen Vito Corleone's idea of the family, bound together by loyalty and, when necessary, by violence, transformed into Michael Corleone's less scrupulous and even bloodier sprawling business empire. The movie never judges Michael—as a man alone, he is not broken or pitiable, but neither is he triumphant. He has survived by seizing power, and he has severed all emotional ties except those with his children.

The scenes of Michael Corleone's large-scale business dealings give the film its scope and much of its melodrama, but the personal tensions within the family give it an emotional resonance. Most affecting is Michael's relationship with his older brother Fredo (John Cazale), who betrays the family out of resentment and weakness. It is here that we see the crucial difference between Michael and his father in their attitude toward unbreakable family ties. When Michael realizes that Fredo has conspired with the enemy, a flicker of pain crosses his face, and he kisses Fredo, crying, "I know it was you! You broke my heart!" But later he turns icy cold ("You're nothing to me now"), and after their mother dies, Michael has Fredo killed. No relationship, however close, can disturb the center of power in Michael's world; the last image is of Michael isolated in his great house. From little Vito Corleone leaping off a ship to swim to the shore of American safety and comfort to this final view of Michael Corleone is a distance much vaster than the span of five recorded decades. *The Godfather*'s first line, spoken by the man

who has come to Don Corleone to ask for help, is "I believe in America." By the end of the second film, we know that the new Don Corleone believes in very little, and that the America of his father has vanished forever. Like its predecessor, *The Godfather: Part II* offers no moral judgment, but the statement is clearly implied: the American dream has been soured by corrupt and greedy men who never really understood what they were inheriting.

Except for *The Friends of Eddie Coyle* (1974), Peter Yates's unusually bleak and realistic crime melodrama, *The Godfather* films marked the last major appearance of the gangster in American films. Audience interest in the seventies shifted to the police, but not necessarily the stalwart, square-jawed police of other decades. Throughout the seventies there were more corrupt, deeply troubled, even dangerous cops than honest ones, while criminals merely became targets. The first truly amoral policeman of the period, however, was Popeye Doyle, the seedy, profane, and sadistic narcotics detective played by Gene Hackman in William Friedkin's Academy Award–winning film *The French Connection* (1971). A swift and expertly made melodrama derived by Ernest Tidyman from Robin Moore's novel, the movie was in the crime-busting tradition that had not produced many memorable entries in other years. Its story, concerning Popeye Doyle's efforts to apprehend a kingpin drug dealer based in Marseille and to confiscate his large shipment of heroin, was hardly original. But by virtue of a relentless pace, ingenious use of New York City locations, and a fine idiosyncratic performance by Hackman, complete with porkpie hat, a pistol ready for whipping suspects, and a permanent sneer, the film is compelling entertainment. The most talked-about sequence was Popeye's car pursuit of a hijacked elevated train, photographed and edited to unnerve every viewer with the sounds of screeching brakes, shrieking passengers, and colliding cars.

It is not likely that the snarling visage of the gangster will appear very often on our screens in the years ahead, especially now that it has been enshrined in grandiose style in the *Godfather* films. The brash and aggressive big-time hood who attracted such topical attention in the thirties has been replaced by a business executive in a three-piece suit, well-groomed, well-heeled, and well-placed. Crime has become big business, but not in the Corleone sense. It is much too discreet for overt large-scale violence.

This is not to say that crime itself will ever go out of movie fashion. Independent-minded people who kill out of power, greed, vengeance, or simply for the-hell-of-it will always attract audience attention. In a world where cataclysms occur much too frequently, we may talk about collective guilt or mankind's capacity for evil. But the dramatic concerns of film remain with the individual, not with the masses, and movies will continue to probe the dark corners of the mind as people harbor thoughts of treachery and murder. Unfortunately, crime never goes away; fortunately, it has provided the impetus for many films we can admire and remember.

Opposite: The French Connection *(Fox, 1971). Gene Hackman (second from left) won an Academy Award for Best Actor for his performance as the brutish narcotics detective Popeye Doyle. Below: Popeye fires at Pierre Nicoli (Marcel Bozzuffi) in a climactic scene from the Oscar-winning melodrama.*

THE LOWER DEPTHS
Great Movies on Society's Outcasts

In movies as in life, everyone loves a winner, even when the triumph is not necessarily clear-cut. We applaud Lou Gehrig in *Pride of the Yankees* on his last day as a ballplayer although we know he is dying. We are buoyed by Mrs. Miniver, standing proudly in the ruins of her war-torn English village. And we cheer for a battered Rocky (in the first *Rocky* movie), even though he loses the bout.

But there are those for whom life holds few or no rewards, except for what a benign scriptwriter metes out at the end of a film as a sop to depressed audiences. These are society's outcasts and losers: the innocent men trapped into lives of crime, the men whose single guilty act sends them hurtling toward doom, those whose lust to be champions makes them forget their humanity—and all the women who plummet to despair and madness. Their woeful stories have provided the fodder for a number of outstanding, often somber films. These are films where sunlight rarely penetrates, where desperate people play out their lives in cramped and dingy quarters or in some metaphoric hell.

Film attitudes toward the lower depths have changed in revealing ways over the decades. Largely ignored in the silent era until the last years, the losers and outcasts moved in and out of the spotlight as time passed. Often fleeing from an implacable law—victims of a callous and heedless society—in the thirties, they scurried into the shadows in the forties, then reemerged reluctantly in the fifties to be exposed in bright light as grotesques living in the wrong era. (Norma Desmond and Blanche DuBois were the period's patron saints of has-beens.) By the seventies, society's lower echelon was treated in films as symbolic of *all* of America's (or even mankind's) ills, inhabiting a tacky dance ballroom or, appropriately, a mental hospital.

For most of the twenties, American filmmakers apparently saw little reason to depress their new and burgeoning audiences with distressing tales from life's underside. On the whole, they felt that this sort of thing was best left to the Europeans, especially the Germans, who delighted in *Weltschmerz* and gloom-laden, tragic views of ruined lives. Prominent examples of German films about men who were utterly destroyed by events or by circumstances of their own making include F. W. Murnau's *The Last Laugh* (1924), E. A. Dupont's *Variety* (1926), and Josef von Sternberg's *The Blue Angel* (1930), all starring Emil Jannings. The stark photography and psychological intensity of these films carried over into American movies of the late twenties and early thirties, especially when Murnau and Von Sternberg themselves came to work in Hollywood.

With the onset of the Depression, bringing America's carefree days to an end, it no longer seemed inappropriate for film to touch on more sordid topics. Among the rash of escapist films—frivolous comedies, elaborate musicals, or even gangster films that made lawlessness seem if not profitable, then entertaining—was an occasional film that strongly suggested that American society was exacerbating the misery of its more unfortunate citizens with a cold and aggressive attitude.

One of the first and strongest of the "society-is-against-us" films came, not surprisingly, from Warner Bros., which drew much of its impetus in the thirties from topical issues. An autobiographical story by one Robert E. Burns, entitled "I Am a Fugitive from a Georgia Chain Gang," had exposed the brutality and corruption of the state's prison system, and Warners, not one to miss the main chance, adapted it into a searing social drama that dropped "Georgia" from its title, for obvious reasons. *I Am a Fugitive from a Chain Gang* created a sensation on its release late in 1932 and even precipitated a clamor for immediate legislation. Its story of Jim Allen (Paul Muni), an ambitious young war veteran who becomes a desperate thief and, finally, a fugitive, was such strong medicine that when the actual fugitive Burns was arrested in New Jersey, there was a flood of appeals for leniency, and the governor refused to extradite him to Georgia. An angry South attacked the movie, calling it a nasty fabrication.

As directed by Mervyn LeRoy, *I Am a Fugitive from a Chain Gang* has the pounding drive and relentless pace of many Warners movies of the period, as well as the overheated dialogue in which every line appeared to be punctuated with exclamation points. It also overstated Allen's innocence so that the exposé was less effective than it might have been; guilty as well as innocent prisoners hardly deserved the humiliation and brutalization that destroys Jim Allen. His punishment is as swift as it is unjustified: we watch with dismay as his role as an unwitting accomplice in a robbery sends him to a chain gang. The scenes in prison have a documentary-like power: we see men at work on a rock pile, or chained to their beds, or watching with bitter indifference as Allen is savagely beaten. His escape is depicted with melodramatic force; the horns, the barking bloodhounds, the flight underwater give these scenes a nightmarish quality.

Allen rises to prominence as a Chicago architect, but he is caught again and returned to the chain gang. At this point, we sense that the writers have truly stacked the cards against him. (The defense of the chain gang system as "beneficial to convicts, physically and morally," seems laughable today.) But when, after false hopes and promises, his pleas for a pardon are adamantly refused, he escapes again, to bring the film to a shattering (and famous) conclusion. Hovering in the shadows at a furtive last meeting with the girl (Helen Vinson) who has stood by him, he tells her hoarsely, "They'll always be after me. No friends, no rest, no peace!" She asks, "How do you get along? How do you live?" Out of the darkness comes his stinging reply: "I steal!"

Of the thirties films portraying society as callous and uncaring—an inexorable force that destroyed innocent lives—the most potent was

Opposite: Midnight Cowboy *(Hellman-Schlesinger/United Artists, 1969). An oddly touching friendship develops between streetwise "Ratso" Rizzo (Dustin Hoffman) and the naïve cowboy Joe Buck (Jon Voight) in the lower depths of New York City.*

Fritz Lang's second American film, *You Only Live Once* (1937). A faulty but often affecting drama, it told a harrowing story of a young couple, Eddie Taylor (Henry Fonda) and his wife Joan (Sylvia Sidney), whose flight from the law ends in their death by gunfire. Eddie, an ex-convict and three-time loser, is accused of a crime he didn't commit, and rather than serve another sentence, he escapes from prison. When the escape results in the death of a sympathetic chaplain (William Gargan), the outcome for Eddie and his faithful Joan can be surmised.

Lang gives the film the same somber intensity, the same Germanic, doom-laden atmosphere he had brought to *Fury* the year before. But here his bitterness is somewhat tempered with an uncharacteristic tenderness and warmth toward the ill-fated couple, and, as played by Fonda and Sidney, they arouse our sympathy and regard. In his thirties films, culminating in *The Grapes of Wrath* in 1940, Fonda always brought exceptional conviction to his downtrodden types, and Sidney, the definitive Depression heroine, reveals the core of steel within the tremulous, frightened young bride. There is not much subtlety in the point of view—Eddie states bluntly, "They made me a murderer," and Joan pleads, "We have a right to live"—but in the last scenes, Lang creates a tragic aura that surmounts the message-mongering. After giving birth, Joan brings the baby to her sister and returns to Eddie's hideout, where a police cortege is waiting for them. Fonda is photographed through the police's telescopic gun sight; the born target has become an actual target.

The principal flaw of *You Only Live Once* is prominent but not fatal. As in *I Am a Fugitive from a Chain Gang*, the cards are very heavily stacked against Eddie and Joan from the very first: a hotel owner tosses them out when he learns that Eddie is an ex-convict; his new boss treats him with vicious contempt and fires him peremptorily; and at his trial (which is never shown) he appears to be convicted on his past record. Only a public defender (Barton MacLane) and the priest show any compassion. Still, despite its one-sided stance, *You Only Live Once* is perhaps the representative film among the "society-as-victimizer" crop of the thirties.

Above: You Only Live Once *(Walter Wanger/United Artists, 1937). In the climax of Fritz Lang's grim melodrama, born victims Joan and Eddie Taylor (Sylvia Sidney and Henry Fonda) make their last desperate attempt to flee from the law.*
Opposite: A lobby card for I Am a Fugitive from a Chain Gang *(Warner Bros., 1932).*
Below: In this film, Jim Allen (Paul Muni, at front) contemplates a hopeless life on a Southern chain gang. The movie created a sensation in its day, and actually sparked legislation to ease prison conditions.

While many Hollywood films of the thirties glibly proclaimed that the roots of crime were embedded in society's hardened indifference, one film portrayed a man at fatal odds with the violence-ridden society in which he lived, unable to cope with its simple demands of loyalty and friendship. Adapted by Dudley Nichols from Liam O'Flaherty's novel, John Ford's *The Informer* (1935) was a grim melodrama concerning one day—in fact, the last day—in the life of Gypo Nolan (Victor McLaglen), a brutish, baffled, childlike giant who, during the Irish "troubles" in 1922, betrays his best friend, Frankie McPhillip (Wallace Ford), to the Black and Tans. Cornered, tried, and finally shot by his fellow rebels, the dying Gypo begs forgiveness of his friend's sorrowing mother.

Produced by RKO with a small budget—dark, expressionistic lighting is often used to conceal the flimsy sets—and many misgivings,

The Informer received greatly admiring reviews and won four Academy Awards. For many years, however, the film has been depreciated by critics who have deplored its heavy-handed symbolism, its maudlin scenes, and the indifferent performances by some actors in key supporting roles. (A legend has even been perpetrated that John Ford extracted an impressive performance from McLaglen by keeping him in a constant state of intoxication.)

Yet the admitted shortcomings of *The Informer* tend to fade beside the many striking scenes depicting Gypo Nolan's downfall in the fog-shrouded streets of Dublin. The scene in which Gypo informs to the British police has a fine cutting edge: Gypo nervous and obsequious, the officer barely concealing his scorn as he pushes the money to Gypo with a stick and snaps, "Twenty pounds. You'd better count it." Despite too many self-consciously "arty" touches, such as the recur-

The Informer *(RKO, 1935). A dying Gypo Nolan (Victor McLaglen) finds forgiveness from the mother (Una O'Connor) of the friend he betrayed to the British police. John Ford's drama of the Irish "troubles" in the early twenties is no longer considered among the director's best films, but many scenes retain their original power.*

ring figure of the blind man, Gypo's increasingly desperate flight from the consequences of his terrible deed takes on a cumulative power as the long night wears on. Ford makes small moments work to maximum effect: the fearful clatter of Gypo's newly acquired coins as they tumble onto the floor at the wake of Frankie McPhillip; the revealing shot that tracks through the boisterous crowd surrounding the drunken Gypo to the face of the rebel (Joseph Sawyer) who suspects his guilt; and, especially, the "trial" scene in which a frantic, sweating Gypo tries to convince the tribunal of rebels that the timid tailor Mulligan (Donald Meek) is the informer. Gypo's death scene in the church has been called mawkish, but it is actually a fitting coda to a somber tale. As Mrs. McPhillip (that splendid actress Una O'Connor) absolves him of guilt, Gypo, with arms outstretched, cries, "Frankie! Frankie! Your mother forgives me!" just before he collapses and dies. Although *The Informer* is far from John Ford's greatest film, it deserves a higher position in the body of his work than critics have afforded it in recent years.

By the 1940s, American society's ostensible guilt was soon replaced by the larger guilt of genocide by madmen across the ocean, and by America's need to pull both victims and victimizers together for the sake of a world war. After the war, two cinematic attitudes prevailed toward the relationship of man and society. On the one hand, there was a flurry of interest in coming to grips with the country's longstanding social problems, such as racism, anti-Semitism, and alcoholism. On the other hand, there was an inevitable turning inward; the theory was that man's tendency to promote evil, to become ensnared in criminal activity, did not come from outer forces acting upon him but from the darkest recesses of his own mind. In film after film, man himself, and not some formless "society," was to blame—he was corruptible, treacherous, reprehensible; often, woman was even worse.

Ultimately, the dark-hued, violent melodrama that flourished in the mid- and late forties came to be known as the *film noir*. Several of the films, however, while sharing the atmosphere and viewpoint of the *film noir*, fell outside its framework, offering not conventional crime stories but portraits of losers making one last futile effort to rise above the abysmal level of their lives.

One was Fox's 1947 film *Nightmare Alley*, directed by Edmund Goulding and adapted by Jules Furthman from William Lindsay Gresham's novel. A highly unusual film to come from the studio of Shirley Temple and Betty Grable, the movie offered a bleak view of the carnival world. It concentrated on an ambitious but small-time barker and "mentalist" (Tyrone Power, cast against his usual type and succeeding admirably), who ends his tawdry career as a wild, alcoholic "geek." The "geek," a freak attraction considered the lowest form of carnival life, specializes in biting the heads off live chickens. (In the opening scene, the resident "geek" goes berserk and has to be restrained.)

Although the director fails to give the movie any real style or texture, *Nightmare Alley* remains one of the more fascinating films of the period. (It also demonstrated the change of attitude from the thirties—the antihero Stan Carlisle is not destroyed by "them" but

by his own corrupt nature.) The early scenes are best, establishing the seedy carny milieu as Stan schemes to take over the mind-reading act performed by Zeena (Joan Blondell, in an impeccable performance) and her alcoholic husband, Pete. It sags somewhat in the middle section, but the last scenes have a chilling effect: Stan alone in a hotel room, screaming for liquor and finally accepting a job as a geek. ("Mister, I was *made* for it!") In an ironic reprise of the beginning, he goes berserk. "How can a guy get so low?" someone asks, and the cautionary answer is, "He reached too high."

Another film that offered an exceptionally graphic, incisive view of a man doomed by his own mean and greedy spirit was Warners's production of *The Treasure of the Sierra Madre* (1948). B. Traven had written a novel about three drifters in 1925 Mexico whose search for gold ends in disillusion and death, and Huston adapted it for the screen, eliminating its heavily Marxian implications. Humphrey Bogart played Fred C. Dobbs, a nasty, hot-tempered vagrant whose dreams of glory end ignominiously in the barren hills, with Walter Huston (John's father) as Howard, the sly, toothless codger who knows "what gold does to men's souls," and Tim Holt as Curtin, the basically decent young man who joins the others in their disastrous quest.

From the first scenes in a grubby Mexican town in which the men come together to plan their search for treasure, the film has a dry, acrid flavor. As they venture into the hills and their avidness for gold turns to obsession, this flavor becomes more pronounced. Subtly, the film depicts the breakdown of the relationship among the three prospectors when they make a strike; we can see the loose camaraderie eroding with each passing day. A look or a glance becomes more meaningful than words: Dobbs's eyes positively gleam as old Howard weighs the gold; a flicker of confusion passes across Curtin's face as he wonders whether to rescue Dobbs from a mine cave-in; the ominous silence of Curtin and Dobbs as they sit opposite each

Nightmare Alley (Fox, 1947). Circus barker Tyrone Power is forcibly restrained by Mike Mazurki. Interested observers at left include Joan Blondell and Coleen Gray. This was an odd movie to come from Fox: a dark view of carnival life and one man's descent into its very dregs.

other, guarding their hoards and fighting sleep, fills the night air. The conventional action scenes may pale beside these quiet expressions of the film's central theme, but the climax, which finds Dobbs trapped by the outlaw Gold Hat and his fellow bandits, is one of the most frightening scenes ever devised for an adventure film. (Alfonso Bedoya's characterization of Gold Hat evokes a truly terrifying, primitive evil.)

The Treasure of the Sierra Madre disappointed at the box office, but it is one of the most impressive films of the forties. At its best, it strongly suggests Erich von Stroheim's *Greed* in its corrosive dissection of the destructive power of gold (and in the final scenes of men trapped in an unyielding desert). But it is very much its own film as well, with a finely honed approach by director-screenwriter Huston that exposes the drifters' mounting fear and suspicion to the camera's merciless glare. As Dobbs, Humphrey Bogart replaced the mysterious, romantic veneer that made him a star in *Casablanca* with the snarling visage of a man whose life is controlled by spite, malice, and greed (a transformation that audiences apparently did not appreciate). When he remarks, "Nobody gets the best of Fred

C. Dobbs," we know that we are watching a born loser who has been bested by just about everyone. Walter Huston, who won the Best Supporting Actor award, made a memorable character of Howard, grinning as he senses the paranoia behind Dobbs's determination or as he is welcomed into a Mexican village with a bottle of whisky and a bevy of attentive girls, and, near the end of the film, standing alone in a sandstorm and laughing as he finds the empty bags that once contained their gold.

Among the rash of late-forties films on the lower echelon of humanity were several interesting films on boxing. A sport that attracts a dramatically promising assortment of petty criminals and pathetic hangers-on, boxing had been a film subject for some time, but within a few years, *Body and Soul* (1947), *Champion* (1949), and *The Set-Up* (1949) peeled away its colorful surface to reveal the grimy underside where arrogant roosters in boxing trunks clawed their way to the championship while broken-down boxers grasped at the last shreds of their self-respect. (Many years later, *Rocky* reconstructed the myth of the true boxing champion.)

Of the three films, RKO's *The Set-Up* had the most stringent

The Treasure of the Sierra Madre *(Warner Bros., 1948). Dour Fred C. Dobbs (Humphrey Bogart) is clearly suspicious of Howard (Walter Huston), his fellow gold prospector. Huston's strong physical resemblance to the leading character in Erich von Stroheim's* Greed *emphasized the other similarities between this film and the earlier classic.*

production and the least impressive credentials, but it proved to be the most successful: a compact and vivid little film that took the viewer into the depths of the boxing world where destroyed fighters dream of one last triumph while the paying customers cry for blood. Under Robert Wise's direction, *The Set-Up* relates the story of one evening in the life of Stoker Thompson, a has-been boxer at thirty-five, whose manager has already arranged to have him throw a fight for fifty dollars. But Stoker, still clinging to his tattered pride, refuses, and, in a bloody fight, he wins. Badly beaten by hoods, he can still cry, "I wouldn't do it! I won tonight! I won!" Played with grittiness and sensitivity by that estimable actor Robert Ryan, Stoker is a heroic figure who stirs pity and admiration. He accepts his fate but he will not allow himself to be knocked out of the ring forever. *The Set-Up* manages well within its small budget, fully conveying the sleaziness and brutality of boxing's lowest order.

By 1950, with the *film noir* beginning to go out of vogue, denizens of the lower depths began to emerge from their private nightmare world into the merciless light. With no resources to fall back on, they found themselves confronting a society that had rejected them out of hostility or indifference, or that they themselves had rejected years ago out of misplaced pride. In two of the most celebrated films of the period, there were searing moments in which

bright lights exposed souls ravaged by life. In *A Streetcar Named Desire*, Blanche DuBois's furious suitor rips off the Chinese lantern covering the lamp—for her, a source of sustaining illusion—and holds her aging face under the cruel light. And in *Sunset Boulevard*, Norma Desmond finally surrenders to total insanity, giving herself over to the bright glare of the cameras that once treated her with reverence.

Billy Wilder's *Sunset Boulevard*, released by Paramount in 1950, was an abrasive study of monstrous self-delusion as well as a bitterly sardonic view of Hollywood as a manufacturer of foolish, evanescent dreams and myths. Laced with touches of satire and Grand Guignol, the Academy Award–winning screenplay by Wilder, Charles Brackett, and D. M. Marshman, Jr., centered on Norma Desmond (Gloria Swanson), a silent-screen goddess whose pathetic belief in

her own indestructibility has turned her into a demented recluse. The crumbling Beverly Hills mansion where she lives with only a butler (Erich von Stroheim) who was once her director and husband has become her self-contained world. Norma's relationship with Joe Gillis (William Holden), a small-time writer who becomes her lover, ends with murder and total madness. (The connections between the characters and the actors are both obvious and subtle—is art imitating or mocking life?)

Sunset Boulevard permits little sympathy for Norma Desmond or for Joe Gillis, who, despite increasing nausea and irritation, allows himself to be "kept" by her. As we watch their relationship, compounded of her self-delusion and sexual hunger and his opportunism, fester in the nearly mummified rooms of her overstuffed home, we are far more repelled than moved. But for all the ugliness and grotesquerie (rats in the pool, a dead pet monkey in the house), we are mesmerized by Wilder's skill and by the audacity and bravura of Swanson's performance as Norma. Eyes bulging, teeth flashing, arms

Left: The Set-Up *(RKO, 1949). Boxer Stoker Thompson (Robert Ryan) fights not only to win the match but also to hold on to his tattered pride. At his side is his manager (George Tobias).*
Right: Sunset Boulevard *(Paramount, 1950). Silent film star Norma Desmond (Gloria Swanson), after having attempted suicide, is attended by gigolo Joe Gillis (William Holden) in Billy Wilder's mordant Hollywood drama. The role of Gillis was originally to be played by Montgomery Clift, who backed out at the last minute.*

waving, this actress—herself a veteran of the silent era—makes Norma an understandable monster, unaware of her obsolescence. Norma clutches at Joe like a drowning woman, then claws at him like an enraged tigress. In her final, demented state, she envelops herself in the self-woven cocoon where pain and rejection cannot enter: "There's nothing but us—just us, the cameras, and those wonderful people out there in the dark!"

The film had its detractors, who scoffed at the device of having the murdered Joe narrate the story from the grave, or who were repelled by Wilder's uncompromising view of Hollywood's dream factory. But we cannot help but admire the film's many subtleties and striking scenes. The suggestions of Joe's creeping entrapment are especially evocative: as Joe tries on new clothing, an obsequious clerk whispers in his ear, "As long as the lady's paying for it . . ."; Norma and Joe dance alone in her huge ballroom while an orchestra plays; her wrists bandaged after an attempted suicide, Norma tells Joe, "Great stars have great pride." From that moment,

Joe cannot leave her. *Sunset Boulevard* is a film like no other: a cold, hard diamond that casts a steady light.

Tennessee Williams's *A Streetcar Named Desire* (1951) also portrayed a woman at the end of her tether, trying to hold on to an illusion that is turning into a nightmare. Blanche DuBois (Vivien Leigh), however, has not withdrawn from life; rather, the drastic dissolution of her serene, ordered existence as an overrefined Southern belle—beginning with the cataclysmic suicide of her young husband—has sent her into genteel poverty, despair, and, ultimately, promiscuity. She comes to live with her younger sister Stella (Kim Hunter), but Stella's brutish husband Stanley (Marlon Brando), afraid of her influence over Stella, taunts, exposes, and finally rapes her, sending her over the edge into madness.

As directed by Elia Kazan from Williams's 1947 stage success (with a screenplay by Williams and Oscar Saul), *A Streetcar Named Desire* is as evocative as the wailing jazz music that wafts through the New Orleans tenement in which the story is set. The theme is

Above: Sunset Boulevard (Paramount, 1950). Surrendering at last to the peace of madness, silent film star Norma Desmond (Gloria Swanson) makes her last appearance before the cameras. Opposite: A Streetcar Named Desire (Warner Bros., 1951). Blanche DuBois (Vivien Leigh) and Stanley Kowalski (Marlon Brando), her boorish brother-in-law, find themselves on a collision course in this film version of Tennessee Williams's stage drama. Below: The moment of truth: Blanche DuBois's angry suitor, Mitch (Karl Malden), realizes that she is not as young as she pretends to be.

sounded with Blanche's arrival; she is a fragile butterfly that cannot be exposed to light. ("I won't be looked at in this merciless glare," she tells her sister, later adding, "Daylight has never exposed so total a ruin.") At her first meeting with Stanley, she is clearly shaken by his forthright masculinity, and his relentless prying into her past becomes an intolerable threat. Skillfully, the film develops the stages that turn Blanche and Stanley into implacable but unequal enemies on a collision course: she the last fading vestige of culture and beauty, too delicate to survive in a hedonistic world; he contemptuous of her fake refinement and proud of his animal lusts. Blanche's relationship with her shy suitor, Mitch (Karl Malden), is also well handled; his delight in her coquettish ways is so genuine and her comfort in his protection so touching that his ultimate disillusionment is all the more shattering.

A Streetcar Named Desire is theatrically effective—perhaps more theatrical than it should have been, since the stylized settings and rather neatly spaced climaxes smack of the footlights rather than the camera. But the film contains more than its share of haunting scenes, many of them depicting Blanche's desperate search for the elusive "magic" she once knew, or her poignant, painful memories of the past. A touching scene in which a young bill collector reminds her of her dead husband ("Did anyone ever tell you you look like a prince out of *Arabian Nights*?") is followed later by her remembrance of the terrible incident that precipitated her husband's suicide (the film eliminates any overt reference to his homosexuality). Each revelation of her sordid past, each confrontation with Stanley takes her further from reality until the darkness she craves ("I like the dark. The dark is comforting to me") envelops her mind completely.

A Streetcar Named Desire is bolstered considerably by its four leading players. As Blanche, Vivien Leigh surpasses all of her other film performances; although her fragile beauty has never seemed more vulnerable, she succeeds in suggesting both the flirtatious Southern belle and the fleshly wanton. As Stanley, Marlon Brando, repeating the stage role that made him a certified star, is funny and repellent. (Curiously, many audience members took him to be the "macho" hero who was justified in his treatment of snobbish Blanche.) Kim Hunter and Karl Malden are commendable in their less colorful roles; both won Academy Awards, as did Leigh and Richard Day and G. J. Hopkins for their art and set direction.

One fascinating fifties movie opted to keep its losers and outcasts in darkness rather than expose them to light. This was *Sweet Smell of Success* (1957), a nasty and compelling drama of the people who thrive in New York City's night world. Directed, surprisingly, by Alexander Mackendrick, an American who had established a reputation in England with a number of enjoyable comedies (including *Tight Little Island* and *The Man in the White Suit*), the film took the viewer into the tinseled nightclubs, deserted streets, and sinister back alleys on or around Broadway, where daylight never seems to arrive and where sleazy press agents vie for the ear of powerful newspaper columnists. The sleaziest agent of them all is Sidney

Falco (Tony Curtis, in possibly his best performance), whose sycophantic fawning over tyrannical columnist J. J. Hunsecker (Burt Lancaster) brings him only grief and puts him in danger.

The screenplay by Clifford Odets (his first in a decade) and Ernest Lehman, from Lehman's novelette, has a rare pungency that explodes on occasion into savage invective. Obsessed with the idea of getting dubious "items" into Hunsecker's column, Falco will resort to anything the columnist requests, however venal or unlawful —he balks only slightly at planting narcotics on the guitarist who loves Hunsecker's sister. After years of being miscast as Arabian princes in costumed swashbucklers, Curtis was given an appropriate role that took full advantage of his streetwise beginnings. Snaking his way through a shadowed milieu inhabited by petty hoods, sadistic cops, and pathetic B-girls, Falco is a repellent figure whom Curtis makes entirely believable. Burt Lancaster is also properly reptilian, although he is not quite successful at suggesting the callous and corrupt man behind the bland demeanor. Working mostly on location, cinematographer James Wong Howe exposed the tawdry atmosphere that gives *Sweet Smell of Success* its especially acrid odor.

By the 1960s, there was no real need for society's outcasts either to hide in darkness or to expose themselves to the light; they were an accepted part of the flotsam and jetsam that moved in and out with the tide. (Also, the increasing permissiveness of the decade made it possible to portray their mean lives more candidly than before.) Fox's *The Hustler* (1961) introduced audiences to a milieu that had seldom been used except as incidental background: the billiard halls in which small-time hustlers rubbed shoulders with would-be and true champions, gamblers, and hangers-on. Robert Rossen directed a cast headed by Paul Newman, George C. Scott,

Sweet Smell of Success (Norma-Curtleigh/United Artists, 1957). Sleazy press agent Sidney Falco (Tony Curtis) tries to catch the ear of powerful columnist J. J. Hunsecker (Burt Lancaster). The unusually abrasive screenplay by Clifford Odets and Ernest Lehman captured the seamy side of New York's night life.

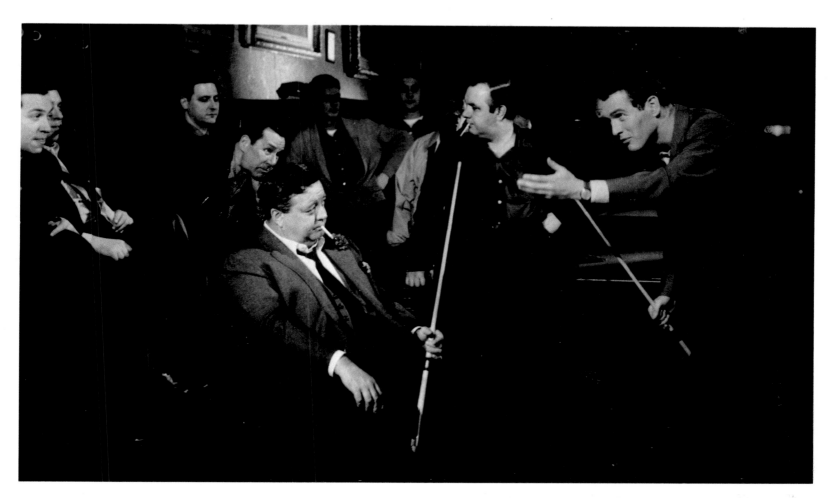

and Jackie Gleason in a story concerning one pool hustler's obsession with beating the country's top player. His determination nearly destroys him, but at the end, broken but proud, he has regained at least some of his humanity.

Rossen and Sidney Carroll's taut if somewhat self-consciously "meaningful" screenplay (from a novel by Walter Tevis), together with Eugene Shuftan's brilliant, Academy Award–winning photography, expresses the tense, bleak, and boozy atmosphere in which the pool shark thrives. Dominating these scenes are Jackie Gleason, massive and deceptively calm as champion Minnesota Fats, and George C. Scott as a malevolent gambler named Gordon. Outside of the poolroom, the film explores a touching romance between two derelicts: Fast Eddie Felson (Newman) and crippled, alcoholic Sarah, whom Piper Laurie plays with a subtlety and passion that belie her earlier days as a starlet. What begins as a pickup develops into a relationship built on need and trust, in which Eddie can confess his dreams and his feelings about pool. Her need is greater than his —his confession of love can only go as far as "You need the words?"—so that when he betrays her in order to win a match, she kills herself. Eddie's discovery of her body constitutes one of Newman's finest moments on film: kneeling, he holds out his hand and rolls his head around in anguish. Out of his private pain, he beats Minnesota Fats and finally faces up to Gordon.

The Hustler (Fox, 1961). Pool hustler Eddie Felson (Paul Newman) challenges champion Minnesota Fats (Jackie Gleason) to a game in Robert Rossen's atmospheric drama of losers and winners in the world of billiards. Below: Eddie, bruised and bleeding, finds comfort with Sarah (Piper Laurie), who has her own burdens to bear.

A common destination for many luckless pool sharks became the focus of attention in a later sixties drama, *The Pawnbroker* (1965). A story of the intolerable suffering that warps a life and the shattering event that redeems it, this unusually powerful film was adapted by David Friedkin and Morton Fine from Edward Lewis Wallant's novel and directed by Sidney Lumet. It concerned Sol Nazerman (Rod Steiger), a pawnbroker in New York's Harlem who had lost his family in the Holocaust. Emotionally barren, he is reminded daily of man's wretched state, not only by the human debris that finds its way into his shop but by the lovely and terrible memories of the past that constantly surge, unbidden, into his mind. At one point, he recalls frolicking in a field with his wife and children; at another, a crowded subway car becomes a cattle car carrying them and hundreds more to an unsuspected doom. The prostitute who bares her breast to him conjures up the dreadful time he watched his wife stripped and raped by concentration camp guards.

As played by Steiger, without the over-intensity and vocal mannerisms that often marred his performances, Nazerman is a deeply scarred war casualty unable to summon up compassion for what he regards as the "rejects, scum" who are his customers. (Among these is a shabby but dignified old black man, played with his usual finesse by Juano Hernandez.) Nor can Nazerman develop a true friendship with the compassionate social worker (Geraldine Fitzgerald) who would like to help him. When his wintry world is at its most unendurable, his young Puerto Rican assistant (Jaime Sanchez) is killed during an attempted robbery. Kneeling beside the boy's dead body, Nazerman rises to slam his hand down on a paper spike; the obvious stigmata reawakens his capacity for pain as he emits a voiceless cry of rage and anguish. It is an uncommonly powerful moment in a haunting film.

No film of the sixties probed more deeply or affectingly into the lives of desperate people living on the fringes of society than

Above: The Pawnbroker *(Landau-Steinmann, 1965). Haunted by bitter memories of his past life, pawnbroker Sol Nazerman (Rod Steiger) reacts with cold indifference toward the pitiful dregs of society who come to his shop and the social worker who wants to help him. Steiger's deeply felt performance was one of his best.*
Opposite: Midnight Cowboy *(Hellman-Schlesinger/United Artists, 1969). On a wintry afternoon, "Ratso" Rizzo (Dustin Hoffman) goes to visit his father's grave, accompanied by his new friend, Joe Buck (Jon Voight).*

John Schlesinger's *Midnight Cowboy* (1969). (Like Alexander Mac-kendrick, the London-born Schlesinger had established his rep-utation in Great Britain, with such films as *Billy Liar* and *Darling*, and also like Mackendrick, he scored his first American success with a film about New York's tawdry night world. Apparently it takes an outside observer, aided, of course, by observant American screenwriters, to grasp this very special milieu.) *Midnight Cowboy* plunged into New York's sleazy Times Square district to tell the story of the curious and moving relationship that forms between two homeless drifters: Joe Buck (Jon Voight), an ingenuous, self-styled Texas "cowboy" who dreams of making it in the city as an active "stud" to rich, lonely women, and Enrico ("Ratso") Rizzo, a lame, chronically ill, street-smart part-time pimp who befriends him. Their scrounging efforts to stay alive in the city's cesspool—and their hope for a new life in sunny Florida—end with Ratso's death.

Waldo Salt's screenplay, based on James Leo Herlihy's novel, approaches but never topples over the edge of exploitation as it takes Joe and Ratso through their grubby little adventures: crashing weird parties, or stumbling into liaisons with an odd assortment of off-the-wall residents, compliant women, and pathetic homosexuals. Joe's descent from a cheerful newcomer innocently accosting women in the street to a wretched, lonely hustler sharing space in an aban-doned building is traced with compassion and a sharp sense for revealing detail, but the movie gains its greatest resonance from his "odd-couple" friendship with Ratso. As they walk the streets together, their contrasting appearances make them an odd duo—Joe with his blond good looks and flashy cowboy outfit, Ratso with his slicked-back hair and shabby clothing and the air of a disreputable rodent. Freezing and penniless in their room, they cling to each other out of necessity, which turns into an unstated but genuine regard. We are moved by Ratso's advancing illness—one view of him trudging through the swirling snow is like a vision of hell—and Joe's increas-ing concern gives dimension to a basically vacuous character. In the film's final scene, as their bus arrives in Florida, the dead Rico slumps against Joe's shoulder, and Joe holds him gently in a final gesture of friendship. Grudgingly, unwittingly, two beings from society's backwater have, for a time, acknowledged their common humanity.

Overleaf, left: They Shoot Horses, Don't They? *(Winkler-Chartoff/Cinerama Releasing Corp., 1969). An exhausted Gloria (Jane Fonda) and her partner, Robert (Michael Sarrazin), try to stay on their feet during one of the dance marathons that took place during the bleakest years of the Depression.*
Overleaf, right: One Flew over the Cuckoo's Nest *(Fantasy Films/United Artists, 1974). Jack Nicholson starred as Randle McMurphy, a freewheeling patient at a mental hospital who fights the establishment by trying to restore the inmates to a semblance of life.*

Although *Midnight Cowboy* resorts too often to Joe's subliminal flashbacks and fantasies of his Texas life, it seldom falters in its scenes of 42nd Street night life. And the acting throughout is exemplary. As Joe Buck, Jon Voight plays with disarming, wide-eyed candor, showing spurts of the temper and impulsiveness that brought him trouble back in Texas. The film's truly remarkable performance is given by Dustin Hoffman, in an astonishing change of pace after *The Graduate*. Using his tight, strangulated voice to maximum effect (his cry of "C'maaa!" sounds like the braying of an arrogant donkey), Hoffman makes Ratso's wheedling pleas for pity and his fleeting attempts at pride ("Don't call me Ratso") the last gasps of a drowning man. As his condition worsens, the fright on his ashen face deepens, and suddenly, unaccountably, we care about this pitiable street rat.

By the close of the sixties and into the seventies, some major films concerned with human pain and degradation went beyond the face value of their stories; they had no social axes to grind, as in the thirties, nor were they content merely to take audiences into the shadowed underworld, as in the forties. In several significant instances, the stories became metaphors for *all* of man's wretched and futile aspirations, or for his abject willingness to remain helplessly trapped in his own life: a willing fly for the spider's web. In a sense, these films were expressions of *mea culpa* for American involvement in the Vietnam War, showing the corruption and decadence at the heart of much American activity, and not only in wartime.

The activity in James Poe and Robert E. Thompson's adaptation of Horace McCoy's novel, *They Shoot Horses, Don't They?* (1969), was marathon dancing. In the Depression years, many desperately poor people had taken part in a combination dance competition and endurance test, in which couples, struggling to win the prize for the longest stretch of dancing, clung to each other until they dropped from exhaustion. Bystanders cheered their favorites on to victory, while a master of ceremonies kept up a continual stream of inane, encouraging banter. *They Shoot Horses, Don't They?* brought together a microcosm of society in a tacky ballroom at the edge of the Pacific Ocean. As the weeks wear on, the hopes, delusions, and private terrors of the dancers are cruelly exposed. The central figures are Gloria (Jane Fonda), a cynical, self-destructive girl, and Robert (Michael Sarrazin), a dreamy-eyed farm boy who shoots Gloria at her despairing request. As the M.C. Rocky, a cheerleader in hell whose favorite expression is "Yowsa!," Gig Young makes his character a mixture of corruption, vulgarity, and weariness beyond caring. (His incisive, unsparing portrait won him an Oscar.)

Director Sydney Pollack presented *They Shoot Horses, Don't They?* as a searing drama that is as ugly as it is unforgettable. The image of the participants as less than human emerges from the start (an aging dancer named Sailor, played by Red Buttons, tells Gloria, "Cattle ain't got it much worse than us," and she replies, "Better. At least they feed them"). Rocky begins his phonily sentimental spiel ("These wonderful, starry-eyed kids"), indifferent to the plight of so many of the dancers, who include Alice, a Jean Harlow look-

alike (Susannah York) on the brink of a breakdown, a worn pregnant girl (Bonnie Bedelia), and the girl's sullen husband (Bruce Dern). As the hours grind on and the effort to stay upright or awake becomes more grueling, it becomes clear that these wretched souls are meant to represent suffering, enduring mankind trapped in a remorseless world. Nowhere is this more evident than in the sequence in which the dancers are obliged to get into gym uniforms to race around the ballroom. In this ten-minute "Human Derby," the last three couples are eliminated from the marathon. Strikingly photographed, this sequence catches the frantic efforts of the participants to stay in the race, their faces distorted with an anguish that becomes almost intolerable to watch. "Isn't that the American way?" the grinning M.C. asks, but he doesn't wait for an answer.

They Shoot Horses, Don't They? confuses with its abundance of flashbacks and flash-forwards (Robert being questioned about his shooting of Gloria), but its cumulative effect is electrifying. Even the inevitable dramatic set pieces (Alice's collapse into madness, Sailor's heart attack) contribute vividly to the overall sense of despair and waste. The outstanding performance is given by Jane Fonda: this remarkable actress never strikes a false note as she tries to cover her transparent sensitivity with a layer of tough, sardonic talk. (Asked what she would buy with her winnings, she replies, "Rat poison.") She taunts the pregnant girl with her willingness to bring life into a vile world, offers herself to Rocky when she learns that Robert has been with Alice (her muttered comment, "Perfect!," is a masterly touch), and she pleads for release from her tortured life with chilling passion ("I'm gonna get off the merry-go-round. . . . Help me! Please! Please!"). Robert shoots her and the marathon goes on . . . and on . . . and on . . .

The film version of Ken Kesey's novel *One Flew over the Cuckoo's Nest* (1974) also used its setting as a metaphor for society, in this case the paranoid society of the sixties in which nonconformity or violent opposition to the establishment was viewed by some as scurrilous, irreligious, and unpatriotic. The 1962 novel had prophesied this attitude, and, in fact, had become a kind of bible of nonconformity. The story of Randle McMurphy (Jack Nicholson), disreputable, defiant, and life-embracing, who, as a patient at a mental hospital, enters into pitched battle with the coolly sinister, unflappable Nurse Ratched (Louise Fletcher), clearly symbolizes nonconformism vs. established society—this vaguely unreal, barbaric hospital is actually Everywhere. There are also suggestions that McMurphy represents sexuality and the life force, Ratched sterility and antilife forces. But the screenplay by Laurence Hauben and Bo Goldman, written long after the age of the rebel and hippie had passed, muted this aspect of the novel, presenting the film as a powerful melodrama in which the McMurphy-Ratched battle assumes both comic and tragic proportions. Although Czech director Milos Forman occasionally seems to make jokes at the inmates' expense, the laughter, more often than not, is genuine—he extracts a good deal of fun, for example, from McMurphy's narration of an imaginary World Series game, the inmates' one-day excursion away from the hos-

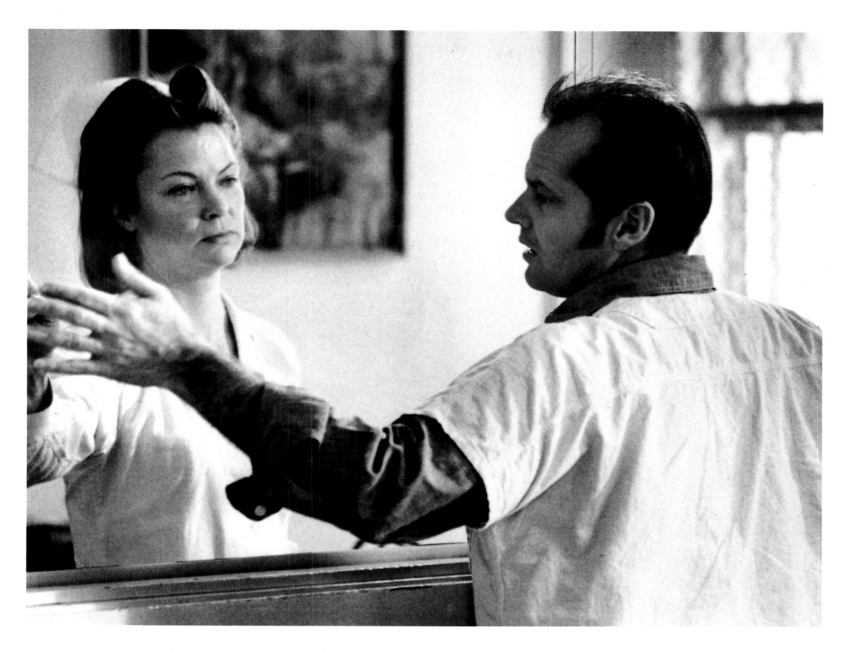

pital, and the wild, nighttime party in the ward—until it culminates in disaster.

However, the viewer's laughter stops as the battle becomes more deadly, and the inmates react with mixed feelings of elation and terror to McMurphy's antics. For them, McMurphy represents the freedom they once surrendered willingly in return for shelter from their private demons, but the increasing clamor surrounding his confrontations with Nurse Ratched unsettles and frightens them. Forman gets splendid performances from the group of actors who play the inmates, notably William Redfield as the prissy Harding, Brad Dourif as the disturbed Billy Bibbit, and (best of all) Will Sampson as Chief, the supposedly mute Indian who, out of compassion, seals McMurphy's final fate. For Nurse Ratched, McMurphy is a nuisance, then a formidable threat that must be removed if the hospital is to function smoothly. As played by Louise Fletcher, she makes reasonableness and patience seem positively chilling attributes. Her quiet

intimidation of Billy Bibbit, leading to his terrible suicide, cannot help but leave every viewer sick at heart. It precipitates the fatal response of McMurphy, whom Jack Nicholson plays in his familiar style, using his uninflected voice and his slightly threatening, off-center, aging-rebel manner to best advantage.

No doubt filmmakers will continue to probe the lower depths for suitable material. There is always an element of risk, of course, since the material is hardly comforting and not all that edifying— but the characters are often so colorful and unusual, and the opportunity to show audiences how lucky they are by comparison is so enticing, that the risk is worth taking. Whether perceived as victims of a hostile society, or as scurrying night figures bent on mayhem, or as glum symbols of a disordered universe, the thieves, derelicts, hustlers, and mad dreamers who inhabit the bottom rungs of the human ladder are unquestionably a fascinating lot.

Above: One Flew over the Cuckoo's Nest *(Fantasy Films/United Artists, 1974).*
Randle McMurphy (Jack Nicholson) locks horns with the establishment, represented by
ice-cold, implacable Nurse Ratched (Louise Fletcher).
Overleaf: Intolerance *(Wark Producing Co., 1916). The people of Babylon celebrate the*
triumphant return of their king, Belshazzar. This set was one of the most spectacular ever built;
it was over a mile in length and could accommodate five thousand people without crowding.

OUT OF THE PAGES, BEYOND THE FOOTLIGHTS
Books and Plays into Film

Pictures made from novels, especially novels everyone is supposed to have read, are usually desperate ventures.

—OTIS FERGUSON, The Film Criticism of Otis Ferguson

When will the movies learn not to adapt great, or even good novels to the screen? . . . Partly out of exploitativeness, but partly also out of stupidity, producers ignore a fact that the very schoolchildren of today have mastered: the form is the content. The shape of the novel on the page, its paragraph and sentence structure, the imagery and cadences of the prose, and all the things that are left to the imagination, these, as much as plot and character, are what the novel is about, and these in good and great novels, cannot be transposed on screen—do not even yield cinematic equivalents.

—JOHN SIMON, Reverse Angle

There are imponderables in a novel that can't be translated.

—S. J. PERELMAN, *interviewed on "The Dick Cavett Show"*

Clearly, novels-into-film have not enjoyed a good press over the years. It is unmistakably true that transposing fiction to the screen is not easy. The "imponderables" that S. J. Perelman mentions, "the shape of the novel on the page, its paragraph and sentence structure, the imagery and cadences of the prose" that John Simon specifies—these are subtleties that resist or defy cinematic translation. There are enough heavy-handed film versions of classic novels to tell us that failure, not success, is most often the result.

Filming a great or even good novel is a difficult task. But is it impossible?

Not necessarily. It is probably accurate to say that the greater the novel, the more complex and intricate its theme and structure, the more formidable the job of adapting it to the screen. It would also be accurate to say that novels of lesser rank, with strong narratives and unsubtle characterizations, usually make the best films. But this is not to deny the value of these films or to dismiss them out of hand. Many of them have provided us with viewing pleasure and, yes, with "visual equivalents" of the printed page, which, while not necessarily the equal of the novels, are entirely satisfactory substitutes.

Messrs. Ferguson, Simon, and Perelman notwithstanding, there have even been superior film versions of great novels. Admittedly, they cannot match the author's prose, and perhaps they deprive moviegoers of using their own imaginations. Yet, through cinematic ingenuity, they make vanished worlds real again, they make favorite characters spring to life. Can many of us now read about Mr. Micawber without seeing W. C. Fields scampering over the rooftops of London to avoid his creditors? Those who fondly remember the film version of *Pride and Prejudice* tend to visualize Elizabeth Bennet and Mr. Darcy in the persons of Greer Garson and Laurence Olivier. We may miss the vigor and color of Charles Dickens's descriptions or the wry and delicate wit of Jane Austen's commentary, but we should not relegate the film versions of their books to oblivion.

Film versions of classic novels were hardly unknown in the silent era. The twenties saw adaptations of books such as *Vanity Fair* (1923), *The Hunchback of Notre Dame* (1923), *The Scarlet Letter* (1926), and *Anna Karenina* (1927, under the title *Love*). These books, after all, were a rich source of film material in the public domain. By the time of the sound era, many studios were turning to the bookshelves for stories, popular contemporary fiction or acknowledged classics, that were well-known to audiences. It was inevitable that the studio with the most prestige and the greatest resources would become the front-runner in book adaptations.

It has never been fully determined who was responsible for the influx of literary adaptations at Metro-Goldwyn-Mayer in the thirties. Most often the credit has been assigned to Irving Thalberg, the head of production who had joined Louis B. Mayer's company in its formative stage back in 1923. Thalberg's closest associate was the erudite Albert Lewin (later a producer and director), and together they steered MGM toward productions derived from famous novels. The films, including *The Barretts of Wimpole Street* and *Mutiny on the Bounty*, were characterized by literate screenplays, elaborate and authentically detailed backgrounds, and fastidious casting of the leading roles.

Thalberg was especially adept at finding suitable vehicles for MGM's star roster. One of his most successful movies in the early thirties was the film version of Vicki Baum's novel and play *Grand Hotel* (1932). The progenitor of many later films on the fateful-meeting-of-strangers theme, the movie was also the first to assemble a cast of the studio's luminaries. *Grand Hotel*'s guest list was headed by Greta Garbo as the world-weary ballerina Grusinskaya, John Barrymore as the penniless Baron von Geigern, Joan Crawford as the hotel stenographer called Flaemmchen, Wallace Beery as boorish business tycoon Preysing, and Lionel Barrymore as Kringelein, a timid, dying clerk who works for Preysing. Director Edmund Goulding, who had the unenviable task of keeping these principals from colliding, managed to keep them on course and to sort out the several strands of plot. Grusinskaya and the Baron share a romantic idyll that ends tragically when the Baron is beaten to death by Preysing during a robbery attempt. Kringelein

Opposite: Grand Hotel *(MGM, 1932). This advertisement for the film was an insert in a 1932 issue of* Fortune *magazine as part of a story on the studio. The artwork was by Vincentini, MGM's top illustrator during the twenties and thirties.*

finally finds the courage to confront his hated boss, and Flaemmchen goes off with him to new places. Life continues; as Doctor Otternschlag (Lewis Stone), intending no irony, tells us, "People come. People go. Nothing ever happens."

Grand Hotel has remained a favorite film for over five decades, but the reason for its continuing popularity is the glamorous presence of its stars—for their cumulative charisma rather than their acting abilities. (Fine performers such as John Barrymore and Greta Garbo are here playing below their best; Garbo, in particular, postures a great deal and overdoes the melancholia.) There are moments in the film that almost define movie stardom, especially John Barrymore's long love scene with Garbo. As they exchange passionate endearments, William Daniels's camera moves in for a close-up of the screen's two greatest profiles. Instantly, Grusenskaya and the Baron fade before the mythic quality of Garbo and Barrymore. It has nothing to do with cinematic art; it has everything to do with the magic of film.

Grand Hotel was an enormous success under Irving Thalberg's aegis, but when he became ill in 1933, Mayer brought back David O. Selznick, who had worked briefly at MGM in the twenties as an associate producer. During his three years at MGM, Selznick, like Thalberg, adapted several classic novels to the screen. His version of Charles Dickens's *A Tale of Two Cities* (1935), directed by Jack Conway, was highly popular, and with good reason: it has spectacle rooted in history (the French Revolution, with its obligatory storming of the Bastille, citizens' courts, and mass executions), high adventure (will Sydney Carton succeed in replacing Charles Darnay in prison and returning him to the girl they both love?), and a starring performance by the elegant actor Ronald Colman.

The film begins with a powerful sequence: the coach of the villainous Marquis St. Evremonde (Basil Rathbone) careens heedlessly through a Paris slum, killing a child and firing the passions of the downtrodden people. It ends with Sydney Carton facing the guillotine, certain of the rightness of his sacrifice and welcoming the peace of oblivion. In between, there are some stirring and well-mounted scenes in the grandiose MGM tradition. Critics who disliked the film seemed to blame Dickens as much as the producers; Otis Ferguson wrote that the movie "emphasized the bathos, smug morality, and provincial missionary spirit" of the author.

A second Dickens adaptation was produced by Selznick and released by MGM in the same year as *A Tale of Two Cities*. *David Copperfield* (1935) also drew fire from some critics (including Ferguson), and it is true that the film has its stodgy moments; it might be one more in a long line of Illustrated Moments from Great Books. But, under George Cukor's sturdy direction, it also has narrative sweep, bountiful humor, some colorful if obviously studio-bound sets, and, above all, a cheerful collection of Dickens eccentrics, played to a fare-thee-well by talented character actors. Leading the pack are W. C. Fields, amazingly right as the impecunious Mr. Micawber, Edna May Oliver as the firm-minded but tenderhearted Aunt Betsey, and Roland Young as the insidious, " 'umble" Uriah Heep. Virtually all of the movie's memorable moments revolve around these three estimable actors. It is rewarding

Opposite: Grand Hotel *(MGM, 1932). Fleeting romance comes to exhausted ballerina Grusinskaya (Greta Garbo) and the insolvent Baron von Geigern (John Barrymore). Below: Joan Crawford recoils in horror at learning that Wallace Beery has killed John Barrymore. Above:* A Tale of Two Cities *(MGM, 1935). The storming of the Bastille, one of the spectacular sequences in this elaborate film version of Charles Dickens's novel. Below: Sydney Carton (Ronald Colman) is solicitous to Lucie Manette (Elizabeth Allan), the girl he secretly loves—and for whom he will later sacrifice his life.*

to see Mr. Micawber, whose rhetorical flourishes are not unlike those uttered by Fields himself, talking brazenly of his nonexistent "prospects," or Aunt Betsey trying to maintain her crusty manner while clearly joyful at the sudden arrival of her nephew, or Uriah Heep cringing before the onslaught of a vengeful Micawber, each cry of "Heep!" like the thrust of a sword.

In its day, *David Copperfield* was received with enthusiasm, but now it typifies the sort of movie product that is vilified by critics who abhor the aura of cultural uplift or the Hollywoodizing of classic books. Yet, like many other of the prestigious MGM releases of the thirties, it has been unfairly maligned. In the same way, perhaps, as the recent stage production of *Nicholas Nickleby* (later presented on television), it offers us an entertaining visual encapsulation of the novel, a reasonable substitute for the full-bodied Dickens prose. It is not the same as reading the novel, nor should it be, and this *Copperfield* may lack the flair or prodigious theatrical skill of *Nickleby*. Yet we need not denigrate its virtues. Carping critics aside, this film shows that it is possible to adapt a literary classic to the screen with taste, honesty, and effectiveness.

Not long after David Selznick left MGM, Irving Thalberg died of heart disease, and his last film was released posthumously. *The Good Earth* (1937), dedicated to Thalberg, adapted Pearl Buck's Pulitzer

David Copperfield (MGM, 1935). The "'umble" Uriah Heep (Roland Young, at far right) finally gets his just deserts from (left to right) David (Frank Lawton), Mr. Dick (Lennox Pawle), Agnes (Madge Evans), Mr. Wickfield (Lewis Stone), Mr. Micawber (W. C. Fields), and Aunt Betsey (Edna May Oliver). Below: An immortal Dickens character, Mr. Micawber, was embodied by a great comedian, W. C. Fields, in this flavorsome version of the novel. Young David was played by Freddie Bartholomew.

Prize—winning novel into a sprawling drama of Chinese life as experienced by a poor farmer named Wang Lung (Paul Muni). Sidney Franklin directed the screenplay by Talbot Jennings, Tess Slesinger, and Claudine West, which traced the cataclysmic events that befall Wang as he moves from desolate poverty to uneasy wealth: the fierce storms, the devastating famine, and the revolution that rocks the country. Ultimately, he comes to understand his deep need and love for the land, represented by O-Lan (Luise Rainer), the shy but resilient slave girl he takes as his bride. At her grave many years later, Wang murmurs, "O-Lan, you are the earth."

The Good Earth won largely admiring reviews for its impressive large-scale production, and Luise Rainer was singled out for her moving portrayal of O-Lan. (Her small, secret smiles and sidelong glances of fear and hope compensate in good part for her Viennese accent.) It is only in recent years that *The Good Earth* has joined other of MGM's literary adaptations in the special purgatory reserved for formerly revered "classics." Actually, there are flaws: the film becomes heavy-handed in the latter portions; the variety of speech patterns, from Oriental to midwestern American, is bewildering; and Paul Muni never makes Wang entirely credible. However, there are strengths as well as weaknesses. Karl Freund's photography is justly famous—it reveals the sweep and unyielding harshness of the land—as is Slavko

The Good Earth *(MGM, 1937). Chinese farmers build fires to ward off the swarms of deadly locusts descending on their crops. This sequence, one of the most spectacular of the thirties, made a fitting climax to the film version of Pearl Buck's novel. Below: Wang Lung (Paul Muni) attends his dying wife, O-Lan (Luise Rainer). While this film version of Pearl Buck's novel has serious flaws, it is impressive in its scope and has many effective scenes.*

Vorkapich's superb montage work, especially in the scenes in which famine forces the peasants on a desperate trek to the cities of the south. There are also scenes of stunning effectiveness, none more so than the climactic attack of the locusts on Wang's land. It is one of the truly memorable sequences in films, generating both suspense and terror as an ominous black cloud of buzzing locusts emerges over the hill and the farmers scramble frantically over the fields to save what they can of the crops.

Although MGM dominated the market in literary adaptations during the thirties, other studios made creditable contributions to America's cultural enlightenment. RKO dusted off Louisa May Alcott's classic novel *Little Women* in 1933, gave it a lavish production, and used it as a vehicle for its new star Katharine Hepburn. She played tomboy Jo March, most forthright of Alcott's little women, who shares joys and sorrows with her New England family and romance with a shy professor (Paul Lukas). The award-winning screenplay by Sarah Y. Mason and Victor Heerman retained all the lace-valentine atmosphere of the original, which was enhanced by the soft glow of Henry Gerrard's photography. The film was more successful in its homely details of family life than in its dramatic portions, but George Cukor, Hepburn's first and favorite director, kept the sentiment from spilling over into sentimentality, and the actress was all quicksilver and girlish enthusiasm.

Another superior film transcription of a classic novel was Samuel

Little Women *(RKO, 1933). The March girls (Jean Parker, Katharine Hepburn, and Frances Dee) share an idyllic afternoon with their mother (Spring Byington) and friends (Douglass Montgomery and John Lodge).*

Goldwyn's production of Sinclair Lewis's *Dodsworth* (1936). Sidney Howard, who had turned Lewis's novel of a retired businessman and his frivolous wife into a play in 1934, adapted it intelligently to the screen, cutting through Lewis's frequently turgid prose to arrive at the heart of a complex marital relationship. Walter Huston repeated his stage role as Sam Dodsworth, a midwestern automobile tycoon seeking contentment after a lifetime of toil. He discovers that his wife, Fran (Ruth Chatterton), is actually a shallow woman concerned only with her own pleasure. After their painful separation, Dodsworth finds peace with a gentle widow, Edith Cortright (Mary Astor).

Guided with a firm hand by William Wyler, *Dodsworth* makes up for what it may lack in cinematic flair with Howard's subtle screenplay. Deftly, the film shows us the growing rift in the Dodsworth marriage: Sam as the decent, honest husband and father, baffled by his wife's social climbing and hurt by her indiscretions, Fran as a woman terrified by the prospect of old age, grasping at what she regards as a last chance at happiness. Their quarrels have the ring of truth about them. Without rancor, she pleads for release from the gray, uneventful existence he craves ("I'm fighting for life—you can't drag me back!"); with infinite sadness, he acknowledges that he is losing her ("Have things gotten *this* bad?"). Finally, however, he leaves her willingly, seeing her at last as a foolish, destructive woman he never really knew.

Walter Huston embodies Sam Dodsworth; he makes us believe that this assured midwestern businessman could recognize his wife's affectations and caprices and still adore her. Although the character of Fran Dodsworth edges toward caricature, Ruth Chatterton gives us glimpses into the pathetic quality behind her social aspirations. But the film's most memorable performance is given by Mary Astor, who projects a womanly warmth in her every scene. *Dodsworth* is a first-rate example of a film that draws on a literary source without damaging it; in fact, it possibly improves on it.

Columbia's production of *Lost Horizon* (1937) was another example of a literary adaptation that did justice to its source, although the source in this case was not exactly in the first rank of fiction. James Hilton's phenomenally popular novel had stirred readers with its concept of a remote fantasy realm called Shangri-La, a place of perfect peace and harmony where all the virtues thrive. Director Frank Capra found the story exceedingly compatible with his essentially optimistic point of view, and, with a screenplay by Robert Riskin, he proceeded to film it with a cast headed by Ronald Colman as Robert Conway, the sensitive intellectual who finds paradise in the serenity of Shangri-La.

Lost Horizon succeeds in generating suspense from its exciting opening sequence, in which Conway and a group of Americans flee in an airplane from a Chinese civil war. They crash-land in a remote part of Tibet, and their journey by foot across the Himalayas ends in the first breathtaking view of Shangri-La, an impressive place with a distinct resemblance to an Oriental luxury hotel. It is amusing to watch the reactions of the Americans to their plight—at first apprehensive, then delighted and appreciative. The film,

however, is concerned with loftier matters. These are pinpointed in the scenes between Conway and Shangri-La's ancient High Lama (played by thirty-eight-year-old Sam Jaffe). Their conversations represent the heart of *Lost Horizon*, the fullest expression of the theme of man's continual search for wisdom in a violent age. At their last meeting, Conway is designated the dying High Lama's specially selected heir: "My son, I am placing in your hands the future and destiny of Shangri-La. . . . You will preserve the fragrance of its history."

After more than four decades, *Lost Horizon* remains one of Hollywood's best-loved films. In its own time, it was welcomed rhapsodically by many who, after the desolate years of the Depression, cherished the dream of a perfect world where poverty did not exist. Today we can still admire its elaborate production, its fairy-tale atmosphere, and the ensemble playing of a good cast ably steered by Frank Capra. However, there is—and probably always was—a problem with the concept of Shangri-La. In place of war, greed, brutality, and other of mankind's many ills, Shangri-La offers the sort of vaporous, all-purpose advice one might find embedded in a Chinese fortune cookie. "Be kind," the High Lama tells Conway. This is "the one simple rule of Shangri-La." His hope is that the creed of brotherly love "will spread throughout the world" so that "the Christian ethic may at last be fulfilled." The sentiment of a

Dodsworth (Samuel Goldwyn/United Artists, 1936). Sam Dodsworth (Walter Huston) finds contentment at last with Edith Cortright (Mary Astor). Sidney Howard adapted his play version of the Sinclair Lewis novel into an intelligent and sensitive film.

Yuletide commercial hardly seems sturdy enough to support the cosmic philosophical theme implied in *Lost Horizon*.

By the forties, studios were less inclined to produce elaborate adaptations of great or near-great novels, although it was clear for a while that Irving Thalberg's "cultural" influence on MGM's films did not die with him in 1937. Well into the forties, the studio continued to produce painstaking versions of classic fiction. Happily, a number of these dispensed with the edifying schoolbook tone to provide satisfying entertainment that made literature, or an acceptable equivalent of literature, available to the public.

One of these was *Pride and Prejudice* (1940). Jane Austen's novel was certainly an accessible classic; it was, after all, an effervescent comedy of manners containing characters as varied, eccentric, and colorful as any in Dickens. The Aldous Huxley–Jane Murfin screenplay drew more on Helen Jerome's stage version than on Jane Austen's book. The result was successful, critically if not financially: a charming period piece that had nothing more serious in its head than the mating and romantic tribulations of the five marriageable Bennet girls. The focus, as in the novel, was on the verbal sparring of two people who are destined for each other: the eldest Bennet girl, Elizabeth (Greer Garson), and the haughty, insufferably snobbish Mr. Darcy (Laurence Olivier).

In attractive settings that never overpower the fragile story, *Pride and Prejudice* captures the spirit if not the letter of Jane Austen: the witty banter, particularly the parry-and-thrust of Elizabeth and Darcy; the glancing commentary on manners and morals; and, especially, the offhand lines that somehow reverberate pleasantly after they are spoken (Mr. Bennet's comment to his plainest daughter after her wretched piano-playing: "You've delighted us long enough"). There are moments of delicious absurdity: the Bennets, mother and daughters, scurrying down the street, their bonnets practically bobbing with excitement at the prospect of a new suitor; the foolish, hypocritical Mr. Collins (Melville Cooper) scampering after Elizabeth and trying to propose to her; the imperious Lady Catherine (Edna May Oliver) arriving at the Bennet house and regaling everyone with her loathing of chickens ("They are incorrigible. They must be killed and boiled! Killed and boiled!").

Guided by Robert Z. Leonard's direction, the cast comes through with splendid performances. Greer Garson's Elizabeth (probably her best acting) is beautifully poised, elegant, and winning, and she is matched by Laurence Olivier's sardonic Darcy, proclaiming that he is "in no humor tonight to give consequence to the middle classes at play." As Mrs. Bennet, Mary Boland never dithered so delightfully ("Look at them! Five of them without dowries! What's to become of them?"), while Edmund Gwenn defines the word "droll" as her quietly exasperated husband. His idea of paradise is a place "where nobody shall talk more than is absolutely necessary."

Other novels with less distinction but wider appeal than *Pride and Prejudice* were adapted by MGM in the forties. Despite declining fortunes, the studio ignored the trend toward controversial subject matter and continued its policy of presenting family entertainment

that could not possibly offend anyone. *National Velvet* (1944), adapted by Theodore Reeves and Helen Deutsch from Enid Bagnold's novel, had no basis in reality, but its idyllic view of English country life, neat, orderly, and Technicolored, was widely popular, and it made a star of ecstatically beautiful, twelve-year-old Elizabeth Taylor. Under

Opposite and above: Lost Horizon *(Columbia, 1937). Jane Wyatt and Ronald Colman enjoy the serenity of Shangri-La, where peace reigns supreme. Above: Robert Conway (Ronald Colman) converses with the High Lama (Sam Jaffe), who has selected Conway to replace him as ruler of Shangri-La. Below and overleaf:* Pride and Prejudice *(MGM, 1940). The Bennets are all atwitter at the arrival of a possible new suitor. Left to right: Greer Garson, Marsha Hunt, Mary Boland, and Maureen O'Sullivan. Overleaf: Proud Elizabeth Bennet (Greer Garson) and the haughty Mr. Darcy (Laurence Olivier) have evidently resolved their differences.*

Clarence Brown's direction, she played horse-crazy Velvet Brown, who rides her horse Pie to victory in the Grand National Steeplechase. Firmly supported by veterans Mickey Rooney, Donald Crisp, and Anne Revere, Taylor gave a luminous performance that inspired critics to panegyrics of praise.

Clarence Brown also directed the film version of Marjorie Kinnan Rawlings's Pulitzer Prize–winning novel *The Yearling* (1946), the warm-hearted story of a boy's devotion to his pet fawn and his discovery that love, and life itself, must sometimes be surrendered. Gregory Peck starred as Penny Baxter, a poor Florida farmer who permits his sensitive young son, Jody (Claude Jarman, Jr.), to raise the fawn but must have it destroyed when the animal becomes destructive. The setting was perhaps too prettified, the color too lush for total conviction, yet Paul Osborn's screenplay, along with the performances of Peck and young Jarman, made the crucial father-son relationship believable, and the details of daily life in the Florida backwoods—a bear hunt, a dog swap, a local feud—were well handled. The climactic sequence, in which Jody must shoot the fawn himself, moved audiences to tears.

One mid-forties literary adaptation seemed a most improbable entry from MGM, home of family-oriented films. *The Picture of Dorian Gray* (1945), Oscar Wilde's story of perversity and muted evil, was made into a curious and often surprisingly effective film. Written and directed by Albert Lewin, who had returned to MGM where he had been Irving Thalberg's closest associate in the thirties, the movie occasionally succeeded in suggesting the decadent life of Dorian Gray (Hurd Hatfield) in late-nineteenth-century London. True to the novel, it showed him surrendering to his darkest impulses under the tutelage of sardonic Lord Henry Wotton (George Sanders). Skulking about the worst sections of the city and covertly committing the seven deadly sins, Dorian remains unchanged over the years while his portrait, hidden in the attic, records the physical changes induced by every vile deed. Lord Wotton's Wildean quips, Dorian's sordid nighttime excursions (recalling those of young Mr. Hyde), and Albert Lewin's arty, symbolic touches make a strange mixture. Even so, there are sequences in this film that are still remembered: the murder of the artist Basil Hallward (Lowell Gilmore)—as Dorian stabs him to death, a lamp swings wildly out of control, casting grotesque shadows on the wall—and Dorian's nocturnal visit to the pub where Sybil Vane (Angela Lansbury), a pathetic victim of his vileness, sings "Little Yellow Bird" in a plaintive voice. The final unveiling of the title portrait, shown in color, while not as horrific as the long buildup would have us believe, jolts the viewer nevertheless.

During the early forties, other studios than MGM found box-office gold (and occasional dross) in film versions of well-known novels and stories. Limited in budget but willing, on occasion and under duress, to experiment with unorthodox material, RKO offered two films that failed to attract audiences on their release but which have survived the years as worthy and fascinating efforts. William Dieterle's *All That Money Can Buy* (1941) adapted Stephen Vincent Benét's story "The Devil and Daniel Webster" (it later re-

verted to that title) into a somber and striking film. James Craig played Jabez Stone, an impoverished New England farmer who sells his soul to the Devil in exchange for wealth. The Devil, depicted here as a crafty old codger named Mr. Scratch (Walter Huston), insists on claiming his due, but the popular politician Daniel Webster (Edward Arnold), who is acquainted with the now-affluent Jabez, demands a trial by jury. At this ghostly trial, Jabez is acquitted through Webster's eloquence in his defense. Within its limitations, including obviously skimpy sets, the movie managed several haunting

Above: The Picture of Dorian Gray *(MGM, 1945). Dorian Gray (Hurd Hatfield) gazes at the portrait that reflects a lifetime of vileness and debauchery.*
Overleaf, left: National Velvet *(MGM, 1944). Elizabeth Taylor as Velvet Brown, who dreams of racing in the Grand National Steeplechase, and Mickey Rooney as Taylor, who helps her train for the race. Below: Velvet rides her horse to victory.*
Overleaf, right: The Yearling *(MGM, 1946). Jody Baxter (Claude Jarman, Jr.) shows his pet fawn to his father, Penny (Gregory Peck).*

wasted words or images, he evokes a genuine nostalgia as he introduces us to the Ambersons in their "magnificent" period, when life was serene and gracious. As the years pass, Welles deftly tempers the nostalgia with a deep melancholy, orchestrating scenes that reveal the decline of the Ambersons through time and circumstance: our last view of old Major Amberson (Richard Bennett), a light from the fire on his face as he reflects on the source of life; the last Amberson ball, at which the camera moves among the Ambersons and their guests while the soundtrack extracts bits of revealing conversation from the babble of voices; and the scene in which a confrontation takes place on the house's great staircase between George and his hysterical, sexually frustrated Aunt Fanny (Agnes Moorehead). Even more skillfully than in *Citizen Kane*, Welles uses all the resources of film to convey an immediate visual sense of the attitudes and emotions fully expressed in Tarkington's novel.

Twentieth Century-Fox in the forties had much greater success with its literary adaptations. In 1941, John Ford temporarily left his beloved Monument Valley to direct a moving film version of Richard Llewellyn's novel *How Green Was My Valley*. The movie concerned the Morgans, a Welsh mining family, and the events that erode and finally destroy them as surely as the mines are destroying their land. The story is narrated by Huw, the youngest son, who, as an adult, recalls his early life with the family ("they are a living truth within my mind"): a brother's wedding, a bitter, disastrous strike, unhappy days at school, where he is abused by a sadistic teacher, and mine accidents that break close ties forever. At the center of the family are his parents—a stern but kindly father (Donald Crisp, in a performance of quiet authority) and a feisty mother (Sara Allgood, lighting the screen with an inner radiance). As their life together worsens, young Huw, played with uncanny appeal by Roddy McDowall, finds solace in their strength and resilience.

Although Phillip Dunne's screenplay is rambling, episodic, and sometimes overly sentimental, *How Green Was My Valley* remains indelible in the memory for scenes that touch the heart with their simple beauty: Morgan and his sons returning from the mines, their voices raised in song as they drop their wages into the mother's lap; Huw strolling with his father in the Welsh countryside or, after a crippling accident, learning to walk again with the help of the minister, Mr. Gruffydd (Walter Pidgeon); townsmen Cyfartha (Barry Fitzgerald) and Dai Bando (Rhys Williams) amiably wreaking their vengeance on Huw's nasty teacher. The film ends with a heartbreaking sequence—the death of the father in a mine collapse. As the lift emerges from the mine, he is held in Huw's loving arms while the women wait with a silent grief that many of them have known before.

While *How Green Was My Valley* is concerned with the plight of the Welsh miners, it is not intended as an angry diatribe against the destructive impact of the mine and its owners. The film concentrates on the family and its place in a turbulently changing community; the literal erosion of the land is only a metaphor for the psychic erosion of the Morgans' spirit and fortitude. John Ford is a conservative rather than a social-minded director. Even in *The Grapes of*

sequences, especially an eerie ball at Jabez's imposing home. Filmed in soft focus, Jabez's guests, a congregation of the damned, move into a dance that becomes strange and otherworldly. Scratch merrily plays a violin with the orchestra. As the music accelerates, Miser Stevens (John Qualen), his soul in thrall to the Devil, whirls with the dancers in a frenzy. When his soul has been claimed, he appears as a moth before Jabez's terrified eyes.

Orson Welles's second movie, *The Magnificent Ambersons*, released by RKO in 1942, was also unable to find an audience. The reasons have never been totally clear; apparently, the studio's new management, still smarting from the controversy over *Citizen Kane* and disappointed by the initial reception of *Ambersons*, insisted on cutting it by one-third and released it to theaters as part of a double bill. The remaining film, really a fragment, still attests, however, to Welles's brilliance as a filmmaker. In his familiar stentorian tones, Welles narrates Booth Tarkington's story of the Ambersons, whose affluent life in a small midwestern town is wrecked by the nation's industrial progress, especially by the impact of the automobile. The focus is on spoiled, snobbish George Amberson Minifer (Tim Holt), who is contemptuous of that progress and who finally (and ironically) gets his "comeuppance" from a speeding automobile, which breaks both of his legs.

Welles's strong cinematic sense was perhaps more evident in this film than in any other he has made. In the opening scenes, with few

Above: All That Money Can Buy *(RKO, 1941). Walter Huston as Mr. Scratch, otherwise known as the Devil. His raspy voice and rascally grin made him a most endearing villain. He was also a formidable opponent for the righteous Daniel Webster.*
Opposite: The Magnificent Ambersons *(RKO, 1942). A typically atmospheric shot from Orson Welles's film, showing neurasthenic Fanny (Agnes Moorehead) and her spoiled nephew, George (Tim Holt). The movie was heavily cut by the studio, which was irritated with Welles for a variety of reasons.*

Wrath, he muted much of John Steinbeck's anger at an uncaring society; the bitterness of the migrants as they face hostility and hunger is not as strongly expressed as the pride in Ma Joad's worn face as she holds her family together. In *How Green Was My Valley*, the bleak view of the striking miners huddled against the cold does not stay in our minds as vividly as that of Mrs. Morgan standing defiantly in the snow as she accuses them of turning their backs on her husband. In John Ford's estimation, issues are not as important as families; commitment to a cause is not as vital as preserving and strengthening family unity.

A Tree Grows in Brooklyn (1945) was another of Fox's well-wrought adaptations of popular novels in the forties. Derived from Betty Smith's best-selling book and directed by Elia Kazan in his feature-film debut, the movie was a long, sentimental, but highly affecting chronicle of a poor family in Brooklyn's Williamsburg district "a few decades ago." The episodic screenplay by Tess Slesinger and Frank Davis centered largely on Francie Nolan (Peggy Ann Garner),

the sensitive, inquisitive young girl who, through a series of joyous and painful experiences, moves a little closer to growing up. Most important in her life are her warmhearted but irresponsible alcoholic father (James Dunn) and her still-young but worn, embittered mother (Dorothy McGuire). During the course of the film, they help her learn about love, resilience, and irretrievable loss.

The film is by no means perfect: it is unfocused and sprawling, its characters are not exactly freshly conceived, and it is much too antiseptic in its view of the time and place—the pungency and color of the setting is only fleetingly apparent. Yet it is moving in its depiction of a family struggling to eke out the barest existence in abject poverty, and it gives one of the screen's best portraits of a young girl tentatively emerging into adulthood. Much of its success in this respect can be attributed to Peggy Ann Garner, who offers what is surely one of the loveliest performances ever given by a child actress. Her plain, eager face betrays every emotion from joy to heartbreak with consummate skill.

Preceding pages and above: How Green Was My Valley *(Fox, 1941). The women of this Welsh mining town await the return of their men from the mines. Above: A lovely quiet moment in the Morgan household as dinner begins.*
Opposite: A Tree Grows in Brooklyn *(Fox, 1945). Young Francie Nolan (Peggy Ann Garner) has a nighttime conversation with her loving father, Johnny (James Dunn). Their relationship was the poignant center of Elia Kazan's film version of the best-selling Betty Smith novel.*
Below: The evocative setting for the film adaptation of Betty Smith's novel.

Most of all, Garner makes something real and moving of the film's core, Francie's relationship with her father. The glow of her love for him is evident in their every moment together: a bedtime conversation in which he fantasizes about their imaginary trip together; her expression of pride, sorrow, and longing as she listens to him playing and singing "Annie Laurie" on their piano; his last words to her before his death ("Don't be afraid. I don't want you should ever be afraid"). At his funeral, Francie's stricken face stands out from all the others; later, when she sobs alone on the roof, shouting "Nobody loved him like I did!" to the heedless sky, Garner lets us feel Francie's intolerable grief.

An adaptation in an entirely different vein came from Paramount in 1945. The postwar years were rife with films that attempted to come to grips with America's social problems, including racial and religious prejudice and alcoholism. Previously, alcoholism had been neglected or treated in comic terms, but Paramount attacked it boldly in a film version of Charles Jackson's novel *The Lost Weekend.* Under Billy Wilder's uncompromising direction, Ray Milland played writer Don Birnam, whose out-of-control drinking sends him plummeting into degradation. The screenplay by Wilder and Charles Brackett gave no quarter in depicting Birnam's frantic search for one more drink—the steps that begin with desperate pleading and lead to the harrowing alcoholic ward of a hospital. Today, much of the film seems contrived and simplistic, but Ray Milland's Oscar-winning performance is persuasive; he conveys Birnam's desperation and self-loathing with every twitch and convulsion. The movie's best-remembered and most horrific moment comes when, at the peak of his alcoholic state, Birnam has a hallucination in which a bat attacks and kills a squealing mouse, and the mouse's blood stains the wall of his room.

In the fifties and sixties, the crop of films derived from classic or popular books included some that strove conscientiously to be true to their sources. When the novel was an acknowledged masterpiece, crammed with complexities in its theme and characterizations, the result was usually not up to the mark. There were some films, however, that offered at least commendable adaptations of well-known novels. At MGM, a version of Stephen Crane's *The Red Badge of Courage* (1951), directed by John Huston, fell far short of its intentions—the film was trimmed down to sixty-nine minutes after complex problems with the studio—but it had many striking images of battle. Vincente Minnelli's production of Irving Stone's *Lust for Life* (1956) made stunningly effective use of color in depicting the wild and shifting moods of Vincent van Gogh (Kirk Douglas). In the sixties, film versions of novels continued to provide plum acting assignments for leading stars: Burt Lancaster in Sinclair Lewis's *Elmer Gantry* (1960); Audrey Hepburn in Truman Capote's *Breakfast at Tiffany's* (1961); and a boatload of luminaries in Katherine Anne Porter's *Ship of Fools* (1965).

Novel adaptations in the seventies included one film that baffled most audiences and won the qualified approval of most critics. John Schlesinger's version of Nathanael West's Hollywood novel *The Day of the Locust* (1975) was a gamble that failed but failed brilliantly, and with more cinematic daring and panache than many other films of the period displayed. West's book was a bleakly satirical vision of California's Dream Factory in the late thirties, peopled with pathetic losers vainly aspiring to fame, and Waldo Salt's screenplay was largely faithful to this vision. Through the eyes of Tod Hackett (William Atherton), a would-be set designer, we observe the monstrous vulgarity and grossness and the desperate manufacturing of dreams that come to symbolize the decline and fall not only of the

Page 262: The Day of the Locust *(Paramount, 1975). Eccentric accountant Homer Simpson (Donald Sutherland) looks with baffled eyes at the strange world of Hollywood in the late thirties. Below: A would-be movie star (Karen Black) and a has-been vaudevillian (Burgess Meredith) in John Schlesinger's pungent adaptation of Nathanael West's novel.*
Preceding page: Lust for Life *(MGM, 1956). Kirk Douglas starred as artist Vincent van Gogh in Vincente Minnelli's adaptation of Irving Stone's book. The visual look of the film often suggested Van Gogh's paintings.*

movie colony but of America itself. In fact, the film's principal sequences, superbly staged by Schlesinger, are meant to support and dramatize that symbol: a set collapses during the filming of the battle of Waterloo; a cockfight turns into a hideous, bloody battlefield; and, in the film's apocalyptic climax, a Hollywood premiere disintegrates into a chaotic riot, a vision of hell.

As a panoramic view of American civilization at its most reprehensible, *The Day of the Locust* resembles Robert Altman's *Nashville*, also made in 1975. However, the former film suffers from the lack of firm control that Altman had wielded over the many characters and intermingling stories. *The Day of the Locust* lacks cohesion, and occasionally it edges into hysteria. Still, the movie is audacious in its overall concept, and it assembles a number of vivid characters who embody West's gallery of grotesques. They include a blonde extra and part-time hooker (Karen Black) who dreams of becoming a star; her drunken father (Burgess Meredith), an ex-vaudeville hoofer; a strange, sexually repressed accountant (Donald Sutherland); a self-styled evangelist (Geraldine Page) who runs "God's gas station"; and a nasty dwarf (Billy Barty). In the film, as in the novel, these people, like specimens under a microscope, are observed without compassion; their mean lives evoke neither pity nor contempt. *The Day of the Locust* is a dispassionate, repellent, but totally fascinating film.

One of the outstanding film adaptations of the seventies was Fred Zinnemann's production of *Julia* (1977), adapted by Alvin Sargent from a story in Lillian Hellman's memoir *Pentimento*. A moving account of the playwright's abiding friendship with a remarkable woman named Julia, the film was an unusual mixture of nostalgic reminiscence, wartime suspense drama, and mystery detection. Jane Fonda played Hellman, who, in a series of flashbacks, tries to remember, in old age, "what was there for me once." She recalls her happy childhood days with Julia and then their adult years apart —herself as a beginning and then successful playwright living with author Dashiell Hammett (Jason Robards), and Julia (Vanessa Redgrave) as a woman totally committed to fighting tyranny. Their paths cross during the early days of Hitler when Lillian is asked to deliver money clandestinely to Julia for underground activities. Soon after they meet in a Berlin café, Julia is murdered by the Gestapo, and Lillian, both angry and sorrowful, is left with an imperishable memory of her friend.

Having been given the nature of an unstructured memoir, *Julia* is diffuse, and occasionally it is difficult to keep the film in focus. But within that limitation, it is a lovely movie, haunting and impressively made. In addition to the meticulously detailed settings of the twenties and thirties, and Douglas Slocombe's exquisite photography, which gives a kind of burnished glow to many key scenes, the film offers portraits of two close friends who are caught up in the tide of history, one dedicated to the point of risking and achieving her own destruction, the other forced by circumstances to test her courage and find her own bravest instincts. The movie's best scenes are those few in which they meet as adults: an extraordinarily touching encounter in a Berlin hospital where Julia, badly beaten by the Nazis and

unable to speak, clasps Lillian's hand, and their brief liaison in the café, in which they must suppress their feelings. (Julia dismisses Lillian abruptly by saying, "My beloved friend, leave!")

Although Jane Fonda gives a strong, feeling performance as Lillian Hellman, it is Vanessa Redgrave, in the much smaller role of Julia, who dominates the film. She conveys Julia's early perception of tyranny in a simple, direct, "It's wrong, Lilly," and when we see her in the thick of the fight, battling Nazi thugs, we understand the selflessness that allows her to risk her life for a cause. Calmly, but with an undercurrent of steely determination, she tells Julia, "We can save five hundred people, maybe a thousand. We can only do today what we can do today." There are sturdy supporting performances by Jason Robards as Hammett and by Maximilian Schell as Johann, the man who contacts Lillian about the mission to Berlin. Shabby, diffident, with a small, apologetic smile, Schell embodies every displaced European whose misfortune could not damage his sense of commitment.

The stage has always provided a bountiful source of material for movies. In the earliest years of sound, with widespread uncertainty about how to use the new production techniques, film versions of stage plays were frequently rigid, studio-bound efforts in which the actors declaimed their lines as if they were still treading the boards. Within a few years, however, filmmakers were able to apply their newfound expertise and a growing spirit of experimentation to theater properties, and began opening them up cinematically. It was not merely a question of expanding settings to other locales (many films continued to betray their stage origins despite the extended locales); it was more of a recognition that the film version of a play called for different rules, new approaches. An imaginative use of the camera could make some stage dialogue superfluous. The charisma of a major film star could add a new (and sometimes unwarranted) dimension to a stage role. A theme or concept that seemed relevant in the theater could flatten out or seem hollow and pretentious when transferred to celluloid. There were undeniable risks in adapting plays to the screen, and in the thirties and forties, many studios (especially Warner Bros.) insisted on taking them, usually with unhappy results. But there were also successes—films that were true to or even improved upon their stage sources.

One such film was *Stage Door* (1937), adapted from the George S. Kaufman–Edna Ferber play. The movie version retained the basic story of aspiring actresses living in New York's Footlights Club, but the entire tone and approach of the play was greatly altered in Morrie Ryskind and Anthony Veiller's scenario. With Gregory La Cava directing, the result was virtually a new version of the material. The play had centered on hopeful actress Terry Randall, daughter of a country doctor, who, out of a lofty regard for the theater and contempt for motion pictures, holds fast to her dream of appearing on the New York stage. During the play, she nobly survives the loss of her ambitious playwriting boyfriend, the suicide of a club resident who cannot get or hold a job, and a botched audition for a role she covets.

Opposite, left: The Lost Weekend *(Paramount, 1945). Bartender Howard da Silva disapproves of Don Birnam's nonstop drinking. Ray Milland's unsparing performance as Birnam highlighted this harrowing drama of alcoholism, derived from Charles Jackson's novel.*
Opposite, right: The Red Badge of Courage *(MGM, 1951). Civil War soldiers pause before their next encounter with the enemy. In the foreground: the Young Soldier (Audie Murphy). Although John Huston's adaptation of Stephen Crane's classic novel was severely cut in its final release print, it managed to convey a sense of how it felt to take part in battle.*

In the film version, the role of Terry Randall was assigned to Katharine Hepburn, and to accommodate her personality, Terry was turned into a snobbish rich girl, in love with the "theatah," who learns humility when another resident of the club (Andrea Leeds), up for the same role she wins, kills herself in despair. Also, a relatively minor role in the play, that of Jean Maitland, a club resident who scores in the movies, was fattened to suit Hepburn's costar Ginger Rogers, who gave it the warmth and the touch of astringency that the play's character lacked. Apart from the changes required by the casting, the film version was markedly superior to the play. Wisely, the screenplay dropped the play's frequent attacks on the movies ("You don't even have to be alive to act in pictures"), discarded Terry's cliché boyfriend, and substituted entire reams of funny, abrasive, and observant dialogue parceled out to the would-be actresses at the Footlights Club. Except for the tear-jerking sequences at the end, the movie seemed newly minted, and such actresses as Rogers, Lucille Ball, Ann Miller, Eve Arden, and Gail Patrick, all quick at repartee, managed to rub away the rather "la-di-da" attitude of the play and find the humanity beneath it.

Occasionally, the freer attitudes of the theater dictated a drastic change when the property reached the screen. Lillian Hellman's first play, *The Children's Hour*, had been a powerful drama concerning two young teachers whose lives are ruined when a vicious student lies about their relationship. In Samuel Goldwyn's film adaptation, under the title *These Three* (1936), the homosexual implications were replaced by a heterosexual relationship between one of the teachers and a young doctor, and there was the suggestion of a standard romantic triangle involving the three principals.

Opposite: Julia *(Fox, 1977). Lillian Hellman (Jane Fonda) and Julia (Vanessa Redgrave), her dear childhood friend, meet for the last time in a Berlin café. Redgrave won a deserved Oscar as Best Supporting Actress for her sensitive performance as a deeply committed woman. Below: On Martha's Vineyard, Lillian struggles to write a play. Part of the film concerned Hellman's emergence as a playwright. Above:* Stage Door *(RKO, 1937). In the clutter of their room at the Footlights Club, hopeful actresses Terry Randall (Katharine Hepburn) and Jean Maitland (Ginger Rogers) discuss the future.*

stage play was a taut drama concerning the Hubbards, an avaricious Southern family dominated by Regina, a Hubbard married to the ill and submissive Horace Giddens. In this theatrically charged story, Regina and her predatory brothers vie for control of Horace's money, with Regina ending up the dubious winner. Although she gains control of the money, she ends up as a lonely figure, defied by her daughter, Alexandra.

It was a well-made play, ripe with melodramatic flourishes and even suggestive of a larger theme: the crushing impact of industrialization on the genteel South. The film version was faithful to the play, opening it enough to provide an idea of the community in which the Hubbards exercised their power. Gregg Toland's deep-focus photography roamed the Giddens house, mixing shadows and sunlight to convey a sense of the menace lurking in the plush surroundings, and William Wyler filmed the key sequences with enormous skill, making them crackle with tension. The final, fatal clash between Regina and Horace is a model of filmmaking craftsmanship. As Regina spits out her venomous hatred, Horace is stricken and begs her to give him the medicine from a nearby table. She sits rigidly in her chair, never moving as he crawls painfully up the stairs for another bottle of medicine in his bedroom. Only when he collapses and dies on the stairs does she begin to scream for

Since the adaptation of the play was done by Lillian Hellman herself, and the direction was in the capable hands of William Wyler, it was not surprising that the altered version worked so well. There was little or no loss of the drama's effectiveness, and with Gregg Toland behind the camera to give the film a smooth professional look, *These Three* made compelling entertainment. As the persecuted teachers, Merle Oberon and Miriam Hopkins gave expert performances, with Hopkins having the edge only because her secretly lovelorn character called for an added measure of pathos. The most remarkable performance came from young Bonita Granville as their scheming nemesis, Mary Tilford. It is a bravura turn calling for sustained intensity, and it is the focus of the film's best scenes, most notably the blistering sequence in which Mary torments and blackmails her fellow student Rosalie (Marcia Mae Jones) into confirming the damaging lie about the protagonists.

The same team that had worked on *These Three*—producer Samuel Goldwyn, author Lillian Hellman, director William Wyler, and cinematographer Gregg Toland—came together with even better results in the film version of *The Little Foxes* (1941). Lillian Hellman's

Left: These Three *(Samuel Goldwyn/United Artists, 1936). Miriam Hopkins, Merle Oberon, and Joel McCrea find their lives shattered by the lie of a vicious girl. This film version of Lillian Hellman's play changed the implication of a homosexual relationship between Hopkins and Oberon to a conventional romantic triangle involving McCrea.*
Right: The Little Foxes *(Samuel Goldwyn/RKO, 1941). The tension mounts as Regina Giddens (Bette Davis) taunts her ailing husband, Horace (Herbert Marshall).*

help. Here the editing, the camera work, the direction, and the acting are impeccably right in a scene as gripping on screen as it was onstage.

Bette Davis gives a strong, somewhat mannered performance as Regina, most effective when she quietly exerts her authority, least effective when she overplays the swaggering villainy, and Herbert Marshall is appropriately cast as a gentle man sickened by the greed of the Hubbards. However, the most impressive acting is done by members of the original stage cast. Charles Dingle and Carl Benton Reid are properly nasty as the Hubbard brothers, who prove to be outmatched by their sister, and Patricia Collinge is especially good as Reid's refined, alcoholic wife, Birdie. Fluttering like a wild bird trapped in a cage, she wins our pity when she reminisces tipsily about the vanished gracious days that can never return.

In subsequent decades, there were movies that made the leap from the stage to the screen without any fatal fractures. The works of leading playwrights offered built-in prestige and bravura roles that attracted many stars. Tennessee Williams and Edward Albee provided Elizabeth Taylor with two of her most challenging roles. In Williams's *Cat on a Hot Tin Roof* (1958), she gave a sensuous and vibrant reading of the role of Maggie, the Southern wife whose marriage with Brick Pollitt (Paul Newman) is troubled. The film deleted the play's suggestion that Brick was tortured by a homosexual past,

concentrating on Maggie's desperate efforts to regain her husband's love and on Brick's stormy relationship with his father, Big Daddy (Burl Ives). It was really steamy melodrama given a thin layer of significance by Williams, but it was acted with vigor and authority. In 1966, Taylor made a brave try at playing the shrewish, vulgar, and contemptuous Martha of Albee's *Who's Afraid of Virginia Woolf?*, but it was more of an audacious stunt than a sustained performance. Richard Burton was better as George, the vitriolic, defeated husband with whom she shares a night of invective and bitter revelation.

The plays of Eugene O'Neill generally have not fared well on the screen—their turgidity seems to become more pronounced on film—but his searing autobiographical drama *Long Day's Journey into Night* made it to the screen in 1962 with most of its power intact. More of a transcription of the play than a film version, the movie repeated the nearly three-hour account of the tortured Tyrone family, stressing the mother's pathetic descent into drug-ridden oblivion. Katharine Hepburn played Mary Tyrone, sustained by morphine and memory, whose disintegration is watched helplessly by her bombastic husband, once-famed actor James Tyrone (Ralph Richardson),

*Cat on a Hot Tin Roof (MGM, 1958). On a steamy Southern night, Maggie (Elizabeth Taylor)
tries to get a loving response from her surly husband, Brick (Paul Newman). Both players
received Academy Award nominations for their performances. Right: An angry confrontation
between a moody Brick and his dying father (Burl Ives). The film version of Tennessee Williams's
play expurgated Brick's homosexual past, leaving the motives for his behavior unclear.*

Opposite: Who's Afraid of Virginia Woolf? *(Warner Bros., 1966). During a long night of revelation, the marriage of Nick (George Segal) and his neurotic wife, Honey (Sandy Dennis), is mercilessly exposed. Below: Playing the bawdy, vitriolic Martha to Richard Burton's defeated George in Edward Albee's dissection of a turbulent marriage, Elizabeth Taylor received her second Academy Award for Best Actress.*
Above: Long Day's Journey into Night *(Ely Landau/Embassy, 1962). Edmund Tyrone (Dean Stockwell) listens sadly to the drug-induced meanderings of his mother (Katharine Hepburn).*

and her sons (Jason Robards and Dean Stockwell). Sidney Lumet directed reverently and capably, offsetting the stretches of tedium with a number of explosively dramatic confrontations between members of the family. There were also isolated sections of quiet beauty in which recollections of the past eased the despair of the present. Although Katharine Hepburn's longtime image of strength and authority worked against her portrayal of Mary Tyrone, she gave a commendable performance as a ruined woman who can only find surcease from pain in narcotics, a wraith presiding at her own funeral.

Another stage adaptation with biographical content was *The Miracle Worker* (1962), derived from William Gibson's long-running play

Helen exultantly understands the sign language for "water," thus beginning her true education, was as moving on film as it had been in the theater.

What takes place when a printed page or a moment of three-dimensional theater is transformed into a strip of film? Detractors of the film medium would tell us that there is a loss: the imagination a reader brings to a book is stunted when the imagined scene is made real on film; the sense of an actual person experiencing a crucial moment—the excitement of live theater—cannot be matched by images projected on a screen.

about Helen Keller and her teacher, Annie Sullivan. The story centered on Annie's fierce and indomitable efforts to turn young Helen from a wild, uncontrollable deaf-mute, pitiable but barely human, into a comprehending and manageable human being. Although the minor defects of the play—the awkward flashbacks, the occasional reaching for emotional effects—were magnified on the screen, the movie still made the titanic struggle for dominance between Annie and Helen an absorbing experience. Arthur Penn directed Anne Bancroft (Annie) and young Patty Duke (Helen), the original stars of the stage version, allowing them to display both their acting skill and their formidable physical prowess. The climactic scene in which

Well, perhaps. Or perhaps any film version of a book or play should not be seen as better or worse, but only different, a medium unto itself in which the components of the older and more venerable media—the narrative, the characters, the point of view, the backgrounds of time and place—are transformed by the camera eye into a mysterious (and sometimes magical) creation called a movie. The relation to its source is of less consequence than what it has become. Moviegoers may continue to ask, "Is it better than the book?" or "How does it compare to the play?," and critics will be glad to give them answers. But in the long view, the film should have a separate existence.

The Miracle Worker *(Fred Coe/United Artists, 1962). A violent battle for supremacy rages between Annie Sullivan (Anne Bancroft) and her wild deaf-mute student, Helen Keller (Patty Duke). Both actresses, repeating their vivid stage performances on film, won Academy Awards. Opposite: Helen runs wild, to the consternation of her mother (Inga Swenson).*

ONE OF A KIND
Movies That Stand Alone

From the formative years to the present, the history of film has included a few rare and deeply influential motion pictures: beacons that cast their light into the future, illuminating new approaches to the art. These are the films that created the language of film, or extended its boundaries, or offered original, imaginative ways of using the techniques that go into the making of a movie. Their mark is plainly evident, or subtly visible, in many films that came after them. Their vibrations can be heard, echoing down the years.

Sadly, we have never paid true homage to those who brought us these seminal films. D. W. Griffith never fully recovered from the shattering failure of *Intolerance*, and after the lovely *Broken Blossoms* in 1919 and the spectacular *Orphans of the Storm* in 1922, his fame declined steadily. He died a bitter and nearly forgotten man. Erich von Stroheim's extravagance and his insistence on complete control made him anathema to the studios, and he was forced to abandon directing and return to acting. Orson Welles was also declared virtually untouchable by the major Hollywood studios, and he was unable to duplicate the early brilliance and innovative excitement of *Citizen Kane*. Hollywood professes to worship talent, but it is uneasy with erratic genius.

Still, their masterworks continue to be seen, to be admired, to be analyzed. These few movies are an ongoing legacy, a recurring tribute. This is the wonder of film: it gives permanence to images cast upon a screen and bestows a kind of immortality on those both behind and in front of the camera, who create these images.

It can truly be said that many of the films discussed in this book had their origins in an epic motion picture that opened on February 8, 1915, at Clune's Auditorium in Los Angeles, and a month later at the Liberty Theatre in New York City. With *The Birth of a Nation*, the eccentric and boldly original filmmaker David Wark Griffith achieved lasting fame; with one nearly three-hour spectacle, he turned film in the direction of art, expanded or refined many of the techniques that make up its grammar, and used film for the first time as a powerful vehicle for the expression of ideas that could deeply affect the audience. A dramatic refutation of those who found movies an amusing toy, *The Birth of a Nation* demonstrated the primitive force of film, its ability to intuitively stir the emotions and fire the imagination. Although a highly controversial work—Griffith had based it on the Reverend Thomas Dixon's blatantly racist novel *The Clansman*—it marked the beginning of film's maturity.

The Birth of a Nation is many things, but it is *not* an accurate re-creation of American history. It is, instead, a highly romanticized view of the South in the turbulent years of the Civil War and the Reconstruction. Basically, it tells the story of two families, the Northern Stonemans and the Southern Camerons, whose children are friends before the war and whose lives are cruelly disrupted and shattered by the conflict. Early in the film, friendship turns to romance when Phil Stoneman (Elmer Clifton) and Margaret Cameron (Miriam Cooper) fall in love, while Ben Cameron (Henry B. Walthall), known as the "Little Colonel," falls for Elsie Stoneman (Lillian Gish), who later reciprocates the feeling. The war brings separation and death, followed by the bitter Reconstruction period in which the South is overrun by carpetbaggers and free blacks. Elsie's fanatic father (Ralph Lewis), with the help of an ambitious mulatto named Silas Lynch (George Siegmann), schemes to crush the white South "under the heel of the black South." When the Little Colonel's young sister Flora (Mae Marsh) is killed escaping from a lustful renegade black, he organizes the Ku Klux Klan to "save the South from the tyranny of black rule." In a double climax, the Little Colonel and the Klansmen rescue Elsie from the evil clutches of Silas Lynch, and also save the Camerons from a cabin where they are being besieged by black soldiers. An allegorical ending offers images of peace and brotherly love.

If *The Birth of a Nation* is a distorted, one-sided view of America in turmoil, it is also an astonishing work of cinematic art. Despite the close scrutiny to which its sweeping action scenes, its moving, intimate details of family sorrow have been subjected, they never lose their power to stir audiences. The Civil War battle scenes are not only amazing in their verisimilitude but also in the artistry with which Griffith selects images for their maximum impact. Especially moving is the scene in which the two youngest Stoneman and Cameron boys meet on the battlefield and die together, or the shot of fallen soldiers accompanied by the simple legend, "War's peace." Sherman's march to the sea is depicted vividly, as is the sequence of Atlanta under siege, with terrified citizens fleeing through the streets. At the same time, we recall small moments that are equally part of film legend. Notable among these is the homecoming of the Little Colonel, in which his mother's arm comes through the open door, motioning him into the warmth and security of the house.

The second part of the film, portraying the horrors of the Reconstruction period, is less spectacular and more problematical. As it shows the South increasingly in the thrall of power-hungry blacks led by Silas Lynch, many of the images are ugly and ominous: grinning, hard-drinking, shiftless blacks brazenly in control of the state legislature; a renegade Negro's attempted rape of young Flora; the Klan's violent revenge. The death of Flora in her brother's arms is touching; we can feel his sorrow as he carries her broken body back to the shocked and grieving family.

Opposite: Gone with the Wind *(David O. Selznick/MGM, 1939). Vivien Leigh as Scarlett O'Hara. She was chosen for the role after one of the most publicized talent hunts in film history.*

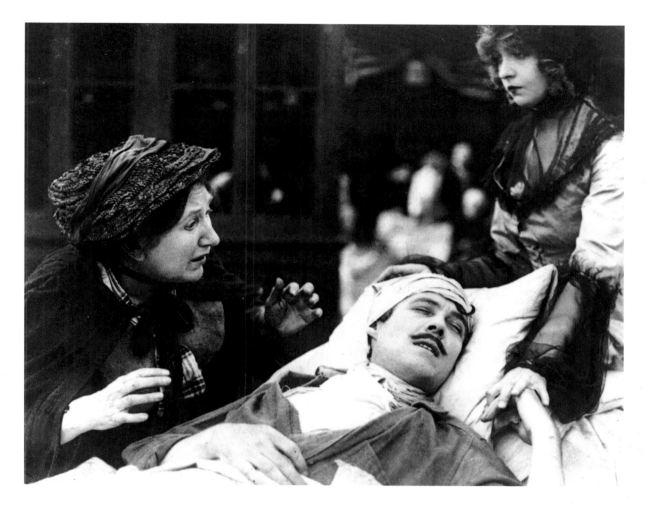

Opposite: The Birth of a Nation *(Epoch Producing Co., 1915). A production still showing General Sherman's march to the sea, one of many historical events re-created in D. W. Griffith's landmark film. Above: Mrs. Cameron (Josephine Crowell) consoles her badly wounded son Ben (Henry B. Walthall) while Elsie Stoneman (Lillian Gish) holds his hand. Below: A victory parade for the Ku Klux Klan. In front: Miriam Cooper, Lillian Gish, and Henry B. Walthall (in his Klan uniform).*

Most thrilling is the long final section in which the Little Colonel and the Klan must bring about the double rescue of the imperiled Elsie in Silas Lynch's house and the equally endangered Camerons in their cabin. For this early period in film history, the cross-cutting between the villains, the victims, and their rescuers is remarkably effective. This sequence, with its carefully orchestrated shifts from the hard-riding Klan to the crazed blacks to the terrified Elsie or the besieged Camerons, spurs almost intolerable suspense. We welcome Griffith's final images of peace, picturing the golden day when "the Bestial War shall rule no more."

There is, of course, no way to discuss *The Birth of a Nation* without confronting the enduring controversy concerning its racist attitudes. In making heroes of its Ku Klux Klan nightriders, in portraying blacks as either lustful monsters or abject but loyal slaves, Griffith made himself vulnerable to charges of flagrant bigotry, which were not long in forthcoming. Black groups vociferously urged the banning of the film, and many showings were accompanied by loud hissing. A number of the reviews were hostile—in *The Moving Picture World* of March 13, 1915, W. Stephen Bush praised "the splendor and magnificence

of its spectacles," but condemned its "undisguised appeal to race prejudices" and its tendency "to inflame race hatred." Francis Hackett, in *The New Republic* of March 20, 1915, was vituperative, calling the film "aggressively vicious and defamatory," one that "degrades the censors that passed it and the white race that endures it."

Many of the contemporary reviews disregarded the film's inflammatory material to praise the brilliance of its execution. Over the more than six decades since its release, critics have thrashed about mightily in their defense of Griffith. They have argued that Griffith had the naïve attitudes of an old Southerner who grew up expecting blacks to be servile. They claim that he did not share Dixon's violently racist views, and was more interested in showing, with some justification, that the South had been deeply wronged by Northern carpetbaggers and free blacks. (After all, his father had been a Confederate participant in the war.) There is little doubt that Griffith genuinely believed he was offering an accurate, impartial account of the Civil War and Reconstruction. Yet it must be questioned whether innocence and naïveté excuse the promulgation of dangerous ideas. We might ask whether critics would defend the son of a Nazi army officer who hon-

The Birth of a Nation (Epoch Producing Co., 1915). A moment from one of the spectacular battle scenes in D. W. Griffith's historic Civil War epic.

estly and innocently believed that the Jews of his country represented a threat to racial purity.

Nevertheless, *The Birth of a Nation* was the screen's first great motion picture, and it remains a masterwork that changed the face of film for all time. We can acknowledge its bigotry and then move on from there, to acknowledge also that it was a monumental achievement that single-handedly moved film out of the nickelodeon and into a higher realm. Film production has changed almost immeasurably since 1915, but the roots of countless movies can be traced back to *The Birth of a Nation*, and to one man's vision of what film could be.

Griffith was shocked by the charges leveled against *The Birth of a Nation* and infuriated that he should be accused of bigotry. By the time of the film's release, he had already completed his next film, *The Mother and the Law*, a modern story of a hapless woman victimized by injustice and overzealous morality. He decided to expand the film into a four-part epic of awesome proportions, aiming to shame those who had accused him of racial hatred as well as to dramatize

man's inhumanity to man over the centuries. It was not an act of contrition or guilt, but an assertion of his belief in the essential brotherhood of all human beings. Produced at a then-staggering cost of two million dollars, *Intolerance* was released in 1916 to admiring reviews and poor business. Audiences were baffled by Griffith's use of interwoven stories, bewildered by the unceasing intensity and the nearly hysterical pace of the last two reels. And, at a time when war with Germany was imminent, a film pleading for tolerance was out of key with the temper of the nation. The failure of *Intolerance* drained Griffith, financially and emotionally.

The irony is both massive and self-evident: *Intolerance* has come to be regarded by many as the greatest silent film, and possibly Hollywood's greatest film of all time. After nearly seven decades, it continues to astonish us with its staggering range, its technical virtuosity, and its visual splendor. Its faults are plain: the simplistic if not foolish "sociological" concepts, the excessive editorializing, the florid titles which, although characteristic of the time, are often hard to

Intolerance *(Wark Producing Co., 1916). The Dear One (Mae Marsh) fights to protect her baby from the grimly moralistic ladies of the Jenkins Foundation. Her performance, sensitive and touching, is one of the greatest in silent films.*

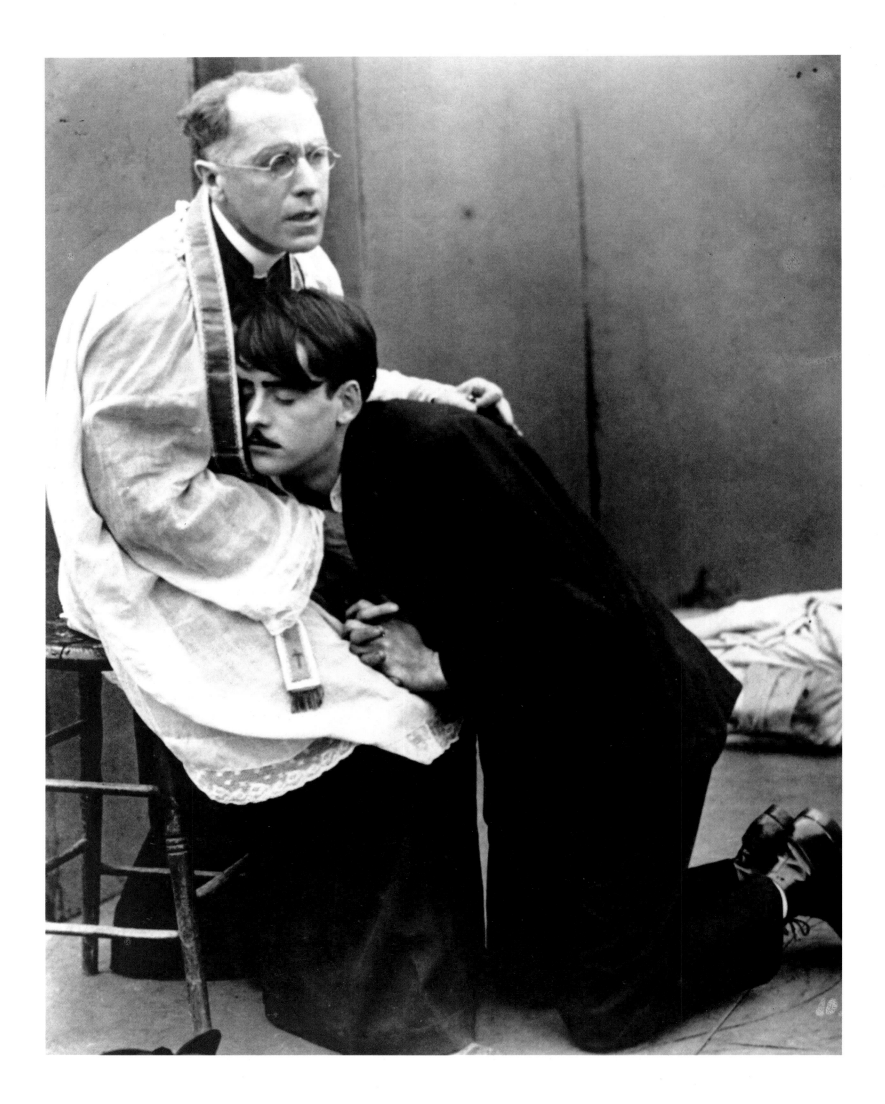

take. The film has even been accused of damaging Hollywood's prestige and turning America's greatest intellectual figures against the medium of motion pictures for fifteen years.

Intolerance is commonly viewed as a cinematic fugue weaving together four separate stories that demonstrate "love's struggle through the ages." Each complements and comments upon the other. These stories are: the fall of Babylon to the Persian conqueror Cyrus the Great in 538 B.C.; the betrayal and crucifixion of Christ; the massacre of the Huguenots in Paris in August of 1572 during the regime of Charles IX; and the modern story, set in an American mill town and city slum. Linking the stories is an image of the Eternal Mother (Lillian Gish), endlessly rocking a cradle to lines from Walt Whitman that call her "chanter of pains and joys, uniter of here and hereafter." Of the four stories, considerable footage is given to the Babylonian section, staged with eye-popping grandeur, in which Babylon's King Belshazzar (Alfred Paget), a champion of religious tolerance, is betrayed to Cyrus by the fanatical High Priest of Bel (Tully Marshall). The modern story, certainly the most dramatic, is also emphasized; it centers on the Dear One (Mae Marsh), who suffers deeply when her young husband (Robert Harron) is falsely convicted of murder and condemned to death and her baby is taken away from her by a callous society of "Uplifters." In the breathtaking climax, linked with the denouements of the other stories, the Dear One races to save her husband from the gallows. The excitement created in these scenes has seldom been duplicated.

After the views of widespread destruction, *Intolerance* ends idealistically, with a vision of "perfect peace" in which soldiers are stopped from fighting by rows of angels, and prisoners rush from their cells as the walls of their prisons disappear. Children play against a background of war weapons now overgrown with flowers, while people walk in the sunshine. The final frame shows the mother, eternally rocking her cradle.

The size and splendor of *Intolerance* are unparalleled, but its place in film history rests on more than its dimensions. It further extended the innovations Griffith had introduced in *The Birth of a Nation*, using them with greater assurance and depth. Specifically, the film demonstrated the many ways in which film techniques could be used to heighten dramatic impact. By imaginative and rhythmic intercutting of the stories, by the use of lighting to enhance the mood of key scenes, and by effective camera work (courtesy of G. W. "Billy" Bitzer) that moved unflinchingly into the action, Griffith was able to create the most *human* of all epic films. He manages to give a sense of immediacy to the large-scale sequences; we cringe with horror during the graphic murder of the Huguenots and during the violent battle between the armies of Cyrus and Belshazzar. Griffith keeps the viewer emotionally involved—he does not even allow the film's most spectacular scene, Belshazzar's premature victory celebration, to entirely overwhelm the personal stories. Unfortunately, Griffith failed to reach his intended audience; his personal expression of protest against bigotry did not erase the cries of racism against *The Birth of a Nation*. But in *Intolerance*, flaws and all, he created one of the seminal works of

motion picture history, and a movie experience that can still enthrall us with its scope and beauty.

Intolerance also boasts a number of extraordinary performances, especially by actresses in the central roles. Griffith may have had a fondness for winsome, twittering heroines, but these women often have fists of iron and backbones of steel. Mae Marsh is truly remarkable as the Dear One, struggling fiercely to protect her baby or fighting, against all odds, to save her husband from the gallows. (It is not easy to forget the shot of her hands at her husband's trial, eloquently communicating her silent anguish as they wring a handkerchief.) Constance Talmadge is also fine—spunky, lively, and finally gallant—as the Mountain Girl who tries to avert the downfall of Belshazzar, and Miriam Cooper is surprisingly "modern" as the spurned Friendless One in the modern story, suggesting the neuroses and tensions that lead her to murder.

Erich von Stroheim, another major figure of the silent years, was a great admirer of Griffith and had worked in Griffith's company in various capacities. The Vienna-born Stroheim had already established a reputation as an actor specializing in thin-lipped, imperious, and sardonic Prussian officers (he was billed as "The Man You Love to Hate") when he persuaded Universal to let him direct his first film, *Blind Husbands* (1919). He also wrote the screenplay, designed the sets, and played the leading role of a lecherous Austrian officer who dallies with a surgeon's neglected wife. The fastidious attention to every aspect of the film, the psychological nuances, and especially the charged sexuality of *Blind Husbands* was even more evident in his 1922 film, *Foolish Wives*. This film, however, was severely cut at the orders of Irving Thalberg, then Universal's head of production, who was irritated by Stroheim's extravagance and arrogant, demanding attitude.

Thalberg figured importantly in the ultimate fate of Stroheim's greatest film, *Greed* (1924). Obsessed with Frank Norris's novel *McTeague*, Stroheim had long entertained the idea of filming it in its entirety, visually duplicating every incident. The film he completed for the Goldwyn Company under the title of *Greed* ran for an astonishing forty-two reels, which Stroheim, under extreme duress, cut down to twenty-four (about five hours in running time). The rest of the story is part of film lore: removed from Stroheim's hands when Goldwyn merged with Louis B. Mayer's company, *Greed* was finally cut to ten reels by Irving Thalberg, who had moved to Mayer and who was still unable to tolerate the director's excesses and tantrums. Stroheim, of course, was outraged by the desecration of his masterpiece, and he minced no words in saying so. His reputation as an unmanageable spendthrift damaged his career as a director for many years.

If *Greed* is a fragment of the original film, it is still an extraordinary fragment and unquestionably a unique work in motion picture annals. It relates the story of a rather brutish and simple dentist named McTeague (Gibson Gowland) who marries his patient Trina (ZaSu Pitts). She becomes a miser out of sexual frustration, and when she refuses to give him the money she has won in a lottery, he

Opposite: Intolerance *(Wark Producing Co., 1916). The Boy (Robert Harron) is consoled by a priest before being led away to his execution for murder. The priest was genuine, chosen by D. W. Griffith for accuracy of detail.*

murders her. Sought by the police, he flees to the blistering waste-land of Death Valley. He is pursued there by Marcus (Jean Hersholt), a former friend and later rival for Trina's love and money; a struggle ends with Marcus dead and McTeague handcuffed to his body. Trina's lust for gold, growing like a weed in untended soil, has become a force that destroys her and the men who loved her.

It is a grim story of implacable fate, but, apparently, it was much more rounded and subtle in its original form. Yet, even with abrupt time lapses and gaps in the narrative, the remaining fragment is not only stunningly dramatic, it also marked a bold advance in cinematic style. Seldom had a film during the silent era depicted the mean and even sordid lives of lower-middle-class Americans in such un-sparing detail. The celebration party for Trina's lottery win and the wedding supper for McTeague and Trina capture every vulgar moment; the camera seems to have intruded on actual events. Nor did any film during that basically romantic period have so gloomy and unre-lieved a sense of foreboding. This is felt from the very beginning: courting Trina, McTeague sings a mournful ditty that ends "left alone in this world's wilderness," a foreshadowing of his ultimate fate in the desert, while during their wedding ceremony, the camera

moves briefly into the street to observe a funeral procession.

Above all, *Greed* is exceptionally frank in its depiction of sexual desire. The moments of raw, "animal" lust—McTeague kissing Trina hungrily while she is under ether, Trina's sudden bursts of passion-ate feeling for McTeague—indicated to twenties audiences that sex-ual activity, movie variety, was not necessarily confined to the decadent rich. (Evidently, the original film had many more of such moments that fell to the cutter's shears.)

Greed rises in crescendo to its final powerful sequences. A series of confrontations between the jobless, increasingly desperate Mc-Teague and the miserly Trina culminate in his beating her to death in a schoolroom ironically festooned with Christmas decorations. Fleeing to the desert, McTeague stands alone in an awesome setting that suggests his own desolation. When he is joined by Marcus, the two men are seen isolated in a pitiless wasteland, with a dead mule and no water. "We're dead men," Marcus says, and soon his battered body lies motionless in the desert. The final frame shows McTeague fatally trapped in what the novel calls "the measureless leagues of Death Valley." The public responded to the film's frankness by re-fusing to attend or rejecting it with laughter when they did.

Above: Greed *(Goldwyn, 1924). Erich von Stroheim's meticulous attention to naturalistic detail is evident in this moment from the wedding dinner for McTeague (Gibson Gowland) and his bride, Trina (ZaSu Pitts). Opposite, above: Furious at her refusal to give him her money, the brutish McTeague bites the fingers of his miserly wife. The released version did not show the complications caused by his act—blood poisoning, resulting in the amputation of several fingers. Opposite, below: The final confrontation in the desert: Marcus (Jean Hersholt) pulls a gun on McTeague, his former friend and now sworn enemy.*

We must leap across seventeen years of screen history to come to the next film of unique distinction and influence. Once again, the film was the work of an inordinately gifted and fiercely individualistic visionary who worked against the grain of the Hollywood studio system. In October of 1938, a flamboyant young man named Orson Welles, who had brought his idiosyncratic Mercury Theatre to radio, created a nationwide sensation with his broadcast of *The War of the Worlds*. His fictional account of a Martian invasion was so convincing that many people across America took it for the truth and panicked. Nelson Rockefeller suggested to George J. Schaefer, President of RKO, that this "boy wonder" might be the miracle needed to save the company from bankruptcy. After some haggling, Welles signed with the company to produce films over which, he insisted, he would have total control.

It was not until three years later that Welles's first film was released. The story of how *Citizen Kane* came to fruition has been often told, especially in Pauline Kael's fascinating essay "Raising Kane." It is still a matter of controversy as to the extent of Welles's contribution to the screenplay, credited to Herman Mankiewicz. In any case, after a long period of gestation, the child of their imagination was born—and then nearly expired. The filming had been conducted largely in secret, and with good reason. To the dismay of a great many people, the subject of the film was evidently the highly powerful publisher William Randolph Hearst; the events in the movie

Above: Citizen Kane *(RKO, 1941). Charles Foster Kane (Orson Welles) and his friend*
Jedediah Leland (Joseph Cotten) stand amid copies of Kane's newspaper, the Inquirer.
Opposite: A candidate for governor, Kane stands proudly before a huge blowup of his
photograph. Only twenty-five, Welles gave a splendidly theatrical performance as Kane.

were strongly suggested by Hearst's public and private life. No previous film had dared to deal so overtly with a living American figure. A campaign engineered by such eminent Hollywoodians as columnist Louella Parsons and Louis B. Mayer clamored to have the movie destroyed before its release. The film's premiere at the Radio City Music Hall in New York was canceled, and bookings were difficult to find. However, Schaefer refused to yield, and *Citizen Kane* opened to enthusiastic reviews and indifferent business.

After more than four decades, *Citizen Kane* remains the most analyzed (if not overanalyzed) of American films. It is not that it is so subtle as that it is made up of so many elements; it is a mystery story, a freewheeling satire on power and ambition in America, a newspaper drama, a flamboyant cinematic experiment, and the biography of an ambitious man: his rise and fall. The man is Charles Foster Kane (Orson Welles), "America's Kubla Khan" and its most influential publisher. He dies with the word "Rosebud" on his lips, prompting a curious reporter to investigate his life. Through interviews with those who knew Kane, leading to a series of flashbacks, we arrive at a composite portrait of Kane as a brazen, outrageous young man, who, through bitter disappointment and personal failure, became a bloated, eccentric hermit living and dying alone in the splendor of his castle called Xanadu. Contrasting views of Kane come from his manager Bernstein (Everett Sloane), his vulgar, alcoholic ex-wife Susan (Dorothy Comingore), his former friend Jedediah Leland (Joseph Cotten), and his enigmatic butler Raymond (Paul Stewart), who speaks his epitaph: "Mr. Kane was a man who got everything he wanted—and then lost it." In the final few minutes, the audience comes to learn the significance of "Rosebud."

Like every true landmark film, *Citizen Kane* looks both backward and forward; it synthesized the past as much as it influenced the future of motion pictures. At age twenty-five, Welles was a brilliant scholar of film, and he absorbed elements of thirties movies into the fabric of his film. A bustling, sensation-minded newspaper had been a familiar setting in many earlier movies. The brash, comic impudence displayed in many scenes echoed the popular screwball comedies of the previous decade. (We tend to forget that much of the film is funny.) The movie even begins like an old-fashioned mystery story, with Xanadu looming out of the darkness like Dr. Frankenstein's domain. Finally, *Kane*'s roots have often been traced back to *The Power and the Glory*, a somber Fox film of 1933, written by Preston Sturges, about a tycoon who comes to grief in his personal life.

More importantly, Welles took many of the basic elements of film and used them in such original ways that film was never quite the same again. With the help of his cameraman, Gregg Toland, and his editor, Robert Wise, he lifted motion pictures into a new era. A viewer can sense his exuberance and delight as he tests the possibilities of film in scene after scene. Much has been written about the dazzling transitions: a shot of young Charlie's sled covered with snow moves abruptly to a group of brief scenes showing the mature Charles brazenly taking charge of the *Inquirer*. The disintegrating

Citizen Kane *(RKO, 1941). Publisher Charles Foster Kane (Orson Welles), caught in his "love nest" with his mistress, Susan Alexander (Dorothy Comingore), confronts Jim Gettys (Ray Collins), Kane's political opponent, who is using Susan to wreck Kane's chances to be governor. Right: At Xanadu, Kane's palatial estate (the "world's largest private pleasure ground"), wife Susan, bored and restless, amuses herself with a giant jigsaw puzzle while Kane looks on.*

marriage of Kane and his first wife Emily (Ruth Warrick) is swiftly dramatized in changing scenes at their dining room table; as the years go by, their conversation becomes increasingly cold and acrimonious. The film is also adept at making a dramatic point in ways that are both economical and effective. When Kane decides to take the consequences of his scandalous association with his mistress Susan, the camera merely has him emerging from darkness into bright light. As Susan (now his wife) is making her opera debut, the camera moves up to the flies, where a stagehand simply holds his nose. Such touches were not original with Welles, but never before had they been used with such deliberate audacity. *Citizen Kane* abounds in moments like these, which tell us that we are watching the work of a gifted young man who is not ashamed to flaunt his knowledge of—and love for—the medium of film.

Citizen Kane is a classic American film, but that is not to say that it is without flaws. The bravura production techniques command so much attention that they cut into our interest in the narrative. And, after a while, the "clever" camera angles and the tricky lighting become wearying. The screenplay, while literate and fascinating, is also rather shallow; we never learn much about the reasons for Kane's supreme power (except that he has a forceful, bullying personality), and we are told, banally, that behind the tyranny was a man seeking love. (What is "Rosebud," after all, but a Hitchcockian "McGuffin" made tritely visible?) However, great films are not necessarily profound films, and we can excuse its shallowness. More troublesome is the film's attitude toward its actual target, William Randolph Hearst. Through Charles Foster Kane, it portrays him as a man with a monstrous ego who, driven by private demons, blusters his way into becoming an American emperor. Yet the film itself is the cinematic equivalent of Hearst's "Yellow Journalism"; it deliberately sensationalizes his story in the same way that he himself exploited people in his newspapers. The question lingers: is this fair game or unfair advantage?

Flaws aside, *Citizen Kane* is one of the great works of cinematic art, a film that led the medium into new directions and left its mark on many films to come. We can attribute its greatness to many factors, and apparently film history will never be able to sort out to everyone's satisfaction the degree of each person's participation. Yet Orson Welles must be regarded as its guiding genius; like Griffith and Stroheim, he had a visionary attitude toward motion pictures, and with the boldness of youth, he gave it shape and form on the screen. There were difficult times ahead for Welles, but *Citizen Kane* endures.

We close this book with a film that is emphatically not Hollywood's *greatest* movie. But it may well be *Hollywood's* greatest movie: a distillation of that magical combination of glamour, technical wizardry, and ballyhoo unique to America's movie colony. In spite of continual revivals and occasional television showings, it continues to draw fascinated viewers, many of whom have seen it more than once. It exists as a movie with its own special cachet, its own

body of lore and legend. (Has any other movie been covered in such voluminous detail?) The film, of course, is *Gone with the Wind* (1939).

The story of how *Gone with the Wind* reached the screen has been told many times and need not be repeated here. Suffice to say that it began with a memorandum dated May 25, 1936, from David O. Selznick to Kay Brown, his eastern story editor, rejecting Margaret Mitchell's phenomenally best-selling book on various grounds. It ended with the film's gala premiere in Atlanta on December 15, 1939. That three-and-a-half-year period witnessed a barrage of publicity such as no film had ever before generated, including, among other things, a veritable storm of activity over the casting of the central roles (especially that of heroine Scarlett O'Hara), considerable brouhaha over the screenplay (playwright Sidney Howard received screen credit), and much *Sturm und Drang* over the director (George Cukor was replaced by Victor Fleming, who died before the film was completed. Sam Wood was rushed in to do the final scenes). Pulling every string in this gargantuan puppet show was David O. Selznick, the film's highly astute and vastly knowledgeable producer, whose lengthy memos on the film are almost as fascinating as the film itself.

It is easy, and possibly irrelevant, to enumerate the shortcomings of *Gone with the Wind*. It is clearly a shameless distortion of history, depicting the American South of pre–Civil War days as a place of grace and breeding, reluctant to surrender its fragrant way of life to the coarse, insensitive North. Its view of slavery and black people is amusing at best, offensive at worst. The "good" blacks are either twittering nincompoops or wise old mammies; when free, they are mostly "bad." Apart from its attitudes, *Gone with the Wind* does not entirely live up to its reputation from a cinematic viewpoint. The second half of the film sags considerably in comparison with the first, and, surprisingly, there is hardly any spectacle at all throughout its three-and-a-half hours of running time. (Even the siege of Atlanta, so brilliantly staged twenty-four years earlier in *The Birth of a Nation*, is confined to some brief shots of the city—actually old sets—in flames.)

Then what is the source of the film's mythic (and deserved) fame? And why is it that such a faulty movie is instantly recognizable by only its initials? A substantial part of its durability is due to the professional skill with which it unfolds a sweeping narrative and to its confident belief in the glamour and magic of the movies. It is also a testament to the power of publicity. Yet there is something more fundamental in its lasting appeal, and it lies in the character of Scarlett O'Hara and her relationship with Rhett Butler. As embodied beautifully by Vivien Leigh in a performance that becomes increasingly impressive over the years, Scarlett develops over the course of the film from a frivolous, lightheaded Southern belle into a tough, resilient woman. Although she never loses her selfishness or even her vanity, she learns to cope with adversity and to fight for what she wants. She is a great fictional heroine, and she gives *Gone with the Wind* some of its heart and much of its bite.

More than any other single factor, it is the fluctuating relationship of Scarlett and Rhett Butler that gives *Gone with the Wind* its perennial romantic appeal. They are well matched; beside the nobility of Ashley Wilkes and the self-sacrifice of Melanie Hamilton, their self-interest and their bristling, knowing attitude toward each other are refreshingly real. Within the limitations of the period (1939, not the 1860s), they generate more than a few sexual sparks. At the Atlanta ball, Rhett insists, "I want more from you than flirting." It is clear that he means it, and she knows it. When he rescues her in the burning city, he tells her, "We belong together." However, he has no illusions about her. After the war, when her only obsession is to hold on to Tara, her plantation, Rhett proposes marriage to Scarlett knowing full well that she needs him more than she loves him. From the first, he is ruled by his sexual attraction to her, and this feeling culminates in the famous scene in which, drunk and

bitter, he carries her upstairs to the bedroom. In Clark Gable's virile performance, Rhett Butler is an irresistible romantic hero, wicked enough to be interesting, and strong enough to be an ideal foil for Vivien Leigh's tempestuous Scarlett. We understand, although we may regret, his final parting from her "to see if somewhere there isn't something left in life of charm and grace."

The Scarlett O'Hara–Rhett Butler relationship may form the core of *Gone with the Wind*, but there is no doubt that David Selznick placed it at the center of a large and shiny apple. Despite the shortage of true spectacle, there are many scenes that remain indelible in film legend. Instead of raging battles we are shown war's devastation, in the moving sequence in which the grieving people of Atlanta look at the casualty lists and in the scenes of Scarlett's experiences as a nurse forced to assist at amputations. (The long tracking shot showing her wandering amid the wounded and dying

*Gone with the Wind (David O. Selznick/MGM, 1939). Even at her wedding to Charles
Hamilton (Rand Brooks, right), Scarlett O'Hara (Vivien Leigh, second from right) gazes
longingly at Ashley (Leslie Howard, left), as Melanie (Olivia de Havilland), his bride-to-be,
stands beside him. Scarlett's parents were played by Thomas Mitchell and Barbara O'Neil (center).*

soldiers is probably the most memorable in the film.) There are also a number of small moments that impress as vividly as the large ones: the guests at Twelve Oaks buzzing excitedly about the war while Scarlett moves heedlessly among them; Scarlett's father (Thomas Mitchell), made mindless by the destruction of Tara, fondling his dead wife's jewelry; Mammy (Hattie McDaniel) telling Melanie, in a long, tearful speech, about Rhett's anguish after his small daughter's accidental death. McDaniel makes her stereotyped Mammy a figure of strength and fortitude (she won the first Academy Award ever given to a black performer). Also contributing to the film's undeniable charisma were William Cameron Menzies's production design, Ernest Haller's striking if overly pretty photography, and Max Steiner's soaring musical score. Together, with David O. Selznick at the helm, they created the quintessential Hollywood movie: the symbol for an era of filmmaking that, unfortunately, has also gone with the wind.

Gone with the Wind (David O. Selznick/MGM, 1939).
One of the film's best-remembered scenes—the weary and wounded
Confederate soldiers are sprawled everywhere on Atlanta's Peachtree Street. Below:
Scarlett, penniless after the war, looks for help from Ashley.

CODA

In this book, I have paid personal tribute to many of the great films that have given me pleasure over the years. Some have left their indelible mark on film history; others have earned their fame through the power of legend. Still others have given me the recurring joy of seeing professionals at the top of their form, in stories that yield up new meanings at every viewing. There is no possible way to set a value on the time spent in the darkness of theaters, dissolved in laughter, moved to tears, or responding to the beauty or magic of a favorite movie.

We continue to watch films, hoping that each one will become another entry in our repository of dreams, another gold coin in our cache of memories. The films I have covered in this book are a permanent part of that treasure. And for that, I am deeply grateful.

For Roxane,
for all the years
and those to come,
with love . . .

ACKNOWLEDGMENTS

How can I adequately thank the many people who helped me complete this massive project? I am deeply and everlastingly grateful for their generous contributions of advice, criticism, and valuable materials, and for their warm support as well.

Once again I want to express my appreciation of the people at Abrams, who share the qualities of patience, professionalism, and pride in their work. These people include Margaret Kaplan, Barbara Lyons, Leta Bostelman, Carol Duffy, Judy Tortolano, Lory Frankel, my diligent and perceptive editor, and Judy Michael, the book's talented designer. I also want to applaud the prodigious and untiring efforts of Susan Grode in arranging permissions to reproduce the photographs.

I should like to thank the people who permitted me to screen essential films, and who provided me with so much beautiful material: Charles Silver and Ron Magliozzi of the Museum of Modern Art's Film Study Center; Mary Corliss of the Museum of Modern Art's Film Stills Archive; Michael King, for his magnificent posters and lobby cards; Jerry Vermilye, whose help, as always, is indispensable in so many ways; Dorothy Swerdlove and the staff of the Billy Rose Collection of the New York Public Library at Lincoln Center; Robert Cushman and Tim Stansbury of the Library of the Academy of Motion Picture Arts and Sciences; the Memory Shop; Movie Still Archives; Frank McGlynn; Mark Van Alstyne; and the extraordinarily knowledgeable and indefatigable Miles Kreuger.

I am very grateful to the people at the film studios who helped me locate and select photographs, and who gave me much useful information: Herbert S. Nusbaum, Dore Freeman, and Ben Washer of Metro-Goldwyn-Mayer; Steve Newman of Twentieth Century-Fox; Jess Garcia and Mark Shepard of Warner Bros.; Nancy Cushing-Jones and Corinne DeLuca of Universal Pictures; Pattie Mears and Mardi Montgomery of United Artists; Mike Berman and Fred Carpenter of Paramount Pictures; Bette LeVine of RKO General Pictures; Bruce Polichar and Tom Bodley of the Samuel Goldwyn Company; Alan Press of Columbia Pictures; Walt Disney Productions; and Lucasfilm Ltd.

There are several people who deserve special mention. One is Curtis F. Brown, whose help with the manuscript was invaluable. Another is Burt Lehrenbaum, my friend of many years, who has endured his frequent role as a sounding board for my ideas with his usual wit and astuteness. Finally, I offer my gratitude and love to my wife, Roxane, who keeps me moving ahead when I start to founder, and to my children, Bob, David, and Karen, who are amused by (and sometimes share) their father's movie madness.

SELECTED BIBLIOGRAPHY

Agee, James. *Agee on Film*. New York: McDowell, Obolensky, 1958.

Bavar, Michael. *Mae West*. New York: Pyramid Publications, 1975.

Baxter, John. *The Cinema of John Ford*. London: A. Zwemmer; New York: A. S. Barnes & Co., 1971.

_____. *King Vidor*. New York: Simon & Schuster, Inc., 1976.

Bayer, William. *The Great Movies*. New York: Grosset & Dunlap, Inc., Publishers, 1973.

Brosnan, John. *Future Tense: The Cinema of Science Fiction*. New York: St. Martin's Press, 1978.

Byron, Stuart, and Weis, Elisabeth, eds. *The National Society of Film Critics on Movie Comedy*. New York: Viking Press, Grossman Publishers, 1977.

Carey, Gary. *All the Stars in Heaven: Louis B. Mayer's M.G.M.* New York: E. P. Dutton, 1981.

Clarens, Carlos. *Crime Movies: An Illustrated History*. New York: W. W. Norton & Company, 1980.

_____. *An Illustrated History of the Horror Film*. New York: Capricorn Books, 1967.

Crowther, Bosley. *The Great Films: Fifty Golden Years of Motion Pictures*. New York: G. P. Putnam's Sons, 1967.

_____. *Reruns: Fifty Memorable Films*. New York: G. P. Putnam's Sons, 1978.

_____. *Vintage Films*. New York: G. P. Putnam's Sons, 1977.

Everson, William K. *American Silent Film*. New York: Oxford University Press, 1978.

_____. *Love in the Film*. Secaucus, N.J.: The Citadel Press, 1979.

_____. *A Pictorial History of the Western Film*. Secaucus, N.J.: The Citadel Press, 1969.

Farber, Manny. *Negative Space*. New York: Praeger Publishers, 1971.

Franklin, Joe. *Classics of the Silent Screen*. Secaucus, N.J.: The Citadel Press, 1959.

Giannetti, Louis. *Masters of the American Cinema*. Englewood Cliffs, N.J.: Prentice-Hall, Inc., 1981.

Gottesman, Ronald, and Geduld, Harry, eds. *The Girl in the Hairy Paw: King Kong as Myth, Movie, and Monster*. New York: Avon Books, 1976.

Halliwell, Leslie. *Halliwell's Hundred*. New York: Charles Scribner's Sons, 1982.

Higham, Charles. *The Art of the American Film*. Garden City, N.Y.: Anchor Press, Doubleday, 1974.

Hirsch, Foster. *The Dark Side of the Screen: Film Noir*. San Diego and New York: A. S. Barnes & Company, Inc., 1981.

Hochman, Stanley. *American Film Directors: A Library of Film Criticism*. New York: Frederick Ungar and Company, 1974.

Kael, Pauline. *Deeper into Movies*. Boston: Little, Brown and Company, 1973.

_____. *5001 Nights at the Movies: A Guide from A to Z*. New York: Holt, Rinehart and Winston, 1982.

_____. *Kiss Kiss Bang Bang*. Boston: Little, Brown and Company, 1968.

_____. *Reeling*. Boston: Little, Brown and Company, 1976.

Kael, Pauline (with Herman J. Mankiewicz and Orson Welles). *The Citizen Kane Book*. Boston: Little, Brown and Company, 1971.

Kagan, Norman. *The War Film*. New York: Pyramid Publications, 1974.

Katz, Ephraim. *The Film Encyclopedia*. New York: Thomas Y. Crowell, Publishers, 1979.

Kauffman, Stanley, ed. (with Bruce Henstell). *American Film Criticism: From the Beginnings to Citizen Kane*. New York: Liveright, 1972.

Kerr, Walter. *The Silent Clowns*. New York: Alfred A. Knopf, 1975.

Knight, Arthur. *The Liveliest Art: A Panoramic History of the Movies*. Rev. ed. New York: Macmillan Publishing Co., Inc., 1978.

Macdonald, Dwight. *Dwight Macdonald on Movies*. Englewood Cliffs, N.J.: Prentice-Hall, Inc., 1969.

Maltin, Leonard. *The Disney Films*. New York: Popular Library, 1973.

Morella, Joe; Epstein, Edward Z.; and Griggs, John. *The Films of World War II*. Secaucus, N.J.: The Citadel Press, 1973.

Moss, Robert F. *Charlie Chaplin*. New York: Pyramid Publications, 1975.

_____. *Karloff and Company: The Horror Film*. New York: Pyramid Publications, 1974.

O'Dell, Paul. *Griffith and the Rise of Hollywood*. New York: A. S. Barnes & Company, Inc., 1970.

Parish, James Robert, and Pitts, Michael R. *The Great Science Fiction Pictures*. Metuchen, N.J.: The Scarecrow Press, 1977.

_____. *The Great Western Pictures*. Metuchen, N.J.: The Scarecrow Press, 1976.

Rosow, Eugene. *Born to Lose: The Gangster Film in America*. New York: Oxford University Press, 1978.

Sarris, Andrew. *The American Cinema: Directors and Directions (1929–1968)*. New York: E. P. Dutton & Co., Inc., 1968.

Schickel, Richard. *His Picture in the Papers: A Speculation on Celebrity in America Based on the Life of Douglas Fairbanks, Sr.* New York: Charterhouse Publishers, 1973.

Sennett, Ted. *Hollywood Musicals*. New York: Harry N. Abrams, Inc., Publishers, 1981.

_____. *Lunatics and Lovers*. New Rochelle, N.Y.: Arlington House, 1974.

_____. *Warner Brothers Presents*. New Rochelle, N.Y.: Arlington House, 1971.

Silver, Alain, and Ward, Elizabeth, eds. *Film Noir*. Woodstock, N.Y.: The Overlook Press, 1979.

Simon, John. *Reverse Angle*. New York: Clarkson N. Potter, Inc., Publishers, 1982.

Slide, Anthony, and Wagenknecht, Edward. *Fifty American Silent Films 1912–1920: A Pictorial Survey*. New York: Dover Publications, 1982.

Suid, Lawrence H. *Guts and Glory: Great American War Movies*. Reading, Mass.: Addison-Wesley Publishing Company, 1978.

Taylor, John Russell, ed. *Graham Greene on Film: Collected Film Criticism (1935–1940)*. New York: Simon & Schuster, Inc., 1972.

Thomas, Tony. *The Great Adventure Films*. Secaucus, N.J.: The Citadel Press, 1978.

Truffaut, François (with Helen G. Scott). *Hitchcock*. New York: Simon & Schuster, Inc., 1967.

Wagenknecht, Edward, and Slide, Anthony. *The Films of D. W. Griffith*. New York: Crown Publishers, Inc., 1975.

Weinberg, Herman G., ed. *The Complete Greed of Erich von Stroheim*. New York: Arno Press, 1972.

Wilson, Robert, ed. *The Film Criticism of Otis Ferguson*. Philadelphia: Temple University Press, 1971.

Wolf, William (with Lillian Kramer Wolf). *Landmark Films: The Cinema and Our Century*. New York and London: Paddington Press Ltd., 1979.

INDEX

Page numbers in *italics* indicate illustrations

FILM COPYRIGHTS

Warner Bros. Pictures, Inc. Renewed 1969 United Artists Television, Inc. All rights reserved. 130 below: *The Big Sleep*, 1946, Copyright © 1946 Warner Bros. Pictures, Inc. Renewed 1973 United Artists Television, Inc. All rights reserved. 131 above: *The Maltese Falcon* (lobby card), 1941, For a film produced by Warner Bros. Inc. 131 below: *Klute*, 1971, © 1971 Warner Bros. Inc. Courtesy Warner Bros. Inc. 132: *Laura*, 1944, © 1944 Twentieth Century-Fox Film Corporation. All rights reserved. 133: *Gaslight*, 1944, © 1944 Loew's Inc. Renewed 1971 Metro-Goldwyn-Mayer Inc. 134: *Rebecca*, 1940, © 1940 Selznick International Pictures, Inc. Renewed 1967 Metro-Goldwyn-Mayer Inc. 135: *Shadow of a Doubt*, 1943, Copyright © Universal Pictures, a Division of Universal City Studios, Inc. Courtesy MCA Publishing, a Division of MCA Communications, Inc. 136: *Notorious*, 1946, © 1946 RKO Pictures. Released to Selznick International Pictures, Inc. All rights reserved. 137: *Strangers on a Train*, 1951, © 1951 Warner Bros. Inc. Courtesy Warner Bros. Inc. 139: *Psycho*, 1960, Copyright © Universal Pictures, a Division of Universal City Studios, Inc. Courtesy of MCA Publishing, a Division of MCA Communications, Inc. 140, 141: *North by Northwest*, 1959, © 1959 Loew's Incorporated 142, 143: *Charade*, 1963, Copyright © Universal Pictures, a Division of Universal City Studios, Inc. Courtesy of MCA Publishing, a Division of MCA Communications, Inc. 144: *Frankenstein*, 1931, Copyright © Universal Pictures, a Division of Universal City Studios, Inc. Courtesy of MCA Publishing, a Division of MCA Communications, Inc. 145: *Dr. Jekyll and Mr. Hyde*, 1920, © 1920 Paramount Pictures 147: *The Phantom of the Opera*, 1925, Copyright © Universal Pictures, a Division of Universal City Studios, Inc. Courtesy of MCA Publishing, a Division of MCA Communications, Inc. 148 above: *The Bride of Frankenstein* (lobby card), 1935, For a film produced by Universal Pictures 148 below: *The Bride of Frankenstein*, 1935, Copyright © Universal Pictures, a Division of Universal City Studios, Inc. Courtesy of MCA Publishing, a Division of MCA Communications, Inc. 150: *Dr. Jekyll and Mr. Hyde*, 1932, Copyright © Universal Pictures, a Division of Universal City Studios, Inc. Courtesy of MCA Publishing, a Division of MCA Communications, Inc. 151: *Dracula*, 1931, Copyright © Universal Pictures, a Division of Universal City Studios, Inc. Courtesy MCA Publishing, a Division of MCA Communications, Inc. 152 left: *The Mummy*, 1932, Copyright © Universal Pictures, a Division of Universal City Studios, Inc. Courtesy MCA Publishing, a Division of MCA Communications, Inc. 152 right: *Freaks*, 1932, © 1932 Metro-Goldwyn-Mayer Distributing Corporation. Renewed 1959 Loew's Incorporated 153 above: *The Wolf Man* (lobby card), 1941, For a film produced for Universal Pictures 153 below: *The Wolf Man*, 1941, Copyright © Universal Pictures, a Division of Universal City Studios, Inc. Courtesy MCA Publishing, a Division of MCA Communications, Inc. 154: *Cat People*, 1942, Courtesy RKO General Pictures. 155: *The Body Snatcher*, 1945, Courtesy RKO General Pictures. 156 above: *I Walked with a Zombie* (lobby poster), 1943, For a film produced for RKO General Pictures 156 below: *I Walked with a Zombie*, 1943, Courtesy RKO General Pictures 157 above: *The Thing from Another World*, 1951, Courtesy RKO General Pictures 157 below: *Rosemary's Baby*, 1968, Copyright © 1968 by Paramount Pictures Corporation. All rights reserved. Courtesy of Paramount Pictures 158: *The Birds*, 1963, Copyright © Universal Pictures, a Division of Universal City Studios, Inc. Courtesy MCA Publishing, a Division of MCA Communications, Inc. 159: *Rosemary's Baby*, 1968, Copyright © 1968 by Paramount Pictures Corporation. All rights reserved. Courtesy of Paramount Pictures 160: *2001: A Space Odyssey*, 1968, © 1968 Metro-Goldwyn-Mayer Inc. 162 left: *The Day the Earth Stood Still*, 1951, © 1951 Twentieth Century-Fox Film Corporation. All rights reserved. 162 right: *The War of the Worlds*, 1953, Copyright © 1952 by Paramount Pictures Corporation. All rights reserved. Courtesy of Paramount Pictures 163 above: *Forbidden Planet*, 1956, © 1956 Loew's Incorporated 163 below: *Invasion of the Body Snatchers*, 1956, © 1956 Allied Artists. All rights reserved. 165 above: *Forbidden Planet*, 1956, © 1956 Loew's Incorporated 165 center: *Fantastic Voyage*, 1966, © 1966 Twentieth Century-Fox Film Corporation. All rights reserved. 165 below: *Planet of the Apes*, 1968, © 1967 Apjac Productions, Inc. and Twentieth Century-Fox Film Corporation. All rights reserved. Courtesy Twentieth Century-Fox Film Corporation. 166: *2001: A Space Odyssey*, 1968, © 1968 Metro-Goldwyn-Mayer Inc. 167: *Star Wars*, 1977, © Lucasfilm Ltd. (LFL) 1977. All rights reserved. 168 above: *Star Wars*, 1977, © Lucasfilm Ltd. (LFL) 1977. All rights reserved. 168 below: *The Empire Strikes Back*, 1980, © Lucasfilm Ltd. (LFL) 1980. All rights reserved. 169: *Close Encounters of the Third Kind*, 1977, Copyright © 1977, 1980 Columbia Pictures Industries, Inc. Courtesy of Columbia Pictures, a Division of Columbia Pictures Industries, Inc. 171: *King Kong*, 1933, Courtesy RKO General Pictures 172: *The Invisible Man*, 1933, Copyright © Universal Pictures, a Division of Universal City Studios, Inc. Courtesy of MCA Publishing, a Division of MCA Communications, Inc. 173 above: *Snow White*, 1937, © Walt Disney Productions 173 center: *Pinocchio*, 1940, © Walt Disney Productions 173 below: *Bambi*, 1942, © Walt Disney Productions 174: *Fantasia*, 1940, © Walt Disney Productions 176–77, 178, 179: *E.T.: The Extra-Terrestrial*, 1982, Copyright © Universal Pictures, a Division of Universal City Studios, Inc. Courtesy MCA Publishing, a Division of MCA Communications, Inc. 180–81: *Our Town*, 1940, © 1940 Sol Lesser. Released through United Artists Associated, Inc. All rights reserved. 182: *Ordinary People*, 1980, Copyright © 1980 by Paramount Pictures Corporation. All rights reserved. Courtesy Paramount Pictures 183: *Alice Adams*, 1935, Courtesy RKO General Pictures 184: *Fury*, 1936, © 1936 Metro-Goldwyn-Mayer Corporation. Renewed 1963 Metro-Goldwyn-Mayer Inc. 185: *To Kill a Mockingbird*, 1963, Copyright © Universal Pictures, a Division of Universal City Studios, Inc. Courtesy MCA Publishing, a Division of MCA Communications, Inc. 186: *The Last Picture Show*, 1971, Copyright © 1971 Last Picture Show Production, Inc. Courtesy of Columbia Pictures, a Division of Columbia Pictures Industries, Inc. 187: *American Graffiti*, 1973, Copyright © Universal Pictures, a Division of Universal City Studios, Inc. Courtesy MCA Publishing, a Division of MCA Communications, Inc. 188: *The Crowd*, 1927, © 1927 Metro-Goldwyn-Mayer Distributing Corporation. Renewed 1956 Loew's Incorporated 189: *Dead End*, 1937, © 1937 Samuel Goldwyn, Jr. Courtesy of Samuel Goldwyn, Jr. and The Samuel Goldwyn Company 190: *On the Waterfront*, 1954, Copyright © 1954. Renewed 1982 Columbia Pictures Corporation. Courtesy of Columbia Pictures, a Division of Columbia Pictures Industries, Inc. 191 above: *The Grapes of Wrath* (lobby card), 1940, For a film produced for Twentieth Century-Fox Film Corporation 191 below: *The Grapes of Wrath*, 1940, © 1940 Twentieth Century-Fox Film Corporation. All rights reserved. 192: *Our Daily Bread*, 1934, © 1934 King Vidor. Released through United Artists Associated, Inc. All rights reserved. 194: *Sounder*, 1972, © 1972 Radnitz/Mattel Productions, Inc. All rights reserved. Courtesy Twentieth Century-Fox Film Corporation. 195: *Make Way for Tomorrow*, 1937, Copyright © Universal Pictures, a Division of Universal City Studios, Inc. Courtesy of MCA Publishing, a Division of MCA Communications, Inc. 196 left: *Kramer vs. Kramer*, 1979, Copyright © 1979 by Columbia Pictures Industries, Inc. Courtesy of Columbia Pictures, a Division of Columbia Pictures Industries, Inc. 196 right: *Ordinary People*, 1980, Copyright © 1980 by Paramount Pictures Corporation. All rights reserved. Courtesy Paramount Pictures 197 above: *Kramer vs. Kramer*, 1979, Copyright © 1979 by Columbia Pictures Industries, Inc. Courtesy of Columbia Pictures, a Division of Columbia Pictures Industries, Inc. 197 below: *Nashville*, 1975, Copyright © 1975 by American Broadcasting Companies, Inc. All rights reserved. Courtesy of Paramount Pictures 198: *Mr. Smith Goes to Washington*, 1939, Copyright © 1939. Renewed 1967 Columbia Pictures Corporation. Courtesy of Columbia Pictures, a Division of Columbia Pictures Industries, Inc. 199: *All the King's Men*, 1949, Copyright © 1950. Renewed 1977 Columbia Pictures Corporation. Courtesy of Columbia Pictures, a Division of Columbia Pictures Industries, Inc. 200 above: *Mr. Smith Goes to Washington* (lobby card), 1939, For a film produced for Columbia Pictures 200 below: *All the President's Men*, 1976, © 1976 Warner Bros. Inc. Courtesy Warner Bros. Inc. 201: *Nashville*, 1975, Copyright © 1975 by American Broadcasting Companies, Inc. All rights reserved. Courtesy Paramount Pictures 202: *The Godfather*, 1972, Copyright © 1972 by Paramount Pictures Corporation. All rights reserved. Courtesy Paramount Pictures 203: *Underworld*, 1927, Copyright © Universal Pictures, a Division of Universal City Studios, Inc. Courtesy of MCA Publishing, a Division of MCA Communications, Inc. 204 above left: *Little Caesar* (lobby card), 1930, For a film produced for Warner Bros. Inc. 204 above right: *Little Caesar*, 1930, Copyright © 1930 Warner Bros. Pictures, Inc. Renewed 1958 Associated Artists Production Corp. All rights reserved. 204 below: *The Public Enemy*, 1931, Copyright © 1931 Warner Bros. Pictures, Inc. Renewed 1958 Associated Artists Production Corp. All rights reserved. 205: *Little Caesar*, 1930, Copyright © 1930 Warner Bros. Pictures, Inc. Renewed 1958 Associated Artists Production Corp. All rights reserved. 206 left: *The Public Enemy*, 1931, Copyright © 1931 Warner Bros. Pictures, Inc. Renewed 1958 Associated Artists Production Corp. All rights reserved. 206 right: *Scarface*, 1932, © 1932 Howard Hughes. Released through United Artists Associated, Inc. All rights reserved. 207: *High Sierra*, 1941, Copyright © 1940 William Riley Burnett. Renewed 1967. All rights reserved. Released through United Artists Corporation. 208 above: *Double Indemnity* (lobby card), 1944, For a film produced for Universal Pictures 208 below: *Double Indemnity*, 1944, Copyright © Universal Pictures, a Division of Universal City Studios, Inc. Courtesy of MCA Publishing, a Division of MCA Communications, Inc. 209: *The Killers*, 1946, Copyright © Universal Pictures, a Division of Universal City Studios, Inc. Courtesy of MCA Publishing, a Division of MCA Communications, Inc. 210: *White Heat*, 1949, © 1949 Warner Bros. Pictures, Inc. Released through United Artists Associated, Inc. All rights reserved. 211 left: *The Asphalt Jungle*, 1950, © 1950 Loew's Inc. Renewed 1977 Metro-Goldwyn-Mayer Inc. 211 right: *The Big Heat*, 1953, Copyright © 1953. Renewed 1981 by Columbia Pictures Corporation. Courtesy of Columbia Pictures, a Division of Columbia Pictures Industries, Inc. 212: *Kiss of Death*, 1947, © 1947 Twentieth Century-Fox Film Corporation. All rights reserved 213: *In Cold Blood*, 1967, Copyright © 1967 by Pax Enterprise, Inc. Courtesy of Columbia Pictures, a Division of Columbia Pictures Industries, Inc. 214, 215: *Bonnie and Clyde*, 1967, © 1967 Warner Bros. Inc. Courtesy Warner Bros. Inc. 217: *The Godfather: Part II*, 1974, Copyright © 1974 by Paramount Pictures Corporation. All rights reserved. Courtesy of Paramount Pictures 218: *The Godfather*, 1972, Copyright © 1972 by Paramount Pictures Corporation. All rights reserved. Courtesy of Paramount Pictures 219: *The Godfather: Part II*, 1974, Copyright © 1974 by Paramount Pictures Corporation. All rights reserved. Courtesy of Paramount Pictures 221: *The French Connection*, 1971, © 1971 Twentieth Century-Fox Film Corporation. All rights reserved 222: *Midnight Cowboy*, 1969, Copyright © 1969 Jerome Hellman Productions, Inc. All rights reserved. Released through United Artists Corporation 224: *You Only Live Once*, 1937, © 1937 Walter Wanger. Renewed 1964 United Artists Associated, Inc. All rights reserved. 225 above: *I Am a Fugitive from a Chain Gang* (lobby card), 1932, For a film produced by Warner Bros. Inc. 225 below: *I Am a Fugitive from a Chain Gang*, 1932, Copyright © 1932 Warner Bros. Pictures, Inc. Renewed 1959 United Artists Associated, Inc. All rights reserved. 226: *The Informer*, 1935, Courtesy RKO General Pictures. 227: *Nightmare Alley*, 1947, © 1947 Twentieth Century-Fox Film Corporation. All rights reserved 228: *The Treasure of the Sierra Madre*, 1948, © 1948 Warner Bros. Inc. Renewed 1976 Metro-Goldwyn-Mayer Inc. 229 left: *The Set-Up*, 1949, Courtesy RKO General Pictures 229 right: *Sunset Boulevard*, 1950, Copyright © 1950 by Paramount Pictures Corporation. All rights reserved. Courtesy Paramount Pictures 230: *Sunset Boulevard*, 1950, Copyright © 1950 by Paramount Pictures Corporation. All rights reserved. Courtesy Paramount Pictures 231: *A Streetcar Named Desire*, 1951, © 1951 Warner Bros. Inc. Renewed 1979 Metro-Goldwyn-Mayer Inc. 232: *Sweet Smell of Success*, 1957, Copyright © Universal Pictures, a Division of Universal City Studios, Inc. Courtesy of MCA Publishing, a Division of MCA Communications, Inc. 233: *The Hustler*, 1961, © 1961 Rossen Enterprises, Inc. and Twentieth Century-Fox Film Corporation. All rights reserved. Courtesy of Twentieth Century-Fox Film Corporation 234: *The Pawnbroker*, 1965, © 1965 Landau/Steinman 235: *Midnight Cowboy*, 1969, Copyright © 1969 Jerome Hellman Productions, Inc. All rights reserved. Released through United Artists Corporation 236: *They Shoot Horses, Don't They?*, 1969, © 1969 Winkler-Chartoff. Courtesy Cinerama Releasing Corp. All rights reserved 237, 239: *One Flew over the Cuckoo's Nest*, 1974, Copyright © 1975 N. V. Zwaluw. All rights reserved. Released through United Artists Corporation. 240–41: *Intolerance*, 1916, Wark Producing Company 242: *Grand Hotel* (advertisement), 1932, For a film produced by Metro-Goldwyn-Mayer Inc. 244: *Grand Hotel*, 1932, © 1932 Metro-Goldwyn-Mayer Distributing Corporation. Renewed 1959 Loew's Incorporated 245: *A Tale of Two Cities*, 1935, © 1935 Metro-Goldwyn-Mayer Corporation. Renewed 1962 Metro-Goldwyn-Mayer Inc. 246: *David Copperfield*, 1935, © 1935 Metro-Goldwyn-Mayer Corporation. Renewed 1962 Metro-Goldwyn-Mayer Inc. 247: *The Good Earth*, 1937, © 1937 Metro-Goldwyn-Mayer Corporation. Renewed 1964 Metro-Goldwyn-Mayer Inc. 248: *Little Women*, 1933, Courtesy RKO General Pictures 249: *Dodsworth*, 1936, © 1936 Samuel Goldwyn, Jr. Courtesy Samuel Goldwyn, Jr. and The Samuel Goldwyn Company 250: *Lost Horizon*, 1937, Copyright © 1937. Renewed 1965 Columbia Pictures Corporation of California, Ltd. Courtesy of Columbia Pictures, a Division of Columbia Pictures Industries, Inc. 251 above: *Lost Horizon*, 1937, Copyright © 1937. Renewed 1965 Columbia Pictures Corporation of California, Ltd. Courtesy of Columbia Pictures, a Division of Columbia Pictures Industries, Inc. 251 below: *Pride and Prejudice*, 1940, © 1940 Loew's Incorporated. Renewed 1967 Metro-Goldwyn-Mayer Inc. 252: *Pride and Prejudice*, 1940, © 1940 Loew's Incorporated. Renewed 1967 Metro-Goldwyn-Mayer Inc. 253: *The Picture of Dorian Gray*, 1945, © 1945 Loew's Inc. Renewed 1972 Metro-Goldwyn-Mayer Inc. 254: *National Velvet*, 1944, © 1944 Loew's Inc. Renewed 1971 Metro-Goldwyn-Mayer Inc. 255: *The Yearling*, 1946, © 1946 Loew's Inc. Renewed 1973 Metro-Goldwyn-Mayer Inc. 256: *All That Money Can Buy*, 1941, Courtesy of W. R. Frank Productions 257: *The Magnificent Ambersons*, 1942, Courtesy RKO General Pictures 258–59, 260: *How Green Was My Valley*, 1941, © 1941 Twentieth Century-Fox Film Corporation. All rights reserved. 261: *A Tree Grows in Brooklyn*, 1945, © 1945 Twentieth Century-Fox Film Corporation. All rights reserved. 262: *The Day of the Locust*, 1975, Copyright © 1974 by Long Road Productions. All rights reserved. Courtesy of Paramount Pictures 263: *Lust for Life*, 1956, © 1956 Loew's Incorporated 264 left: *The Lost Weekend*, 1945, Copyright © Universal Pictures, a Division of Universal City Studios, Inc. Courtesy MCA Publishing, a Division of MCA Communications, Inc. 264 right: *The Red Badge of Courage*, 1951, © 1951 Loew's Inc. Renewed 1979 Metro-Goldwyn-Mayer Inc. 266: *Julia*, 1977, © 1977 Twentieth Century-Fox Film Corporation. All rights reserved. 267: *Stage Door*, 1937, © 1937 RKO Radio Pictures Inc. All rights reserved. Courtesy Twentieth Century-Fox Film Corporation 268 left: *These Three*, 1936, © 1936 Samuel Goldwyn, Jr. Courtesy Samuel Goldwyn, Jr. and The Samuel Goldwyn Company 268 right: *The Little Foxes*, 1941, © 1941 Samuel Goldwyn, Jr. Courtesy Samuel Goldwyn, Jr. and The Samuel Goldwyn Company 269: *Cat on a Hot Tin Roof*, 1958, © 1958 Loew's Incorporated and Avon Productions Inc. 270: *Who's Afraid of Virginia Woolf?*, 1966, © 1966 Warner Bros. Inc. Courtesy Warner Bros. Inc. 271: *Long Day's Journey into Night*, 1962, © 1962 Ely Landau/Embassy 272, 273: *The Miracle Worker*, 1962, Copyright © 1962 Playfilm Productions, Inc. All rights reserved. Released through United Artists Corporation. 274: *Gone with the Wind*, 1939, © 1939 Selznick International Pictures, Inc. Renewed 1967 Metro-Goldwyn-Mayer Inc. 276, 277, 278: *The Birth of a Nation*, 1915, Epoch Producing Company 279, 280: *Intolerance*, 1916, Wark Producing Company 282, 283: *Greed*, 1924, © 1924 Samuel Goldwyn 284, 285, 286: *Citizen Kane*, 1941, Courtesy RKO General Pictures 288, 289, 290–91: *Gone with the Wind*, 1939, © 1939 Selznick International Pictures, Inc. Renewed 1967 Metro-Goldwyn-Mayer Inc.

ENDPAPERS:
Gone with the Wind *(David O. Selznick/MGM, 1939)*. *A classic film moment:*
Scarlett O'Hara (Vivien Leigh), dressed in her widow's weeds, shocks Atlanta society by
dancing with the dashing Captain Rhett Butler (Clark Gable).

HALF-TITLE PAGE:
The Gold Rush *(Charlie Chaplin/United Artists, 1925)*. *Prospecting for gold in the Klondike,*
a starving Charlie Chaplin boils his shoe and eats it with the enthusiasm and finesse of a
gourmet in a four-star restaurant.

TITLE PAGE:
Close Encounters of the Third Kind *(Columbia, 1977)*. *The "third kind" of encounter—*
actual contact with beings from other worlds—occurs when this massive spaceship lands in
Wyoming. Director Steven Spielberg has said that he wanted the ship to resemble an oil refinery
at night, a kind of city of light.

CONTENTS PAGE:
She Wore a Yellow Ribbon *(RKO, 1949)*. *Captain Nathan Brittles (John Wayne) looks out on*
the land he has loved and defended. The film was another of director John Ford's heartfelt
tributes to the U.S. Cavalry and to America's pioneer spirit.

PAGE 291:
Clockwise from upper left: Top Hat, E.T.: The ExtraTerrestrial, King Kong, The Wizard of
Oz, A Streetcar Named Desire, Citizen Kane, The Treasure of the Sierra Madre, City Lights,
Sunset Boulevard, The African Queen. *Center:* Singin' in the Rain

PAGE 292:
Pride and Prejudice
PAGE 301:
Our Town
BELOW:
The Maltese Falcon

PROJECT DIRECTOR: *Margaret L. Kaplan*
EDITOR: *Lory Frankel*
DESIGNER: *Judith Michael*
RIGHTS AND REPRODUCTIONS: *Barbara Lyons*

LIBRARY OF CONGRESS CATALOGING IN PUBLICATION DATA
Sennett, Ted.
Great Hollywood movies.

Bibliography: p.
Includes index.
1. Moving-pictures—United States—History—
Pictorial works. I. Title.
PN1993.5.U6S43 1983   791.43'75'0973   83-2683
ISBN 0-8109-0980-4

Published in 1983 by Harry N. Abrams, Incorporated, New York

Printed and bound in Japan